The influence of Civil Society on Japanese Nuclear Disarmament Policy

This book is the fruit of an outstanding piece of research on the relationship between Japanese NGOs advocating nuclear disarmament and successive Japanese government policies on nuclear issues. Few pieces of large scale research have to encounter and overcome such deeply seated institutional reluctance to discuss their attitudes to a major issue as this has done. Dr. Tobisawa has nonetheless persuaded them out of their tents and produced a work of great interest and importance. Anyone with an interest in nuclear politics both in respect of Japan and more globally will find it fascinating, as will students of NGOs functioning more broadly in contemporary global politics.

Professor Richard Langhorne

The influence of Civil Society on Japanese Nuclear Disarmament Policy

Kazuhiro Tobisawa

University of Buckingham Press

British Library Cataloguing in Publication Data
A catalogue record for this book is available from the British Library

ISBN 978-1-912500-02-4

Printed and bound in Great Britain by
Marston Book Services Ltd, Oxfordshire

Table of Contents

Acknowledgements

It is with deep gratitude and great pleasure that I dedicate this book to My Mentor in Life:

Dr Daisaku Ikeda
Doctor of Letters Honoris Causa, the University of Buckingham 2011
President of Soka Gakkai International

It is with deep gratitude and great pleasure that I dedicate this book to My Academic Memtor:

Professor Richard Langhorne

It is with deep appreciation and great pleasure that I dedicate this book to the following persons:

Professor Terence Kealey
Sir Anthony Seldon
The Lord Tanlaw
Mr Peter and Mrs Leonie Thorogood
Professor Alistair Alcock
Professor Martin Ricketts
Mr Gerry Loftus
Professor John Drew
Professor John Clarke
Dr Philip Towle
Professor Martin Blakeway
Ms Fujiko Hara
Professor James Rafferty
Professor Susan Edwards
Mr Jae Sundaram
Ms Anne Matsuoka
Ms Joanna Leach
Ms Linda Waterman
Ms Alison Smith
Ms Felicity Roberts-Holmes
Ms Akemi Tobisawa

Foreword

The town of Buckingham, the central base for my DPhil research, was originally a traditional English castle town where the castle of the Duke of Buckingham once stood. Located in a picturesque streetscape of a town that has changed very little since the 18th century is the University of Buckingham, Great Britain's first independent university, where students from over 85 countries from around the world are currently studying. Not far from the castle ruins is Hill House, a stately white mansion belonging to Mr Peter and Mrs Leonie Thorogood, whom I consider to be my British parents. It is here that I began writing my DPhil thesis. This beautiful and culturally rich environment formed the foundation of my intellect. I wrote this book based on my doctoral thesis, which I completed in 2015. There has been no essential change in regard to the nuclear weapons issue for half a century. However, I published this book because I believe a basic understanding of the fundamental structure of the issue is essential for understanding and analyzing the nuclear weapons issue.

On July 8, 2017, The United Nations adopted the Treaty on the Prohibition of Nuclear Weapons. This is a treaty that acknowledged the *hibakusha* (atom bomb survivors) in international law for the first time. On the other hand, the five major nuclear powers (P5) along with the Japanese government and some other countries refused to sign the treaty on the grounds that it fails to take into consideration the actual security environment. The refusal of these countries to sign the treaty significantly diluted the treaty's legal and political effectiveness. However, because the treaty was adopted, the moral responsibility of countries that dare violate it will at the very least be called into question by international society. Along with increased global awareness of the inhumanity of nuclear weapons, the moral resistance against their use is growing stronger.

With the nuclear powers at the lead, the notion of relying on nuclear weapons as a deterrent based on the view that a country will be exposed to threats if it abandons its nuclear weapons is gaining ground around the world today. In fact, the world is exposed to the real threat of nuclear weapons as North Korea has already reached the stage where it can conduct trial ICBM launches. Consequently, it is not difficult to imagine that the nuclear deterrent theory will gather further momentum. In addition to posing the fundamental question as to whether peace can really be achieved in a world that has abolished all nuclear weapons, this book offers numerous analyses of theories by nuclear armaments advocates for comparison. Since the Treaty on the Prohibition of Nuclear Weapons has been adopted, and ICAN was awarded the Nobel Peace Prize, people's awareness about nuclear disarmament may increase globally for a while. Once people become more composed and emotions cool, however, the true status of nuclear disarmament will be questioned.

While long-established antinuclear weapon CSOs are giving their full support to the groundswell of consensus for nuclear disarmament in recent years, they have not changed their stance of carefully examining international affairs in a cool-headed manner. Rather than the transient emotions often observed in popular social movements, their realistic viewpoint goes much deeper, is on an equal footing with states, and forms the basis for developing a massive movement that will have an impact on decision-making beyond national boundaries on a global scale. In interview surveys presented in this book too, various organizations including Komeito express the opinion that the conclusion of the Treaty on the Prohibition of Nuclear Weapons is premature and that there is a need to take more realistic steps. Nevertheless, these organizations do not necessarily oppose the Treaty on the Prohibition of Nuclear Weapons. Their concern has been the push to adopt the treaty simply because it exists, without making efforts to find realistic solutions. In terms of effectiveness, their concern is right to the point. Essentially, they are seriously considering from a calm viewpoint how to maintain effectiveness of this treaty by involving the P5 and the Japanese government. The total abolition of nuclear weapons can never be achieved by ignoring this viewpoint. There are many international treaties that are treaties in name only and simply espouse idealistic theories. In this sense too, Dr Ikeda's private diplomacy was one case that enhanced the presence and the influence of nuclear issues in civilian society to the same level or higher than national diplomacy, and indeed produced results. There is a fundamental ideological difference between anti-nuclear weapon CSOs and advocates of nuclear deterrence. For example, CSOs view nuclear weapons as an absolute evil while advocates of nuclear deterrence consider nuclear weapons as a necessary evil. Building on the viewpoint of this fundamental difference, this book presents a comparative study.

During my doctoral course, I studied under Professor Richard Langhorne, who is a world authority in global politics and history. In 1998, when I was a high school student in Japan, I was deeply impressed after watching a Japanese television program where Professor Langhorne gave a brilliant commentary on Winston Churchill's diplomacy during the Second World War. I took the video recording of this documentary with me later during my study in the United States and then in Great Britain, and I watched it repeatedly to increase and maintain my motivation to study abroad and research life. When I enrolled in graduate school to do a master's course in 2007, Professor Langhorne also took up the position of Professor in Global

Politics at the University of Buckingham to take charge of the teaching of global governance. Although this encounter was purely coincidental, I was deeply moved by this uncanny coincidence. When I went on to study in the doctoral course, Professor Langhorne kindly accepted to be my academic advisor and patiently mentored me. In 2010, when I visited New York for field work during my doctoral studies, Professor Langhorne kindly accompanied me on an interview survey of the SGI UN Liaison Office.

In 2011, Professor Langhorne managed to fit in a visit to Japan in his busy schedule to give keynote lectures at various institutions and to attend the presentation of an honorary doctorate to Dr Ikeda. During a packed schedule of less than a week, I accompanied the professor on visits to various academic and other institutions every day, and this elevated and refined intellectual journey remains a great honor in my life and a source of deep pride. Even in my present work, the fact that I once studied under Professor Langhorne and that I was one of his students makes me feel proud and is a source of encouragement to me in my daily work and academic research. From the bottom of my heart, I would like to express my profound appreciation for all that Professor Richard Langhorne has done for me.

The dedicated support I received from my mother, Akemi Tobisawa, and her presence were also indispensable in completing this thesis. When she was still a young woman, my mother participated in Josei Toda's Declaration Calling for Nuclear Abolition at Mitsuzawa Stadium in Japan on September 8, 1957, and the inauguration ceremony of Dr Ikeda as the 3rd President of Soka Gakkai in 1960. As a living witness to the principles of the individuals, she adopted their philosophies on arms control and international peace as her lifelong guiding principles. Since that time, nuclear disarmament and international peace have been the cornerstone of our family precepts. When I was 8 years old, the Gulf War erupted, and on the news everyday there were reports on the invasion of other countries and massacres committed under the Hussein regime. At that time, I asked my mother why the United States was not dropping nuclear bombs on Iraq. In my mind as a child, nuclear weapons were a way of overcoming opponents at a single go, and a deep psyche was at work in my mind that made me feel the use of such powerful weapons could stop further invasions of other countries and massacres by the Hussein regime in dreadful situations that caused casualties among the multinational forces led by the US military, and also created many refugees. When I look back now, it was a naïve question from a child. My mother calmly answered me in a manner that was easy to understand by telling me that the destructive power of nuclear weapons was too great and would also indiscriminately kill ordinary people who were not involved in war. She also said that there would be serious problems from radiation contamination after the use of nuclear weapons. She never admonished me in an angry manner, and at our house, freedom of thought was always respected. In high school, when I belonged to the debate club and studied about the problem of war, my mother told me about the theory of the possibility of nuclear substances carried by temperate westerlies reaching Japan if nuclear weapons were ever used, and she taught me the importance of Japan's role in disarmament. Moreover, she taught me to consider phenomenon from a global perspective. Verifying the potential of temperate westerlies aside, I believe that having a family environment where such discussions and dialogue were a regular part of life became a catalyst for my entry into academic life.

This book represents both the results of my research and the culmination of my family's quest for nuclear disarmament and international peace for half a century. Based on my own personal experience, I would like to add, if I may, that I believe education at home and higher education are mutually important in forming a person's humanity and intellect. In any case, since this is an academic study, needless to say, I proceeded with my research unemotionally based on the facts, from a fair and impartial viewpoint.

I would like to extend my sincere gratitude to numerous global CSOs and government institutions, as well as many other people who gave their kind cooperation and encouragement in my DPhil research while they themselves were so busy.

Kazuhiro Tobisawa

October 25, 2017

PART 1: Introduction

Introduction

The dissertation investigates the influence of Japanese Civil Society Organisations (CSOs) on Japanese official policy in respect of nuclear disarmament.

PART 1 consists of an introduction, a literature review and a description of the research methodologies used.

PART 2 describes the basic definition of influence and how it could be measured. It also describes the policies and attitudes of the Japanese government on the one hand, and the structure and attitude of important Japanese CSOs in the field of anti-nuclear weapons on the other hand. Some comparative discussion of similar non-Japanese CSO activities has been included.

PART 3 is a case study of a particularly significant figure involved in Japanese CSO activity over a very long period, Daisaku Ikeda. In addition to creating the CSO which has the longest history in Japan, his career included several episodes of private diplomacy conducted at the highest level.

PART 4 contains the conclusion, which discusses the effectiveness of Japanese CSO activities in the light of the research upon which this dissertation has been built.

Nuclear disarmament is a complex diplomatic issue. First of all, it is a mistake to attempt to resolve it as a security issue. Furthermore, the issue cannot be resolved merely by analysing nuclear weapons or by discussing the legal framework for prohibiting the weapons. Disarmament of nuclear weapons will not advance unless the background reasons for nuclear development are pursued and causes resolved.

The role of civil society was first recognized in the field of security through the collaboration between NGO (Non-Governmental Organisation) "International Campaign to Ban Landmines (ICBL)" and government agencies, during the process of establishing the Convention on the Prohibition of Anti-Personnel Mines, the so-called Ottawa Treaty, (signed 1997, effective as of 1999). There are some CSOs aiming for nuclear disarmament in Japan grouping together to apply the Ottawa Process to nuclear disarmament.

The collaboration between NGOs and government organisations was pivotal to the success of the Ottawa Process. There was no possibility of NGOs going it alone in successfully establishing the Convention on the Prohibition of Anti-personnel Mines. Also, at this point (in 2014), the US, Russia and China have not yet ratified the Convention. It is not easy to persuade military powers to ratify international conventions regarding security.

Since the development of nuclear weapons, nuclear disarmament has been pursued roughly in two ways. The first, similar to the Ottawa Process is a legal approach attempting to establish international law at the global level, and this was represented during the Cold War by the Nuclear Non-Proliferation Treaty (NPT) of 1969. Since the end of the Cold War, there has been the Nuclear Weapons Convention (NWC), submitted jointly by Costa Rica and Malaysia to the United Nations (UN) in 2007 and was adopted in 2017. The other is a diplomatic approach pursued by inter-governmental diplomatic negotiations. The representative example of this type was the US-USSR mutual agreement to reduce the number of nuclear warheads during the Cold War. In the post-Cold-War-multi-polar-world, nuclear disarmament of North Korea is sought through the Six-Party Talks, which include the US, Japan, China, Russia, North Korea, and South Korea. However, neither approach can be said to be functioning effectively. The Six-Party Talks have not been reconvened since the 6th, that took place in March 2006, and again there is no plan for the next meeting. Further, North Korea conducted its second nuclear test in May 2009, questioning the efficacy of the Six-Party Talks that took place from 2003 to 2006. In spite of the efforts of the parties concerned, the number of nuclear powers continues to increase.

The Ottawa Process was a successful collaboration between NGOs and the governments; however, there are no NGOs willing to engage in removing nuclear weapons, which are after all not placed where civilians can lay their hands on them. There is a need to note carefully whether there is any NGO that has nuclear weapons' knowledge and knowhow. Every time there is any nuclear test around the world CSOs conduct street demonstrations and anti-nuke conventions. Although they cannot participate directly in the political decision making process as sovereign citizens with voting rights, they can boost national and international public opinion against nuclear weapons and perhaps influence voting behaviour. Having stated this, nuclear issues have become a highly politicized matter, so much so that leaders who may espouse anti-nuclear sentiment may be restrained from taking the position publicly, given the current situation of neighbouring countries and the international political scene, and remain passive on the issue. Japan presents a typical case.

Northeast Asia is a particularly serious region where nuclear issues are concerned. With the exception of Japan and South Korea, three countries in the region (Russia, China and North Korea) all possess nuclear weapons. In the event of the reunification of South Korea and North Korea, unified Korea could well be a nuclear power and that means Japan alone will be deterred by its policy prohibiting development, use and transfer of nuclear weapons. Japan does, however, have a military alliance with the USA under which it is automatically protected by the US nuclear umbrella. Even after the end of Second World War, Japan has had a growing level of disputes with Russia and China over territorial and historical issues. Against this insecure background, some members of the Japanese parliament, albeit a small section, are for nuclear armament of Japan. As the only victim of the atomic bombs, the Japanese people have taken the destruction brought about by atomic bombs as a subjective experience, but with generational changes such feelings are diminishing.

Since 1945, no nuclear weapons have been used in wars, but due to the recent trend of globalization, and the dramatic development of free movement of information and material, there is an increasing possibility of nuclear weapons falling into the hands of terrorists and being used by them. In order to maintain the present non-use of nuclear weapons into the future, there is no other way but to totally abolish nuclear weapons from the earth. This is what Henry Kissinger and other US conservative strategists, as well as President Barack Obama, have come to assert. That said, however, the USA does not have any concrete plans to totally abolish its own nuclear weapons. There is no point if the US were to be alone in totally abolishing such weapons. While it is ideal for all nuclear powers to abolish them all together, it is not realistic. No nuclear state will willingly go for total abolition unless other nuclear powers do so. This is to say, that nuclear weapons are not just weapons but they have become diplomatic cards to play. And the reason for the failure to totally abolish these deadly weapons is mutual distrust among the states. Even when a nuclear power makes a public announcement through its government, there remains the possibility of it secretly producing nuclear weapons. Announcements alone are not trustworthy. This is the difference between landmines and nuclear weapons. It is not that nuclear weapons are the causes of mutual distrust and confrontation. Up to now all governmental negotiations are deadlocked, including the UN nuclear disarmament talks such as the Conference of Disarmament in Geneva (CD), as well as the Six-Party Talks. The Talks were a series of inter-governmental conferences, which were held six times between 2003 and 2006, to prevent North Korean nuclear development. It firstly started following North Korea's official announcement to withdraw from the NPT in 2003. Then the IAEA sent this case to the UN Security Council. The origin of the Talks can be traced back to the meeting between Jimmy Carter and Kim Il-sung in 1994 when Carter visited the country to initiate a dialogue to mitigate North Korea's hard-line policy including concern about developing nuclear weapons in the future. In particular, the United States has been seriously concerned about this issue, which possibly threatens the integration of Northeast Asia and the area of the Pacific Ocean. In the year 2002, North Korea had already admitted their plan of developing highly enriched uranium, but agreed to join the Six-Party Talks. The members of the Talks were the United States, China, South Korea, Russia, Japan, and North Korea. There was always political horse-trading with North Korea, which wanted to win concessions including economic aid, and the other governments, which tried to make the country abandon all their nuclear plans. The situation got a little better but then it had a relapse. The Talks were dead-locked following North Korea's announcement withdrawing from the Talks and its second test of nuclear weapons, which happened just two months after the 6th Six-Party Talks on March 2006. The Talks have not been held again (as of 2014).

Of the two approaches to nuclear disarmament, the NWC was drafted by an international CSO, the International Association of Lawyers Against Nuclear Arms (IALANA), headquartered in Germany. The Ottawa Treaty as well as other international legal documents has been drafted with the cooperation of CSOs and civilians. It is easy to surmise that the USA and other nuclear powers will find it difficult to accept the Convention, which regards nuclear weapons as totally unlawful. Anti-nuclear CSOs and the presenters of the Convention will need to put their heart and soul into finding ways to convince nuclear powers to sign and ratify it. Concluding the Convention is the ultimate objective, not the means.

There are various anti-nuclear CSOs working around the world; however, for the purpose of this thesis, this study will focus on the anti-nuke CSOs in Japan, Japan being the one and only country attacked with nuclear weapons. Anti-nuclear CSOs in Japan, with their experiences of coping with the fallout of the atom bomb blasts, are alone in being able to be subjectively involved in the anti-nuclear movement. Another reason for choosing Japanese CSOs is that they are passionately committed to their cause. The successful Ottawa Process also signalled that the role, presence and decision of governments are essential. It is therefore important to shed light on the relations between anti-nuclear CSOs and the government in Japan. While international treaties are final objectives, there is another effective diplomatic approach towards nuclear disarmament, which it is considered important for this thesis to focus on, namely that CSO diplomacy could open the window of the deadlocked inter-states negotiations. To explain this effectively could lead to the resolution of half-a-century old attempts at nuclear disarmament and justify the purpose of this research.

Literature Review

To begin with there are hardly any research papers let alone books referring to the roles of CSOs in nuclear disarmament studies. This is due to the fact that nuclear matters are considered political issues to be handled by governments or an exclusive agenda to be handled by governments and experts. On the other hand, the role of CSOs and their impact on nuclear disarmament is basically two-fold: to form an anti-nuclear public opinion from the grass-roots and to win the privilege of participating and deliberating at the NPT Review Conference.

In 1997 "A Study on People-to-People Diplomacy", a collection of case studies, was published in Japan by Hisakazu Usui, Professor of the Faculty of Global and Inter-Cultural Studies, Ferris University and Mikio Takase, Associate Professor Faculty of Law, Kanto Gakuin University together with twelve other academics. Among them, Takuya Sasaki, Associate Professor Faculty of Law, Rikkyo University, alone covered NGO diplomacy in the field of nuclear disarmament in a twenty-five-page-chapter. [1] The research was entitled, "The US Diplomacy and Nuclear Weapons" and covered the effects and limits of a moratorium on nuclear weapons during the first half of the 1980s and its effect and limits on the Reagan administration.

According to Sasaki, a nation-wide anti-nuclear movement meeting arranged by civil societies took place in March 1981 at Georgetown

---

[1] Takuya Sasaki, Kokusai Shakai Ni Okeru NGO No Tenkai: 1, Amerika Gaiko To NGO (NGO Activities in the International Society: 1, American Diplomacy and NGO), Minsai Gaiko No Kenkyu (Studies of People-To-People Diplomacy), Sanrei Shobo 1997, p75-p99

University. There were over 300 activists present from 33 states representing areas of peace, religion and environmental protection. According to Sasaki, this meeting of civil societies demanding a nuclear weapons moratorium was arranged due to fear that the Reagan administration with its all out confrontational attitude towards the USSR might pull the trigger for nuclear war between the two states. The meeting created a new organisation "The Nuclear Weapons Freeze Campaign (known as the Freeze). In May 1983, despite a prior call for restraint from the administration, the US National Conference of Catholic Bishops adopted "The Challenge of Peace: God's Promise and Our Response – A Pastoral Letter on War and Peace".[2] This gave ethical and moral legitimacy to the Freeze campaign and had a strong impact on political circles in Washington D.C. In February 1982, Democratic Congressman Ed Markey, submitted to the US Congress a draft resolution on freezing nuclear weapons. Edward Kennedy, a Democrat and Mark Hatfield, a Republican Senator jointly submitted the same draft to the US Senate. Both were, however, rejected. In the results of the referendum on Nuclear Freeze that took place at the same time as the November 1982 Midterm Election, 9 states out of 10 and 34 cities out of 35, including Chicago, Denver, Philadelphia and Washington D.C., approved of a freeze of nuclear weapons.

It was in Europe that the anti-nuclear citizens movement took off. The ideological source of European anti-nuclear movements went-back to the Russell-Einstein Manifesto of 1955. The Manifesto led to the

---

[2] The National Conference of Catholic Bishops, *The Challenge of Peace: God's Promise and Our Response – A Pastoral Letter on War and Peace*, 3rd May 1983
http://www.usccb.org/upload/challenge-peace-gods-promise-our-response-1983.pdf (accessed on 17th December 2012)
"We support immediate, bilateral verifiable agreements to halt the testing, production and deployment of new nuclear weapon systems.", p3

convening of the Pugwash Conference on Science and World Affairs in 1957 with the participation of eleven prominent scientists. The Conference received a Nobel Peace Prize in 1995 for promoting nuclear disarmament. Europe has been a centre of anti-nuclear movements. It was Sasaki's understanding that after 1980 the anti-nuclear movement became active in Western Europe where any limited nuclear war would most likely take place between the US and USSR and that this had impacted the nuclear freeze movement in the US. Central to the European anti-nuclear movement were peace, disarmament and environment NGOs, the IKF (Inter-denominational Peace Council) in Holland, the CND (Campaign for Nuclear Disarmament) in the UK and the Green Party in Germany.

In January 1984, President Reagan called on the USSR to begin "a constructive dialogue" for the reduction of military arsenal and in September prior to the Presidential election he had a first meeting with Andrei Gromyko, the USSR Foreign Minister (1957-1985) and proposed the reopening of arms control negotiations that had been broken off at the end of 1983. In January 1985 George Shultz, US Secretary of State (1982-1989) met Gromyko in Geneva, and agreed to the reopening of negotiations on strategic nuclear weapons, intermediate nuclear weapons, and space weapons, thus putting the US-USSR military arms control negotiations back on track. Sasaki had two questions: what role did the Nuclear freeze movement in the US contribute to the political process, and can one assert that the Nuclear Freeze movement had moved the Reagan Administration again towards arms control negotiation? He concluded that, for the USSR to return to the negotiation table and in the final analysis to accept the terms US offered and conclude the Intermediate Range Nuclear Forces Treaty 1987, was not the outcome of the CSO movement but the result of power politics, i.e., that the US's consistent strength, particularly the effect of military containment could not be denied. In today's post-Cold War, multipolar world, this theory of power politics is much less likely to have currency. This dissertation will investigate through Japan's anti-nuclear CSO activities whether or not Sasaki's theory of the limits of anti-nuclear CSO activities still holds.

Claudia Kissling, University of Bremen, Germany, claimed nuclear matters belong to high politics in her book, "Civil Society and Nuclear Non-Proliferation: How do States Respond? (2008)", but she also asserted that CSOs play important roles. According to Kissling, it all started with CSO representatives being invited to participate in the Preparatory Committee meetings at the NPT Review Conference that began in 1995 and being asked to share their opinions regarding contents and direction of the items to be discussed. She further said the participation of NGOs made the NPT Review Process transparent. However, Kissling concluded that the NPT Review Conference itself was not productive due to the attitudes of the nuclear powers, particularly that of the US Government which was national interest oriented.[3]

The conclusion to be drawn from the above is the fact that the nuclear issue cannot be resolved without convincing governments,

---

[3] Claudia Kissiling, Civil Society and Nuclear Non-Proliferation: How do States Respons?, Ashgate 2008

"However, in the case of the NPT, the lack of interaction cannot only be attributed to inadequate preconditions for civil society involvement and its exclusion from an intergovernmental core of decision-making in the field of security. The hardening of many State positions and the tenacity with which they were hold lets to true delibration and preferred classical bargaining with no intention to adapt their positioning instead… In the case of the NPT RevCon, some actors, most prominently the US, indeed had fixed interests and preferences, resorted to strategic bargaining directed towards utility maximization and used rhetoric as justification, meaning that they were not prepared to change own beliefs". p175

particularly the nuclear powers. Another point is that the conventional anti-nuclear CSO movements are outside the political decision-making framework or even at the opposing end. When anti-nuclear CSOs come together to form a federation, agreements are hard to come by, thus inevitably exposing its structural weakness. And worse, the anti-nuclear CSO movement itself suffers from ebbs and flows affected by the atmosphere of the moment.

To date no one, not even scholars in Japan have made Japanese anti-nuclear CSO movements their subject of inquiry. This dissertation is significant in that it focuses on the private diplomacy of CSOs, in mitigating inter-state conflicts that lie behind nuclear issues as well as involving governments in social movements of nuclear disarmament.

Methodology

The source of material for this thesis is basically the diplomatic documents of the government of Japan. For the government's nuclear policies and the relations with China and the USSR, I have referred to a Diplomatic Blue Book, the materials collected and edited by the China Affairs Bureau of the Ministry of Foreign Affairs (MOFA), including statements by governments, and other basic Japan-China related materials and the minutes of the Diet (parliament) of Japan. I have researched in the official MOFA website, the National Diet Library Japan, the Diplomatic Archives of the MOFA, the Institute for Advanced Studies on Asia (University of Tokyo) data base. In 2010, I made a visit to the Permanent Mission of Japan to the International Organizations in Vienna to interview the First Secretary in charge of nuclear policy. In the same year, a visit was also made to the Arms Control and Disarmament Division, Disarmament, Non-Proliferation and Sciences Department of MOFA where I personally met and discussed issues with the officials in charge and was presented with a copy of the Disarmament and Non-Proliferation Policy of Japan which is a White Paper compiled and edited by the Division. The views collected from my interviews provided valuable materials for understanding the nuclear policy of the Ministry and its attitude concerning nuclear weapons.

There is no public record concerning the activities of the Japanese anti-nuclear CSOs or their private diplomacy, nor are they referred to in government official or diplomatic documents. I therefore personally researched the four CSOs referred to in this dissertation and directly received their reports, as well as their records of activities, quarterlies and official reports. Interviews were also conducted to learn of the distinguishing features of their nuclear abolition activities, their strategies, relations with the Japanese government as well as their views on the situation regarding the Northeast Asian region. The Japan Physicians for the Prevention of Nuclear War (JPPNW) provided me with the minutes of their meetings as well as their basic materials. In 2012, I visited its headquarters (in Hiroshima City), and interviewed the Secretary-General and the Senior Managing Director. I have also referred to their official website for the record of their activities and minutes of their Board of Directors' meetings. The Mayors for Peace (MP) referred me to their official website on which most of the information of their activities was made public both in Japanese and English. I also made a personal visit to their headquarters in the City of Hiroshima and had a personal interview with the Secretary-General. The Japanese Association of Lawyers against Nuclear Arms (JALANA) invited me to be its member. I was given the opportunity to participate in their annual general meeting and understand their point of view. For the purposes of my thesis I was able to gather information from their regularly distributed mail magazine, bulletin and official website. I also conducted an interview with the Secretary-General. The Soka Gakkai International (SGI) provided me with their annual report on NGO activities, quarterly, bulletin and materials and leaflets used for their Exhibition on the Abolition of Nuclear Weapons, and Daisaku Ikeda's Annual Peace Proposals and books. And from 2010 a number of interviews were held with the Chairman and the Secretary General of the SGI Peace Committee in charge of SGI's nuclear abolition movement. I was invited to one of their main activities, Exhibition on Nuclear Abolition, "From a Culture of Violence to a Culture of Peace Transforming the Human Spirit" that took place at the UN Office in Vienna on 16th October 2010 and was able to directly observe and learn about their thoughts and action strategies. In 2010, I visited their overseas bases of NGO activities, the SGI UN Liaison Office in New York and in Geneva, interviewed their representatives regarding nuclear abolition activities as well as receive materials. In 2012, I made a visit to the Soka Gakkai Hiroshima Peace Committee, the base of the SGI nuclear abolition activities, the Soka Gakkai Hiroshima Peace Committee, interviewed the Chairman and staff as well as receiving materials on the history of the activities of the Committee. I have also attended a number of times the Japan NGO Network for Nuclear Abolition (JNNNA) that was established in 2010. The Network has regular participation by the major anti-nuclear CSOs, such as JALANA and the SGI. At times, a representative of the International Campaign to Abolish Nuclear Weapons (ICAN)[4], international NGO alliance, is invited as a guest speaker. I would especially like to mention how I was able to receive most valuable testimonies concerning what took place

4 Nobel Peace Prize 2017

(including the situation and the direction of the Japanese government), at the meeting convened after the representatives returned from the Conference: Humanitarian Impact of Nuclear Weapons held in Oslo, Norway from 4-5 March 2013. Also in 2010, I made a visit to the Komeito Committee of Promoting the Abolition of Nuclear Weapons (KCPANW) and interviewed its Chairman, who is a member of the Japanese parliament, and was able to learn of the relationship between a political entity and CSOs, and their possible collaboration. Komeito is a Japanese political party and was founded by Daisaku Ikeda in 1964. The anti-nuclear ideology espoused by Ikeda and the SGI has its origin in the 13th-century philosophy of the Buddhist Monk Nichiren who preached the sacrosanctity of human life. I studied Nichiren's philosophy as well as the records of the military government's inquisition of Tsunesaburo Makiguchi, the Soka Gakkai's first president who was arrested and jailed by the military government during the Second World War (1944). Another document referred to was published only in Japanese as a collection (therefore, a joint publication) of Ikeda's deliberations with Richard Nicolaus von Coudenhove-Kalergi, Andre Malraux, Henry Kissinger and Norman Cousins, from which I found references to nuclear disarmament. And for the purpose of comparative analysis I checked what Japanese scholars have written about Japan's philosophy of nuclear armament. With regard to Ikeda's private diplomacy vis-à-vis China and the USSR in the cold-war era, the Soka Gakkai Office of International Affairs provided me with important materials on SGI's official positions. They included articles from its bulletin at the time and personal notes made public. Since SGI staff members in charge of SGI's relations with China and the USSR had already retired, I was provided for the purposes of my thesis a written document in Japanese with a particular focus on the SGI's relations with the Soviet Union, prepared by successors of the staff members to the best of his knowledge. Ikeda's interview articles in public media as well as books in Japanese were consulted.

My sources of objective materials were memoirs and testimonies of Japanese media correspondents and bureau chiefs stationed in China and the USSR at the time as well as notes and books written in Japanese by former MOFA experts on Russia as well as articles in major Japanese newspapers. I have only used articles that are reliable, having checked the dates and place of events and, clearly stating who (which organisation) did what, when and where. The books I referred to for the core matters of my research were published only in the Japanese language.

PART 2: Setting the Context

Chapter 1: Influence

This chapter provides an examination of Japan's political climate and social culture that make up the background of the history of its CSO activities as an introduction to the main theme of this dissertation on nuclear disarmament.

Japan's CSOs have an extremely short history of being involved in the political arena. To begin with the term "citizen" means a person with an independent identity, with clear concept of his rights, able to present his ideas on governmental and administrative issues, and act and take part in social activities.[1]

The concept of 'a citizen' in the West goes back to ancient Rome when citizens meant being responsible for the defence of polis as a member of the heavy infantry ("polites" in Latin), as well as participating in the administration/government of their cities and meant persons who possessed civil rights.

Such a tradition was weakened during the later Roman Empire and lost in the Dark Ages when Europe developed a discriminatory social hierarchy robbing citizens their rights of direct participation in political matters. Citizens won back such rights through the Puritan Revolution and the French Revolution. These developments in Western Europe of reinstallation of civil societies and the rights of the citizens had very little impact on Japan which until the end of the Second World War

[1] SHARE (a NGO that engages in international cooperation through health promotion), Interview with Professor Michio Ito of Rikkyo University Graduate School of Social Design Studies, Ima NGO Ga Hatasu Yakuwari Vol. 1 (Role of NGO Today Volume. 1), http://share.or.jp/opinion_advocacy/think/ito_michio_interview01.html (accessed on 1st May 2015)

maintained its feudal social system. In fact there has never been a civil revolution that would overturn the political system of the Japanese state, albeit there were times when famine and economic depression led to uprisings of peasants against the government. They, however, did not result in radical reform or collapse of the feudal system leading to citizens obtaining direct voting rights.

This has created a political climate and convention up to this day whereby people are expected to totally accept that the governments and administrators of the time are mandated to take care of all political decision making from diplomacy to national security, education as well as public welfare and social services on their behalf.

The Russian Revolution of 1917 and Marxism-Leninism, however, did affect Japan. From about 1910 proletarian movements claiming protection of rights of the working class caught on and developed into a cultural movement that involved intellectuals who produced Proletarian literature. This developed into a radical and violent movement that resulted in a High Treason Incident of 1910 which involved an anarchist socialist Shusui Kotoku (1871-1911) plotting to assassinate Emperor Meiji (1852-1912). The attempt at the assassination of the Emperor was prevented and in 1911, 24 socialists and anarchists including Shusui were sentenced to capital punishment, and 2 to prison terms. The Japanese Communist Party was initiated in 1922 but until the end of the Second World War it was considered illegal and therefore remained as an underground movement. While some regard these communist and socialist movements as the emergence of civil society in modern Japan, it is really only in the post Second World War era that a full-blown civil society and civil society movements came into existence.

However, there was another opportunity for people to be engaged in direct political participation. This was the establishment of the Imperial

Diet (Parliament) and the creation of the right to choose politicians through election. That is to say, bi-cameral elections were held in the House of Peers and the House of Representatives and eligibility for election was limited to men above the age of 25 who had paid a certain amount of taxes. Against the background of a democratic current in the post First World War period, the requirement for tax payment was abolished in 1925 and all men older than 25 years were granted voting rights (with the enactment of the General Election Law). Against this background ordinary citizens without peerage and governmental office were elected as representatives and a number of political parties were established. Representatives of citizens, without peerage and officialdom were called partisans as they developed political careers within political parties. However, political participation by citizen's representatives was blocked by the emergence of militarism.

This began with what is referred to as the 15th May Incident in 1932, the assassination of Prime Minister Tsuyoshi Inukai (1855-1932) by young Japanese naval officers which was followed by the 26th February Incident in 1936. This was an attempt at a coup d'etat by young army officers killing former Prime Minister Korekiyo Takahashi (1854-1936) and other leading government officials. Following these two incidents the military leaders occupied the majority of the important government posts while politicians, dreading attack and assassination, were not able to oppose the military. The military's radical and violent drive was brought to an end by Japan's defeat in the Second World War, but many liberal opinion leaders and CSOs, including the Soka Gakkai, were devastated by the harsh repression (see Chapter 3 and 4).

Nevertheless, popular suffrage did give birth to a Japanese CSO that continues to this day. Yukio Ozaki (1858-1954) [2] elected as a

---

[2] Yukio Ozaki 1858-1954,

representative of the people at the first House of Representatives Election stood uncompromisingly for constitutional government. He was the first to publicly criticize feudalistic clans and military governments that monopolized the cabinet and government offices usurping the name of the Emperor and the imperial mandate. He was committed to establishing the 'rule of law' and democracy. The "*Goken*" (constitution) movement, for defence of the Constitution (1912-13) which he led spread throughout the country and drove the clan-clique government of the Choshu-clansman General Taro Katsura (1847-1913) into resignation in a matter of 53 days. Ozaki's impeachment address of 1913 stands as a symbol of the Constitutional History of Japan and Ozaki is even today considered the 'Father of Constitutional Government'. The event can be said to have been the first time a citizen made a direct impact in changing a political regime.

> "They pay lip service to loyalty and patriotism, as if these were their monopoly…but just look how they behave. They hide behind the throne, lying in wait to ambush their political foes. They have made the throne their breastplate, and the rescript (imperial charter) their bullets to destroy their enemy"[3]

Inheriting Ozaki's commitment to defend rules and principles of democracy in spite of the will and intention of the government of the

---

Member of the House of Representatives Japan 1890-1953, Minister of Education 1898, Mayor of Tokyo City 1903-1912, Minister of Justice 1914-1916, Honorary Member of the House of Representatives, Honorary Citizen of Tokyo Metropolitan City

[3] Translated by Fujiko Hara, with a foreword by Marius B. Jansen, *The Autobiography of Ozaki Yukio: The Struggle for Constitutional Government in Japan*, Princeton University Press 2001, pp271

day, his daughter Yukika Sohma[4] established in 1979, a CSO Association to Aid Indochinese Refugees, today's Association for Aid and Relief (AAR Japan), by calling on the Japanese people to donate 1 yen each to provide shelter and humanitarian relief to Southeast Asian refugees from Indochina, driven away from their countries that were being socialized as well as provide material and medical goods to refugee camps. [5]

The actions Sohma took were different from those of the Japanese government. For while the Government ratified in 1981 the international convention relating to the Status of Refugees 1951, it has been extremely passive regarding the acceptance of refugees. The Japanese Government has certified and accepted 6 refugees in 2013 against the application from 3,260 refugees and in 2014, a limited 11 refugees against the 5,000 persons who applied.[6]

This is an extremely low number of people granted refugee status among developed countries. [7] Reuters, an international media

---

[4] Yukika Sohma 1912-2008,
President of the AAR, the first woman interpreter of English and Japanese languages, and were in executive positions in many CSOs in Japan.

[5] AAR Japan, History of AAR Japan the Ministry of Justice http://www.aarjapan.gr.jp/english/about/history.html (accessed on 15th June 2015)

[6] Ministry of Justice Japan, *Press Release: Immigration Bureau of Japan 20th March 2014: Number of Refugee Status 2013 (in Japanese)* http://www.moj.go.jp/nyuukokukanri/kouhou/nyuukokukanri03_00099.html (accessed on 15th June 2015)
Ministry of Justice Japan, *Press Release: Immigration Bureau of Japan 11th March 2015: Number of Refugee Status 2014 (in Japanese)* http://www.moj.go.jp/nyuukokukanri/kouhou/nyuukokukanri03_00103.html (accessed on 15th June 2015)

[7] UNHCR's Data in 2008
USA (application: 45,179. Granting refugee status 16,742), France (application: 38,089. Granting refugee status: 9,648), Canada (application: 14,338. Granting refugee status: 7,554), Germany (application: 14,614. Granting refugee status: 7,291), UK (application: 21,072. Granting refugee status: 4,752)

organisation based in the UK., carried one expert's opinion, 'there is no other country among the industrialized countries that has consistently recorded this low rate of refugee designation'. The German international broadcaster, Deutsche Welle, also carried an opinion to the effect that South Korea too has an extremely low acceptance of refugees and that this was the trend of East Asian countries 'a result of giving priority to economic development over human rights in the name of protecting national interest and domestic markets. [8]

The Ministry of Justice in Japan claimed that the reason for the low number of acceptance of refugees is because most of the applicants were not refugees but job seekers. Even though that may be so, it is still an extremely low number of refugee recognition.[9]

The ministry's allegation is also at odds with the future health of the Japanese economy. For the Ministry of Health, Labour and Welfare Japan (MHLW) just released its forecast that due to declining birth rate and an aging population there will be a need for 2,480,000 care-givers by 2025 but the number of staff will be limited to 2,150,000. [10] The future of the Japanese economy cannot be sustained by the Japanese labour force so that an active immigration policy is becoming urgently required. The trend, however, is towards refusing job-seeking

---

The Network Aiming at the Coexistence with the Refugees in Japan http://www.rafiq.jp/event/101205nanmin_report.pdf (accessed 15th June 2015)

[8] NewsSphere 13th March 2015, Nihon No Nanmin Nintei 5000Nin Chu 11Nin To Senshinkoku Chu Saitei Shimaguni Ha Iiwakeni Naranai Kaigai Kara Hihan (Japanese Government gave only 11 people the refugee status out of 5,000. Their word "island country" cannot become a reason to refuse refugees) http://newsphere.jp/politics/20150313-1/ (accessed on 15th June 2015)

[9] Ibid

[10] The Nikkei (newspaper) 13th February 2015, Kaigoshoku No Fukushoku Shien Nado Teian (30Man Nin Busoku De Koro Sho (It will be 300,000 employees short: the MHLW suggested supporting staffs, who were in nursing or care for aged, to reinstate)
http://www.nikkei.com/article/DGXLASFS13H4N_T10C15A2EE8000/ (accessed on 15th June 2015)

immigrants not just refugees. Regarding the Syrian refugee crisis, Germany and other EU countries announced they would receive a large number of refugees in 2015. The United States also announced an increase in its annual number of immigrants accepted from 70,000 to 100,000 by 2017. [11] This is to support Syrian refugees. [12] The Japanese government accepted only three Syrian people[13] in spite of the fact that the UN High Commissioner for Refugees (UNHCR) asked them for support (as of September 2015).[14] This is evidence that Japan is passive about becoming a diverse society after the model of Western countries.

What Sohma did was to support refugees wherever they were instead of action by the government of Japan. In 2015, the AAR's refugee support activities have expanded to cover 60 countries and regions around the world. It has become a successful case of CSO activities independent of the government. Today, Sohma's daughter Fujiko Hara is carrying on the commitment of Ozaki and Sohma to

---

[11] CNN Politics, *Kerry: U.S. to accept more Syrian Refugees*, 20th September 2015 (accessed on 21st September 2015)
http://edition.cnn.com/2015/09/20/politics/syrian-refugees-john-kerry/index.html

[12] Ibid

[13] Asahi Shimbun Digital, Syria Nanmin No Wakamono Seifu Ga Gentei Ukeire O Kento (The Japanese government will accept young Syrian asylum seekers as international students not refugees) 25th September 2015 (accessed on 1st October 2015)
http://www.asahi.com/articles/ASH9S761TH9SUTFK025.html
60 Syrian people applied for refugee status to the Japanese government. But the government accepted only three people.

[14] Asahi Shimbun Digital, Syria Nanmin Ukeire O Nihon Seifu Ni Yosei UNHCR Kyokucho (Director of UNHCR requested the Japanese government to receive Syrian refugees) 21st June 2015 (accessed on 5th July 2015) http://www.asahi.com/articles/ASH6N443BH6NUHBI00D.html
Amin Awad, UNHCR Director for Middle East and North Africa Operations, visited Japan and requested the Japanese government to receive Syrian refugees.

establish constitutionalism and a civil society. In accordance with the spirit of the Constitution she presides over Gakudo-kai, a study group established with a like-minded group of people, to live up to the rights and responsibilities (sovereignty) bestowed by the new constitution to accept such national issues as our own. Top level scholars, politicians and those who served with UN organizations are invited as speakers to learn of the issues before us and to examine what each one of us can do to improve the situation. [15] "Gakudo" is a nom de plume of Ozaki. For a CSO's activities to spread over 3 generations and over 100 years can be said to be a rare case of a successful civil movement initiated in Japan.

In Japan, women's suffrage and eligibility for election were granted under the occupation policy led by the US Forces following the Second World War. For Japan it was a national imperative to regain independence from the occupation and recover sovereignty. The Shigeru Yoshida government in power, however, chose secret diplomacy as means of achieving the most important objectives.

During the negotiation process of the 1952 Treaty of Peace with Japan that endorsed its independence, Yoshida sent his Minister of Finance, Hayato Ikeda (1899-1965) to the US in 1950 ostensibly to explain to the US government the state of Japan's economy and to facilitate introduction of foreign capital and its reconstruction.[16] At the same time, Yoshida arranged for Ikeda to have a secret meeting

---

[15] Gakudo-kai Official Website http://gakudo-kai.com/ (accessed on 20th June 2015)

[16] The House of Representatives Japan, Questions from Jintaro Yokota (Member of the House) on 13th December 1950 and Answer from Prime Minister Yoshida on 11th January 1951,
http://www.shugiin.go.jp/internet/itdb_shitsumona.nsf/html/shitsumon/010025.htm (accessed on 28th April 2015)

concerning security and diplomatic affairs with Joseph Dodge[17] and others, to allow stationing of the US armed forces in Japan following reconciliation and regaining independence. This secret diplomacy was made public by a testimony given by Kiuchi Miyazawa[18] an official of the Ministry of Finance who had accompanied Hayato Ikeda as his secretary.

> "At the time there were two groups in Japan, those who were for early peace and those for total peace. The former was mainly represented by conservatives and they thought that it was better to reach an early, even though limited, peace with democratic states led by the United States of America. Conservatives mainly represented this group. On the other hand, the Socialist Party of Japan and the Communist Party Japan were for peace on all fronts, claiming that separate peace would not enable Japan to resolve the state of war with the USSR, therefore, peace should be made at the same time with both the US and the Soviet groups. There was difficulty in reaching an early peace apart from arranging peace on all fronts that the conservatives wished. And that issue was none other than the defence of Japan following the peace. Realistically, while in reality Japan needed to be under the protection of the US it was difficult to find an easy explanation to convince the majority of the people how an independent state can possibly allow foreign armed forces to be stationed... In any case, Hayato Ikeda was informed of

---

[17] Joseph Doge (1890-1964). Chairman of the Detroit Bank, now Comerica. Dodge also served as an economic advisor to the US government for postwar economic stabilization programme in Germany and Japan.

[18] Prime Minister of Japan 1991-1993, Minister of Finance 1998-2001, Member of the House of Representatives 1967-2003, Member of the House of Councillors 1953-1965

Yoshida's intentions only just before his departure. Looking back it appears that it was there and then that PM Yoshida leaked what we know today, the concept written in the US-Japan Security Treaty, that he gave the go ahead for Japan to request the stationing of US troops." [19]

(Translated by Fujiko Hara)

Yoshida was a former diplomat, a bureaucrat turned politician. One could say that his political attitude was one that had been inherited from the pre-war bureaucratic structure of government and he had no regard for freedom of information or participation by citizens. He was known to have a penchant for appointing ex-bureaucrat politicians to cabinet posts that included Hayato Ikeda from the Ministry of Finance and Eisaku Sato from the Ministry of Railways who in the end served as prime ministers. This system was euphemistically called the Yoshida School.

Important post war political decisions were made not based on the will of the people or a popular referendum. True, Japan was poor and in a chaotic situation following its wartime defeat, nonetheless it has clearly missed important opportunities for nurturing civil society and developing the power of public opinion on diplomatic and security issues.

It appears that Japan has a well-rooted institutional habit, perhaps designed to avoid unnecessary frictions, for part of the top echelon secretly to make important decisions on implementation of important policies and undertakings. The Constitution of Japan too had been drafted by the Occupation Army, and in that sense, it can be said that the post war reconstruction policy had been established within a framework

[19] Kiichi Miyazawa, Tokyo-Washing No Mitsudan (The Secret Conversation between Tokyo and Washington), Chuokoronsha. Ltd 1999, p46-p47

that had not had any participation by the general public. The Post War Japanese democracy had been bequeathed by the Occupation Army, in particular the US, and was not won by the Japanese people by themselves. That said, however, policy decisions of the Yoshida government, did play an important role in building today's economic power and without doubt the Japanese Constitution itself has provided a sure foundation for Japan to prosper as a peace-loving nation.

As a result, however, such historical footprints have caused the Japanese people to develop a mentality to the effect that they could leave it up to the government to make political decisions. The Puritan Revolution in the United Kingdom built the basic system of today's parliamentary democracy in the UK and the French Revolution spawned the well-known present day national slogan of "Liberté, Égalité, Fraternité" in France. For the Japanese, however, we may be able to read history books and text books, novels and other materials to learn about and imagine those historic events but we find it difficult to personally feel and experience the spirit and energy of the people dedicated to changing government and achieving their objectives.

The absence of any historical experience of the citizens taking the situation into their own hands to change it has left the majority disinterested and cynical about their inability to act. This is the reality of the Japanese way of thinking, no doubt unbelievable to Westerners who have a history of achieving reforms. The SGI's Daisaku Ikeda too has the following to say about the thinking pattern of the Japanese society.

> "Japanese society has an age-old tendency to avoid seeing things from the perspective of whether they are good or evil which has given rise to adages and proverbs such as 'better bend than break (don't kick against the pricks) or 'look for a big tree

when you seek shelter (if you rely on someone, rely on the powerful). They represent spiritual climate that encourages one to seek self-protection and self-interest rather than seek good over bad and right over wrong. Such social soil of vacillation and indecision can be said to have allowed atrocious invasion of other countries (the Second World War) and denial of the freedom of speech under the rampant militarism back home."[20] (Translated by Fujiko Hara)

This trend continues to this day. It was only in 1998 that the government of Japan passed the Non-Profit Organisation Act. It was to grant legal status to organizations, such as CSOs, undertaking specific non-profit activities to promote free social activities of citizens.

The government created a system with this law that recognized 20 areas[21] of activities officially authorized by local governments on submission of plans of action as well as financial foundation. This was

---

[20] Stuart Rees and Daisaku Ikeda, Heiwa To Tetsugaku To Shigokoro O Kataru (Dialogue on Peace, Philosophy and Poetic Inspiration), Daisan Bunmeisha, Co., Ltd 2014 p268-p269

[21] 1: welfare including promoting medication and insurance, 2: social education, 3: town planning, 4: tourism, 5: promoting developing fishing and agricultural villages, 6: promoting activities of academics, culture, arts or sports, 7: environmental conservation, 8: disaster rescue, 9: regional safety, 10: protection of human rights and peace promotion, 11: international cooperation, 12: promoting gender-equal society, 13: education for children, 14: promoting information society (information technology), 15: promoting science and technology, 16: promoting economic activities, 17: human resource development and developing employment opportunities, 18: consumer protection, 19: helping activities of the 18 areas above, 20: other activities equivalent to the 18 areas above (especially authorised by each local prefectural government).
Cabinet Office of Japanese Government, *Tokutei Hieiri Katsudo Towa (What is the Activities of Non-Profit Organisation?)*
https://www.npo-homepage.go.jp/about/npo-kisochishiki/nposeido-gaiyou
(accessed on 1st May 2015)

the first law that publically recognized civic activities freely undertaken by citizens and was put in place by civic organizations and associations of supra-partisan members of parliament.[22] Originally the bill was named 'The Act to Promote Citizens' Activities' but the use of the term 'citizens' was opposed by some of the conservative politicians who in turn proposed a "Law for Civic Service". Finally, those involved agreed to the current naming of the law.[23]

The term 'citizen' has a special place in Japan and is not popularly used by the public. Further, conservative politicians interpret the word to mean communists, socialists or anarchic anti-establishments figures. In its place, 'common people' is the term generally used in Japan, understood as a community of people who stay away from tackling political and economic issues that are beyond their brief, content to submit to be ruled. Thus, 'common people' does not suggest autonomous individuals.[24]

Even today, some time since the law had been enacted, the Cabinet Office reported that 40% of Japanese people are uninterested in voluntarily participating in civic activities (as of 2013). Since it is reported that in the wake of the Great East Japan Earthquake of 2011, 18.9% of the people volunteered to help the victims, it follows that prior to 2011, some 60% of the Japanese people were uninterested in volunteer activities. As of 2013, 65% of the Japanese people have no experiences in participating in such activities.[25]

---

[22] Professor Michio Ito of Rikkyo University Graduate School of Social Design Studies, *Ima NGO Ga Hatasu Yakuwari Vol. 1 (Role of NGO Today Volume. 1)*, SHARE (a NGO that engages in international cooperation through health promotion)
http://share.or.jp/opinion_advocacy/think/ito_michio_interview01.html
(accessed on 1st May 2015)

[23] Ibid

[24] Ibid

[25] Cabinet Office of Japanese Government, Hokokusho: Heisei 25Nendo

Following the enactment of the law there were 23 recognized juridical corporations, but by 2015 this had increased to 50,147, (of which 839 enjoy a special-tax break on their donations received.[26] Most of the well-heeled and active corporations receive commissioned undertakings or subsidies from the government, while those organizations engaged in areas the government has no interest in or those that carry out independent activities against governmental policies are mostly financially weak. It must be pointed out that this is often a result of a lack of strong commitment as citizens and temptations to receive government subsidies.[27]

Also, unlike in Western countries, there is little custom among the Japanese to make personal donations. It follows, therefore, that unless organizations have sufficient foundations for their activities including their financial base, many of the successful NPOs (Non-Profit Organisations) and NGOs are submissive to government policies and often are commissioned to carry out governmental programmes. As such, it is difficult for them to develop independent activities opposing,

---

Shimin No Shakai Koken Ni Kansuru Zittai Chosa (Report: Factual Survey of People's Contribution to Society 2015), p11
https://www.npo-homepage.go.jp/uploads/h25_shimin_chousa_all.pdf (accessed on 1st May 2015)
The Cabinet Office entrusted a survey company named the Navit in Tokyo to make this survey. It targeted 10,000 Japanese citizens in all areas of Japan (male 47%, female 53%. Age: 20-69), and spent 45 days (7th September – 22nd October 2013).

[26] Cabinet Office of Japanese Government, *Tokutei Hieiri Katsudo Hojin No Ninteisu No Suii (Transition of Number of Certified Non-Profit Organisations)*, https://www.npo-homepage.go.jp/about/toukei-info/ninshou-seni (accessed on 1st May 2015)

[27] Professor Michio Ito of Rikkyo University Graduate School of Social Design Studies, *Ima NGO Ga Hatasu Yakuwari Vol. 1 (Role of NGO Today Volume. 1)*, SHARE (a NGO that engages in international cooperation through health promotion)
http://share.or.jp/opinion_advocacy/think/ito_michio_interview01.html (accessed on 1st May 2015)

or taking clearly different positions, from the government.

CSOs in Japan are clearly increasing but the effectiveness of their activities is a different matter. In the field of nuclear disarmament, the subject of this thesis, it is noteworthy that the positions of non-nuclear CSOs and the policies of the government do not always agree.

The four CSOs researched in this dissertation represent organizations with independent financial bases, independent and powerful physicians, lawyers, local governments and religious organizations but they are not certified by the Non-Profit Organisation Act. They represent independent civic activities clearly beyond the frame of the government and are creating an interesting history of civic activities in Japan where diplomatic and security issues are broadly considered as the sole prerogative of the government.

Here, definition of 'influence', included in the title of the dissertation is examined. It means close relations between things and organizations, having large effects and causing changes and reactions on others.

Also, having an impact on international or domestic policies means incorporating one's ideas to initiate certain activities that would otherwise have taken place. That is to say, if a certain organization with a specific policy recommendation had participated in the policy making process and its policy had been adopted, one could say that the organization had contributed to developing a policy.

There is, however, little possibility in Japan today for the government and a particular CSO to sit down at a table to develop a policy together.

Therefore, the effect of a social movement on policy making depends on how effectively it can project its policy recommendation during the process of policy making, from their presentation to their adoption and final evaluation. It also means that if the CSO can provide perspectives or logical positions that were missing in the government's sphere of interests and also that a CSO can expand its work through its civilian network with which the county the government has no official diplomatic relations. This will help to establish a foundation on which national governments can develop relations and start negotiations. This can be one way of recognizing CSOs to have had an impact. Even when such efforts do not always produce a large and clear outcome. For CSOs to continue to work on the government so that it shows interest in nuclear disarmament, this should be recognized as having an impact.

Generally speaking, CSOs have impact on such issues as the economy, the military, using messages sent via the media, by information and communication technology (ICT), SNS (Social Networking Service) as well as their specialized knowledge, and diplomatic power (including having access to foreign countries and other organizations, networking and power of negotiation). Some organizations and states often combine those factors to exert their leverage.

For example, one of the ways the Japanese government exerted its influence over the international community was to provide economic assistance, including the Official Development Assistance (ODA) starting in 1954.

This was a strategic policy beyond adopting the theory of redistribution, of the 'haves' assisting the 'have nots' or based on humanitarianism. In fact, in 2015, the Japanese government, from the standpoint of active pacifism based on international cooperation, announced that the role of ODA was becoming ever greater. Seeking a greater position for Japan in the international community, it adopted strategic viewpoints, namely, sharing universal values, collaboration for peace and stability of the international community, strategic expansion of ODA towards economic growth of developing countries and Japan, promotion of human security, and building strategic partnerships.[28]

Clearly, this strategy is in response to the abduction and killing of two Japanese nationals in February 2015 by a terrorist group, the ISIL (Islamic State in Iraq and the Levant) and the need to expand collaboration against global terrorism as well as to the unstable security environment in Northeast Asia caused by Japan's friction with China and Russia (see Chapter 5 and 6). Japan has set aside 423 billion yen for the 2015 ODA budget.[29]

Since Japan does not possess nuclear weapons and since its Constitution clearly denies the right of belligerency and possessing military power, its economic power is the way to exert its influence. Also, Japan's contribution to the UN is second only to that of the United States (see Chapter 2). Japan also aims to be a member of the Security Council, using the same kind of pressure.

That would require a fundamental reform of the UN Security Council. On the other hand, it is interesting to note that Japan, an economic power but, by its law, not in possession of military power has been elected 11 times to the non-permanent member of the Council between 1958 and 2015, with the support of UN members. This may be recognized as a fruit of its ODA policy.

Indeed, Japan has been elected the most frequently. Just for comparison, Italy and Canada had served 6 times, and Germany 5 times; this gives Japan a big lead. It can be said that this is a symbolic case of how the power of an economy can have a great impact on

---

28 MOFA, *ODA Budget (13th May 2015)* http://www.mofa.go.jp/mofaj/gaiko/oda/shiryo/yosan.html (accessed on 10th May 2015)

29 Ibid

international relations. In addition, Japan served as the host nation at the 7th Pacific Islands Leaders Meeting (PALM 7) in 2015.[30]

Prime Minister Shinzo Abe announced in a keynote lecture Japan's financial assistance amounting to a total of 55 billion yen, was spent with a view to staving off China's influence in the South Pacific as well as to supporting Japan in its efforts at reform of the UN. What is meant by UN reform is clearly for the Japanese government to have a greater impact on the UN and in the end to be a permanent member of the UN Security Council.

> "In order for us to face up to the fury of nature and also recover even better from disasters, we must bring to each other our wisdom and experiences while maintaining connections in which we help each other out at any time. What will help us achieve this goal well is a community committed to (the) equality of all before the law, which places importance on democracy and has great regard for the human rights of each individual. What we should have are two-way relations that are as level as the horizon itself and entirely free of threats using force or coercion. That is the order for a society of Pacific citizens…one is that Japan is now working to boost momentum towards reforming the United Nations. I would like very much to ask for your understanding and cooperation in this area…I am looking forward to being able to meet you, the leaders of island nations, again this autumn on the side-lines of the United

---

[30] Participating Countries: Japan, Kiribati, Cook Islands, Samoa, the Solomon Islands, Tuvalu, Tonga, Nauru, New Zealand, Niue, Vanuatu, Papua New Guinea, Palau, Fiji, Marshal, Micronesia, Australia and the United States (US started to participated in from PALM 6 in 2012)
MOFA, PALM http://www.mofa.go.jp/mofaj/area/ps_summit/ (accessed on 1st June 2015)

Nations General Assembly."[31]

After its defeat in the Second World War, Japan has, through its economic power staked out a certain amount of presence and influence in the international community, but this provided cause for criticism at the time of the Gulf War (see Chapter 2). It was a criticism of Japan's lack of human contribution by countries that were paying the cost of losing the lives of men participating in the multilateral forces.[32]

This was an emotional criticism, demanding Japan shed blood together rather than appreciating how much Japan's actual contribution of a total of $130 billion had gone to support the joint forces. However, this was a case of acknowledging that economic power does not necessarily have positive effect in gaining respect and support.

Military force is one of the vehicles that have had the longest impact on the history of man. For example, it had led to military dictatorship, as a method of governing the masses. Military dictatorship usually governs through an undemocratic decision-making process, does not recognize diverse perspectives and opinion, including anti-establishment views, and leads government to resort to all out information control. It brainwashes people by providing information favourable to the government, and by censoring and shutting out information from abroad.

These are cases of premodern use of power. Today, when the masses

---

[31] MOFA, "A Beacon for Diplomacy toward PICs: Working to Establish a Society of Pacific Citizens" Keynote Speech by Prime Minister Shinzo Abe during the Opening Session of the Seventh Pacific Islands Leaders Meeting (PALM7) May 23, 2015 Iwaki, Fukushima http://www.mofa.go.jp/mofaj/files/000081724.pdf (accessed on 1st June 2015)

[32] Hiroshi Nakanishi (Professor of Kyoto University), *Wangan Senso To Nihon Gaiko (The Gulf War and Japanese Diplomacy)* http://www.nippon.com/ja/features/c00202/ (accessed on 12th June 2015)

are able to directly access all sorts of information, that sort of regime has collapsed, with a few exceptions. Egypt, for example, where the thirty-plus years of Hosni Mubarak regime collapsed due to SNS inspired anti-regime mass insurgency. One could cite this as a case where information technology defeated military power. Peculiar cases are Thailand and North Korea. North Korea has created an isolated spot by shutting out the Internet and all information networks and strictly regulating its people from leaving the country.

In Thailand, a military regime was established by the 2014 coup-d'état. However, the king holds a strong power in this country and is deeply loved by his people. As a result the loyalty of the national army is to the king rather than to the government. It is generally accepted by the people that the army rose up to stabilize the confused state of the country. A September 2014 opinion poll showed that ninety per cent of the people are satisfied with the military administration.[33] Since freedom of speech is controlled the facts of the poll are unclear, but it is said that the military is not abusing the power, as did its Thaksin Shinawatra regime. The case, however, is not a simple case of saying that military power is effective in correcting corrupt democratic government.

Osamu Akagi, [34] a specialist on Thai politics pointed out "The military may be on its way to building a 'democratic state' but there are limits as it leaves room for military intervention at any time. Without the growth of Civilian Control true democratization cannot take place

---

[33] Mainichi Shimbun 27th October 2014, Yureru Okoku: Thai "Kai Kaku" No Yukue /2 Sizi Eru Gunsei "Minshuka" (Shaking Kingdom: Thai "Road for Reformation" Part 2, Military Government is getting support) http://mainichi.jp/shimen/news/20141027ddm007030127000c.html (accessed on 12th June 2015)

[34] Special Appointed Professor of Osaka University of Tourism (Japan) and Honorary Professor of Osaka University of Foreign Studies

(translated by Fujiko Hara)".[35] Military power can be likened to powerful medicine, with a high possibility of adverse reactions. Changes brought about by the use of military power have strong possibilities of leaving deep roots of problems in the future.

Escalation of military power has left deep scars of history, such as Nazi Germany and the Pol Pot Regime in Cambodia. Among military power nuclear weapons are prime examples of military power for their destructive force and remain today as symbols of international power politics. Needless to say, it is out of the question to expect CSOs to exert military influence for they do not possess military power to pressure governments.

The media and ICT belong to the same category in that they create public opinion and thus affect policy making. Newspapers and the media have plainly been the means by which citizens shared information. Newspapers and other media are expected to have a high level of reliability but, in the final analysis, they provide standardized information unilaterally.

On the other hand, the Internet, 'whirlpool information' as it is called, provides a massive amount of 'facts', including information that has no credibility, even false information, for users to choose from. While the Internet provides advantages for users to choose and acquire the information they seek, the trustworthiness of the information is inferior to newspapers and media. According to a 2011 survey conducted by the Ministry of Internal Affairs and Communications Japan (MIAC), citizens relied 94.9% on television as source of

---

[35] Mainichi Shimbun 27th October 2014, Yureru Okoku: Thai "Kai Kaku" No Yukue /2 Sizi Eru Gunsei "Minshuka" (Shaking Kingdom: Thai "Road for Reformation" Part 2, Military Government is getting support) http://mainichi.jp/shimen/news/20141027ddm007030127000c.html (accessed on 12th June 2015)

information (92.1% in 2005 survey) while newspapers stood at 77.3% (86.5% in 2005 survey) and Internet users 61.4% (41.4% in 2005 survey). This shows that users of the Internet as source of information are rapidly on the rise.

However, for reliability as a sources of information television scored 63,3%, newspapers, 72.7% and the Internet remained at 28.9%.[36] Nevertheless, the large-scale anti-government movement that took place in Arab countries in 2012, the so-called "the Arab Spring", mostly used Facebook to mobilize people. According to a survey conducted by the Dubai School of Government, a government managed think tank, during the Arab Spring people used Facebook to learn more about the background of the protest, including transmission of information on the protest movement and related information, plans for action and control of activities, in excess of 80% of the users used Face book to exchange information regarding movements.[37] Also, citizens of Egypt used SNS 88.1%, local and non-government media 62.7%, and regional and international media 56.85%.[38] This means that ICT was effectively used not just as a source of information but in sharing as well as transmitting information. It proved efficient in establishing citizens' movements towards bringing down long-term despotism.

However, in the case of nuclear disarmament, the purpose is not to bring down the government but the point is to find ways for governments to promote nuclear disarmament policies. The four anti-nuclear CSOs, the subject of this paper, have official websites as

---

[36] MIAC, *2011 White Paper: Information and Communications in Japan* http://www.soumu.go.jp/johotsusintokei/whitepaper/ja/h23/html/nc213230.html (accessed on 18th June 2015)

[37] MIAC, *2012 White Paper: Information and Communications in Japan* http://www.soumu.go.jp/johotsusintokei/whitepaper/ja/h24/html/nc1212c0.html (accessed on 18th June 2015)

[38] Ibid

well as specialized pages on nuclear disarmament. Their effects are considered in Chapter 3.

A major of US think tanks is that their influence is specialized. That is to say, their think tanks are divided into non-ideological and ideological think tanks that are polarized into conservative and liberal ideologies.[39] One of the reasons there are a huge number of think tanks in the US is the 'spoils system' of the administration. At the time of the change of administration there is a huge demand for recruiting specialists and think tanks are one of the suppliers of such talents. On the other hand, think tanks are precious employers of retired administration officials. Another reason for their existences is that they can expect large donations, since non-profit organizations are promised preferential tax treatments by law.

Ideological think tanks are considered to encourage ideological conflicts within the US political scene. Conservative think tanks are part of the Republican network while liberal think tanks work with Democrats both providing constant policy recommendations and related information. Politicians, therefore, depend a great deal on think tanks and appreciate their worth.

On the other hand, non-ideological think tanks due to their neutrality, credibility of their policy suggestions and information, are rated higher than their ideological counterparts. According to the 1997 survey conducted among the US Congress staff and journalists, the Brookings

---

[39] <Conservative think tanks>: Heritage Foundation, American Enterprise Institute (AEI), Cato Institute, Hoover Institute and Hudson Institute, etc
<Liberal think tanks>: Center for American Progress (CAP), Center on Budget and Policy Priorities, Economic Policy Institute, Institute for Policy Studies and Third Way, etc
<Non-Ideological think tanks>: Brooking Institution, Carnegie Endowment for International Peace, Council on Foreign Relations, RAND Corporation, Center for Strategic and International Studies, etc

Institution had the highest credibility, followed by the RAND Corporation. The third was the AEI, the fourth, Council on Foreign Relations and the fifth, the Carnegie Endowment for International Peace[40]. The Heritage Foundation which is a conservative think tank was ranked the most influential but ninth in its credibility.[41] Non-ideological think tanks contribute talents regardless of whether they are Republicans or Democrats and they maintain their impact on policy recommendation as their ideology-free views are treasured.[42]

On the other hand, the Japanese government employs French type elite government officials rather than the US spoils system; there is hardly any way for private citizens to become bureaucrats. Also, since there is no legal status for think tanks in Japan, they grow out of civil organisations and business corporations also conduct research activities

---

[40] Tomoyuki Yoshida of University of Tokyo, *Amerika Ni Okeru Ideorogi Teki Bunkyokuka To Sinku Tank (Ideological Polarization: American Think Tanks)*, US-Japan Research Institute (USJI) 21st July 2011
http://www.us-jpri.org/en/reports/seminar/miyata20110721_2.pdf (accessed on 17th June 2015)

[41] Andrew Rich, War of Ideas: Why mainstream and liberal foundations and the think tanks they support are losing in the war of ideas in American politics, Stanford Social Innovation Review, Graduate School of Business, Stanford University Spring 2005 pp24
http://www.ssireview.org/pdf/2005SP_feature_rich.pdf (accessed on 17th June 2015)

[42] "Richard N. Haass (former Director for Policy Planning for the US Department of State under the George W. Bush administration. He worked for the Brooking Institutions), James Steinberg (former Deputy Secretary of State under the Obama Administration. He worked for the RAND Corporation and the Brooking Institutions) and Susan Rice (former US Ambassador to the UN and Assistant to the President for National Security under Obama Administration. She worked for the Brooking Institution), etc"
Tomoyuki Yoshida of University of Tokyo, *Amerika Ni Okeru Ideorogi Teki Bunkyokuka To Sinku Tank (Ideological Polarization: American Think Tanks)*, US-Japan Research Institute (USJI) 21st July 2011
http://www.us-jpri.org/en/reports/seminar/miyata20110721_2.pdf (accessed on 17th June 2015)

as think tanks.[43] Only 48% of them carry out research, and unless they are public foundations or public associations, they do not have any preferential tax treatment.[44]Also, only about 10% (19 institutions) give priority to political and administrative fields as well as international issues. The majority of their research areas are limited to local autonomy and economic issues.

Specialized research institutes on nuclear disarmament are limited to the Centre for the Promotion of Disarmament and Non-Proliferation [CPDNP] (public foundation) established by MOFA and universities in Hiroshima and Nagasaki.[45] Each research institute has excellent accomplishments in nuclear disarmament research but they have yet to have large impacts on government's policy decisions. They have neither a system nor the custom of dispatching talents to the government as seen in the US think tanks. Not only that, since the CPDNP employs MOFA staff and diplomats, it acts as MOFA's external organ. As such it is difficult for it to totally oppose the government's diplomatic and security policies.

Diplomatic power is mainly composed of accessibility to and networking among nation states, private and public sectors and among citizens. Diplomacy other than that between governments is referred to

---

[43] "There are about 300 private organisations and corporations are working as "think tanks" in Japan (as of 2014). National Institute for Research Advancement (Japan) [NIRA] could receive replies and reports from 181 organisations (out of 300). Its ratio is general incorporated foundations (17%), public foundations (18%), general incorporated associations (7%), public associations (1%), non-profit organisations (NPT) and incorporated general educational institutions (universities and colleges, etc) [9%]." National Institute for Research Advancement (Japan) [NIRA], Outline of Survey Result of "Information of Think Tanks 2014", http://www.nira.or.jp/pdf/tt2014_gaiyo.pdf (accessed on 17th June 2015)

[44] Ibid

[45] The Institute for Peace Science (Hiroshima University), the Hiroshima City University Peace Institute, the Nagasaki University Research Centre for Nuclear Weapons Abolition

as non-official diplomacy, private diplomacy, civil diplomacy or civilian diplomacy but for the purpose of this paper it will be referred to as private diplomacy. Through cultural and international exchanges conducted by CSOs and private organisations private diplomacy contributes to highlighting national interests and values to other parties and the international community as well as to realizing mutual understanding through resolving tensions. These provide a standard in deciding whether diplomatic power has been manifested.

When diplomatic relations cease, or when political tensions increase, it is difficult to have official meetings and even non-official meetings are restrained. In such an atmosphere it is difficult even to contemplate holding meetings, and the parties are left to sound out each other's intentions inviting danger of inflexibility on both sides. In such times diplomatic channels can be opened through exchanges between citizens and civic organizations. Relations between the US and Iran is one such example. In 2008, President Ahmadinejad of Iran went to the US for the 63rd UN General Assembly but the White House did not meet him. However, a small group of American peace and human rights activities did have a talk with him. Their purpose was to introduce him to the American community and to tell him their commitment to anti-war and disavowal of violence.[46]

Ahmadinejad apparently told the group that he was ready for further IAEA inspections. The neutrality of the Peace and Human Rights Group is suspect as it used expressions praising Ahmadinejad's speech and behaviour. Nonetheless, such doubt and criticism come with private

---

[46] Ed Hale, White House Does Not Meet with Iran President Ahmadinejad during UN General Assembly Meeting But a Small Group of American Citizens Does, Peace with Iran 25th April 2007 http://www.peacewithiran.com/white-house-does-not-meet-with-iran-president-ahmadinejad-during-un-general-assembly-meeting-%E2%80%93-but-a-small-group-of-american-citizens-does/#more-86 (accessed on 16th June 2015)

diplomacy. What is important is that it was able to draw out Ahmadinejad's words concerning nuclear inspections.

Among examples of Japanese private diplomacies, an outstanding one was the 3,000 cherry blossom trees presented to Washington DC in 1912 and planted along the Potomac River as a symbol of friendship by Yukio Ozaki, as the Mayor of Tokyo. Cherry blossoms are the floral emblems of Japan. And in Japan planting trees mean 'planting life', thus conveying a wish for eternal friendship to prosper. Ozaki's presentation, strictly speaking was diplomacy by a local government body. Since the MP referred to in this dissertation is also involved in diplomacy by local governments (see Chapter 3), this research has categorized non-government diplomacy as private diplomacy. During the Second World War the cherry blossom trees were renamed as 'Eastern trees' and some branches were cut as acts of retaliation against Japan. However, soon after the end of the war cherry blossom queens were elected in both countries and they continue to represent the history of Japan-America friendship.

The National Cherry Blossom Festival begun in 1935 continues to be a celebrated place where over forty thousand people visit from the length and breadth of the United States of America.[47] They present opportunities to promote mutual understanding and peace and friendship by holding events at which Japanese Americans who were compulsorily confined are invited to share their experiences.[48]

---

[47] National Cherry Blossom Festival http://www.nationalcherryblossomfestival.org/ (accessed on 17th June 2015)
The Japan-American Society of Washington DC, *55th Annual Sakura Matsuri Japanese Street Festival* http://www.sakuramatsuri.org/japanese/ (accessed on 17th June 2015)

[48] Sankei Shimbun 29th March 2015, "Nihon No Isan O Hokori Ni Sogo Rikai O" Zenbei Sakura Matsuri De Nikkeizin No Rekishi O Kataritsugu Shikiten (Be proud of Japanese legacy and promote mutual trust: holding event to share history of Japanese American at the National Cherry Blossom Festival)

The leverage of anti-nuclear CSOs is based on expertise and diplomacy. Therefore, the impact of the four anti-nuclear CSOs focused on by this paper is examined through their media coverage and opinion polls. Details of their activities are described in Chapter 3.

Japan's five major national newspapers[49] candidly report the anti-nuclear activities of the four CSOs but refrain from stating their attitude of pros and cons. This phenomenon represents a fixed idea in Japan that diplomacy and security issues are the exclusive prerogative of the government. At the same time, the papers know they can ill afford to ignore influential CSOs. An island country like Japan is not a migrant or diverse society as in Europe and the United States, so international issues are not part of people's daily lives. Therefore, even in today's highly developed information society international issues are not felt closely.

It follows that most Japanese public are focused on domestic issues. The Great East Japan Earthquake that triggered nuclear power plant incidents has opened another opportunity for the people to rethink nuclear issues. While the newspapers do not make known their attitudes concerning CSOs activities on recent incidents, it is possible to figure out their opinion by which public activities the papers choose to report.

With regard to their interest in SGI, all newspapers unfailingly carry Ikeda's annual Peace Proposals, including his main theme concerning total abolition of nuclear weapons, which is that Japan should play a

---

http://www.sankei.com/world/news/150329/wor1503290024-n1.html (accessed on 17th June 2015)

[49] The Yomiuri Shimbun (Newspaper) circulation: 9,263,986 (June-December 2014), the Asahi Shimbun (Newspaper) circulation: 7,101,074 (June-December 2014), the Nikkei circulation: 275,534 (June-December 2014), the Mainichi Shimbun (Newspaper) circulation: 329, 8779 (June-December 2014) and the Sankei Shimbun (Newspaper) circulation: 161, 5209 (June-December 2014). This survey was made by the Japan Audit Bureau of Circulations http://www.jabc.or.jp/ (accessed on 4th May 2015)

central role in negotiating a NWC.[50]

Ikeda's Peace Proposals are not focused merely on nuclear abolition but cover a wide range of issues which include human rights and environmental issues, however, Japan's main media and public opinion mainly focus on his commitment for a nuclear free world. For example, his recent 2014 Peace Proposal had a huge impact throughout Japan. Since the Great East Japan Earthquake in 2011, the country has been divided in two, between those who were for restarting nuclear power plants and people who were for denuclearization. In local elections including the Tokyo gubernatorial election, the nuclear power plant was a point at issue.

The Yomiuri Shimbun of that year, uncharacteristically, reported a day before Ikeda's annual Peace Proposal that he planned to recommend denuclearization.

> "Soka Gakkai Honorary President Daisaku Ikeda to recommend denuclearization.
> On 26th Soka Gakkai Honorary President Ikeda will offer his opinion on account of the accidents of the Tokyo Electric Power Company's Fukushima No. 1 nuclear power plants (2011). He will announce a "peace recommendation" calling for an urgent

---

[50] Asahi Shimbun 27th January 2015, Soka Gakkai Ikeda Shi Ga Heiwa Teigen O Happyo (Mr. Ikeda of Soka Gakkai presented his peace proposal), http://www.asahi.com/articles/DA3S11571431.html (accessed on 3rd May 2015)
Mainichi Shimbun 26th January 2015, Soka Gakkai: Ikeda Shi Ga Teigen (Soka Gakkai: Mr. Ikeda proposed), http://mainichi.jp/shimen/news/20150126ddm041040100000c.html (accessed on 3rd May 2015)
Sankei Shimbun 26th January 2015, *Soka Gakkai No Ikeda Meiyo Kaicho Ga Heiwa Teigen (Honorary President of Soka Gakkai Ikeda presented his peace proposal),* http://www.sankei.com/life/news/150126/lif1501260028-n1.html (accessed on 3rd May 2015)

examination of energy policy transformation so as to be freed from dependence on nuclear power generation. This could affect the energy policy of the Komeito party, as the Soka Gakkai is its main supporting organization. Mr Ikeda, pointing out Japan experiences one tenth of the number of earthquakes that occur globally and tsunamis are not rare, there are possibilities of recurrences of accidents. Japan should, therefore, aim at the introduction of renewable energy and promote 'collaboration with countries that are forerunners in the field', 'should consider joint development to reduce cost' and 'promote technological innovation to enable easy adoption by developing countries'".
(The Yomiuri Shimbun 25th January 2014)[51]
(Translated by Fujiko Hara)

Conventionally, newspaper companies choose 26 January when the Peace Proposal is made to print such opinion. The unusual turn of events reflected the fact that the public was eager to learn what Ikeda, who had over the years pressed for denuclearization, had to say. The Yomiuri Shimbun stated that the Proposal should have an effect on the ruling party's energy policy. Its judgement was underscored by the fact that the Komeito Party (see Chapter 2, 3, 4 and 5) that Ikeda had established was part of the ruling party government's coalition. In fact not just the Komeito but the largest ruling Liberal Democratic Party that had over many years promoted nuclear power publicly promised to reduce as much as possible the country's dependence on nuclear energy

---

[51] The Yomiuri Shimbun 25th January 2014, Ikeda Meiyo Kaicho Datsu Genpatsu Izon He: Komeito Ni Eikyo Mo (Honorary President Ikeda will propose abandoning nuclear power generation: It will influence the Komeito), http://www.yomiuri.co.jp/politics/news/20120125-OYT1T01096.htm (accessed on 25th January 2014)

in the future.[52]

Since 2011 the nuclear power issue has divided public opinion in two between those who believe that nuclear reactors should be completely abolished in order not to repeat the tragedy of a nuclear power plant accident and the other view that nuclear power has to be promoted as long as alternative energy does not exist. If nuclear power plants were stopped there would be a serious energy issue. The Japanese people wished to know what Ikeda who had being playing a leading role over half a century in nuclear abolition movement, thought about the issue.

The Chugoku Shimbun (Newspaper) with its headquarters in Hiroshima city continuously reports all moves related to nuclear abolition from its Hiroshima Peace Media Centre.[53] It has special columns for Ikeda's Peace Proposals, visitors to Hiroshima City such as political and social leaders from around the world and foreign ambassadors serving in Japan,[54] as well as the result of regular SGI's attitude survey on nuclear weapons (see Chapter 3). Social and political leaders from around the world as well as ambassadors to Japan featured in the newspaper have been invited to Hiroshima to give speeches at the SGI sponsored commemorative lectures on Nuclear Abolition. Then they customarily visit the Mayor of Hiroshima City and have press

---

[52] The Yomiuri Shimbun 26th November 2014, *Summary of Manifesto: Liberal Democratic Party Japan* http://www.yomiuri.co.jp/election/shugiin/2014/commitment/20141126-OYT8T50052.html (accessed on 5th May 2015)

[53] Hiroshima Peace Media Centre (Chugoku Shimbun) http://www.hiroshimapeacemedia.jp/?lang=ja (accessed on 3rd May 2015)

[54] F. W. de Klerk (former President of South Africa) November 2010
H. E. Mykola Kulinich (Ambassador of Ukraine to Japan) July 2011
Elard Escala (Ambassador of Peru to Japan) May 2013
Oscar Arias (former President of Costa Rica) April 2014

meetings as well.[55]

Hiroshima and Nagasaki cities are eager to have world leaders visit the sites of the atomic bombing for them to understand the true state of affairs[56] and the media notes that SGI is acting as the intermediary between the two cities and political and social leaders and ambassadors with whom it has developed contacts through its own diplomacy. The newspapers that unfailingly post the result of the attitudinal survey on nuclear weapons recognize SGI's prominent power of survey through data banks and think tanks from its global network.

Each CSO and government agency has its own self-assertion and philosophy and, although they may have the same objective of nuclear abolition there can be irreconcilable differences in their approach and direction (see Chapter 2 and 3). In order to overcome such differences, CSOs have to develop their skills to collect data and conduct research to keep up with present realities. Since the object of this paper is to study the realistic impact CSOs have on nuclear abolition, it has focused on CSOs that possess legal and medical expertise in particular.

The JPPNW is well known in Japan and is often covered in the news, and its headquarters, the International Physicians for the Prevention of Nuclear Weapons (IPPNW), has received Nobel Peace Prize (1985). Following The Great East Earthquake in 2011, the IPPNW pointed out the health hazards of nuclear power plants and through its

---

[55] Hiroshima Peace Media Centre (Chugoku Shimbun), Kakuheiki Haizetsu He Renkei Yakusoku Peru Taishi Ga Hiroshima Shicho Hyokei (Agreed to cooperate for the nuclear abolition: Ambassador of Peru to Japan visited Mayor of Hiroshima City) 27th May 2013,
http://www.hiroshimapeacemedia.jp/?p=9821&query=%E5%89%B5%E4%BE%A1%E5%AD%A6%E4%BC%9A (accessed on 3rd May 2015)

[56] Hiroshima City 23rd January 2015, *Request to US President Obama to visit Hibakuchi*,
http://www.city.hiroshima.lg.jp/www/sp/contents/1422240749304/index.html (accessed on 3rd May 2015)

investigation of thyroid gland cancer in Fukushima Prefecture[57] is focused as an organization on powerfully asserting the total abolition of nuclear reactor. This, however, is not necessarily a consistent view of the JPPNW (see Chapter 3). Both the IPPNW and JPPNW are recognized for the IPPNW Congresses that regularly take place around the world.

The 20th IPPNW World Congress 2012 (see Chapter 3) that took place in Hiroshima City was particularly covered by major newspapers such as the Mainichi Shimbun.[58] Also, The Hiroshima Peace Media Centre (the Chugoku Shimbun) and others that have strong footholds in Hiroshima had included special columns with experiences of A-bomb victims and favourably reported on the significance of the Congress held in Japan.

On the other hand, the Mainichi Shimbun, of the national press, focused on the point that 'de-nuclearization' was missing in the final document Hiroshima Peace Appeal, in spite of the fact that one of the three days of the Congress was devoted to a general session that had Tokyo Electric Power Company's Fukushima No. 1 nuclear power plant accidents as well as a debate on the pros and cons of nuclear energy as its themes.[59]

---

[57] Shizuoka Shimbun 3rd March 2015, Fukushima Ziko Rinken Demo Kojosen Kensa O Ishidantai Ni Shisa (The Accident in Fukushima, A group of medical doctors (IPPNW) indicated that it needs to hold thyroid function test in neighbour prefectures), http://www.at-s.com/news/detail/1174173295.html (accessed on 6th May 2015).
This article was provided by the German Chapter of KK Kyodo News to Japanese newspapers.

[58] Mainichi Shimbun, IPPNW Sekai Taikai: Seimei Ni 'Datsu Genpatsu' Morazu Heimaku Hiroshima (IPPNW World Congress: It did not add 'abandoning nuclear generation' in the final document. Hiroshima) http://mainichi.jp/select/news/20120827k0000m040076000c.htm (accessed on 30th August 2012).

[59] Ibid

This was due to a divergence of views between the IPPNW Headquarters, devoted to total denuclearization, and the JPPNW, which stresses the need to separate nuclear power and nuclear weapons and other divergences of opinion of other branches. The media report on this resulted in introducing to the Japanese public the notion that nuclear weapons and nuclear energy could be different issues. However, the Chugoku Shimbun did not refer to the differences of opinion but emphasized in its coverage that the content of the outcome statement strongly urged there to be no new nuclear victims, through the abolition of nuclear weapons and avoidance of nuclear power accidents.[60]

It is believed that the article deliberately suggested that nuclear abolition and nuclear power should be treated as the same issue. It points to the fact that there are two public opinions, on the one hand the national opinion saying that nuclear issues must be calmly inspected, and on the other hand an emotional view from the A-bombed area saying that nuclear power plant victims are the same as A-bomb victims so they should be treated on the same basis.

The IPPNW is a trailblazer anti-nuclear CSO and recognized as such by the MP and other fellow CSOs. As such it has a huge leverage. And since the IPPNW is an organization of physicians it has emotional support that can be likened to patients' trust of their doctors. Their medical perspectives warning nuclear issues can cause serious health damage and their medical surveys are much more powerful than the general CSOs campaigning on the streets with their placards for nuclear abolition.

Furthermore, the IPPNW leads the world's largest anti-nuclear NGO alliance "ICAN (International Campaign to Abolish Nuclear Weapons)" (see Chapter 3). If the organization decides, in the debate between

---

[60] Ibid

nuclear weapons and nuclear power, to be positive on nuclear abolition but negative on de-nuclearization of nuclear power, its perception could well be a standard for anti-nuclear public opinion. In reality, the assertion of JPPNW is correct, since the debates on the two issues would have to be conducted separately. Now that the long-held view of nuclear power plant safety has collapsed, there is a need in earthquake prone Japan to stringently discuss the issue of nuclear power as much as nuclear abolition.

Japanese people generally understand the MP as part of the activities organized by Hiroshima and Nagasaki cities to enlighten people on the real consequences of A-bombing. The media also reports with trust and confidence the MP's activities as those of public anti-nuclear organizations. They even report on organizational changes including personnel change of its secretary-general. Official websites[61] of member cities with keen interests on important nuclear matters report on the MP's activities in their category of 'peace cities'. This suggests that for local inhabitants the MP stands out above other CSOs.

However, the high level of recognition and awareness of the MP do not necessarily translate into them having influence in changing policies and public opinion. A full account of the assessment of their leverage will be given in Chapter 3.

There has been a big change recently in the so-called "nuclear allergy", an unconditional hatred of nuclear weapons due to the experience of being bombed with A-bombs. In 1999, a Vice-Minister of

---

[61] Kyotanabe City (in Kyoto Prefecture), *Heiwa Toshi: Heiwa Shucho Kaigi Ni Tsuite (Peace City: About the Mayors for Peace)*, http://www.kyotanabe.jp/0000004984.html (accessed on 6th May 2015) Takarazuka City (in Hyogo Prefecture), *Hiewa Shyucho Kaigi Heno Kamei Ni Tsuite (About Joining the Mayors for Peace),* http://www.city.takarazuka.hyogo.jp/kyoiku/jinken/1000113/1000479.html (accessed on 6th May 2015)

Defence of Japan (a member of the House of Representatives) was immediately recalled for asserting that Japan should possess nuclear arms.[62] For a long time there was a tendency in Japan to regard any discussion of nuclear armament as taboo. Recently, even the A-bombed areas regarded their experience as a historical tragedy and saw the need for making realistic decisions on nuclear security issues as two separate issues (see Chapter 2 and 3).

In 2006, when executive officers of the Liberal Democratic Party Japan (LDP Japan), which was the ruling party, and the Minister of Foreign Affairs Japan both spoke of the need for discussion on nuclear armament following North Korea's nuclear test conducted in 2006, the Yomiuri Shimbun carried its editorial entitled, "It's wrong to bar 'nuclear discussion'".

> "Shoichi Nakagawa, the Chairman of Policy Research Council of the Liberal Democratic Party Japan raised the need for nuclear debate, "In the face of North Korea's nuclear test, how will Japan's peace and safety be protected. It should be good to discuss the issue from various perspectives." Foreign Minister Taro Aso supported Nakagawa's proposition and said, "Discouraging discussion will only invite criticism that we are denying freedom of speech...
>
> "...In the face of North Korea's nuclear test, isn't he a sincere and responsible politician to raise the question, 'what countermeasures do we have short of possessing nuclear weapons?" We want to know how the decision was made on the Three Non-Nuclear Policy? Given the present circumstances, it

---

[62] The Obuchi Administration recalled Shingo Nishimura (Member of the House of Representatives and Vice-Minister of Defence)

would do well for us to deliberate on that issue as well."[63]

(Translated by Fujiko Hara)

The opinion poll conducted by the Yomiuri Newspaper showed that 51% of the respondents were negative about having discussions on the possibility of possessing nuclear arms and 46% were in favour, that is, more or less matching results. The Mainichi Shimbun's opinion poll showed approximately 80% were against Japan's possession of nuclear arms, but 61% were in favour of having discussion while opposing the possession of nuclear arms.[64]

Although a limited 8% of the respondents were in favour of discussion with a view to possessing nuclear arms, those who were even against discussion, for fear of Japan's intentions being misunderstood, were now down to 8%, and those who were against discussing the issue since it could lead to possessing nuclear arms were reduced to 14%. Thus there is today a big change from the time when even discussion was denied.[65] Furthermore, the Sankei Shimbun's 2010 opinion poll on Japan's nuclear armament registered 85% in favour of nuclear armament and 96% were in favour at least of discussing the issue in the public arena.[66]

The opinion poll of the same paper in 2011 showed, in the light of China and Russia possessing nuclear arms in Japan's vicinity and North

---

63 Yomiuri Shimbun 8th November 2006, Shasetsu: "Kaku Rongi" Giron Sura Fuziru No Ha Okasii (Leading Article: "Discussion for Nuclear Armament: it is strange to even prohibit discussing about nuclear armament")

64 Mainichi Shimbun 27th November 2006, Kaku Hoyu No Giron Ha Yonin – Saita No 6Wari Shimeru (No to Nuclear Armament But Accept to Discuss about That – This Opinion Poll Reached 60%)

65 Ibid

66 Sankei Shimbun 16th December 2010, *Opinion: Nippon No Kaku Buso (Opinion Poll on Japanese Nuclear Armament)* http://sankei.jp.msn.com/life/trend/101216/trd1012161852013-n1.htm (accessed on 3rd January 2010)

Korea carrying out nuclear tests twice, that 86.7% of respondents were in favour of the government and the parliament discussing nuclear issues while those against were down to 8.5%.[67] With regard to the government policy of the Three Non-Nuclear Policy, 55.9% were for maintaining it while those who were for its revision increased to 39%.[68] The results of these opinion polls showed that the deeply embedded national allergy to nuclear matters had declined due to strained security circumstances surrounding Japan. What should be focused on here is how Japanese public opinion is formed.

This nuclear debate did not come about as a result of national deliberations, but rather it has the aspect of being promoted by politicians and defended by the media through their editorials. It cannot be denied that typical Japanese processes may have intervened in the process of creating national opinion, that is to say the government has the prerogative on matters of diplomacy and security, and since the nuclear issue was raised by politicians who are supposed to be experts it should be right.

The Article 73 of the Constitution of Japan clearly states that managing foreign affairs is the sole prerogative of the Cabinet[69]. It is

---

[67] Sankei Shimbun 14th February 2011, *Opinion: Nippon No Kakubuso (Opinion Poll on Nuclear Armament),* http://sankei.jp.msn.com/politics/news/110214/stt11021422510013-n1.htm (accessed on 19th August 2011)

[68] Ibid

[69] "Article 73: The Cabinet, in addition to other general administrative functions, shall perform the following functions:
Administer the law faithfully; conduct affairs of state.
Manage foreign affairs.
Conclude treaties. However, it shall obtain prior or, depending on circumstances, subsequent approval of the Diet.
Administer the civil service, in accordance with standards established by law.
Prepare the budget, and present it to the Diet.
Enact cabinet orders in order to execute the provisions of this Constitution and the law. However, it cannot include penal provisions in such cabinet orders

natural that it is written in law as a matter concerning the whole nation, nevertheless the Government of Japan attaches strong self-interest to the clause and is extremely nervous about persons and parties outside the government debating or negotiating foreign and security affairs.

For example, in 2001 when the MOFA learned that the governor of Okinawa planned to visit the US and directly request the US Administration to lighten the heavy burden Okinawa bears towards the maintenance of the US military base, the Ministry called a press conference to publicly express concern that diplomacy carried out by local government could infringe the right of the national government to conduct diplomatic affairs stating, "Negotiations and talks regarding foreign affairs and defence are the sole prerogatives of the two governments, as long recognized by governors of Okinawa. Even if the visit is made, it is unlikely that a request (for reducing the burden) will be made.[70]

As shown above, in Japan it is likely that public opinion on matters regarding diplomatic affairs and national security originate from the government and politicians. It follows, therefore, that there is a need to influence both the government and public opinion.

The other point has to do with the lessening of the impact of the bombed areas with the passage of 70 years from the bombings. Unlike

---

unless authorised by such law.
Decide on general amnesty, special amnesty, commutation of punishment, reprieve, and restoration rights."
Ministry of Justice Japan, *Japanese Law Translation Database System, The Constitution of Japan*
http://www.japaneselawtranslation.go.jp/law/detail_main?re=&vm=02&id=174 (accessed on 11th June 2015)

[70] Ryukyushinpo (a newspaper in Okinawa Prefecture) 8th May 2001, *Gaiko Ha Kuni No Senken Ziko: Hashimoto Okinawa Taishi (Diplomacy is State Monopoly by Hashimoto the Ambassador to Okinawa)* http://ryukyushimpo.jp/news/storyid-112148-storytopic-86.html (accessed on 5th June 2015)

debates on nuclear armament the government and politicians are not involved. This is an issue which the children from 6 to 15 years old are taught in their history and morality courses as part of national compulsory education policy at elementary and junior high schools. For the Japanese people, the areas on which nuclear bombs were dropped represent symbols of anti-nuclear movement and determination never to repeat the tragedies. Indeed, many schools have made it a customary practise to organize school excursions for students to visit the area, meet and listen to *hibakusha,* persons exposed to A-bomb radiation.

However, there was an incident in Nagasaki City in May 2014 during a school excursion trip. As reported by the Asahi Shimbun, five 14 and 15 years old male students mockingly called out to a *hibakusha* who was sharing his experiences with the visitors, "You, sorry survivor!" and encouraged their fellow students to 'laugh' and 'clap their hands'.[71]

Later, the school and the students did offer their apologies but according to The Nagasaki Atomic Bomb Survivors Council, the host organization, there had been at times some inattentive students but not those who disturbed the meeting. The man whose role it is to share his experiences as an A-bomb victim also said that the incident was his first experience of that kind. And he said he was troubled that after sixty-nine years the atomic bombing seemed somebody else's problem to the young generation.[72] There was also an incident in 1997 also in Nagasaki, where a middle high school students threw candies and shouted swear words at an A-bomb victim while he was acting out his

---

[71] Asahi Shimbun 8th June 2014, Shugakuryokosei 5Nin Nagasaki No Hibakusha Ni Bougen Yokohama No Chugakko Shazai (5 students of school trip used offensive languages against a hibakusha in Nagasaki, their junior high school in Yokohama City apologized), http://www.asahi.com/articles/ASG673RG9G67TOLB001.html (accessed on 7th May 2015)

[72] Ibid

own dramatized experience.[73] However, not only high schools try to place Japan's A-bomb experiences at the starting point of their activities, so also do anti-nuclear CSOs (see Chapter 3).[74]

It is unlikely that any anti-nuclear activists and A-bomb victims will deny the impact bombed out areas have on the movement, nevertheless, they cannot escape noticing declining impact of such concerns on public opinion. Even the Chugoku Shimbun, the most ardent believer in nuclear abolition, warned that there is a declining number of people participating in the peace movement. Its 2001 national consciousness survey on atomic bombing revealed that 13% of those polled responded 'its high time to forget it' and 2% said 'its something of the past that has nothing to do with me'.[75]

The 2010 Japan Broadcasting Corporation's nuclear bomb consciousness survey revealed that 70% of Hiroshima citizens knew the day on which the bomb was dropped but nationwide it was limited to 23% who gave the correct answer.[76] Similarly, 64% of the Nagasaki citizens were able to give the correct answer, while nationwide the number was 23%. Citizens in their 20s and 30s were 52% correct in Hiroshima and 64% in Nagasaki. Indeed, half of the younger generation

---

[73] Ibid

[74] Ibid

[75] Hiroshima Peace Media Centre (Chugoku Shimbun), Genbaku No Hi Maeni Zenkoku Yoron Chosa (National Opinion Poll before Day of Atomic Bomb) http://www.hiroshimapeacemedia.jp/abom/01abom/yoron/yoron.html (accessed on 13th June 2015)

[76] NHK (Japan Broadcasting Corporation) Broadcasting Culture Research Institute, Shakai Ya Seiji Ni Kansuru Yoron Chosa: Genbaku Toka Kara 65Nen Kienu Kaku No Kyoi (Opinion Polls on Politics and Society: 65th Anniversary of Dropping Atomic Bombs – Fear of Nuclear Weapons has not been disappeared) October 2010 https://www.nhk.or.jp/bunken/summary/research/report/2010_10/101005.pdf (accessed on 12 June 2015)

were not aware when nuclear bombs were dropped on their cities.[77]

With regard to the future of nuclear weapons, the greatest responses were that, "they will be reduced but not all that much". More than 50% of the people answered the same in Hiroshima and Nagasaki as well as nationwide.[78] Over 70% of the people in Hiroshima and Nagasaki as well as nationwide were pessimistic concerning the danger of terrorists using nuclear weapons in the near future.[79] All those opinion polls suggest that it is clear that the younger the generation's perception of atomic bombings itself) is fading, albeit gradually.

The JALANA has not grown enough to have a large impact on the Japanese public opinion. Its scale, compared with three other organizations is extremely limited and less known. Its activities and opinion are barely reported in national and local newspapers. This research has examined papers for the purposes of this dissertation but it failed to find any relevant reportage. The reason for this dissertation focusing on this organisation is because the law itself is a field of study essential in examining movements for nuclear disarmament. Many anti-nuclear CSOs including the four organisations (JPPNW, MP, JALANA and SGI) have been promoting the establishment of the NWC. The aim of founding the ICAN was, and its main activity is, to promote international law.

> "IPPNW launched the International Campaign to Abolish Nuclear Weapons – ICAN – following our 17th World Congress in Helsinki. The focal point of the campaign – a Nuclear Weapons Convention – is the means by which abolish will be

[77] Ibid
[78] Ibid
[79] Ibid

achieved an enforced under international law"[80]

Legal activities are essential to achieve JALANA's objectives. Its activities are limited and have little effect on public opinion. However, JALANA plays a leading role in the operation and management of the Japan NGO Network for Nuclear Weapons Abolition (JNNNWA (see Chapter 3). In fact, JALANA is represented on JNNNWA's five-member board[81]. The other three organisations[82] have not taken seats on the board (as of 2015).

Also, JALANA is a member of the IALANA, which serves as the drafting organization of the NWC together with the International Network of Engineers and Scientists Against Proliferation. Therefore, JALANA's expertise and knowledge serves as a powerful and effective legal and theoretical pillar. In fact, they serve as the legal advisor to the biggest Japanese anti-nuclear CSO alliance (see Chapter 3).

---

80 JPPNW, *IPPNW 18th World Congress, Delhi, India: DELHI DECLARATION March 9, 2008*, http://www.hiroshima.med.or.jp/ippnw/sekaitaikai/18ippnw200839.html (accessed on 7th May 2015)

81 JNNNWA, *NGO Renraku Kai Ni Tsuite (About the Organisation)* https://nuclearabolitionjpn.wordpress.com/about/ (accessed on 7th May 2015)

82 JPPNW, Mayors for Peace and SGI

Chapter 2: Japanese Government Nuclear Policy

This chapter provides a comparative analysis of the structure of the government's foreign policy on nuclear arms control and anti-nuclear movement of the Japanese CSOs. The purpose is to authenticate fundamental roles CSOs must play regarding the issues of nuclear weapons.

Historically, issues of security, military and weapons were matters of state-based decisions and negotiations. In terms of international law, the 1925 Geneva Convention was a major example of an attempt to prohibit the use of weapons such as biological weapons, which kill indiscriminately. The 1925 Geneva Convention was a milestone in banning the use of bacteriological and other weapons of indiscriminate killing. The UN has organized a number of disarmament conferences including the Special Session on Disarmament of its General Assembly (SSD) 1, 1978, SSD2 1982 and SSD3 1988. Constituents were, however, only the member states. In recent years, the roles of civil society organisations (CSOs) have been recognized particularly in the fields of the environment as policy-making experts in international conferences including the UN. The area of security remains different from environmental issues although quite a few anti-nuclear NGOs have been granted advisory status in some UN organisations including the UN Social and Economic Council. But all parties and members there are states. In recent years particularly in the fields of the environment, the role of CSOs as experts for policy-making have been highly valued and they have often been allowed to participate in the worldwide decision-making conferences including in the UN. The security fields are still very different from environment matters even though many anti-nuclear NGOs have been granted advisory status in some UN sections including the UN Social and Economic Council.

The Cold War period raised the nuclear arms race to a peak between the US and USSR, the two superpowers. There was a global angst, a sense of crisis since if the nuclear weapons were used in a global war on the scale of the Second World War they might annihilate the human race. The Cuban crisis of 1962 could have developed into just that. Most critical for the Japanese government's nuclear policy was the Northeast Asian situation during the post-Cold War period. The Soviet Union conducted its first nuclear test in 1949; China's nuclear weapons development began in the 1960s, with its first nuclear test conducted in 1964 in the autonomous region of Uyghur. In recent years post-Cold War nuclear test were carried out on the Indian subcontinent, in Indo-Pakistan conflicts. India conducted tests in 1978 and 1998, and in 1998 Pakistan did so as well. North Korea withdrew from the NPT in 2003, and carried out its nuclear tests (2006, 2009 and 2013). Japan's encounter with nuclear weapons was in August 1945 when the US military dropped atom bombs on Hiroshima on 6th and Nagasaki on the 9th August 1945. Victims from the bombings, including those who died years later from radiation and other diseases, numbered 250,959[1] in Hiroshima and 158,754[2] in Nagasaki. Japan remains the only atom-bombed country since 1945 as no nuclear weapons have been used in war since the atomic bombs were dropped on Hiroshima and Nagasaki.

Japan has not even once developed or possessed nuclear arms. This policy is based on the negative sentiments developed from the experience of the enormous damage suffered by people of Hiroshima

---

[1] Hiroshima City, List of *hibakusha* (official information) http://www.city.hiroshima.lg.jp/www/contents/0000000000000/1283234802275/index.html (accessed on 15th December 2011)

[2] Nagasaki City, List of *hibakusha* (official information) http://www1.city.nagasaki.nagasaki.jp/gentai/irei_tuitou/houan.html (accessed on 15th December 2011)

and Nagasaki[3] Japan has consistently stressed nuclear disarmament and the need to abolish nuclear weapons in the international community but it has hardly been able to make an impact in the matter. The reason stems from the dilemma that Japan's national security policy in the Northeast region of Asia constantly relies on the nuclear umbrella of the Unites States of America. The Japanese government policy on nuclear arms is premised on the alliance with the US and the diplomatic relations between China and Russia in Northeast Asia. The axis of relations was most evident during the Cold War. In the post-Cold War times, there has been progress in diplomatic negotiations on nuclear disarmament and non-proliferation through negotiations for the Comprehensive Nuclear Test Ban Treaty (CTBT) and the NPT Review Conferences (held every 5 years since 1995) discussions held at the UN or international organisations, as well as establishing international laws such as recommendations from the International Court of Law (1996). However, diplomatic negotiations concerning the reduction of the development, possession and use of nuclear arms involving the nuclear states continue to be limited to bilateral dialogues between the US and Russia.

Diplomatic negotiations for actually reducing the development and possession of, and use of nuclear arms, however, remain limited today to New Strategic Arms Reduction Talks in bilateral negotiations, for example between the US and the Russian Federation. The New Strategic Arms Reduction Treaty (START) and the Six-Party Talks established in order to resolve the issue of North Korea's nuclear development were started in 2003; however North Korea's withdrawal

---

[3] Ministry of Foreign Affairs Japan (MOFA), *Gunshuku To Waga Kuni No Torikumi: Gaikan (Japan's Approach for Disarmament and Non-Proliferation)*, http://www.mofa.go.jp/mofaj/gaiko/fukaku/torikumi.html (accessed on 6th May 2010)

in 2004 and its testing in 2009, has meant that no plans are in place for reopening the talks. Multilateral talks by the six countries, the US, Russia, China, Japan, Korea and North Korea, the UN Security Council and other subsidiary organs such as the UN Disarmament Conference and the First Committee of the UN General Assembly for debating disarmament and international security issues, and inter-government talks among states remain the main areas for discussion. The Abolition of nuclear arms requires a high level political and or diplomatic involvement not merely limited to a military framework. However, most intergovernmental negotiations remain deadlocked and while there has been some momentum towards nuclear disarmament, at present there is no concrete roadmap towards it.

The government of Japan stated in a White Paper issued in 2002 (later White Paper on "Japan's Disarmament and Non-Proliferation Policy") that "the country's disarmament policy, an initiative prohibiting possession and use of weapons of mass destruction (WMDs, including nuclear, biological and chemical weapons) as well as anti-personnel mines, cluster bombs and unlawful small arms that involve the general public in conflicts causing unacceptable inhuman consequences, promotes it as one of the important pillars of diplomacy".[4] This clearly stated policy[5] has not been changed as of 2013 and remains one of the consistent foreign policies of the government.[6]

---

[4] MOFA, Arms Control and Disarmament Division, Disarmament, Non-Proliferation and Science Department, *Japan's Disarmament and Non-Proliferation Policy (white paper, 2nd Edition, 2004)*, p24

[5] MOFA, Arms Control and Disarmament Division, Disarmament, Non-Proliferation and Science Department, *Japan's Disarmament and Non-Proliferation Policy (white paper, 1nd Edition, 2002)*, p13 http://www.mofa.go.jp/mofaj/gaiko/gun_hakusho/2002/hon1_1.pdf (accessed on 8th October 2011)

[6] MOFA, Arms Control and Disarmament Division, Disarmament,

With regard to its nuclear disarmament and non-proliferation policies, the government has made it clear since 2004 that its basic approach consists of four factors, "commitment to peace and a self-assigned mission as the sole atom-bombed country, perspectives of security, humanitarian approach, and a Human Security perspective.[7] The first approach based on the principles of peace enshrined in Japan's New Constitution, expresses the view that tragedies of the Second World War and atomic bombing should never again be repeated. It further states that nuclear weapons should be abolished and that Japan has the mission to declare its resolve to the peoples of the world.[8]

The government of Japan has adopted and declared as its national principle/credo the three non-nuclear principles, of not possessing, not manufacturing and not allowing other states or parties to bring nuclear weapons into the country. The declaration was adopted as a resolution at the November 1971 sitting of the House of Representatives as "Resolution of the House of Representatives concerning non-nuclear arms and the reduction of the US Military Bases on Okinawa". This was followed by the adoption at the Foreign Affairs Committee of the House of Representatives in April 1976[9] as well as at the Foreign Affairs

---

Non-Proliferation and Science Department, Japan's Disarmament and Non-Proliferation Policy: Chapter 1 "Outline" of 1st (2002), 2nd (2004), 3rd (2006), 4th (2008), 5th (2010), and 6th edition (2013)

[7] MOFA, Arms Control and Disarmament Division, Disarmament, Non-Proliferation and Science Department, *Japan's Disarmament and Non-Proliferation Policy (white paper, 2nd Edition, 2004)*, p23-p26

[8] Ibid p27

[9] MOFA, Resolution at the Japanese Diet regarding the Three Non-Nuclear Principles
Resolution approved by House of Representative Committee on Foreign Affairs, 27th April 1976, following the Nuclear Non-Proliferation Treaty (NPT) http://www.mofa.go.jp/mofaj/gaiko/kaku/gensoku/ketsugi.html (26th March 2012)

Committee of the House of Counsellors in May of the same year[10] and finally adopted in 1982 as the joint resolution of the two houses.[11]

The Three Non-nuclear Principles were adopted at the time of the return to Japan of the Ogasawara Islands occupied during the Second World War by the United States of America. At that time there was fear in Japan that nuclear arms and nuclear fuel might be brought into the islands. The adoption of the resolution was a response by the government to the questioning of the Komeito-Party, then in opposition, at the General Session of the House of Representatives on 8 the December 1967, asking if the government could clearly state that "the three non-nuclear principles of not producing, installing and bringing in (nuclear fuel and nuclear wastes)" to the islands will be honoured at the time of the return to Japan of the Ogasawara islands.[12]

Three days later on 11th December 1967, Prime Minister Eisaku Sato proposed what is known today as the Three non-nuclear principles, i.e., "Japan will not possess, produce or allow others to bring in nuclear weapons" in response to the questions (interpellations) from political partiess.

With regard to the second issue, the reasons for promoting disarmament and non-proliferation policy are not limited to references

---

[10] MOFA, Arms Control and Disarmament Division, Disarmament, Non-Proliferation and Science Department, Japan's Disarmament and Non-Proliferation Policy (white paper, 2nd Edition, 2004), Chapter 1, Section 4: Japan's Basic Standpoint and Approach for Disarmament and Non-Proliferation

[11] Ibid

[12] Formal Questioning Session at the House of Representative Japan by Komeito (political party), *Minutes of Plenary Session of the House of Representatives Japan [094/099]57-Shu-Honkaigi-4Go, 8th December 1967,* http://kokkai.ndl.go.jp/cgi-bin/KENSAKU/swk_dispdoc.cgi?SESSION=24165&SAVED_RID=2&PAGE=0&POS=0&TOTAL=0&SRV_ID=3&DOC_ID=23407&DPAGE=5&DTOTAL=99&DPOS=94&SORT_DIR=1&SORT_TYPE=0&MODE=1&DMY=28412 (accessed on 14th September 2011)

made in. It also takes into consideration an unstable security environment surrounding Japan at the time, such as the existence of China and Russia, the two big powers with a vast territory and arsenal, including nuclear weapons. It refers further to North Korea as an unstable factor in possession of ballistic missiles and carrying out repetitive nuclear weapons tests as well in the Taiwan Straits.

The Government also saw possibilities of new threats in the post-Cold War era due to existing tensions and unclear and unstable factors in northeast Asia surrounding Japan, and cited the launch by North Korea of its ballistic missile Taep'odong in August 1998, and its secession from the NPT (1969) in January 2003. It also referred to the terrorist bombing in Bali, Indonesia in February 2002 as a possible new form of terrorist threat with WMDs in Northeast Asia.[13]

On the third point, the Japanese Government asserts there is an increasing momentum to address disarmament and non-proliferation issues from humanitarian standpoints, given the accelerated increase in destructive and deadly powers of weapons.

The Government believes that the St Petersburg Declaration (1868) which established technical standards for the use of a certain level of explosives from humanitarian considerations as well as the Geneva Protocol (1925) prohibiting the use of toxic gases are early examples of humanitarian approaches. More recently, the government endorsed the Ottawa Treaty that banned the use of anti-personnel mines, as an international rule based on humanitarian principles and was one of the original signatories (1997). The treaty was successfully concluded in

---

[13] MOFA, Arms Control and Disarmament Division, Disarmament, Non-Proliferation and Science Department, Japan's Disarmament and Non-Proliferation Policy (white paper, 2nd Edition, 2004), Chapter 1, Section 4: Japan's Basic Standpoint and Approach for Disarmament and Non-Proliferation

1998 and the government considers humanitarianism as an essential factor in reducing WMDs and banning weapons that are unnecessary but responsible for frightful consequences. The government, however, does not make any reference to the inhumanity of nuclear weapons (see Chapter 3). In summarizing its foreign policy in the fourth point, the government noted, against the lack of a political framework that existed during the cold war period, that there have been a soaring number of cross-border conflicts that are not necessarily due to ideological differences, such as swelling refugees, surging international crimes involving narcotics, cross-border contagious diseases, terrorism, environmental destruction and unexpected economic crisis such as the Asian currency crisis:

> "…under these circumstances, it is becoming all the more crucial for the state to strengthen initiatives that focuses on human security in order for each citizen to live with dignity in addition to the traditional notion of protecting lives and property of citizens through ensuring national security and prosperity".[14]
> (Translated by Fujiko Hara)

This reference to human security may be stated within the framework of disarmament and non-proliferation diplomacy covering the disposal of anti-personnel mines and small arms that endanger the lives and safety of people in the conflict zone. Even in post-conflict times it is extremely important to ensure the safety of the lives of the

---

[14] MOFA, *Diplomatic Blue Book 2002, Section 3: Approaches to Global Issues, No 6: Human Security* http://www.mofa.go.jp/mofaj/gaiko/bluebook/2003/gaikou/html/honpen/index.html (accessed on 7th May 2010)

people in conflict zones.[15] Here again, no reference is made to nuclear weapons.

That the government clearly stated in 2002 its posture concerning disarmament and non-proliferation underscores the importance it places on security spelled out in the second point. In 2002, the Government placed as its top diplomatic priority the fight against terrorism and non-proliferation of WMDs, etc.[16] This was in response to the 9.11 terrorist attacks in New York in the preceding year.

The government recognized terrorism as a threat to its security and established in November 2001 Special Measures Law on Terrorism in order to supply fuel to Anglo-American forces dispatched to Afghanistan. It further decided to dispatch members of the Self Defence Forces as logistical support extending the period to May 2003.[17]

In January 2001, the Government convened a conference in Tokyo to discuss Afghanistan in collaboration with the US, the European Union and Saudi Arabia and decided to provide support up to 500 million dollars. The Government considered that establishing peace in Afghanistan and its reconstruction was important for avoiding the country becoming a hot bed of terrorism.[18] The priority given to fighting terrorism was to avoid the worst-case scenario of terrorists possessing and deploying WMDs.[19]

The government demanded an immediate and unconditional

---

[15] Ibid

[16] MOFA, *Diplomatic Blue Book 2002, Chapter 1: Outline "International Situation and Japanese Diplomacy 2002*
http://www.mofa.go.jp/mofaj/gaiko/bluebook/2003/gaikou/html/honpen/index.html (accessed on 7th May 2010)

[17] Ibid

[18] Ibid

[19] Ibid, *Chapter 3: Diplomacy in Each Field, No 7: Arms Control, Disarmament, and Non-Proliferation*
http://www.mofa.go.jp/mofaj/gaiko/bluebook/2003/gaikou/html/honpen/index.html (accessed on 7th May 2010)

acceptance of inspection with regard to the alleged suspicion of Iraq's development and deployment of WMDs. Further, apart from its security policy, a great deal of reference is made to anti-terrorism policy. Regarding economic policy, it recognizes that globalization is likely to bring about further efficiency in economic activities, thereby essentially bringing about benefits to all countries and all peoples; however, there is also a negative aspect to expanding the gap between the rich and the poor. The government thus states:

> …From the perspective of <u>not creating hotbeds of terrorism</u>, the international community has taken positive initiatives in order that benefits of globalization may be enjoyed by the international society as a whole including the developing countries and to realize sustainable development.[20]
> (Translated by Fujiko Hara)

While the government referred to the issues of Iraq's WMD and the potential possession and use of WMDs by terrorists, there was no reference made to the principles of the Peace Constitution referred to as the first point, nor any declaration from the only country that had atom-bombs dropped on Hiroshima and Nagasaki. Despite continuing conflict in Afghanistan and renewed warfare in Iraq, the security threat to Japan has become the territorial issues with China and Russia that continue from the end of the Cold War period and remains the priority in disarmament and non-proliferation diplomacy.

The government promotes its nuclear disarmament and non-proliferation policies based on the following three main factors:

---

[20] Ibid, "Approaches on Tendency of World Economics and Sustainable Development"

strengthening of the NPT regime, acceleration of bilateral and multilateral consultation on concluding the CTBT and its ratification, and the "expansion of non-nuclear zone".

Also, in the White Paper on Disarmament and Non-proliferation Policy of 2002 up to the present in 2013, the government clearly explained its position and initiatives in a chapter dealing with "Roles of civil society" and "Dialogue with citizens" within its Policy White Paper (on Japan's disarmament and non-proliferation policy).[21] It regards the role of civil society in the security area began with its involvement in the process of concluding the Treaty Banning Anti-Personnel Mines (known also as the Ottawa process). The government is of the opinion that relations with CSOs on nuclear weapons are limited to nuclear disarmament and the strengthening of the NPT regime. It believes there are no CSOs that seek collaboration regarding CTBT and expansion of non-nuclear zones.[22]

The government asserts that it is collaborating with CSOs on nuclear disarmament on the following five points, recognizing the high public aspirations of the people for the abolition of nuclear weapons and active movements by *hibakusha,* the local governments of *hibaku* cities of Hiroshima and Nagasaki, and NGOs in abolishing nuclear weapons. The first point is participation at the annual Peace Memorial Ceremonies organized by the Cities of Hiroshima and Nagasaki held in August with the attendance of dignitaries including the prime minister and members of the cabinet as well as meetings organized by *hibakusha* held in conjunction with the events. The second point is inviting experts

[21] * Arms Control and Disarmament Division, MOFA, has made the Chapter about the role of civil society titled "Role of Civil Society" or "Dialogue and Cooperation between the Japanese government and Civil Society" in all editions of its white paper "Japan's Disarmament and Non-Proliferation Policy" since 2002

[22] Interview with Yasuyuki Ebata 2010

and knowledgeable persons to serve as co-chair and as advisors at the Tokyo Forum on Non-Proliferation/Nuclear Disarmament Forum (1998).[23] The third is co-sponsorship and support of NPT Operation Study Conference and side events of the preparatory committees. Other occasions were at the NPT as side event conducted at the UN, as side event of the NPT Operating Study Conference (2010) and when at Disarmament/Non-Proliferation Education Seminar (2009),[24] business enterprises of Hiroshima City and the Japan-US academic organisations sponsored "Committee on Computer Graphic Reconstruction of Peace Park and its surroundings" before the bomb was dropped, was presented at the UN Headquarters as a side event of the NPT Operation Study Conference (2010).[25] The fourth is that the Government cooperates every year in the organisation of UN Disarmament Conference held throughout Japan and their main conferences and side events,

---

[23] MOFA, Arms Control and Disarmament Division, Disarmament, Non-Proliferation and Science Department, Japan's Disarmament and Non-Proliferation Policy (white paper, 1nd Edition, 2002), Chapter 8: Role of Civil Society, Section 2: Symposium and Workshops, p157-p159
http://www.mofa.go.jp/mofaj/gaiko/gun_hakusho/2002/hon8.pdf (accessed on 7th May 2010)
MOFA, Arms Control and Disarmament Division, Disarmament, Non-Proliferation and Science Department, Japan's Disarmament and Non-Proliferation Policy (white paper, 2nd Edition, 2004), Chapter 8: Role of Civil Society, Section 8: Symposium and Workshops, p237-p238

[24] MOFA, Arms Control and Disarmament Division, Disarmament, Non-Proliferation and Science Department, Japan's Disarmament and Non-Proliferation Policy (white paper, 5nd Edition, 2011), Chapter 7: Dialogue and Cooperation with Civil Society, Section 4: Japan's Basic Standpoint and Approach for Disarmament and Non-Proliferation, Section 2: Symposium and Workshops, and Dialogue and Cooperation with Civil Society, "Side Event of the 3rd Preparatory Session for 2010 NPT Review Conference in 2009, sponsored by MOFA, UN Office of Disarmament Affairs, UN Institute for Disarmament Research, and Center for Nonproliferation Studies of Monterey Institute of International Studies" p129

[25] Ibid, Chapter 3: Disarmament, Non-Proliferation, and Education, No 1: Submission of Working Papers about Disarmament and Non-Proliferation Education

recognizing their importance as part of the disarmament and non-proliferation education of the general public, high school and university students.[26] The importance of disarmament and non-proliferation education is recognized as a uniquely Japanese initiative, and the need for promoting it is noted in the final resolution of the NPT Operation Conference (2010). The fifth is cooperation provided to NGOs and embassy-sponsored atomic bomb exhibitions overseas.[27] It appears that the government approach is for having

---

[26] Ibid p132

[27] MOFA, Arms Control and Disarmament Division, Disarmament, Non-Proliferation and Science Department, Japan's Disarmament and Non-Proliferation Policy (white paper, 4nd Edition, 2008), Chapter 8: Role of Civil Society, Section 2: Symposium and Workshops, No 5: Collaboration to hold exhibitions regarding Atomic Bombs in Overseas, p148

"History of Japan's Exhibition regarding Atomic Bombs in the world"

1, In Porto Alegre, Brazil, January and February 2006, sponsored by City Hall of Porto Alegre, supported by Japanese Consulate-General in Curitiba

2, In Minsk, Belarus, April 2006, sponsored by Committee on Nuclear Accident in Chernobyl, and Japanese Embassy to Belarus

3, In San Salvador, El Salvador, May 2006, sponsored by Student Association of Department of Social Information of UCA, supported by Japanese Embassy to El Salvador

4, In Kazanlak, Bulgaria, August 2006, sponsored by Kazanlak City and Kazanlak Art Gallery, supported by Japanese Embassy to Bulgaria

5, In Sao Paulo, Brazil, August and September 2006, sponsored by Modern Cultural Space and Japanese Consulate-General in Sao Paulo

6, In La Paz, Bolivia, August 2006, sponsored by La Paz City, Japanese Expat Organisation in La Paz, Bolivian Library Association, and Japanese Embassy to Bolivia

7, In Tegucigalpa, Honduras, July and August 2007, sponsored by Japan Overseas Cooperation Volunteers, supported by Japanese Embassy to Honduras

8, In Curitiba, Brazil, sponsored by Parana State Department of Culture, Supporting Association of Japanese-Brazilian Culture in Curitiba, and Japanese Consulate-General in Curitiba

9, In Dacca, Bangladesh, Study in Japan, Alumni Association of "Study in Japan" and Japanese Embassy in Bangladesh

10, In Asuncion, Paraguay, sponsored by Centro Paraguayo Japonesa, Japan Society in Paraguay, JICA and Japan Overseas Cooperation Volunteers, and Japanese Embassy to Paraguay

11, In Chicago, the United States, sponsored by Hiroshima Peace Culture

greater opportunities for public-private contacts rather than collaborating on nuclear disarmament with CSOs. With regard to the government's support for A-bomb exhibitions, it must be pointed out it has low efficacy in inspiring international public opinion since most events take place in smaller cities and in countries without nuclear weapons. As for the government's claim for co-sponsorship of A-bomb exhibitions with NGOs, it must be noted that the co-sponsor is usually the Overseas Youth Cooperation Organization or the Japan International Cooperation Agency (JICA), established by the Foreign Ministry or the government, or overseas research organisations. The NGOs that the government refers to are not financially and otherwise independent anti-nuclear grassroots CSOs.

The anti-nuclear policy of the Japanese government is for the total abolition of nuclear weapons, to clear all nuclear weapons from the earth. Its policy, however, is not in favour of partial abolition, which makes its stance look ambiguous.

Every year from the 49th UN General Assembly (UNGA 1994) up to the present, draft resolutions were submitted and adopted by a majority including the P5 countries, the United States, the USSR (Russia today), France, China, and the United Kingdom, that legally possess nuclear weapons. These resolutions ("Nuclear Disarmament Towards Ultimate Abolition of Nuclear Weapons",[28] "Roadmap to Total Abolition of

---

Foundation and Hiroshima Peace Memorial Museum, DePaul University, Hiroshima City, Nagasaki City, and Nagasaki Atomic Bomb Museum, and supported by Japanese Consulate-General in Chicago
12, In Salcedo, Dominica, sponsored by Salcedo Prefecture, Republic of Dominica, JICA volunteers, Japanese Embassy to Dominica
[28] MOFA Archives 1994
http://www.mofa.go.jp/mofaj/gaiko/un_cd/gun_un/ketsu_94.html (accessed on 8th January 2013)
MOFA Archives 1999
http://www.mofa.go.jp/mofaj/gaiko/un_cd/gun_un/ketsu_99.html (accessed on

Nuclear Weapons" [29], "Draft Resolution on Nuclear Disarmament",[30] Compliance to the NPT, Early effectuation of the CTBT, Cut-off Treaty (Treaty to Prohibit Production of Fissionable Materials for Military Use, Strengthening of the International Atomic Energy Agency (IAEA), and Proliferation of Weapons of Mass Destruction), presented with the objective of avoiding materials that can lead to the proliferation of WMD and falling into the hands of terrorists, asserted the importance of their keeping, management and protection (after 2001).[31]

The Japanese government is opposed as are the P5, to the notion of illegality of the use of nuclear weapons, as the first step for building a framework for total abolition of nuclear arms. The government continues to abstain from 1966 to this day (2013) concerning the Recommendatory note of the International Court of Justice submitted by 28 countries including Malaysia, "Follow-up resolution on "Recommendation Advice concerning the legality of the use and or threat of nuclear weapons" (1966). As an explanation, the Japanese representative stated at the UNGA that: "Japan supports the unanimous vote concerning the advisory opinion of the International Court of Justice (ICJ) 1996" concerning "the obligation to reach nuclear disarmament through sincere negotiation", however, it believes "it is too early to expect all nations to immediately carry out their obligations by

---

8th January 2013)

[29] MOFA Archives 2000-2001
http://www.mofa.go.jp/mofaj/gaiko/un_cd/gun_un/ketsu_2001.html (accessed on 8th January 2013)

[30] MOFA Archives 2002-2012
http://www.mofa.go.jp/mofaj/gaiko/un_cd/gun_un/archive.html#ketsugian_others (accessed on 8th January 2013)

[31] MOFA Archives 2001: Disarmament and Non-Proliferation – Japan's Proposal at the UN Assembly 2001 titled "Approach to Abolition of Nuclear Weapons"
http://www.mofa.go.jp/mofaj/gaiko/un_cd/gun_un/ketsu_2001.html (8th Jan 2013)

commencing multilateral negotiation for an early conclusion of the Treaty Prohibiting Nuclear Weapons".[32] The statement was criticized even within the Diet (Parliament) of Japan. Masayoshi Hamada (Member of House of Counsellors and the Chair of the KCPANW) presented a written question to the Government, through the President of the House, as to why Japan abstained from voting on the Follow-up Resolution that more or less coincided with the policy of the NPT Review Conference in which the Japanese government participates and which it supports.[33] The Japanese government expressed its clear stand, saying, there was a need to win understanding of the nuclear weapons countries, and it could not support a resolution that did not get the support or understanding of the nuclear powers.

> "With regard to the draft resolution (the Follow-up Resolution), we have abstained from voting at the UNGA First Committee, based on our country's stand that it believed it important to continue to carryout realistic and sincere efforts for nuclear disarmament with a view to achieving, with the understanding

---

[32] Japan NGO Network for Nuclear Weapons Abolition, Kokuren Sokai Daiichi Iinkai Oyobi Raishun No Osuro Kaigi Ni Kansuru Shitumon (Questions on No 1 Committee of the UN Assembly and the Oslo Conference in Spring Next Year), p2
http://nuclearabolitionjpn.files.wordpress.com/2012/11/20121119_ngoquestions.pdf (accessed on 19th April 2013)

[33] House of Councillors Japan, Sangiin Shitumon Dai 82 Go ""Kakuheiki No Ikaku Mataha Shiyo No Gohosei Ni Kansuru Kokusai Shiho Saibansho Kankokuteki Iken No Follow UP" Ni Kansuru Shitumon Shui" – Migi No Shitumon Shuisho O Kokkai Ho Dai 74 Jo Ni Yotte Teishutsu suru. Heisei 22 Nen 11 Gatsu 4 Ka, Hamada Masayoshi. Nishioka Takeo Sangiinn Gicho Ate.
(No 82 of Question at the House of Councillors Japan "Memorandum on Questions regarding UN Resolution "Follow up of ICJ Advisory Opinion on Legality of Threat or Use of Nuclear Weapons"". Interpellator: Masayoshi Hamada, a member of the House and Komeito, to Speaker Takeo Nishioka)
http://www.sangiin.go.jp/japanese/joho1/kousei/syuisyo/176/syup/s176082.pdf (accessed on 7th January 2012)

of both nuclear weapons states and non-nuclear states, a peaceful an safe world without nuclear weapons."[34]
(Translated by Fujiko Hara)

As for the legal recognition concerning the illegality of the use of nuclear weapons, states with nuclear weapons, the US, the UK, France and Russia are opposed to it.[35] The Japanese Government takes an ambiguous stance and continues to state the importance of the abolition of nuclear weapons, emphasizing its conventional stance as the only A-bombed country. Thereafter, the Japanese government, continued to abstain or refuse signature on resolutions that condemned the inhumanity of nuclear weapons at the 2012 UNGA and the First preparatory meeting for the 2015 NPT Review Conference, and was sternly criticized by the governments of South Africa and Norway that promote non-nuclear policies and even by Japan's anti-nuclear CSOs

---

[34] House of Councillors Japan, Sangiin Tobeinsho Dai 82 Go "Naikaku Sanshitsu 176 Dai 82 Go Heisei 22 Nenen 11 Gatsu 12 Nichi, Naikaku Sori Dajin Rinji Dairi Kokumu Daijin Sengoku Yoshito. Nishioka Takeo Sangiin Gicho Ate.
(No 83 of Written Answer [176-No82, 12 November 2011] from Acting Prime Minister / Minister of State Yoshito Sengoku to Speaker of the House of Councillors Takeo Nishioka)
http://www.sangiin.go.jp/japanese/joho1/kousei/syuisyo/176/toup/t176082.pdf (accessed on 7th January 2012)

[35] Asahi Newspaper, (21 countries admitted [illegality of use of nuclear weapons] and 35 countries made statements to the International Court of Justice), 6th December 1994.
This article appeared the answers of 35 countries regarding illegality of use of nuclear weapons, and the IALANA's research about each state's standpoint. Under this research result, the IALANA evaluated that the Japanese government has not clarified its standpoint regarding illegality of use of nuclear weapons. The Japanese government has not said "agree or disagree with the ICJ Advisory Opinion 1996", but only said "nuclear weapons are against humanitarian spirit based on international law. As the only victim of atomic-bombs, we underline importance of nuclear abolition. In order for that, we have to make an nuclear non-proliferation regime based on the NPT to be effective and universal"

(see Chapter 3). It is pointed out that for the only country that has suffered from nuclear weapons to refuse or abstain from placing its signature would drastically reduce its significance when a UN resolution is adopted, and reduce the international drive against nuclear weapons.[36] What is required to raise the momentum for nuclear disarmament is the constructive engagement of the "parties", nuclear states and the victim state, Japan. The reason for Japan not being able to make a total commitment is closely related to the complexity of the post-Cold War Northeast Asian political situation and the need because of it for its defence and foreign policies to depend on the US's "nuclear umbrella".

Yasuyuki Ebata, the First Secretary in charge of nuclear policy of the Permanent Mission of Japan for the UN and Other International Organs in Vienna, stated that government policy on nuclear issues was essentially that it should be conducted balancing the four categories of nuclear disarmament, nuclear non-proliferation, peaceful use of nuclear energy and national security.[37] Basically, he said that while nuclear disarmament, nuclear non-proliferation and peaceful use of nuclear energy constitute the main pillars of the present framework of the NPT Regime, national security is de facto of foremost importance since most of the neighbouring countries possess nuclear weapons today.

Under the circumstances, the government believes it is not enough to discuss and promote what CSOs advocate, the total abolition of nuclear weapons and the establishment of a treaty banning nuclear

---

[36] Akira Kawasaki (Secretary-General of Japan NGO Network for Nuclear Weapons Abolition)'s Remark, Public Seminar "Towards Abolition of Nuclear Weapons: the World Situation and Japan – Report on 1st Preparatory Session for the 2015 NPT Review Conference and the Future", at Meiji Gakuin University, Tokyo, 12th May 2013

[37] Interview with Yasuyuki Ebata 2010

weapons.[38] Also, the Arms Control and Disarmament Section of the MOFA that produced the White Paper "Nuclear Disarmament and Nuclear Non-proliferation Diplomacy" stated that while it edits and publishes the White Paper at the instruction of the government, it by no means exclusively represents diplomatic policy. While the Arms Control and Disarmament Section is dedicated to the promotion of disarmament and non-proliferation policies, there are sections in the same Foreign Affairs Ministry that implement policies with a focus on Japan-US Alliance and national security, and furthermore, the Ministry of Defence Japan also produces defence policies. The government, therefore, states that it takes appropriate diplomatic stance in response to a given situation.[39] As far as the Arms Control and Disarmament Section is concerned, while the government promotes nuclear disarmament in accordance with the Article 6 of the NPT, it also necessarily believes in taking realistic approaches. From the above, it suggests that the present state of national security remains a great challenge in Japan's anti-nuclear policies.

Japan's national security policy system over the years has seen the complicated blending of its constitutional principles and the realistic policy deployed under the Japan-US Security Treaty. Japan's post-Second World War constitution provides in its Article 9 the renunciation of war, and refusal to maintain arms as well as practice the right of war (engagement). This article has been the target of many controversies over pros and cons as well as differences in interpretation. However, it is generally referred to as the Peace Constitution because of its clauses renouncing war and non-maintenance of armed forces.

Land, sea and air self-defence forces (formerly, the National Police

---

[38] Ibid

[39] Interview with Haruna Abe 2010

Reserve) is kept not as an army but to provide minimum defence in case of urgent and unjust infringement/invasion, absence of other appropriate means of removing it, and as necessary minimum use of force.[40]

> "Following the Second World War our country resolved never again to repeat the ravages of war and made continuous efforts to build a peaceful state, Lasting peace is the hearts' desire of the Japanese people. The Constitution of Japan that upholds the ideal of pacifism has in Article 9 provisions concerning renouncement of war, not possessing war-making capabilities and disavowal of the right of belligerency. Naturally, this provision does not repudiate the intrinsic right of self-defence of a sovereign state. The government understands, therefore, that unless the right of self-defence is denied, the possession of a minimum level of military power is recognized under the Constitution. With this tin mind our country maintains, services and operates forces exclusively for national defence under our constitution". [41]
>
> (Translated by Fujiko Hara)

For reasons stated above, the government perceives that possession of minimum levels of defence, weaponry and ordinance is allowed by the Constitution but not ballistic missiles and attack type aircraft

---

[40] Ministry of Defense Japan, "Kenpo To Zieitai" 2, Kenpo 9 Jo No Shushi Ni Tsuite No Seifu Kenkai, (2) Zieiken Hatsudo No Yoken (Constitution and Self-Defense Force" 2, Japanese Government's Opinion on Meaning of Article 9 of the Constitution, (2) Conditions for Invoking Right of Self-Defense) http://www.mod.go.jp/j/approach/agenda/seisaku/kihon02.html (accessed on 23rd February 2012)

[41] Ibid

carriers.[42] Japan, however, could not be totally aloof to the framework for international security issues. Japan's diplomatic stance regarding international security, therefore, is changing. During the Gulf War (1990-1991) the Japanese government provided financial assistance of a total of 13 billion dollars, in lieu of dispatching self-defence forces to join the US-centred multinational force. The amount exceeded those of Kuwait, Saudi Arabia and Germany that followed Japan's suit but Japan's failure to send personnel to join the effort was greatly criticized.[43] Public opinion in Japan was aroused gradually in favour of sending supplies and goods to support non-combative efforts. Learning from this experience the government changed its policies and deployed forces on the ground based on the "supreme principles/purposes" noted in the preamble of the constitution.[44]

> "We, the Japanese people….determined to preserve our security, and existence, trusting in the justice and faith of the peace-loving peoples of the world", "We desire to occupy an honoured place in an international society striving for the preservation of peace, and the banishment of tyranny and slavery, oppression and intolerance for all time from earth", "We recognize that all peoples of the world have the right to live in peace, free from fear and want", "We believe that no nation is responsible to itself alone, but that laws of political morality are

---

[42] Ibid

[43] MOFA, Diplomatic Blue Book 1991, Chapter 2: Gulf War and Japanese Diplomacy, Section 2: Response to Gulf War, No 3: Support to Restore Peace in the Area of Gulf, No 5: Evaluation by the International Society http://www.mofa.go.jp/mofaj/gaiko/bluebook/1991/h03-2-2.htm (accessed on 9th August 2011)

[44] MOFA, Diplomatic Blue Book 1991, Chapter 1: Changing of International Situation and Japanese Diplomacy, Section 2: Issues to Japanese Diplomacy, No 3: Issues to Japanese Diplomacy

universal; and that obedience to such laws is incumbent upon all nations who would sustain their own sovereignty and justify their sovereign relationship with other nations". [45]
(Translated by Fujiko Hara)

After 2001, Japan lost no time in deciding to dispatch Self-Defence Forces (SDF) to Afghanistan and Iraq to join US forces. The Act on Special Measures against Terrorism (2003) provides the legal ground for this decision. The SDF were dispatched to assist activities of the US-led coalition in their attempt to achieve the objectives of the UN Charter by contributing to the removal of terrorist threats such as those from the Taliban. Their activities involved ship to ship refueling, transporting ship fuel and air lifting manpower and material, conducting repair and maintenance, providing medical services, and port service.[46]

The dispatch of SDF aroused serious debate whether or not it violated the constitution and litigation took place across the country. In May 2008, the Nagoya High Court (in Aichi Prefecture), one of the Higher Courts in Japan, ruled that SDF activities in Iraq were unconstitutional. It is unlikely that a ruling of a regional court of law will be reflected in a government decision but it is a fact that there was a legal judgment that the matter in question was unconstitutional. The government's view was that it was not unconstitutional since SDF was not participating in any combat.

---

[45] Sanseido Co., Ltd., Shin Roppo: Nihonkoku Kenpo (New Compendium of Laws Japan: Constitution), p11, 2001

[46] Prime Minister of Japan and His Cabinet (Prime Minister's Office Japan), Tero Taisaku Tokuso Ho Ni motozuku Taio Sochi No Zissi Oyobi Taio Sochi Ni Kansuru Kihon Keikaku Ni Tsuite, Anzenhosho Kaigi Kettei, Kakugi Kettei (Cabinet Decision and Decision of Security Council of Japan on Basic Plan of Measures for Action and Measures based on Special Anti-Terrorism Law) http://www.kantei.go.jp/jp/kakugikettei/2001/1116keikaku.html (accessed on 9th August 2011)

"...Whereas, Special Measures Act concerning Humanitarian Reconstruction and Safety Support Activities in Iraq (No. 137 Act, 2003, hereafter, Iraq Special Measures Act) limits our country's contribution to non-use of military power (i.e., as well as that implementation will be limited to areas where presently no combat is taking place (actions that accompany international armed conflicts such as kill and injure people and or destroy goods) and where areas where no combat is likely to take place during the period involved. In other words, the act is structured so as to ensure that the activities of our country will not be part of the coalition activities.

All said, the government's intention regarding the area in which the SDF will be involved (involvements as provided for in Article 2, Section 1 of the Special Measures Act Concerning Iraq) is defined as areas where no combat is taking place at present as well as not likely to take place during the period of implementation, based on information uniquely collected and received from other countries....."

(Written response of Prime Minister Yasuo Fukuda to queries concerning the Final Decision of the Nagoya High Court) [47]

(Translated by Fujiko Hara)

---

[47] Ministry of Defense Japan, Shokan Horei To – Shitsumon Shuisho Tobensho – 2008 Nen 4 Gatsu 27 Nichi No Nagoya Koto Saibansho Kakutei Hanketsu Ni Kansuru Shitsumon Ni Taisuru Tobensho (Fukuda Yasuo Naikaku Sori Daijin) (Related Laws – Memorandum on Questions and Written Response – Written Response to Questions on Final Judgement of Nagoya High Court on 27th April 2008 (by Prime Minister Yasuo Fukuda) http://www.mod.go.jp/j/presiding/touben/169kai/syu/tou352.html (accessed on 9th August 2011)

The Japan-US Alliance remains from the end of Second World War to this day the axis of the government's diplomatic and defence policies. Its purpose is,

> "The Japan-US Alliance based on Japan-US Security System is the cornerstone of Japan's diplomacy. It has effectively functioned to bring peace and prosperity to Japan and the Far East as well as a basic framework for the security and development of the Asia-Pacific Region. It continues to have an essential role in the Asian Pacific region where instabilities persist after the end of Cold War". [48]
> (Translated by Fujiko Hara)

At the time of the conclusion of the Japan-US Security Treaty (1952), the Japanese Government expected to totally depend on the US for Japan's post-war national security so as to concentrate on the reconstruction of the devastated land and economy (the so-called Yoshida Doctrine. Shigeru Yoshida was prime minister from 1946 to 1952). Following the end of the war (1945) Japan was under the occupation of the allies, with the US Army playing a central role until the effectuation of the San Francisco Peace Treaty and the recovery of national sovereignty (1952). After regaining independence under the Japan-US Security Treaty, the US Army would establish military bases in Japan where men-in-uniform would be stationed. At the same time, Japan would be protected by the US nuclear weapons, under the so-called nuclear umbrella. Since that time Japan's national security

---

[48] MOFA, *Nichibei Kankei – 1, Nichibei Kankei Soron (Japan-US Relation -1 , Outline of Japan-US Relation)* http://www.mofa.go.jp/mofaj/area/usa/kankei.html (accessed on 24th January 2013)

would depend on nuclear deterrence from an international political perspective.

The Japanese government headed by Prime Minister Yoshida and the Allied Forces were of the strong opinion that resurgence of the old militarism must be avoided, for example through rearmament, as Japan regained independence. Shigeru Yoshida as well as most of the high government officials at the time had been detained or imprisoned by the military during the war for having opposed its policies. Yoshida had been a pro-Anglo-American diplomat who served as Japan's ambassador to the Court of St. James. Prior to the opening of the war, he collaborated with Joseph Clark Grew, the then US Ambassador to Japan and others to avert it but to no avail. After the war started, he organized a group to engineer its end, but was arrested and imprisoned. This background won him the trust of the allied forces at the end of the war. The Allied Forces as well, fearing deeply that rearmament of Japan may lead to a possible resurgence of its militarism had it stated clearly in the draft new constitution that Japan would not possess armed forces.

> "ARTICLE 9. Aspiring sincerely to an international peace based on justice and order, the Japanese people forever renounce war as a sovereign right of the nation and the threat or use of force as means of settling international disputes. (2) To accomplish the aim of the preceding paragraph, land, sea, and air forces, as well as other war potential, will never be maintained. The right of *belligerency* of the state will not be recognized."
>
> (Article 9 of the present Constitution of Japan)
>
> (Translated by Fujiko Hara)

The draft treaty (1950) reflects the background of the final

Japan-US Security Treaty (1952). That is to say, the national security of Japan will totally depend on the US forces stationed in Japan that will not possess military forces.

> "…….The Constitution of Japan will make clear that the Japanese people wish to protect their safety and life trusting in fairness and trust of the peace loving countries, and to pursue sincerely international peace based on justice and order, will renounce war and not possess armas. The United States determined that it was the ultimate objective of the Unitedd Nations to build a world where such country can live in security, as well as invasion against such a country must be, in accordance with the principles of the UN Chatter, rapidly and effectively stopped…"
>
> Draft Japan-US Security Treaty (11 October 1950)[49]
>
> (Translated by Fujiko Hara)

The United States of America will be responsible for ensuring the safety of Japan, which does not possess armaments, on behalf of the UN. The Japan-US Security Treaty (1952);[50]

> "…There is danger to Japan in this situation because irresponsible militarism has not yet been driven from the world. Therefore Japan desires a Security Treaty with the United States of America to come into force simultaneously with the Treaty of

[49] MOFA and MOFA Diplomatic Archives, Nippon Gaiko Shuyo Bunsho Nenpyo (1) (Japanese Diplomatic Main Papers and Chronological Table (1)), p119-p112

[50] Joyakushu, 30-6. Japan's Foreign Relations-Basic Documents Vol.1, p444-p448.

Peace between Japan and the United States of America."
(Translated by Fujiko Hara)

However, with the establishment of the People's Republic of China (PRC, 1949) and the Korean War (1950-1953) the US began to strongly feel the danger of communization of Asia. Thus rearmament of Japan and the Japan-US collective would defend the security of the Asia Pacific Region. This became the prime objective of the Security Treaty. The US concern about the communization of East Asia was based on the Domino theory which was its mainstream ideology during the cold war. In other words, if one country fell to communism in the region, neighbouring countries would also be communized as per the Domino theory. With regard to the rearmament of Japan, the Defence Agency was established in 1954 and with it, Ground, Maritime and Air SDFs allowing also the possession and use of arms.

The Japan-US Security Treaty was revised in 1960 with a view to strengthening it and Japan-US Alliance signified a breakwater against the communization of Northeast Asia and created a bulwark of liberalism. The two countries, as equal allies shared military information and engaged actively in joint exercises. This kind of mutual defence agreement is a typical bilateral security setup during the cold war period.

In 1949, for example, the US and the Philippines concluded a mutual security treaty to counter China. The Cold War was intensified by the Korean War (1950 – 1953), and the US Administration concluded a mutual security treaty with the Philippines, its colony up to 1946. The US also concluded a mutual security treaty with South Korea in 1953. In fact the Korean War was the first armed conflict between the Eastern and the Western blocs. The grisly battle ended in an armistice after the North Korean army supported by the Soviet Union and China created a stalemate with the South Korean army and the allied forces led by Douglas MacArthur. This resulted in the US Administration concluding hasty mutual security treaties with the Republic of Korea and nations of Northeast Asia.

The treaty allowed the US forces to be stationed in South Korea giving them the right of operational control. The control was to be transferred to the South Korean forces in 1993 after the Cold War with the proviso that the treaty allows the US forces to have full control in case of an emergency.

The US military concerns in northeast Asia can naturally be associated with expanding Soviet influence. It is interesting to note that there were concerns over China's emergence as well. Chiang Kai-shek's Kuomintang that had ruled the Chinese continent was driven to Taiwan having lost the war against the Communist forces. The US supported the Kuomintang during its war with Japan (1937-1945) but supported neither the Communists nor the Kuomintang during the civil war. During the Cold War, however, to prevent further expansion of Communism, the US returned to the support of Taiwan and placed it within the Western sphere of defence. The Taiwan government concluded a mutual defence agreement with the USA fearing the Chinese Government might attack Taiwan after the Korean War. The treaty became void after Taiwan lost its UN representation to China in 1971.

During the Cold War, the Japanese Government normalized diplomatic relations with the Soviet Union in 1956 and with China in 1972. Further in 1978 the government concluded a peace treaty with China (Sino-Japanese Peace and Amity Treaty). As of 2013 the Russian Federation effectively controls the disputed territories. In drafting a peace treaty with the Soviet Union the Japanese government included in Article 5 a clause "all Northern territorial islands shall be returned to Japan". The Soviet government had, on the other hand, a clause with an opposite effect: "The Japanese government should renounce all rights of claim and right of possession over the Northern Territories".[51] These claims made the confrontation over the territorial issue definite. Since then, the Japanese government's basic policy has been to desist from having any negotiation over a peace treaty with the Soviet Union and the Russian Federation later unless and until the northern territorial issues are resolved, that is to say until the northern territories are returned.

These have been suggestions made by experts and anti-nuclear CSOs. For the Japanese government threats to national security come from relations it has with neighbouring countries, especially China and Russia. Deterrence to their threats had to be a security policy dependent on the US nuclear umbrella. Both China and Russia are legally recognized nuclear powers under the NPT.

Regarding relations with China and Taiwan, there are issues concerning understanding of history and territorial disputes over the Senkaku Islands for which Japan has effective rule as part of its territory. Since the late 2000 the issue has become one that could develop into

---

[51] Kajima Institute of International Peace, *Gaiko Shuyo Nenpyo 1 (Chronological Table of Japanese Diplomacy Vol. 1 [1941-1960])*, Hara Shobo Co., Ltd., 1983, p718-p719
Suggestions for Peace Treaty by Japan and the USSR, 16th August 1955, London
Japanese suggestions:Article 5 "editorial note: Draft revision of 30th August" 1, Of the Japanese territories occupied by the Union of Soviet Socialist Republics ans the result of the war, Sovereignty of Etorof, Kunashiri, Shikotan, and Habomai islands shall be totally recovered. With regard to the Karafuto south of north xxx 50 degrees as well as islands in the neighbourhood and the Chishma archipelago, negotiation between allied countries including the USSR and Japan.

serious diplomatic and defence problems (Sino-Japanese relations are taken up in Chapter 5 and Japan-Soviet relations in Chapter 6).

North Korea cannot exist without China's assistance and close economic relationship. According to the South Korean Statistical Agency, North Korea's trade with China was 70 % ($5.629 billion). [52] Should China stop economic exchange and support, North Korea would de facto dissolve from economic bankruptcy. US Secretary of State John Kerry called on China given its impact on North Korea, to exercise Chinese power to stop its aggressive stance in conducting the third nuclear test (2013) as well as abrogating the ceasefire agreement reached to end the Korean War. [53] For the resolution of the issue of nuclear arms in northeast Asia depends mainly on easing tensions between Japan and China as well as Japan and the Russian Federation. Indeed these issues confuse Japan and stagnate policy on nuclear disarmament.

Tadatoshi Akiba, the former mayor of Hiroshima and MP President (1999-2011), agreed that the Japanese government had a consistently

---

[52] Sankei Newspaper, Kita Chosen No Taichu Boeki Izon, Hazimete 7 Wari Ni (Ratio of North Korean Dependency on Trade with China reached 70%), * this article appeared analysis of South Korean National Statistical Office, 27th December 2012
http://sankei.jp.msn.com/world/news/121227/kor12122723290005-n1.htm (accessed on 5th March 2012)

[53] World News 15th April 2013 [Kerry: China must to do more to resolve North Korean missile crisis]
http://worldnews.nbcnews.com/_news/2013/04/15/17757742-kerry-china-must-do-more-to-resolve-north-korean-missile-crisis?lite (accessed on 19th April 2013)
"That done, I think it is very important to the Chinese to focus on the fact that ... if they're not prepared to put the pressure on the North -- and they have the greatest ability to have an impact on the North -- then this can become more destabilizing,"...
"It is obvious that China is the lifeline to North Korea. Everybody knows that China provides the vast majority of the fuel to North Korea. China is their biggest trading party, their biggest food donor and so forth," he added.

negative stance as regards the nuclear arms but said if the US moved towards their abolition then Japan would follow suit.[54] This shows how the nuclear powers have had a heavy bearing on the Japanese government as well as the international structure of nuclear disarmament. That is to say, that the global power balance including the attitudes of the US, the Russian Federation and the nuclear powers has great power on decisions and actions of governments around the world on nuclear disarmament. Akiba has been engaging in nuclear abolition activities since his student days at the University. After earning his doctorate at the Massachusetts Institute of Technology, he has been a researcher, member of the Japanese House of Representatives as well as mayor of the City of Hiroshima. He is an authority on anti-nuclear policies. He believes that the realistic road map towards nuclear disarmament and abolition lies in nuclear powers, especially the US and the Russian Federation reducing their arsenal, abandoning them, in other words reducing the value of nuclear arms. These suggestions have come from learned persons and anti-nuclear CSOs. For the Japanese government threats to national security come from relations it has with neighbouring countries, especially China and Russia. Deterrence from their threats must be based on security policy dependent on the US nuclear umbrella. Both china and Russia are nuclear powers legally recognized by the NPT.

In the 46th House of Representatives election of December 2012 forces that spoke for the nuclear armament of Japan seized the momentum. The cause is issue of the Senkaku Islands that lie between Japan and China that suddenly stirred up political and military tension. The faction in favour of nuclear armament is the new Japan Restoration

---

[54] Kazuhiro Tobisawa (writer of this dissertation) and Tadatoshi Akiba had a meeting on 2nd December 2011. Then Akiba showed his view on nuclear disarmament.

Party organized by politicians who have for long asserted the need for it. The party won 54 seats (11 seats before the election) out of a total of 480 seats, while the Liberal Democratic Party Japan (LDP) snapped up 294 seats (pre-election strength of 119 seats), The Komeito established by Daisaku Ikeda won 31 seats (pre-election strength 21 seats). The LDP and Komeito formed a coalition commanding a strength of 325 seats (it had a coalition from 1998 to 2009). The Japan Restoration Party snatched third position. There has been no other time in the post-war political history of Japan that parties calling publically for uclear armament have won so many seats in the parliament. The result can be ascribed to the deep sense of concern about the political friction the country has had with China and Russia, both nuclear power states, rather than the neglect of the horrific experiences of Hiroshima and Nagasaki.

It is clear that the root of Japan's nuclear armament goes back to the political tension between China and Russia since the cold war years. Some conservative politicians, critics, journalists and scholars have asserted over the years that nuclear armament was essential for the security of Japan. Their reasons are as follows: China and Russia will eventually pose threats to Japan due to East West confrontation during the cold war and the territorial issues[55]. States without nuclear weapons have low status and therefore no voice in the comity of nations.

Shintaro Ishihara[56] has in his almost half a century long political activities been an outspoken critic of Japan-US Security Treaty and the

---

[55] Terumasa Nakanishi, Kimindo Kuasaka, Yoshiko Sakurai, Tsutomu Nishioka, Kan Ito, Nisohachi Hyodo, Nihon Kakubuso No Ronte – Kokka Sonritsu No Kiki O Ikinukutameni (Viewpoints of Japanese Nuclear Armament – To Survive in Crisis of the Nation's Existence), PHP Institute Office2006

[56] Member of the House of Representatives 1972-1995 and 2012-2014, former Governor of Tokyo 1998-2012, and Member of the House of Councillors 1968-1972

threat that China poses. According to him, the present situation with the US forces stationed in Japan is not different from the allied occupation in the aftermath of Second World War, Japanese citizens should realize complete independence of Japan by possessing national defence forces that will protect our territorial land free of influence from any country. He has also been asserting over the years his doubt that the US would really come to our help with all its might just because Japan is an ally.[57] In the House of Representatives election of 2012 during the campaign Ishihara reiterated his long held thoughts on nuclear armament.

> "States that do not have nuclear power in today's world are diplomatically weak. Without nuclear power one has little say. North Korea makes the US anxious because it is engaged in nuclear development..... Russia has taken our territories (northern territories) and it has nuclear power. China is attempting to take away Japan's territory (Senkaku Islands) with its nuclear arms. Japan is lives in delusion of peace...Japan should at least conduct simulation of nuclear weapons. That can be a sort of deterrence. Whether to have it or not is a question that can be postponed. Japan-China friendship is important but Japan should not become the second Tibet."[58]
> (Translated by Fujiko Hara)

On issues of the Chinese threat and Japan's security, Pema Gyalpo[59],

---

[57] Shintaro Ishihara (Governor of Tokyo Metropolitan City), *Nihon-yo (Japan), Sankei Newspaper*, 8th June 2010

[58] Shintaro Ishihara, Lecture at Japan Foreign Correspondence Club, 20th November 2012

[59] Naturalized Japanese citizens, Professor in Political Science, Toin University of Yokhama, Kanagawa Prefecture, Japan, Advisor to the Prime Minister of Bhutan, and former Representative of 14th Dalai Lama to Japan

who served as the first representative of the Asia Pacific Region of the Tibetan government in exile, has analysed the reality of the northeast Asian situation based on his long-term academic research. Pema Gyalpo believes that the Constitution of Japan should have been revised from the perspective of national security at the time when China possessed nuclear weapons. There are a number of people who were involved in the drafting of both the Japanese Constitution and the UN Charter who share the same objectives and the spirit enshrined in the principles of peace.

There was a plan to state clearly the establishment of the UN Forces in the UN Charter but it failed to do so due to opposition including from the US government. If the UN Forces had ever existed then the Japanese Constitution would have become a realistic law but without them there is no way Japan can respond to emergencies or to international conflicts. The Constitution, therefore, should be revised to recognize its rights of belligerency and collective self-defence, with the objective of defence against countries with which it is in conflict such as China.

Pema Gyalpo, opposes the rise of pre-war militarism in Japan but believes patriotism is natural if not excessive. He believes that the extremely abstract nature of the Constitution that holds up hollow pacifism and lacks a realistic approach to national security is driving some people towards nuclear armament and revision of the Constitution.[60]

Here it is necessary to clarify the role of the UN forces. The UN forces differ fundamentally from the defence forces of various countries in that they are not permanent forces. Article 7 of the UN Charter

---

[60] Pema Gyalpo, Lecture at Gakudo-kai Seminer "Japanese Original Power, Danger of China, and Possibilities of India", at Hibiya Library & Museum, Tokyo, 13th May 2013

clearly states that the United Nations can take military sanctions against a threat to peace, and this forms the legal basis that enables the organization of UN forces.[61] Article 42 of the charter empowers the UN Security Council to assume command of the UN forces.[62] However, under Article 43, UN member states that have signed a special prior agreement with the Security Council to provide military forces are to do so at the request of the Security Council; but to-date no member state has signed this agreement (as of 2015).[63] Moreover, no UN forces have ever been organized or mobilized according to this process.

In the first place, throughout the Cold War period a number of permanent members of the UN Security Council such as the United States, the USSR and China were at loggerheads with each other, and for a prolonged period the situation was such that even the framing of any kind of agreement itself would have been difficult. Therefore, even if a conflict arose between Japan and China, there would be no countries to provide military power, so there would effectively be no mobilization of UN forces in such a case. Even if there were countries prepared to provide military forces, it is obvious that Russia and China, which have territorial disputes with Japan, would use their veto against the mobilization of UN forces as permanent members of the UN Security Council.

However, there is one special exception. Immediately after the outbreak of the Korean War, the UN Security Council passed a resolution deeming North Korea to be an aggressor in South Korea, and at the instigation of the United States, forces were formed with the

---

[61] UN, C*harter of the United Nations* http://www.un.org/en/documents/charter/chapter3.shtml (accessed on 20th July 2015)

[62] Ibid

[63] Ibid

participation of 22 countries. These received approval from the United Nations and were to be called UN forces. Douglas MacArthur of the US army became Supreme Commander, but as these forces strongly reflected the intentions of countries of the West to provide assistance to Korea, they were closer to being multinational forces than true UN forces. Although the USSR was in a position where it should have exercised its veto in defence of North Korea, another socialist country, but it had absented itself at the time of the resolution in protest over the leadership struggle between the Kuomintang and the Communist Party in China.

Immediately after the cease fire of the Korean War, the countries[64], which joined the UN forces for the Korean War, signed the Official Minutes to the Agreement Regarding the Status of the UN Forces in Japan.[65] This was an agreement allowing for the stationing of UN forces in Japan in the event of a resumption of the Korean War. In 2015, the cease fire has continued, and this agreement remains effective more than half a century later, with seven military bases where US armed forces are stationed that have become bases for stationing such UN forces. Moreover, the 10 countries participating in these UN forces, including US and Australian forces, conduct joint military exercises.[66] This exceptional case, which was created by the Cold War, is without precedent.

---

[64] The United States, Canada, New Zealand, the United Kingdom, South Africa, Australia, Republic of the Philippines, France and Italy

[65] MOFA, Agreed Official Minutes Relating to the Agreement Regarding the Status of the United Nations Forces in Japan (signed at Tokyo, February 19, 1954. Published, June 1, 1954)
http://www.mofa.go.jp/mofaj/gaiko/treaty/pdfs/B-S38-P1-3_4.pdf (accessed on 20th July 2015)

[66] Kadena Air Base (US Stationary Forces in Japan), *Base hosts 1st RAAF training in Japan (by Tech. Sgt. Rey Ramon: 18th Wing Public Affairs)* 10th November 2007 http://www.kadena.af.mil/news/story.asp?id=123071589 (accessed on 9th August 2015)

In view of the above, the possibility that UN forces will be mobilized to defend Japan if the security of Japan is threatened is extremely small and, therefore, Pema's analysis cannot be considered appropriate.

The Japanese government has always welcomed the rising momentum for the abolition of nuclear arms as a victim of atomic bombs (*hibaku* country) and desires that international opinion turn towards it. However, dependence on the US Nuclear deterrence and political frictions with nuclear powers in northeast Asia leave Japan unable to forcefully demand nuclear disarmament of its allies starting with the USA that lawfully possess nuclear weapons under NPT. From materials of the MOFA and interview researches it must be stated that while proclaiming the need for nuclear disarmament and abolition, it could only gradually advance by balancing it with national security. Moreover, nuclear disarmament will not advance unless the nuclear powers themselves steer that way.

This attitude causes CSOs to be critical of the government's passive stance regarding nuclear disarmament and abolition. From the perspective of national security, it is the basic concept of the Japan-US Security Treaty that the US nuclear umbrella is essential. The Japanese government in 2012 was asked to sign a statement prepared by 16 states including Switzerland and Norway to strengthen efforts to declare nuclear weapons unlawful, at the UN First Commission on strengthening efforts to make nuclear weapons unlawful. On 18th October 2012 the Japanese government decided to refuse. The explanation for the refusal was that by signing the statement logical consistency will be lost since Japan does depend on national security for deterrence including the US nuclear arms. The single country that had nuclear bombs dropped on it did not support a statement stressing the inhumanity of nuclear weapons.[67]

In October 2013 the First Committee of the UN General Assembly adopted the Joint Declaration on the Inhuman Effects of Nuclear Weapons and Their Non-use presented by sixteen non-nuclear states, with New Zealand, Norway, Costa Rica, Egypt and South Africa playing pivotal roles. The Joint Declaration was adopted by 125 countries including Japan, and was the greatest number of countries to have signed, compared with three previous joint declarations. As might be expected, the P5, countries legally holding nuclear weapons refused to sign. Signatory countries welcomed Japan's signature following its refusal to do so during the last three occasions. The number of signatories has now reached two thirds of the 193 UN member countries. The Joint Declaration stated that while the inhumanity of nuclear weapons has not been the core issue of nuclear disarmament and non-proliferation, but that finally their inhumanity was established as a global issue. "The survival of humankind depended on the non-use of nuclear weapons under all circumstances" – it was for this single reason that the Japanese government could not sign because of the dependence on the US nuclear deterrence for its national security and diplomatic issues it has with China and North Korea. As this sentence had not been taken out of the Joint Declaration it was a dramatic move on the part of Japan.

There were a number of reasons for the Japanese government to finally sign the agreement, one of which was that Foreign Minister, Fumio Kishida comes from Hiroshima. Both his grandfather and father

---

[67] Chugoku Newspaper, Nihon, Kaku Higohoka No Shomei Kyohi: Kokureni No 16Kakoku Seimeian (Japan refused to sign a document that describes nuclear weapons as inhumane, which was submitted by 16 countries to the UN committee), Masakatsu Oota (Kyodo Press Co., Ltd.), 19th October 2012 http://www.chugoku-np.co.jp/News/Sp201210190065.html (accessed on 21st October 2012)

were members of parliament and both were avid promoters of nuclear abolition. Also it seems that the coalition partner the Komeito has been strongly pressing for Japan to accept the inhumanity of the nuclear weapons. When the government refused to sign the 2012 joint declaration it is said that Kishida had been persuading the MOFA official in charge to sign the document until the day before.[68]

The Komeito is demanding the Japanese government sponsor a nuclear abolition summit in Hiroshima and Nagasaki cities, saying that the sole country with the experience of being atom bombed has the responsibility as well as the rights in the international community.[69] The idea behind this proposition was for national leaders to see for themselves the actual situation on the ground and to follow with realistic deliberations on the abolition of nuclear weapons.

With regard to the inhumanity of nuclear weapons, the KCPANW delivered to the Minister of Foreign Affairs in October 2012, "An urgent proposal concerning the inhumane aspects of nuclear weapons" through the Head of the Disarmament, Non-Proliferation and Science Department. The proposal referred to the deliberation on nuclear disarmament taking place at the First Committee of the UN General Assembly just at the time, as well as the rising concern for the inhumanity of nuclear weapons and appealed that Japan being the only atom-bombed country has the responsibility to lead international deliberation.

---

[68] Akira Kawasaki's Presentation, Report Session of Oslo Conference, which was held in support of the Japan NGO Network for Nuclear Weapons Abolition, 19th March 2013

[69] Komei Newspaper, *Kakuhaizetsu Sekai No Choryu Ni-Kakuchi De Shusenkinen Gaito Enzetsukai* (Let's make nuclear abolition as a worldwide common sense, New Komeito Party gave speeches in cities and towns in Japan for the memorial day of finishing of the Second World War,), 16th August 2011, p1

Specifically, a three-point suggestion was made to the government; namely: Japan to immediately start talks with the proposing states to enable it to sign the revised version of "the Inhumane aspects of Nuclear Weapons" as a joint proposer; secondly, Japan must contribute, with combined wisdom of public and private sectors, to deliberations at the "Conference: Humanitarian Impact of Nuclear Weapons" to be held in March 2013 in Norway; and thirdly, as the first step to the Komeito proposed Nuclear Abolition Summit to take place in Hiroshima and Nagasaki, at the 2014 "Non-Proliferation and Disarmament Initiative (NPDI)" that the Komeito is proposing, and as the first step, Japan should take the leadership as the presiding country to send a clear message regarding "the inhumanity of nuclear weapons" at the Non-Proliferation and Disarmament Initiative (NPDI) Hiroshima Conference in 2014.[70] Also, in the December 2012 election of the House of Representatives that returned the coalition government to power, the Komeito was the only party that clearly described nuclear disarmament as a foreign policy initiative in its Manifesto (the strengthening of the NPT regime and the retention by the government of the Three Non-Nuclear Principles).[71]

Foreign Minister Fumio Kishida stated that he judged that there were no inconsistencies between Japan signing the Joint Communique and the presenting Japan's security policy depending on the US nuclear umbrella and coping with threats of China and North Korea.[72] The

---

[70] Komei Newspaper, Kokusai Giron O Shudo Seyo, Kakuheiki Hizindosei Meguri Kinkyu Teigen, To Kaku Haizetsu Suishin Iinkai (Komeito Party Committee on Promoting of Nuclear Abolition called Japanese government should lead discussion about humanitarian consequences of nuclear weapons in the international society), 20th October 2012

[71] Nihon Keizai Shimbun (Japanese Economic Newspaper Co., Ltd), Shuin Sen Koyaku Shuu (Manifestos of All Political Parties on the Diet for General Election 2012), 15th December 2012

[72] MOFA, Kishita Gaimu Daizin Kaiken Kiroku 2013 October 11th 12:35pm-

present Joint Communique had some changes made, that is to say, "all approaches and initiatives towards nuclear abolition must be supported" added at the suggestion of the Japanese government. The Japanese government is essentially in the position to support nuclear abolition. However, its foreign policy and political bearings are not radical, such as suddenly prohibiting worldwide use of nuclear weapons and demand total abolition by nuclear weapons states, rather they are to create a framework towards gradual nuclear abolition by depending on the US nuclear deterrence policy. The Japanese government interpreted that the last Joint Statement allowed the present circumstances. It is also a fact that this had made it easier for counties that hither-to-fore rejected to sign it. It was a big step forward in the history of nuclear disarmament that the largest ever number of signatories, including Japan, the only atom-bombed country, went a long way to diffusing the understanding that nuclear weapons are inhumane weapons. The Joint Statement did clearly state the non-first use of nuclear weapons but did not include the promotion of nuclear weapons abolition. One has to say that there is a long way to go to be able to say that this Joint Statement has reduced the regional nuclear threat in Northeast Asia as well as the global threat of nuclear terrorism that US President Obama has cited. Also in the absence of the signature of the P5, the standing members of the UN Security Council, there is a need for diplomatic efforts to work on the P5.

At the same First Committee of the UN General Assembly Session, the "Joint Statement on the Humanitarian Consequences of Nuclear

---

Daijin Kaikenshitsu Mae (Record, Press Conference of Foreign Minister Kishita, 12:35pm in front of the Meeting Room of Foreign Minister Japan), October 2013
http://www.mofa.go.jp/mofaj/press/kaiken/kaiken4_000011.html (accessed on 10th December 2013)

Weapons", a joint statement put together by seventeen US allies[73] including Australia was submitted. The Japanese government did sign it. In fact it was only the government of Japan that signed both the New Zealand proposal and the Australian Joint Statement. The Australian proposal compared to that of New Zealand's is considered retrogressing and moderate.[74] Reasons for it is the following two sentences in the Australian draft concerning "banning nuclear weapons alone will not eliminate them", and "recognizing the importance of both humanitarian and security aspects".

> "Banning nuclear weapons by itself will not guarantee their elimination without engaging substantively and constructively those states with nuclear weapons…"[75]
> "...and recognising both the security and humanitarian dimensions of the nuclear weapons debate."[76]

Most of the signatory states to the Joint Statement proposed by Australia were countries dependent on the US nuclear umbrella. This

---

[73] Delivered by Ambassador Peter Woolcott, Australian Permanent Representative to the United Nations, Geneva and Ambassador for Disarmament, *Joint Statement on the humanitarian consequences of nuclear weapons*, 21st October 2013, p1
Submitted by "Australia, Belgium, Canada, Finland, Germany, Italy, Japan, Latvia, Lithuania, Luxembourg, the Netherlands, Poland, Portugal, Slovakia, Spain, Sweden, and Turkey"

[74] Asahi Shimbun Digital (Asahi News Paper Digital), Kaku Fushiyou No Kyodo Seimei Ni Nihon Hatsusando (Japan signed the joint statement of non-use of nuclear weapons for the first time), 16th November 2013
http://www.asahi.com/articles/TKY201311160069.html (accessed on 10th December 2013)

[75] Delivered by Ambassador Peter Woolcott, Australian Permanent Representative to the United Nations, Geneva and Ambassador for Disarmament, *Joint Statement on the humanitarian consequences of nuclear weapons*, 21st October 2013, p1

[76] Ibid

shows the difficult position of the Japanese government, while it knows only too well the inhumanity of the nuclear weapons from the experience of Hiroshima and Nagasaki, it still believes it essential for security to have the US nuclear umbrella given the East Asian situation.[77] This is proof that the situation in East Asia is a big factor that accounts for Japan's passive nuclear disarmament policy.

This chapter clarified how much and why the Japanese government have been negative on nuclear disarmament despite the country being the only victim of atomic-bombs. But, there are highly-motivated and influential anti-nuclear CSOs in Japan. In the next chapter, this dissertation explores the role of anti-nuclear CSOs and their relations with the Japanese government, CSOs in other countries, and international organisations including the United Nations.

---

[77] Komei Graphic Winter 2014, Comment by Nobumasa Akiyama, Professor of Hitostusbashi University and former senior research fellow of the Centre for the Promotion of Disarmament and Non-Proliferation Japan, January 2014, p10-p11

Chapter 3: Japanese Civil Society Organisations' Activities against Nuclear Weapons

Background:

This chapter will analyse the Japanese four anti-nuclear CSOs and will begin by reviewing anti-nuclear CSO activities in the United Kingdom as a point of comparison and contrast. The United Kingdom is recognized as a victor of the Second World War, and under the Treaty on the Non-Proliferation of Nuclear Weapons (NPT) is also recognized as a nuclear weapon state. Japan, on the other hand, is a non-nuclear weapon state, and therefore its CSO activities and approaches toward nuclear disarmament naturally differ.

According to Mark Fitzpatrick,[1] the United Kingdom is the most passionate country in Europe regarding nuclear disarmament, and he also identified the United Kingdom as the only country in Europe where support for nuclear disarmament by the general public is viewed as being important, politically, at the ballot box.[2] The British government's official nuclear policy is based on reliable, independent nuclear deterrence at the minimum level required for the defence of the country and its allies.[3] The Campaign for Nuclear Disarmament (CND), established in 1958, is the oldest CSO in the United Kingdom and has

---

[1] Director, Non-Proliferation and Disarmament Programme, the International Institute of Strategic Studies (IISS)

[2] Mark Fitzpatrick,

[3] Satomi Kyuko (National Diet Library Japan), Eikoku No Kaku Seisaku O Meguru Keii To Giron –Trident Koshin O Chushin Ni – (Process and Discussion about the British Nuclear Policy –Updating the Trident System -), National Diet Library Japan, November 2011 http://ndl.go.jp/jp/diet/publication/refer/pdf/073005.pdf (accessed on 21st July 2015) p94

exercised direct influence on decision-making in the British government, particularly on Labour governments. This is because Michael Foot[4] and other Labour Party members of Parliament (MPs) were founding members of CND. CND's activities as a CSO focus on the elimination of nuclear weapons held by the government, and its method is non-violent, direct action. CND has held demonstrations at British nuclear submarine bases and other places, and many of the participants have been arrested[5] In1962, members of CND also established the Independent Nuclear Disarmament Election Committee, whose members included Pat Arrowsmith[6] and Vanessa Redgrave,[7] to exert influence on other political parties. This committee conducted campaigns to unseat candidates opposed to nuclear disarmament in general elections, irrespective of their political affiliation, and threw its support behind candidates that agreed with nuclear disarmament in a number of constituencies but they suffered a crushing defeat.[8] (The anti-nuclear movement of the CND as of 2015 is not limited to nuclear disarmament but extends to the peaceful use of nuclear power including nuclear power generation). Of particular concern to CND members in regard to nuclear disarmament has been the strong military alliance between the United States and the United Kingdom. Their understanding was that under the US-UK Mutual Defence Agreement of

---

[4] Member of Parliament 1945-1955 and 1960-1992, Secretary of State for Employment 1974-1976, Leader of the Labour Party 1980-1983

[5] CND, *171 arrests at Faslane nuclear base*, 1st October 2007, http://www.cnduk.org/cnd-media/item/465-171-arrests-at-faslane-nuclear-base (accessed on 21st July 2015)

[6] British author and peace campaigner

[7] British actress

[8] The Committee stood candidates in the British general election 1964 in Bromley and Twickenham, but they achieved only 1,534 votes.
Hawaii Book Library, *Radical Alliance*
http://www.hawaiilibrary.com/articles/radical_alliance (accessed on 21st July 2015)

1958, the two countries signed an agreement not only for both countries to share nuclear technology and nuclear weapons but also to cooperate in foreign policy matters regarding these.[9] This agreement is familiarly known by another name, the US-UK Nuclear Cooperation Agreement, but contains no mention of the word "diplomacy" nor engaging in cooperative foreign policy in regard to nuclear weapons.[10] The British Labour Party, which has a close relationship with CND, has long maintained a negative nuclear policy as its basic policy, which dates back to after the Second World War. On the other hand, the Margaret Thatcher (Conservative Party) Administration, which came to power in 1979, forged ahead with a positive nuclear policy and established the Trident Systems.[11]

Opposing the government, the Labour Party, led by Michael Foot, issued a manifesto in which it made a unilateral commitment to the abolition of nuclear weapons in the United Kingdom during the General Election of 1983 but the party suffered a crushing defeat. A factor

---

[9] IWJ Independent Web Journal, *Interview with Kate Hudson (CND Secretary-General) in London 21st February 2013 (written in Japanese)* http://iwj.co.jp/wj/open/archives/60424 (accessed on 21st July 2015)

[10] British American Security Information Council, *US-UK Nuclear Cooperation, 1958 US-UK Mutual Defence Agreement* http://web.archive.org/web/20041221225546/http://basicint.org/nuclear/1958MDA.htm (accessed on 21st July 2015)
Atomic Weapons Establishment (AWE), *UK/US Agreement* http://web.archive.org/web/20080118030158/http://www.awe.co.uk/main_site/about_awe/history/timeline/1958/ (accessed on 21st July 2015)

[11] The UK Trident Systems encompasses the development, procurement and operation of the current generation of British nuclear weapons, and the means to deliver them. Trident itself is an operational system of four Vanguard-class submarines armed with Trident II D-5 ballistic missiles, able to deliver thermonuclear warheads from multiple independently targetable re-entry vehicles.
UK Government, *Announcement, Strategic Defence and Security Review Published, 19th October 2015*
https://www.gov.uk/government/news/strategic-defence-and-security-review-published--2 (accessed on 21st July 2015)

contributing to this was the inability of many British voters to embrace the party's manifesto, which had extremely strong socialist tones, including advocating aggressive interference in industry, abolition of the House of Lords, and withdrawal from the European Economic Community (EEC).[12] This manifesto also received harsh criticism from within the Labour Party as being "the longest suicide note in history."[13] This was during the Cold War when there were also threats from the USSR, which had re-ignited the issue of nuclear development, and many British people opted for nuclear deterrence over nuclear abolition. In the General Election of 1997, Tony Blair of the Labour Party clearly stated in his political manifesto that he would maintain the Trident Systems but, after rising to power, conducted a review of the existing Trident Systems and significantly reduced nuclear weapons.[14] The rationale behind this reduction was that the Cold War had ended and the government would maintain nuclear weapons at a minimum level for self-defence. While the two extremes of total nuclear abolition advocated by CND and the Labour Party, on the one hand, and the aggressive nuclear deterrence promoted by the Thatcher government, on the other hand, existed during the Cold War, in the process of debating the two, a middle-of-the-road policy that was supported by the majority of British people emerged. This policy, which combined aspects of both sides, recognized the importance of nuclear deterrence and at the same time made a commitment to gradually reduce the number of nuclear

---

[12] Political Stuff Site, *Archive of Labour Party Manifesto 1983* https://web.archive.org/web/20150330053201/http://www.labour-party.org.uk/manifestos/1983/1983-labour-manifesto.shtml (accessed on 21st July 2015)

[13] UK Labour Party MP Gerald Kaufman
BBC News, *Foot's message of hope to left*, 14th July 2003 http://news.bbc.co.uk/2/hi/uk_news/politics/3059773.stm (accessed on 21st July 2015)

[14] The House of Commons, Research Paper 98/91, The Strategic Defence Review White Paper, 15th October 1998

weapons. Due to unstable conditions resulting from Russia's annexation of Ukraine's Crimea in 2014, however, there is a possibility that changes will occur in the nuclear policies of European countries (see Chapter 5).

As an anti-nuclear CSO, CND has had a strong impact on the Labour government and the Labour Party manifesto. While it would be difficult to wholly reflect the views of CND on political decisions, it can be acknowledged that CND played a substantive role in deepening discussion and in mature decision-making by providing unique arguments and views. The criterion for determining whether or not a CSO has exerted a powerful impact on decision-making cannot be judged simply on the basis of whether or not that organization's views have been adopted across the board. CND's assertions and activities are often radical and impractical, and on many occasions are viewed as being based on idealistic theories that ignore the security environment of the United Kingdom and its national interests. Nevertheless, its strong affirmations have contributed to initiating moves to reduce the United Kingdom's nuclear weapon stocks. This view of CND is also common to many anti-nuclear CSOs.

Likewise, a number of the four Japanese anti-nuclear CSOs, which are the focus of this dissertation understand that not all their views are supported, and while they make strong affirmations and do not fail to calmly analyse the current situation, they realize that nuclear abolition will take a long time.[15] Moreover, in recent years, they have been engaging in active dialogue with the Japanese government. However, they believe that treaties including disarmament agreements among countries are solely the domains of politics, and that they should be concluded through formal negotiation between states. Consequently,

---

[15] Interview with Kenichi Okubo 2013, and see Chapter 4

they do not engage in discussion of specific provisions of agreements on behalf of the Japanese government (see Chapter 5).

The number of CND members reached 100,000 in 1984 at the end of the Cold War, and subsequently contracted to half that number following the Cold War; however, CND has continued its vigorous activities up until the present (as of 2015).[16] Moreover, Labour CND, a campaign for peace and nuclear disarmament within the Labour Party, was established as a specialist section of CND in 1979. Although it is not a formal section of the Labour Party, MPs such as Jeremy Corbyn[17], Alice Mahon and Walter Wolfgang became members, and Tony Blair and former Foreign Secretary Jack Straw are former members. Labour CND has taken up the former platform of CND and Labour Party, calling for the abandonment of the Trident Systems.[18] However, the Conservative government led by David Cameron (in coalition within the Liberal Democratic Party) decided to update the Trident Systems in 2010. This means that the United Kingdom will not retire its nuclear submarines until the 2060s, in other words, it will not abandon nuclear weapons until the 2060s. However, there is a possibility of a change in policy with a change in government through the will of the British people.

Among numerous anti-nuclear CSOs in the world, it is no exaggeration to say that their Japanese counterparts lead the world's anti-nuclear CSO movements in the strength of their commitment which is in sharp contrast to the passive stance of the government of Japan. There has not been any actual collaboration between Japanese

---

[16] Paul Byrne, *Social Movements in Britain*, Routledge London 1997, pp91

[17] Very recently (12 Sep 2015), Jeremy Corbyn was elected as Leader of the Labour Party.

[18] Labour CND, *Labour PPCs say Scrap Trident* http://www.labourcnd.org.uk/2015/02/labour-ppcs-say-scrap-trident/ (accessed on 22nd July 2015)

anti-nuclear CSOs. The Japanese government has believed that they have exclusive rights in the fields of diplomacy and security including nuclear policy, and do not need any cooperation with private organisations. However, it has been gradually changing with some Japanese CSOs' efforts in recent years. This chapter will now explore this change.

Since the end of the Second World War, a lot of anti-nuclear CSOs have been established in Japan. It is because of language barriers and a different motivational basis with CSOs in other countries that, many of their activities have been noted only inside Japan. Many of their quarterlies and internet websites have been created only in Japanese. Also, Japanese anti-nuclear CSOs' motivation is based on the tragedy of Hiroshima and Nagasaki in 1945. It is very emotional and many Japanese CSOs have believed that nuclear weapon issues cannot be resolved only through logic. Some CSOs in other countries, which have never experienced damage from nuclear weapons, have difficulty in understanding the stance of Japanese CSOs'. For example, there is a basic question whether the memories of Hiroshima and Nagasaki can be a symbol for worldwide anti-nuclear activities today. However, there are some successful Japanese CSOs, which have led regional and global nuclear disarmament in good relations with governments and other organisations.

This chapter focuses on the four representative organisations leading the anti-nuclear activities; JPPNW, the Japan Branch of International Physicians for the Prevention of Nuclear Weapons (IPPNW), the MP, the JALANA, and the SGI.

These four organisations are large in scale, have a long history and each contribute with their unique expertise. Unlike their domestic counterparts their activities are global, or are collaborative organisations or a branch of internationally recognized anti-nuclear bodies. The four organisations represent anti-nuclear CSOs in different areas including medicine, local governments, law and religion. This dissertation focuses on these four organisations and excludes others, as their activities, scale and history are limited to within national borders. Nuclear weapon issues are global issues, which have happened during the Cold War. Therefore, CSOs, which aim to abolish nuclear weapons, must have global scale activities through having their bases overseas or collaborating with organisations in other countries. Many of the Japanese anti-nuclear weapon CSOs' activities have been developed only inside Japan. They have not been able to directly influence any international movement against nuclear weapons. The four organisations have been working globally and are also members of international anti-nuclear CSO alliances. Some of them have a very long history of activities against nuclear weapons following the end of Second World War.

From the 1990s to the early 2000s there was growing global public opinion in favour of the abolition of nuclear weapons, with leaders speaking up and a number of submissions made to the United Nations of draft conventions banning nuclear weapons. These developments greatly encouraged anti-nuclear CSOs in Japan and around the world.

In 1996 the ICJ published its advisory opinion stating that the use of nuclear weapons was a highly political matter that could not be judged by law but it went on to clearly state that the use of nuclear weapons conceptually constituted a violation of international law. In 2007 George P. Shultz, William J. Perry, Henry A. Kissinger and Sam Nunn sent the Wall Street Journal a joint statement calling for a World Free of Nuclear Weapons. CSOs and international public opinion hailed it as a recommendation of the four wise men. It was a dramatic development, unthinkable during the Cold War period, that those men who were in charge of diplomacy and national defence within the US administration during and after the Cold War period would encourage anti-nuclear public opinion. The possibility of nuclear terrorism becoming a real threat prompted them to urge the abolition of nuclear weapons.[19] This represents a common angst seen in the US President Obama's Prague speech. The essence of the Obama speech was an expression of a serious alarm concerning the possibility of terrorists possessing and using nuclear weapons. To prevent that from happening the only way was their global dismantlement. That is to say, the four wise men and Obama perceived that the threat of nuclear terrorism is graver than the advantage of possessing nuclear weapons.[20]

> "...Today, the Cold War has disappeared but thousands of those weapons have not. In a strange turn of history, the threat of global nuclear war has gone down, but the risk of a nuclear attack has gone up. More nations have acquired these weapons. Testing has continued. <u>Black market trade in nuclear secrets and nuclear materials abound. The technology to build a bomb has spread. Terrorists are determined to buy, build or steal one. Our efforts to contain these dangers are centered on a global non-proliferation regime, but as more people and nations break</u>

---

[19] Shultz, Perry, Kissinger, Nunn, *A World Free of Nuclear Weapons*, Wall Street Journal 2007,
http://online.wsj.com/news/articles/SB116787515251566636
http://www.pugwash.org/reports/nw/nuclear-weapons-free-statements/NWFW_statements_USA.htm (accessed on 11th October 2010)

[20] Katsuya Kodama (Vice-President Professor, Mie University, Japan), *Hiroshima Nagasaki Purosesu: Kaku Haizetsumade No Genzitsuteki Gutaitekina Rodo Map* (Hiroshima Nagasaki Process: A Realistic Road Map for Nuclear Abolition) , 2013
http://bylines.news.yahoo.co.jp/kodamakatsuya/20130807-00027073/
(accessed on 3rd June 2013)

> the rules, we could reach the point where the center cannot hold. Now, understand, this matters to people everywhere. One nuclear weapon exploded in one city -- be it New York or Moscow, Islamabad or Mumbai, Tokyo or Tel Aviv, Paris or Prague -- could kill hundreds of thousands of people. And no matter where it happens, there is no end to what the consequences might be -- for our global safety, our security, our society, our economy, to our ultimate survival. Some argue that the spread of these weapons cannot be stopped, cannot be checked -- that we are destined to live in a world where more nations and more people possess the ultimate tools of destruction. Such fatalism is a deadly adversary, for if we believe that the spread of nuclear weapons is inevitable, then in some way we are admitting to ourselves that the use of nuclear weapons is inevitable…[21]

He has not, however, denied the role and value of nuclear weapons in ensuring national security including his own. He was awarded the Nobel Peace Prize for his commitment to realizing a world free of nuclear weapons but a pre-critical nuclear test conducted under his administration (5th December 2012) speaks for it. Also, the US administration has yet to show a definitive road map towards the abolition of nuclear weapons. What is more, should the administration change hands to the Republican Party there is a high possibility of it entirely dismissing the Obama Prague speech. Even if the next president were a Democrat there is no certainty that his or her priorities will not differ greatly, so that he may not strongly persist with nuclear abolition,

[21] Obama's Prague Speech on Nuclear Weapons: FULL TEXT http://www.huffingtonpost.com/2009/04/05/obama-prague-speech-on-nu_n_183219.html (accessed on 3rd February 2010)

as does Obama. Policies, whether at the national or local levels, may change greatly with the political party or leader in power. Decisions regarding nuclear weapons are naturally the exclusive prerogative of national governments. The role, therefore, of anti-nuclear CSOs is to prevent any regression of the nuclear abolition momentum with the change of governments and policies and to create a flow of nuclear abolitionism at national, regional and international levels. It is common for governments to regard abolition of nuclear weapons as a national security issue. The four wise men's worry and the Prague speech were born out of a strong shared sense of crisis in the face of the reality that nuclear proliferation is uncontainable and there is a want of concrete ways to prevent it. There is a possibility of proliferation of WMDs that single super power, agreements among nations or government level diplomacy are difficult to control. The ideological credo and activities of Japanese anti-nuclear CSOs were historically considered to conflict with the government's diplomatic guidelines and policies. Anti-nuclear CSOs, however, base their activities on winning recognition of the inhumanity of nuclear weapons as well as their unlawfulness. Their activities are based on achieving the illegality of nuclear weapons by putting in force a treaty banning the use of nuclear weapons, establishing non-nuclear zones in Northeast Asia and Middle Eastern regions and achieving a successful outcome of the NPT Review Conference. There are large discrepancies between these objectives and views of national governments, including Obama's Prague speech, that regard it as a security issue although objectives are the same.

In fact, the United States and the USSR (later Russia) achieved significant historical reductions in nuclear weapons as a result of the Strategic Arms Limitation Talks 1 (SALT 1). The United States achieved an 85% reduction in nuclear warheads, which numbered

31,255 at the peak period in 1967, to 4,804 in 2013.[22] Under the New Strategic Arms Reduction Treaty (New START) 2011, both the United States and Russia agreed to reduce their number of nuclear warheads to 1,550. Furthermore, they also reached agreement on arms reduction from the perspective of protection of the environment. Western countries have also actively cooperated in securing the safety of Russian nuclear facilities inherited from the USSR and the Russian government also received cooperation in maintaining facilities it had been unable to maintain. In 1992, the Munich G7 Summit made a decision to cooperate in resolving the problem of the disposal of weapons and environmental problems of the former republics of the USSR.[23] At the Tokyo G7 Summit in the following year in 1993, a decision was made to provide grants-in-aid of $100 million to the countries of the former USSR, and various forms of assistance were initiated in earnest to dispose of nuclear weapons, prevent pollution of the surrounding ocean areas due to the leaking of radioactivity from retired nuclear submarines, and prevent the theft of nuclear fuels of the former republics of the USSR.[24]

---

[22] Weekly Standard, *State Dept: U.S. Nukes Down 85%, From 31,255 to 4,804*, 19th December 2014
http://www.weeklystandard.com/blogs/state-dept-us-nukes-down-85-31255-4804_821888.html (accessed on 1st August 2015)
Rose Gottemoeller, US Undersecretary for Arms and International Security of the Department of State announced.
CNN, *U.S. reveals it has 5,113 nuclear warheads*, 3rd May 2010 http://edition.cnn.com/2010/POLITICS/05/03/us.nuclear.warhead.count/ (accessed on 1st August 2015)

[23] G8 Information Centre, 1992 Munich Summit, *Political Declaration: Shaping the New Partnership*, Munich, 7 July 1992 http://www.g8.utoronto.ca/summit/1992munich/political.html (accessed on 7th July 2015)

[24] Technical Secretariat on Cooperation for the Elimination of Nuclear Weapons Reduced in the Former Soviet Union, G8 Global Partnership: Nichiro Hikakuka Kyoryoku Russia Taeki Sensuikan Kaitai Kyoryoku Zigyo: Kibo No Hoshi (G8 Global Partnership: Russo-Japanese Cooperation on Denuclearization: Russo-Japanese Cooperation on Demolishing Retired

> "Article II (7) of the Political Declaration: Shaping the New Partnership Arms control agreements which have been signed by the former Soviet Union, in particular the START and CFE[25] treaties, must enter into force. The full implementation of the CFE Treaty will create the foundation for the new cooperative security framework in Europe. We welcome the far reaching follow on agreement on strategic nuclear weapons concluded by the US and Russia in June as another major step towards a safer, more stable world. Further measures, in particular the unilaterally announced elimination of ground launched short range nuclear weapons by the United States and the former Soviet Union, should be carried out as soon as possible. We support Russia in its efforts to secure the peaceful use of nuclear materials resulting from the elimination of nuclear weapons. The Geneva negotiations for a convention on the effective global ban on chemical weapons must be successfully concluded this year. We call on all nations to become original signatories to this convention."

As part of the G8 Global Partnership Against the Spread of Weapons and Materials of Mass Destruction, an agreement concluded at the Kananaskis G8 Summit in 2002,[26] the Japanese government also

---

Nuclear Submarines), September 2008 http://tecsec.org/pdf/kibounohoshi_j.pdf (accessed on 7th July 2015)

[25] Treaty on Conventional Armed Forces in Europe

[26] G8 Information Centre, 2002 Kananaskis Summit Documents: Statement by G8 Leaders: The G8 Global Partnership Against the Spread of Weapons and Materials of Mass Destruction, 27th June 2002 http://www.g8.utoronto.ca/summit/2002kananaskis/arms.html (accessed on 19th July 2015)

allocated a budget of 790 million yen for the Star of Hope, a program for the dismantling of Russia's decommissioned nuclear submarines. As a result, six decommissioned nuclear submarines were dismantled from 2005 to 2009, and Russia expressed its gratitude to Japan.[27]

While many anti-nuclear CSOs welcomed the trend in nuclear arms reduction established through this diplomacy and dialogue, they were emotionally dissatisfied. It cannot be denied that these nuclear arms reductions were achieved through the efforts of countries out of economic need and a need for environmental protection to avert radiation pollution in their territorial waters. However, if Russia's financial situation and economy improved and it became capable of maintaining and managing its own nuclear weapons and if some conflict should occur, the possibility that a nuclear arms race would resume could not be ruled out. As suggested by Thomas C. Schelling and as discussed (See Chapter 5), it is realistic to assert that political tension among countries and international society will not disappear even if the abolition of nuclear arms is achieved, and that the world will have other crises and tensions.

The ultimate form of nuclear disarmament envisaged by Japanese anti-nuclear CSOs is founded on the view that the development and use of nuclear weapons are absolute evils that go against the dignity of human life. Thus, while they applauded the large-scale reduction in US and Soviet (later US and Russian) nuclear weapons, they were not wholly satisfied. The most extreme view among these organizations, like that of JALANA, is the conviction that the US government should

---

[27] MOFA, Russia Taieki Gensen Kaitai Kyoryoku Zigyo "Kibo No Hoshi" (Cooperation on Demolishing Russian Retired Nuclear Submarines "Star of Hope"), 5th April 2010 http://www.mofa.go.jp/mofaj/gaiko/kaku/kyuso/star_of_hope.html#4 (accessed on 19th July 2015)

first apologize for dropping the atomic bombs on Japan during the Second World War and then lawfully provide compensation to the *hibakusha* victims of the bombs.[28] In this case, however, the United States has a firm belief that the dropping of the atom bombs made it possible to bring the Second World War to an early end through the unconditional surrender of Japan. Therefore, this view would not serve to bridge the emotional gap with the CSOs.[29] Even if CSOs cannot compromise emotionally or philosophically as in the cases of the JPPNW and the SGI, it can be said that their modus operandi has been to come to practical terms with existing nuclear issues by using their respective influence, as well as cooperating with the Japanese government to exercise their influence, on nuclear disarmament.

There are several examples of multilateral agreements for the abolition of nuclear weapons in the South American Region. Fourteen Latin American countries signed in 1967 the Treaty for the Prohibition of Nuclear Weapons in Latin America that came into force in 1968. It is called The Treaty of Tlatelalco, named after the location of the Mexican Foreign Office where the signing ceremony took place. The main substance of the Treaty covered the prohibition of testing, use, manufacture, production, acquisition, stockpiling and deployment of nuclear weapons in the domains of the parties to the Treaty. This was the world's first regional treaty that declared a nuclear free zone. Other regional Nuclear Free Zone treaties that followed more or less applied the same content. In 1986 the South Pacific Nuclear Free Zone came

---

[28] Masanobu Inoue (Member of the JALANA Board of Directors), *Hiroshima Hanketsu No Gani (Meaning of the Judicial Decision in Hiroshima)*, JALANA official website http://www.hankaku-j.org/data/jalana/001.html (accessed on 19th July 2015)

[29] BBC News, *Enola Gay crew 'have no regrets*' 4th August 2005 http://news.bbc.co.uk/2/hi/americas/4743061.stm (accessed on 20th July 2015)

into force (Treaty of Rarotonga)[30] and the governments of the United Kingdom and France, both nuclear powers, ratified it in 1996. France, however, conducted in 1995 a nuclear test in the South Pacific, a year ahead of the ratification and this invited controversy. In 1997, the Southeast Asia Nuclear-Weapons-Free Zone Treaty[31] came into force with the ratification of the 10 member states of the Association of Southeast Asian Nations (ASEAN). Two years later, in 2009 an African Nuclear Weapons Free Zone Treaty came into force with 29 countries out of the 54 covered by the treaty.[32] In the same year, a Treaty on a Nuclear Weapon Free Zone in Central Asia came into force by the ratification of five Central Asian Republics.[33] These nuclear free zone treaties effectively function to prohibit the use of nuclear weapons in the region as well as to promote their non-proliferation. Countries that are party to nuclear weapons free zone treaties are, however, non-nuclear states and are yet to successfully work on the reduction and abolition of nuclear weapons of the major nuclear powers starting with the P5. Moreover, in regions where the threat of the use of nuclear weapons and conflicts abound, such as in Northeast Asia and the Middle East, no nuclear free zone treaty has been concluded. There are, however, a number of CSOs including the Japan's four anti-nuclear organisations that are engaged in various initiatives towards enacting a treaty designating Northeast Asia a nuclear weapons free zone. These will be

---

[30] US Department of State, South Pacific Nuclear Free Zone Treaty http://www.state.gov/www/global/arms/treaties/spnfz.html (accessed on 5th January 2013)

[31] Association of Southeast Asian Nations, SANWFZT http://www.aseansec.org/asean-anthem/ (accessed on 5th January 2013)

[32] US Department of State, *African Nuclear Weapons Free Zone Treaty,* http://www.state.gov/www/global/arms/treaties/afrinwfz.html#1 (accessed on 5th January 2013)

[33] United Nations Office for Disarmament Affairs, *Treaty on a Nuclear-Weapons-Free-Zone (CANWFZ)* http://disarmament.un.org/treaties/t/canwfz/text (accessed on 5th January 2013)

referred to later.

In 2007 the governments of Costa Rica and Malaysia jointly proposed

to the United Nations a draft NWC. The draft convention prohibits development, testing, production, stockpiling, transfer, use and threat of use of nuclear weapons. The drafting of the nuclear weapons prohibition treaty has been worked on since 1996 by three organisations; the International Network of Engineers and Scientists Against Proliferation (INESAP), the IALANA, and the IPPNW.[34] Japanese CSOs, as well as numerous anti-nuclear CSOs around the world, are actively working to achieve their major objective, the establishment of the NWC. A second-generation *hibakusha*, Katsuya Kodama, Vice-President of Mie University, Japan proposed in 2007 an NWC roadmap called The Hiroshima Nagasaki Process (HNP) by way of adopting the successful Ottawa Process that led to the establishment of the Convention on the Prohibition of Anti-Personnel Mines (CPAPM).[35] The CPAPM movement was initiated in 1991 when the Foundation of US Vietnam War Veterans and a German NGO, Media International, agreed to start an International Campaign to Ban Landmines (ICBL). Its drafting conference took place in Oslo in 1997 and the Convention was signed in Ottawa the same year and made effective in 1999. This process was applied to a treaty banning cluster bombs as well. The Norwegian government began its campaign in 2006 and the following year, it

[34] INESAP, *Nuclear Weapons Conventions* http://www.inesap.org/publications/nuclear-weapons-convention (5th January 2013)

[35] Katsuya Kodama, Hiroshima Nagasaki Purosess: Kakuheikihaizetsu Madeno Genzitsuteki Gutaiteki Na Rodomapu 1 (Hiroshima Nagasaki Process: Drawing A Roadmap to the Total Abolition of Nuclear Weapons 1), 2013 http://bylines.news.yahoo.co.jp/kodamakatsuya/20130807-00027073/ (13th June 2013)

hosted an international conference banning the use of cluster bombs, leading 46 countries to adopt the Oslo Declaration. International NGOs actively supported the initiative while the International Red Cross as well as the so-called middle power states participated in the process. The same year 111 counties unanimously adopted the International Cluster Bomb Ban Treaty (ICBBT) at an international conference that took place in Dublin.[36] Kodama pointed out that the road to peace and arms limitation would not have met this success had the process depended on the leadership of the military powers, the US and Russia, whereas, he said, the Ottawa and Oslo Processes succeeded because the middle powers and NGOs cooperated together, working around the military powers. The times, he said, were shifting in a big way from military-powers led disarmament negotiations to those led by global citizens.[37] Kodama also points out that the NWC initiative, prepared by three NGOs and submitted by the Costa Rican and other governments do not have a high possibility of immediate adoption while its significance is not inconsiderable. The 2020 Vision Campaign proposed by the MP with the 75th anniversary of Hiroshima and Nagasaki bombing in mind, according to Kodama, is desirable in strengthening the international framework for nuclear abolition, even though it has not had the success of moving international opinion in a powerful surge similar to the case of NWC.[38] The 2020 Vision Campaign was initiated at the Geneva NPT Review Preparatory Meeting when the MP presented "The Hiroshima/Nagasaki Protocol, a Roadmap to the Total

---

[36] ICBL, *Ban History*
http://www.icbl.org/index.php/icbl/Treaty/MBT/Ban-History (accessed on 13th June 2013)

[37] Katsuya Kodama,1, 2013
http://bylines.news.yahoo.co.jp/kodamakatsuya/20130807-00027073/
(accessed on 13th June 2013)

[38] Ibid

Abolition of Nuclear Weapons by 2020". This Protocol promotes the implementation of nuclear disarmament negotiations based on Article 6 of the NPT Treaty, while at the same time hopes to establish a methodology for a comprehensive nuclear disarmament in all areas. This is to encourage implementation of disarmament obligations by all nations based on the ICJ Advisory Opinion 1996 concerning the illegality of the use of nuclear weapons and threat of such use.[39] In other words, the 2020 Vision would not fulfill obligations for achieving the conditions unless the P5 at least implement Article 6 of the NPT. Since President Obama's speech at Prague there has not been any concrete action or policy towards nuclear disarmament and non-proliferation taken by the P5s. Therefore, it can be said that in reality the vision faces an extremely tall hurdle. The HNP advocated by Kodama will happen when the four relevant international conventions (Treaty Prohibiting the use and threat of use of nuclear weapons, Treaty prohibiting the development of nuclear weapons, Treaty for the abolition of nuclear weapons and the Treaty establishing global non-nuclear zones) are established step by step. Supporters for their establishment are international NGOs including *hibakusha* organisations and non-nuclear countries. The features of the treaty prohibiting the use and threat of the use of nuclear arms do not have the premise of involving nuclear powers including the P5. Instead the aim is to develop the treaty from the statement issued in 1996 by the ICJ Advisory Opinion, namely, that the use of nuclear weapons violates the generally applied principles and rules of international law to armed conflicts. Kodama points out that while resolutions prohibiting the use of nuclear arms have been continuously adopted every year since 1994,

---

[39] Mayors for Peace, *Mayors for Peace 2020 Vision Campaign* http://www.2020visioncampaign.org/en/about-us.html (accessed on 13th June 2013)

the Japanese Government unfortunately always gives priority to the whim of the United States. Moreover, while it agrees to the abstract resolution it submits, it has abstained from voting in favour of resolutions prohibiting the use of nuclear arms that are more concrete in nature.[40] Since other nuclear powers also either abstain or reject their adoption, the UN resolutions have no effect. He further states that while it is unthinkable for the Middle Powers and NGOs together to promote the process of prohibiting the use and threat of use of nuclear weapons and have all nuclear powers immediately sign and ratify a treaty, it is important to have many non-nuclear countries ratify it thereby establishing an international norm. Such a treaty would prohibit nuclear weapons, including conducting pre-criticality tests, prohibiting actions that aim to improve nuclear warhead performances. Nuclear powers would be prohibited from making more nuclear weapons than they already possess, that is to say freeze the state of nuclear weapons.[41] While it appears impossible today, the treaty abolishing nuclear weapons, Kodama explains, can be reached by taking a step at a time towards banning the use as well as the threat of use of nuclear weapons. The last treaty, declaring a global non-nuclear zone, should not be a conventional regional treaty but it should enable all countries that wish to be party to it to do so and their total landmass should be declared a nuclear free zone.[42]

During the interpellation that followed the prime minister's

---

[40] Katsuya Kodama, *Hiroshima Nagasaki Process: Kakuheikihaizetsu Madeno Genzitsuteki Gutaiteki Na Rodomapu* 2 (In English 'Hiroshima Nagasaki Process: Drawing A Roadmap to the Total Abolition of Nuclear Weapons 2'), 2013
http://bylines.news.yahoo.co.jp/kodamakatsuya/20130807-00027074/ (accessed on 13th 2013)

[41] Ibid

[42] Ibid

general-policy speech delivered at the opening of a Diet session on 3 October 2008, a Komeito party representative proposed that the best contribution the Japanese can make towards building world peace was to promote the HNP as the material form that represented the minds of the people of Hiroshima and Nagasaki. That is to say, the Japanese government should actively support and promote the HNP as the Nuclear Abolition Roadmap as a first step initiating the process towards a treaty banning use of nuclear weapons. While it was unlikely that nuclear powers would immediately ratify the treaty, it is nonetheless an important role for non-nuclear countries to limit the use and threat of use of nuclear weapons. As the only country to have been atom-bombed and with a Peace Constitution, there could be no better contribution Japan can make in building world peace.[43] In his response, Prime Minister Taro Aso said that the government of Japan does share the objective in realizing as soon as possible a world without nuclear arms and emphasized the importance of steadily putting in place realistic measures. As for concrete actions he did not go beyond stating that continued efforts would be made patiently to work on all nuclear powers through submission of nuclear disarmament resolutions to the United Nations.[44] In 2009, the chair (Member of the House of

---

[43] Kokkai Kaigiroku Kensaku Sisutemu, *Hamayotsu Toshiko Ni Yoru Komeito Daihyo Shitsumon*, Kokuritsu Kokkai Toshokan 3rd October 2008 (Search System of Record of the Proceedings of the Diet (Japan), Query by Representative of Komeito (Toshiko Hamayotsu, Acting Representative of Komeito) at Plenary Session of the House of Councillors, Japan, National Diet Library, 3rd October 2008) http://kokkai.ndl.go.jp/cgi-bin/KENSAKU/swk_dispdoc.cgi?SESSION=13227&SAVED_RID=2&PAGE=0&POS=0&TOTAL=0&SRV_ID=9&DOC_ID=5123&DPAGE=1&DTOTAL=1&DPOS=1&SORT_DIR=1&SORT_TYPE=0&MODE=1&DMY=15438 (accessed on 10th July 2010)

[44] Kokkai Kaigiroku Kensaku Sisutemu, *Aso Taro Naikaku Soridaijin No Toben*, Kokuritsu Kokkai Toshokan 3rd October 2008 (Search System of Record of the Proceedings of the Diet (Japan), Answer by

Councilors) of the KCPANW took all his assigned time in explaining at the House of Councillors Committee on Foreign Affairs and Defence that the Government of Japan should take action on the HNP and spelled out concrete proposals to Hirofumi Nakasone, the Minister of Foreign Affairs. During the interpellation that followed, he said that KCPANW's proposal on nuclear abolition and disarmament depended on whether or not the US would ratify the CTBT, but that it was important to start acting on what could be done right now, and that was the HNP – first stage nuclear abolition as the target and work backwards to see what must be done thereafter. He explained that the HNP represented a conventional way of addressing the issues of nuclear disarmament by ministries of foreign affairs, including the Japanese. As a result much time was spent on defining 'nuclear weapons' and 'nuclear disarmament' which resulted in the production of numerous documents but little action, hindered by particular circumstances of the times. He proposed instead, that the way to go forward was to set the objective of establishing a global standard, an international norm stating that nuclear weapons were evil and then to consider what actions should be taken.[45] This approach is similar to one proposed by Daisaku Ikeda,

---

Prime Minister Taro Aso to Toshiko Hamayotsu (Komeito), National Diet Library, 3rd October 2008)
http://kokkai.ndl.go.jp/cgi-bin/KENSAKU/swk_dispdoc.cgi?SESSION=13227&SAVED_RID=2&PAGE=0&POS=0&TOTAL=0&SRV_ID=9&DOC_ID=5123&DPAGE=1&DTOTAL=1&DPOS=1&SORT_DIR=1&SORT_TYPE=0&MODE=1&DMY=15438 (accessed on 10th July 2010)

[45] Kokkai Kaigiroku Kensaku Sisutemu, Hamada Masayoshi (Komeito) No Shitsugi, Sangin Gaiko Boei Iinkai, 2009nen 7gatsu 2ka
(Search System of Record of the Proceedings of the Diet (Japan), Questions by Masayoshi Hamada (Komeito) , Committee on Foreign Affairs and Defence, House of Councillors, National Diet Library, 2nd July 2009) http://kokkai.ndl.go.jp/cgi-bin/KENSAKU/swk_dispdoc.cgi?SESSION=1333&SAVED_RID=2&PAGE=0&POS=0&TOTAL=0&SRV_ID=9&DOC_ID=5846&DPAGE=1&DTOTAL=3&DPOS=2&SORT_DIR=1&SORT_TYPE=0&MODE=1&DMY=2222 (accessed on 10th July 2010)

that is, deductive private diplomacy rather than the mainstream inductive diplomacy of governments (see Chapters 5 and 6). The KCPANW continued to state that, given past history, the CSO type of nuclear disarmament movement tended to be regarded as compromising Japan's security, and that nuclear disarmament would disable Japan's maintenance of its security. The speaker continued to state that reducing nuclear threats from North Korea and China would only strengthen Japan's security, and the HNP would strengthen nuclear disarmament and allow harmonious coexistence. As North Korea continues to conduct nuclear tests, the speaker was made aware on her/his visit to the US as part of the ruling party's delegation, that it was important for the government to make clear its initiative concerning nuclear disarmament since there were not a few members of the US administration as well as the Congress who assumed that Japan would go nuclear.[46] Foreign Minister Nakasone said that he shared the need to establish an objective of creating a peaceful and secure world without nuclear weapons, but stated that in order to advance nuclear disarmament and non-proliferation, one has to cope with the challenging situation surrounding Japan, including that of North Korea; and to ensure peace and security in the Northeast Asian region, the presence of the Japan-US Security Treaty and extended deterrence of the US (i.e., nuclear umbrella) were essential while Japan continues to build and construct frameworks towards nuclear abolition.[47]

---

[46] Ibid

[47] Kokkai Kaigiroku Kensaku Sisutemu, Nakasone Hirofumi Gaimudaijin No Hamada Gin Heno Toben , *2009nen 7gatsu 2ka*
(Search System of Record of the Proceedings of the Diet (Japan), Answer by Minister of Foreign Affairs Hirofumi Nakasone to Hamada, Committee on Foreign Affairs and Defence, House of Councillors, National Diet Library, 2nd July 2009)
http://kokkai.ndl.go.jp/cgi-bin/KENSAKU/swk_dispdoc.cgi?SESSION=1333&SAVED_RID=2&PAGE=0&POS=0&TOTAL=0&SRV_ID=9&DOC_ID=5846

In 2010 the KCPANW, in an interview conducted by this author, emphasized the importance of the roles played by CSOs. Since the Japanese government tends to be shy in raising issues of nuclear disarmament with nuclear powers, including its ally the US, it is all the more important for the anti-nuclear CSOs to collaborate in communicating opinions to their governments. Also as there are no Japanese parliamentarians who have personal connections with their counterparts in countries with nuclear weapons, connections among CSOs become extremely important.

The KCPANW exchanges views with many anti-nuclear CSOs, not just with the Soka Gakkai (Japan), its main support organisation and invites Japan's Foreign Ministry staff to be part of the tripartite nuclear abolition team including the government, public and private sectors.[48] At the 2010 the KCPANW meeting, anti-nuclear CSOs proposed to the Foreign Ministry to clarify what is meant by "reduced role of nuclear weapons", referred to in the Japan-US Joint Declaration during President Obama's 2009 visit to Japan, to ensure "passive security" that nuclear weapons will not be used against non-nuclear states as well as for Japan to take the leadership in bringing into effect the Treaty Banning Nuclear Weapons.[49] The KCPANW also functions as a bridge between the Japanese government and its ministries including the MOFA as well as anti-nuclear CSOs. It attempts to reflect views of anti-nuclear CSOs in government policies, while prompting a change in the presently passive attitude of the government regarding nuclear

---

&DPAGE=1&DTOTAL=3&DPOS=2&SORT_DIR=1&SORT_TYPE=0&MODE=1&DMY=2222 (accessed on 10th July 2010)

[48] Interview with Masayoshi Hamada 2010

[49] Komeito News, *To Suishi-ni Nichigokyodosengen De Iken Kokan: NGO Mo Sanka* (KCPANW held a session on the Joint Statement of Japanese and Australian Governments, and NGO joined the session), 20th February 2010 https://www.komei.or.jp/news/detail/20100220_496 (18th August 2010)

disarmament. The KCPANW, however, believes that it is not realistic to have governments, including those of nuclear powers, to sign and ratify the NWC and believes that it should also invest energy in building a realistic political process such as the HNP.[50]

It was only since the 1998 Tokyo Forum for Nuclear Non-Proliferation and Disarmament (The Tokyo Forum) that the government of Japan contacted the private sector to exchange views. The Forum was organized at the initiative of Japanese Prime Minister Ryutaro Hashimoto (1996-1998), and Foreign Minister Keizo Obuchi[51], following the nuclear tests conducted by India and Pakistan in May 1998. The purpose was to maintain and possibly strengthen the non-proliferation set up in South Asia and to find ways to further promote global nuclear disarmament. For this purpose some twenty-three internationally active scholars were invited from countries[52] including Pakistan that just conducted nuclear tests, and

---

50 Interview with Masayoshi Hamada, 2010

51 Keizo Obuchi, Japanese Foreign Minister 1997-1998, Prime Minister 1998-2000

52 Member List:

Lt. Gen. Nishat AHMAD (Former President of the Institute of Regional Studies, Islamabad), Mr. Yasushi AKASHI (Former President of Hiroshima Peace Institute), Amb. Marcos Castrioto DE AZAMBUJA (Ambassador of Brazil to France), Prof. Sergei Yevgenevich BLAGOVOLIN (Deputy Director World Economics and International Relations Institute (IMEMO, Moscow), Amb. Emilio Jorge CARDENAS (Executive Director, HSBC Argentine S.A. Former Ambassador of Argentina to the United Nations), Dr. Therese DELPECH (Director, Strategic Affairs, Atomic Energy Commission (CEA, Paris) , Amb. Rolf EKEUS (Ambassador of Sweden to the United States), Dr. Robert GALLUCCI (Dean, School of Foreign Service, Georgetown University), Prof. HAN Sung-Joo (Professor of Korea University), Mr. HU Xiaodi (Deputy Director-General,

Department of Arms Control and Disarmament, Ministry of Foreign Affairs, China), Amb. Ryukichi IMAI (Distinguished Fellow, Institute for International Policy Studies, Tokyo), Dr. Joachim KRAUSE (Deputy Director, Research Institute of the German Society for Foreign Affairs (DGAP, Berlin), Mr. Michael KREPON (President, Henry L. Stimson Center, Washington), Mr.

nuclear powers the US, France, China and Great Britain.[53] However, no anti-nuclear Japanese CSOs or for that matter members of NGOs were included. Members were limited to professionals and researchers who were relatively close to the government or those who focused on government diplomacy, United Nations and Security policy professionals. The conference did not have any opportunities to exchange opinions with the civilian sector and acted de facto as an advisory organ to the government on nuclear disarmament and non-proliferation. It was no place to discuss the inhumanity of nuclear weapons. The Tokyo Forum, on the other hand, does analyse and make propositions on nuclear disarmament and non-proliferation that are related to today's Northeast Asian situation. To begin with, it defined nuclear development and nuclear tests by India and Pakistan that were

---

Pierre LELLOUCHE (Member of the Council, International Institute of Strategic Studies, London), Dr. Patricia M. LEWIS (Director, United Nations Institute for Disarmament (UNIDIR, Geneva), Amb. Margaret MASON (Director of Council Development, Canadian Council for International Peace and Security, Ottawa), Mr. Nobuo MATSUNAGA (Vice Chairman, Japan Institute of International Affairs, Tokyo), Dr. Joseph S. NYE, Jr. (Dean, JFK School of Government, Harvard University, Boston), Prof. Robert O'NEILL (Chichele Professor of the History of War, All Souls College, University of Oxford), Dr. Abdel Monem SAID ALY (Director, Al-Ahram Center for Political and Strategic Studies, Cairo Egypt), Prof. John SIMPSON (Director, Mountbatten Center for International Studies, Department of Politics, University of Southampton), Amb. Hennadiy UDOVENKO (Former Minister of Foreign Affairs, President of 52nd Session of United Nations General Assembly, Member of Ukrainian Parliament), Prof. ZAKARIA Haji Ahamad (Dean, Faculty of Social Science and Humanities, Universiti Kebangaan Malaysia (National Univ. of Malaysia)
The Report of the Tokyo forum for Nuclear-Non Proliferation and Disarmament http://www.mofa.go.jp/mofaj/gaiko/t_forum99/tokyo_f.html (8th August 2010)

[53] Arms Control and Disarmament Division, Disarmament, Non-Proliferation and Science Department, MOFA, Japanese Disarmament and Non-Proliferation Diplomacy 2002 (White Paper), Chapter 8: Role of Civil Society, http://www.mofa.go.jp/mofaj/gaiko/gun_hakusho/2002/hon8.pdf (accessed on 25th October 2010)

outside the NPT framework, as the gravest concern at that time, and posited them as "new nuclear risks". It also pointed out the that the universality of the NPT was broken, seeing the tests as new risks, and showed the following four ways and means of reducing Asian nuclear risks.

The first way was to recognize the UN as an important organisation in building cooperative relations on international security matters. It especially emphasized the need to ensure new fiscal resources as well as to comply with fiscal rules, strengthening operations, reforming the Security Council, establishing new rules and principles, implementation devices and compliance with fiscal rules as well as specifying especially the need to ensure new fiscal resources.[54] Japan was the second largest contributor to the UN ($276,100,000 in 2013 with the contribution ratio of 10,833%)[55] after the US ($618,500,000 in 2013 with the contribution ratio of 22%)[56]. No new concrete policies found their way into the final Tokyo Forum document to ensure new fiscal resources. The Japanese government, however, did point out that strengthening of the UN was necessary to promote nuclear disarmament and non-proliferation worldwide. Secondly, it proposed the need to amend strategic relations with the nuclear powers and the surrounding countries in order to reduce nuclear risks. It further pointed out that the future of non-proliferation and nuclear disarmament was not bright. As far as the government of Japan is concerned, given the existing nuclear powers

---

[54] MOFA, *Report of Tokyo Forum: Part 1, The New Nuclear Dangers*, MOFA Archives, http://www.mofa.go.jp/policy/un/disarmament/forum/tokyo9907/report-1.html (25th October 2010)

[55] MOFA, *Financial Contribution to the United Nations 2003,* http://www.mofa.go.jp/mofaj/kids/ranking/un.html (accessed on 25th October 2010)

[56] Ibid

and those with the possibility of arming themselves with nuclear weapons, the future of non-proliferation and nuclear disarmament was not bright, due to the distrust and competitive mentality of these nuclear powers as well as those with the potential of obtaining nuclear armaments. It was the view of the government that the issue should be addressed by three major nuclear powers, the US, Russia and China as well as those in the three regions in which nuclear confrontation could possibly take place, namely, South Asia, Middle East and Northeastern Asia (hereafter, the three regions). Relations among the three powers must be repaired so as to remove strategic mistrust among them and create an environment in which nuclear disarmament and non-proliferation can proceed. It also asserted that states, big or small, in the three regions, should adopt serious policies towards advancing nuclear disarmament and non-proliferation.[57] The final document also strongly urged the leadership of both the US and Russia to give higher priority to nuclear disarmament and non-proliferation policies to pick up speed to reduce nuclear arms according to the bilateral START initiative.[58] A new partnership was urgently required between the US and China in order to reduce nuclear risks, recognizing that while the leaders of the two countries exchanged frequent visits immediately following the cold war, the intricate differences between them could not be ironed out;, after all, most of the nuclear weapons are in the possession of the US and Russia. It is a given that China will increase its political and economic power not just in the East Asian region but also around the world. The government pointed out that how the

---

[57] MOFA Archives, *Report of Tokyo Forum: Part 2, Mending Strategic Relations to Reduce Nuclear Dangers* http://www.mofa.go.jp/policy/un/disarmament/forum/tokyo9907/report-2.html (25th October 2010)

[58] Ibid

Chinese government will employ that power would directly affect the presence of the United States in East Asia and went on to express misgivings that the recent Chinese military build-up has created insecurity and bilateral relations would suffer. Indeed it was feasible that Chinese and Russian nuclear weapons could become equal in both numbers and quality. It is evident that China would become a political and economic power not just in the East Asia but globally. The Japanese government expressed concern that the recent build-up of Chinese military power was causing insecurity not just in its neighbourhood but also other regions as well.[59] While the settlement between China and Russia over their borders in 1999 was welcome and there was hope for the continuation of such friendly relations, nevertheless scepticism remained about whether bilateral relations would improve in the future. The reasons lay in the possible future friction between the two countries on one hand and the United States of America on the other. And if China and Russia would increase their military strength nothing good would come of the bilateral relations to the extent that in the future, the number and qualities of Chinese and Russian nuclear arsenals may reduce. If the two countries adopted policies of nuclear deterrence, this would contribute not only to inculcating trust but also to the stability of East Asian region. The Tokyo Forum put together recommendations on other matters in detail as well. To wit, the Forum expressed a strong concern that the North Atlantic Treaty Organisation (NATO), a US ally, and Russia continued to maintain the option of the first-use of nuclear weapons and suggested that the regime of IAEA management should not mandate just the P5 but also states such as India and Pakistan that are today outside the framework of NPT. The Government of Japan clearly stated also that building mutual trust among nuclear states and

---

[59] Ibid

the neighbouring countries would lead to reducing nuclear risk. This could be a concrete way of resolving the issue but the government has not been able to take the initiative to improving relations between the US, Russia and China. Particularly, Sino-Japanese and Japanese-Russian relations had become difficult since the Second World War and the Cold War. Following the Cold War, territorial issues have increased in the decade after 2000 (see Chapters 5 and 6).

On the other hand, the Disarmament, Non-Proliferation and Science Department (DNPSD) of the MOFA compile every two or three years a White Paper, "Disarmament and Non-Proliferation Policy of Japan" (issued in 2002, 2004, 2006, 2008, 2011, and 2013). In addition to nuclear weapons, the White Paper describes disarmament and non-proliferation of other WMDs including biological weapons and anti-personal land mines as well as conventional weapons (see Chapter 2).

There is a chapter entitled "Dialogue and Cooperation with Civil Society" in all editions of the White Papers.[60] The chapter explains the collaboration between the government and Civil Society as well as their outcome. The content appears to be similar for each edition and one often finds the same sentences repeated. One, therefore, suspects either there is little progress in the collaboration between the government and the civil society or there exists a consistent action guideline on the part of the government. The White Paper refers to the role of civil society and concludes that it has become increasingly essential to have collaboration with NGOs, national governments and international organisations especially in providing post conflict emergency assistance.

---

[60] White Paper "Disarmament and Non-Proliferation of Japan" in 2002, 2004, 2006, 2008, 2011 and 2013

In the field of nuclear weapons, the government favourably recognized the 2020 Vision Campaign adopted by MP with the participation of mayors from around the world as well as that an NGO representing fifteen NGOs, including that of the *hibakusha* was given an opportunity to speak at the NGO session of the 2010 NPT Review Conference.[61] The government, however, made no reference to its cooperation with the 2020 Vision Campaign or concrete collaboration with the MP. On the other hand, an explanation may be that in the field of conventional weapons, as witnessed in the so-called Ottawa Process over anti-personnel bombs, there is a definite strengthening of international collaboration and consequently greater impacts on governments.

As for concrete actions by the government of Japan, one notes that the prime minister as well as heavy weights of the government are present at the Peace Memorial Ceremonies conducted by Cities of Hiroshima and Nagasaki every year in August as well as participating at the Dialogue meetings with *the hibakusha* held in conjunction. Secondly, the government took part among others in the 66th First Committee of the UN General Assembly (2011), co-organized with the UN, in which, in a side-event "Testimonies of Hibakusha" 2 Special Communicators for a World without Nuclear Weapons shared their experiences of the atomic bomb and explained that meaningful exchange took place with the mass media.

The Government established special Communicators for a World without Nuclear Weapons in 2010 in order to formally include

---

[61] Arms Control and Disarmament Division, Disarmament, Non-Proliferation and Science Department, MOFA, Japanese Disarmament and Non-Proliferation Diplomacy 2013 (White Paper), Chapter 8: Dialogue and Collaboration with Civil Society, p1
http://www.mofa.go.jp/mofaj/gaiko/gun_hakusho/2013/pdfs/hon1_8.pdf (accessed on 9th November 2013)

hibakusha who had been working on their own and/or in collaboration with other organisations in order to give them a greater voice within and without the country.[62] Anti-nuclear CSOs had recognized the need for passing on the *hibaku* experience as they age and therefore civil society has since the Cold-War period, been deeply engaged in the process. The formal creation of the organisation in the 65th year after the A-bombing was indeed a deadly slow political response. It is evidence that the government has long neglected to give credence to the importance of testimonies and indeed shows a passive attitude regarding nuclear weapons themselves. Another activity is the organisation of the UN Disarmament Conference in Japan. Following the address of Prime Minister Noboru Takeshita (1987-1989) at the third UN Special Session on Disarmament in 1988, Japan has hosted the sessions almost yearly from 1989, adopting themes such as "Non-Proliferation of Weapons of Mass Destruction and Conventional Weapons" in 1992, "Non-proliferation of Weapons of Mass Destruction and Conventional Weapons – Security and Confidence Building Measures in Northeast Asia" in 1992, and "Towards a World Without Nuclear Weapons" in 1998, all session themes which reflected issues that concerned nuclear weapons. From the session-theme in 2006, "Concerns for Risk of Nuclear Proliferation and Regional and International Peace and Safety", to "Urgent Joint Action towards a non-Nuclear World" in 2011, all sessions dealt with nuclear issues.[63] One can read the concern of the

---

[62] Arms Control and Disarmament Division, Disarmament, Non-Proliferation and Science Department, MOFA, *Japanese Disarmament and Non-Proliferation Diplomacy 2011 (White Paper), Chapter 7: Role of Civil Society,* p7
http://www.mofa.go.jp/mofaj/gaiko/gun_hakusho/2011/pdfs/hon1_7.pdf (accessed on 9th November 2013)

[63]Arms Control and Disarmament Division, Disarmament, Non-Proliferation and Science Department, MOFA, Japanese Disarmament and Non-Proliferation Diplomacy 2013 (White Paper), Chapter 8: Dialogue and Collaboration with

Government of Japan from the years when nuclear weapons were taken up. The session in 1992 reflected the post-cold war structure and security concerns, in 1998 issues about India and Pakistan becoming nuclear states and from 2006 onward, the North Korean nuclear issue and those of the Northeast Asian situation.

Although they were named UN Disarmament Conferences they were different from the UN General Assemblies and Geneva Conferences on Disarmament that were composed of government representatives adopting resolutions and making appeals. Instead, high-level government officials and disarmament experts participated in their personal capacities to debate issues along adopted themes.[64] The White Paper claimed that holding UN Disarmament Conferences in Japan were meaningful since they signalled Japan's positive attitude towards disarmament within and without Japan as well as making an international contribution in activating international deliberations on disarmament. At the same time organizing the conferences in different local cities served to raise important awareness broadly among citizens. Additionally, the White Paper further pointed out that the conferences as well as the side events acted as important disarmament and non-proliferation education for men and women on the street as well as to the young generation of high school and university students.[65]

The Government provides total cooperation for the holding of the Conferences and its representative gives the opening address.[66] These Conferences could not be said to activate international discussion on nuclear disarmament as claimed, nor have they been taken up in a big

---

Civil Society, p158
http://www.mofa.go.jp/mofaj/gaiko/gun_hakusho/2013/pdfs/hon1_8.pdf (9th November 2013)

[64] Ibid, p157

[65] Ibid

[66] Ibid

way by domestic Japanese media. They promote disarmament and non-proliferation education. The Government of Japan places education as the supportive foundation of its various initiatives as well as that of the civil society towards global disarmament and non-proliferation. These include such initiatives as sending 'Special Communicators for a World without Nuclear Weapons, multi-lingual testimonies of *hibakusha*, seminars for young international diplomats at the bomb sites, as well as supporting and organizing Atom Bomb exhibitions overseas (see Chapter 2).

The White Paper betrays the present status of the Government as being in touch with the civil sector' rather than 'collaborating with civil society'. Also it could not be said that the White Paper would be the mainstream foreign policy given that it depends on the US nuclear umbrella that it hopes is provided under the Treaty of Mutual Cooperation and Security between the United States and Japan. It could well be said that the White Paper is that of DNPSD alone for it cannot be said to have become the mainstream foreign policy of the Government. The Section regards collaboration with CSOs and researchers as so important that its head and members participate as panellists from the government when CSOs conduct symposiums on anti-nuclear issues as well as taking time to exchange views on a personal basis. The MOFA and anti-nuclear CSOs have meetings on nuclear disarmament and non-proliferation starting in 2008. Nuclear disarmament and non-proliferation policies of various governments were focused on in preparing for the 2010 NPT Review Conference.

The Governments of Japan and Australia had established a joint initiative on "International Commission on Nuclear Non-Proliferation and Disarmament [ICNND]" between 2008 and 2010 with respective foreign ministers, Yoriko Kawaguchi for Japan and Gareth Evans for

Australia acting as joint chairs and conducted research on NPT review and exchanged views.[67] The Commission met on four occasions, December 2008 and May, November and December 2009, all at the Japanese foreign office and had meetings with the NGOs. Yoriko Kawaguchi and Hideo Suzuki, the Director of the Arms control and disarmament Division in charge of disarmament and non-proliferation diplomacy represented ICNND at each meeting and the Australian Foreign Minister Gareth Evans was present at the last ICNND and NGO meeting of December 2009[68]. The meetings were attended by representatives of JPNNW, JALANA and SGI and from almost all anti-nuclear CSOs in Japan, 22 CSOs (at December 2008 meeting), 23 CSOs in May 2009, 17 in November 2009 and 23 in December 2009[69]. The meetings did not go beyond sharing the respective views of the CSOs, the Government of Japan and the ICNND.[70] The reply made in 2009 in response to the NGO request by Yoriko Kawaguchi, the Japanese Foreign Minister and the Co-Chair of the ICNND represents the views of the ICNND. The following is a summary of her views: in the past there were many reports and resolutions about abandoning nuclear weapons, but these ceased. Then, when under the Obama Administration things were beginning to move even in the USA, she wished to make a proposition that could lead to concrete actions. To start with she wanted to set as short term objectives, putting CTBT into effect, agreement by P5 for non-first-use of nuclear weapons and negotiation on the Fissile Material Cut-Off Treaty (FMCOT). She wanted to refer to the NWC as a stage towards the universal prohibition

---

[67] ICNND http://icnnd.org/Pages/default.aspx (9th November 2013)

[68] MOFA, *List of Attendees at Meeting between ICNND and NGOs,* http://www.mofa.go.jp/mofaj/gaiko/icnnd/ (accessed on 9th November 2013)

[69] * circulated based on the number of attendees

[70] Interview with Kenichi Okubo 2013

of the use of nuclear weapons. She made a remark that she understood that the NGOs' demand is that the ICNND should not stop at reducing nuclear weapons but should indicate concrete deadlines for nuclear for abolition of nuclear weapons while *hibakushas* were alive. Kawaguchi personally wanted to clarify what it would take to abolish nuclear weapons. When the US was asked to ratify the CTBT the response was that it had to keep the option of conducting nuclear tests open, in order to maintain the credibility of nuclear weapons and in order to live up to the obligations of defending NATO countries as well as Japan and Korea. Japan would do well not to discourage the US from ratifying CTBT. Also, if there are advances in reducing nuclear weapons, the time would then come when the US will tell Japan that it could not provide the extended deterrence including the nuclear umbrella. There are suggestions as to the need for starting studies on reducing and eventually doing away with extended deterrence by and among governments and civil societies that are today under the US nuclear umbrella. There are, however, voices in Washington DC that Obama's Plague Speech was much too idealistic. Non-aligned Nations are watching carefully, while nuclear states are negatively reacting against it. She concluded President Obama's speech should be supported so that what he said could come true.[71] From the views stated above one senses the sorry state of the Japanese government and the ICNND lost between their objective for nuclear abolition but caught in the quagmires of real politics.

The atomic bombings on Hiroshima and Nagasaki in 1945 left deep horror among the Japanese people against nuclear bombs. The anti-nuclear CSOs also share strong feelings as they focus their global

---

[71] *Hiroshima Ishikai Sokuho (Dai 2053 Go)* (Report of Hiroshima Prefectural Medical Association (No. 2053)', 2009, p3

activities appealing for agreement never to repeat the horrendous experience anywhere in the world. The JPPNW and MP have their headquarters in Hiroshima and while the JALANA has one in Tokyo, its President Kenya Sasaki, a lawyer, is a *hibakusha* from Hiroshima. SGI is headquartered in Tokyo as well but it has the Soka Gakkai Hiroshima Peace Committee located in Hiroshima actively carrying out Peace seminars as well as organizing occasions for *hibakushas* to share their experiences so as to inform as many people as possible of what took place.

In March 2011 Fukushima Nuclear Power Plants suffered from mega accidents spewing a vast amount of radiation caused by the tsunami that itself was caused by the Great East Japan Earthquake. The nuclear power plant accidents have given a new impact to the policies and activities of anti-nuclear CSOs in Japan. As a result, they are now divided between those that are against the use of nuclear power as well as nuclear weapons and those that argue that anti-nuclear weapons and anti-nuclear energy are two different issues and therefore believe in focusing their activities only on anti-nuclear weapons. The JPPNW and MP's policies are not to oppose nuclear power generation. For example, The JPPNW explains that since the Great East Japan Earthquake of 2011, the anti-nuclear power plant movement has taken to being extremely emotional as witnessed by a large-scale demonstration that takes place every Friday in front of the Prime Minister's residence. It believes what is needed is verification of nuclear power plant technology from a scientific standpoint. It believes that a cool-headed judgement is needed before a headstrong decision is made to decommission all nuclear power plants, considering the lack of energy resources as well as viable alternative energy in Japan. The JPPNW believes that a cool headed judgment is needed about whether a total abolition of nuclear power plants is a realistic decision in the light of the need for energy.[72] The JPPNW knows well the IPPNW Headquarters is against nuclear generation of electric power but is of the opinion that rather than confronting the government, it should influence politicians as much as possible whether on nuclear powered electricity or nuclear abolition.[73] The JALANA take both anti-nuclear and anti-nuclear energy stands considering both the nuclear weapons and nuclear power generation as posing threats to human lives. Mitsuhei Murata, retired Japanese senior diplomat and former Ambassador to Switzerland who has pointed out the danger of nuclear power plants in Japan prior to the Great East Japan Earthquake is convinced that "The use of nuclear material should be prohibited for both civil and military use".[74] The SGI published its message in the words of President Daisaku Ikeda urgently calling for a change in energy policy to one that does not depend on nuclear energy in the 2012 Annual Peace Proposal published every year on 26 January, the founding day of the SGI.[75] The Proposal always provides the guideline for SGI and CSO activities. The SGI, unlike the JALANA, makes separate approaches as well as activities on anti-nuclear weapons campaign and the use of nuclear power generation.

The IPPNW (headquartered in USA), the umbrella organisation of JPPNW, the MP and the SGI were all initiated during the Cold War period and are pioneers of anti-nuclear CSOs. Most of the many anti-nuclear CSOs around the world were established in the post-Cold War era. Entangled in the maelstrom of East-West military and political tension centred on the nuclear arms race, anti-nuclear movements, both

---

[72] Ibid

[73] Ibid

[74] Interview with Mitsuhei Murata 2013

[75] * Ikeda has submitted his peace proposals to the United Nations every year

governmental and civilian, were slow in gaining momentum. Japan was no exception. Since then Japan has belonged politically to the Western camp, and shared the US administration's diplomacy. With major Eastern powers such as the USSR and China nearby, the government of Japan was unwilling to promote concrete actions towards the abolition of nuclear arms. And as for the citizens, while there were extremely strong pressures against war, and for peace and the abolition of nuclear arms following the awful consequences of the Second World War, it did not culminate in organizing CSOs and raising voices internationally. The Soka Gakkai (SGI today) established in1930 was alone in actively organizing international citizens' anti-nuclear movements throughout the Cold War period following its 1957 Declaration[76] proposing the abolition of nuclear arms as bombs, because they would be counter to the dignity of life. One could, therefore, say that SGI was Japan's first anti-nuclear CSO with a definite international agenda. On the international scene, the IPPNW, a physicians' group, was the recognized pioneer of the citizens' anti-nuclear movement.

Following the end of the Cold War many anti-nuclear organisations were established throughout the world, including the Japanese CSOs starting with the JALANA and the MP. They shared the objectives of opposing nuclear weapons and building a world free of nuclear weapons but their beliefs on nuclear issues were as diverse as their activities. The JALANA and the MP remain critical of the Japanese government for its passivity as well as for its continued opposition to recognising the inhumanity of nuclear weapons. The JPPNW, on the other hand, has a flexible attitude in dealing with the government. For a start, it believes that the anti-nuclear movement should not be radical and stresses the

[76] Declaration calling for the abolition of nuclear arms by Soka Gakkai Second President http://www.joseitoda.org/vision/declaration/ (accessed on 1st December 2012)

importance of taking time. Furthermore, Japan's CSO activities were divided after 2011 when the *tsunami* destroyed the nuclear power plants in Fukushima proliferating doses of radiation. The division was between those who believe that decommissioning of nuclear power plants should be embedded within the conventional anti-nuclear movement and those who believe they are two separate issues to be discussed separately, making it a strong issue of dissension.

The IPPNW, the physicians' anti-nuclear movement has an older history among anti-nuclear CSOs. The nuclear tests conducted during the 1950s and the '60s gave rise to serious anxiety about the effects of radiation on human bodies. As a result the Physicians for Social Responsibility (PSR) was organized in 1961.[77] The IPPNW was officially established in December 1980 in Geneva by physicians in both the US and USSR amid rising concern with the nuclear development that began in the 70s. The process began with the written exchange of views between Bernard Lown, Professor at the Harvard School of Public Health at the time and Yevbeny Chazov, a cardiologist and former Soviet Health Care Minister. At present the IPPNW has its headquarters in Boston, Massachusetts and has branches in 63 countries including Japan (as of 2013) with a membership of over 100,000 physicians from 83 countries.[78] The Nobel Peace Prize was awarded in 1985 for its contribution in spreading reliable information and understanding regarding the devastating effects of nuclear war.[79]

---

[77] PSR official website http://www.psr.org/about/ (accessed on 1st December 2012)

[78] IPPNW official website, IPPNW Affiliate Directory http://www.ippnw.org/affiliates-directory.html (accessed on 1st December 2012)

[79] Nobel Peace Prize 1985 http://www.nobelprize.org/nobel_prizes/peace/laureates/1985/press.html (accessed on 1st December 2012)

(i) Japan Physicians for the Prevention of Nuclear War (JPPNW) / International Physicians for the Prevention of Nuclear War (IPPNW)

The principle of IPPNW is based on the belief that as physicians they will not condone any action that threatens human health. The IPPNW believes that the radioactive contamination resulting from the use of nuclear bombs must not be condoned. The IPPNW's anti-nuclear activities are based on its commitment that physicians must never ignore any activity that may harm human health. They strongly believe that nuclear radiation does severe damage to human health. Chazov, the IPPNW's co-founder, served as Minister of Health Care in the Gorbachev administration and became his close associate. It is said that the first concrete US-USSR nuclear disarmament summit between Donald Reagan and Mikhail Gorbachev that took place in 1986 was the result of Lown advising Reagan and Chazov advising Gorbachev.[80]

During the Cold War the IPPNW World Congress took place in nuclear power countries, the United States in 1981, 1996, and 2002 (Washington DC), the United Kingdom in 1982, the USSR in 1987, and China in 2004 (Beijing), India in 2008 (New Delhi) and, as an exception in Japan in 1989 and 2013 (Hiroshima). Representatives of governments, medical communities, CSOs and the media attended the Congress, where active exchanges of views took place. Of the branches of IPPNW the JPPNW is the most active and supports the IPPNW headquarters financially at its request. At these World Congresses, workshops and

---

[80] Tadatoshi Akiba, Specially Appointed Professor, University of Hiroshima, Former Mayor of Hiroshima, *the 29th Seminar on International Cooperation, "Elimination of Nuclear Weapons by 2020! Peace and the Role of Citizens"*, at the University of Tokyo, 21st October 2011
http://inter.k.u-tokyo.ac.jp/seminar_event/is_seminar/pdf/event_29.pdf
(accessed on 1st December 2012)

educational lectures are actively held, focusing on medical analyses of radiation casualties from the atomic bombing of Hiroshima and Nagasaki cities.

During the 18th World Congress in New Delhi, India 2008, a workshop was held under the theme: "Creating Nuclear-Free Zone in Northeast Asia learning from the negative legacies of Hiroshima and Nagasaki – assumptions of nuclear damages on the cities of today and possibilities of evacuation of residents, with Hiroshima as an example". This was an attempt to analyse from the physicians' points of view the assumed damage and the evacuation possibilities of residents if and when nuclear weapons were used on cities today.[81] The government of Japan enacted the Protection of Citizens Act in 2004 to protect the lives and properties of citizens if and when military attack were to be made against the country, and instructed that a guideline be established to protect citizens by all local governments following the Basic Guideline set by it. The City of Hiroshima had misgivings concerning the central and local governments' guidelines, which lacked consideration of nuclear attacks. As the first city in the world that suffered the blast of the atom bomb, Hiroshima established a "City of Hiroshima Citizens Protection Plan". The Plan contained 4 scenarios – a 16-kilo ton atom bomb exploding 600 meters above the ground, 1-megaton bomb exploding 2,400 meters above the ground, and 1 and 16 kiloton atom bombs exploding on the ground. It was estimated that, with a 16 kilo-ton atom bomb exploding in the air, the blast would reach 4.5 kilometres from the epicentre and the preliminary radiation and heat

---

[81] *Hiroshima Ishikai Sokuho (Dai 2022 Go)* (Report of Hiroshima Prefectural Medical Association (No. 2022), Hiroshima Nanao Kamata (Member of JPPNW Board of Directors, and Professor emeritus Hiroshima University), *'Dai 18 Kai IPPNW Sekai Taikai Waku Shopu* (18th IPPNW World Conference Work Shop)', 5th September 2008, p1

radiation would reach 2.5 kilometres killing and injuring 270,000 citizens within a radius of 4.5 kilometres. In the case of a 1 mega ton atomic bomb, were it to explode at 2400 meters above the ground, 850,000 people out of 1.3 million people living within a 18 kilometre radius would be killed or injured. And if a 16-kiloton atomic bomb were to explode on the ground, it is calculated that the initial radiation would reach 2.2 kilometres and 200,000 residents out of 460,000 living within 3.5 kilometres of the epicentre would suffer death or injury. The analysis assuming a ground explosion can be applied to a terrorist attack with an atom bomb. This, therefore, is a valuable contribution from the city that experienced the terrible effects of the atom bomb. The four scenarios had a common conclusion, that "the evacuation of citizens at the time of nuclear explosion was impossible since no real time information can be communicated or shared. Most of the hospitals and medical institutions would be reduced to radiation polluted rubble. No one would be able to go near the epicentre region due to high radiation levels. It would be extremely difficult in any state for its emergency planning and guidelines to function under a nuclear explosion or attack.[82] The JPPNW urged that people should recognize, drawing on the City of Hiroshima's analysis, that when under nuclear attack not even the greatest efforts made would protect the safety of communities, and that the best way to avoid nuclear attack is to strengthen programmes towards the abolition of nuclear weapons as well as to strengthen programmes to deter nuclear arms and nuclear material from falling into the hands of terrorists.[83]

The JPPNW was established in 1992 with its Headquarters located within the Headquarters of the Hiroshima Prefectural Medical

---

[82] Ibid, p2
[83] Ibid, p3

Association. The original source was to provide medical support and assistance by volunteer physicians to the *hibakusha* in Hiroshima and Nagasaki. The JPPNW considers the nuclear issue to be a health issue and not a political one.[84] Their aim is to prevent nuclear wars from medical and biological perspectives, and organize towards the achievement of their objectives using study groups and lecture meetings as well as participation in the world Medical Association conferences, and to distribute information and materials from the headquarters.[85] Their strong conviction is that the actual experiences of atomic bombings on Hiroshima and Nagasaki should be the starting point of the global anti-nuclear movement.

One of its concrete initiatives is the research on residual radiation. Its purpose is, in collaboration with the Research Institute for Radiation Biology and Medicine, Hiroshima University[86] and the IPPNW, to win legal recognition of *hibakusha* who are not covered by the present legal framework, by dispatching inquiry missions to Chernobyl and Fukushima.[87] Four anti-nuclear CSO cited in this dissertation conduct activities based on the real circumstances caused by the dropping of the atomic bombs. For example, it was the lawyers who represented victims to win for them formal recognition as *hibakusha* who founded the JALANA. (This will be taken up later). Anti-nuclear movements which do not incorporate personal experiences will eventually lose steam, be reduced to conceptual activities and disappear. CSOs are rightly

---

[84] Interview with Katsuko Kataoka 2012

[85] IPPNW Japan Chapter, *About us*, http://www.hiroshima.med.or.jp/ippnw/nihonshibu/index.html (accessed on 14th October 2012)

[86] Research Institute for Radiation Biology and Medicine, Hiroshima University http://www.rbm.hiroshima-u.ac.jp/ (accessed on 14th October 2012)

[87] IPPNW Japan Chapter, *About us*, http://www.hiroshima.med.or.jp/ippnw/nihonshibu/index.html (accessed on 14th October 2012)

concerned that the fact of aging and dying *hibakusha*, as well as the nuclear issue itself, will become prey to political strategies and bargaining.

Zitsuro Yanagida, a Vice International Trustee of the IPPNW and a Director of the JPPNW is a second-generation *hibakusha*. In fact JPPNW members include many *hibakusha* and their second generation offspring. Furthermore, the JPPNW movement owes its presence to the conviction of physicians who took care of *hibakusha* amid unspeakable sights immediately following the atomic bombing of Hiroshima and Nagasaki that the use of nuclear weapons and nuclear wars result in the worst kind of damage to human health. They thus believe that physicians must play a big role in annihilating nuclear weapons, underlined by their professional knowledge on how radiation causes damage to human health.[88]

As of 2013 the JPPNW has approximately 3,000 members (who endorse and support its principles and activities) from 14 out of 47 Prefectural Medical Associations. About 1,000 or so belong to the Hiroshima Prefecture Branch. It is customary for the President of the Hiroshima Prefectural Medical Association to serve as the JPPNW President. It is noted that, while the JPPNW is a separate civic organisation, it receives total financial and personnel support from the Hiroshima Prefectural Medical Association. Also, the Japan Medical Association, the parent organisation of the Hiroshima Branch, provides financial aid (usually one million yen every year and five million yen when functions are held) as well as support in strengthening relations with the government.[89] While the Japan Medical Association does not compel all Japanese physicians to belong to it, it has in addition to the

---

[88] Ibid

[89] *Hiroshima Ishikai Sokuho (Dai 2048 Go)* (tentative translation: 'Report of Hiroshima Prefectural Medical Association (No. 2048)', p2

47 prefectural medical associations, local associations in 920 cities. It has a total of 165,000 members, or sixty per cent of physicians in Japan (as of 2012).[90] Furthermore, the Japan Medical Association along with the Japan Dental Association and the Japan Pharmaceutical Association, are referred to as Japan's Three Large Medical Associations and have a close relationship with the government and the ruling party. They are called on to advise them in their decision making about social security and medical systems. In 1995, Teruaki Fukuhara, the President of the Hiroshima Prefectural Medical Association and his collaborators successfully presented Tomiichi Murayama, the Prime Minister of Japan 1994-1996, with a Resolution Against Nuclear Tests and Abolition of Nuclear Weapons adopted by the Board of Directors of the Japan Medical Association.

> "The effects nuclear weapons tests and their use have on humankind and the earth's environment are unfathomable. Japan as a country has been damaged by the world's first atomic bomb. Given this untold experience it is the united wish of all citizens of Japan that the tragedy should never again be repeated, that a world without nuclear weapons must be created.
>
> The Japan Medical Association, committed to its mission of protecting human life and health, resolutely opposes nuclear tests of any country and demands that all future nuclear tests be immediately stopped. And at the same time calls on all states in possession of nuclear weapons to immediately and sincerely undertake initiatives towards their abolition."
>
> (The 93rd Japan Medical Association Ad Hoc Board of

---

[90] Japan Medical Association http://www.med.or.jp/english/about_JMA/index.html (accessed on 1st December 2012)

Directors Resolves, 24th October 1995)[91]
(Translated by Fujiko Hara)

In 2009, the Kyoto and other JPPNW Branches repeatedly demanded that the Japan Medical Association, following new developments surrounding nuclear issues, including threat of nuclear terrorism, strenuously adopt another resolution. With the tenacious efforts of Sizuteru Usui, the President of The Hiroshima Prefectural Medical Association (JPPNW President) and a Member of the Board of Directors of the Japan Medical Association, the Japan Medical Association unanimously adopted a "Resolution on Nuclear Abolition" and presented it by hand to Taro Aso, the Prime Minister of Japan (2008-2009).

> "Looking back on the last ten years, many lives were lost and lives of citizens have been destroyed throughout the world due to the expansion of local conflicts and terrorism. There appears to be no end to this trend, and what is more the fear of the proliferation of weapons of mass destruction is a shared global concern. Furthermore, we have seen even recently the development of nuclear weapons and repetitive nuclear tests. Particularly, the nuclear tests continue to take place ignoring the opposition of the international society.
>
> In particular, the continuation of nuclear tests has taken place ignoring the opposition of the international society, which today protests loudly against the use of cruel weapons that far transcend regional conflicts and terrorism.

---

[91] Japan Medical Association, '*Nihon Ishikai Soritsu Kinenshi: Sengo Gojunen No Ayumi* (Magazine of 50th Anniversary of Japan Medical Association), 1997, p220

The World Medical Association had adopted in 2001 a resolution condemning terrorism, further it had both in 1998 and 2008 adopted the WMA Declaration calling on every government to diligently work towards nuclear weapons abolition. These were the voices of physicians of the world earnestly urging knowing the untold misery of nuclear weapons as medical professionals. The medical effects of nuclear weapons are immeasurable, not to mention the effects experienced in Hiroshima and Nagasaki. Sixty-three years after the atomic bombing, hibakusha continue to suffer grave after-effects. The Japan Medical Association feels strongly today that they were entrusted with the mission to save lives of people and at the same time demand nuclear states to sincerely undertake an immediate abolition of nuclear weapons."

(The 120th Regular Board of Directors of the Japan Medical Association resolves, 29 March 2009, in Japanese)[92]

(Translated by Fujiko Hara)

Notwithstanding the submission of these resolutions there were no particular changes on the part of the Japanese government concerning nuclear issues. The government's general position is in favour of the abolition of nuclear arms, but given the political situation with neighbouring countries it can only be passive, in reality (see Chapter 2). As long as there is no breakthrough in stalemate political confrontation or opening of government to government negotiation, Japan will remain passive on nuclear issues, and the Northeast Asian situation will remain a crucible for nuclear weapons. The JPPNW recognizes the situation

[92] Kakuheiki Haizetsuni Kansuru Ketsugi (Resolution of Japan Medical Association for Elimination of Nuclear Weapons), 2009, http://www.antiatom.org/Gpress/?p=470 (accessed on 16th December 2012)

and unlike the JALANA and the MP, is working actively to exchange opinions and keep up relations with the government and elected members of parliament. They see nuclear abolition as a long range issue, they are prepared to build a cooperative system with the government of Japan against the complex political and diplomatic relations around the world as well as in the Northeast Asian region[93]. For example, the JPPNW continues to exchange views as well as petition MPs that are affiliated with the Parliamentarians for Nuclear Non-Proliferation and Disarmament, Japan (PNND Japan)[94] organized by like-minded parliamentary colleagues. As far as the JPPNW is concerned, however, they feel that it is rather difficult to encourage concrete involvement by the government or the MPs in specific issues such as that of the North Korean nuclear arms.[95]

The JPPNW, however, organizes and participates in a series of North Asia Regional Conferences as part of their international activities. The IPPNW organizes World Congress and regional conferences alternately. The North Asia Regional Conference is participated in by the IPPNW Chapter in China (official name unknown. The IPPNW Official Website lists it as the Chinese Medical Association), the Chapter in South Korea (official name unknown. The IPPNW Official Website gives no reference), the Korean Anti-Nuke Peace Physicians (KANPP) (IPPNW Official Website provides no information), the Chapter in North Korea and the Mongol Physicians for the Prevention of Nuclear Weapons (MPPNW), the Chapter in Mongolia as of 2013. The North Asia Regional Conference is de facto led by the JPPNW covering organisation expenses, airfare and accommodation expenses

[93] Interview with Katsuko Kataoka 2012

[94] PNND Japan http://www.pnnd.jp/about.html (accessed on 16th December 2012)

[95] Interview with Katsuko Kataoka, 2012

for members of the KANPP and the MPPNW to participate. The purpose of the Conference is denuclearization of the North Asian Region[96] and is largely civilian diplomacy carried out by JPPNW. The predecessor of the conference was the 50th anniversary of atomic bombing organized by JPPNW in 1995 in which members of the IPPNW branches of South Korea, North Korea and China were present. In time they developed friendships and at the 12th IPPNW World Congress in 1996 a decision was made to establish the North Asia Regional Conference by the four countries including Japan.

The First North Asia Regional Conference that took place in 1997 in Nagasaki City issued a Joint Declaration to promote mutual understanding among North Asian countries where personal exchange and the political situation keeps them apart in spite of their geographical proximity, and requested all nuclear states to follow the Chinese Government's example in agreeing to the non-first use of nuclear weapons.[97]

The Second was held in 1999 in Beijing, China. In addition to China, Japan, and North Korea, physicians, researchers and medical students from seven other countries participated in the two-day conference. The Conference pointed out that mutual relations among countries of North Asia suffered from lack of communication and cooperative relations and concluded that they were hampered due to deep-rooted military and political factors. It was recognized in particular that the strong tensions dividing the Korean peninsula was aggravated by the intervention of external powers, the US and the USSR, causing arms expansion to

---

[96] *Kita Azia Chiiki Kaigi (North Asia Regional Conference)* http://www.hiroshima.med.or.jp/ippnw/ippnwnitsuite/kitaasia.html (accessed on 22nd November 2012)

[97] *Dai Ikkai Kita Azia Chiiki Kaigi (1st North Asia Regional Conference)* http://www.hiroshima.med.or.jp/ippnw/ippnwnitsuite/1ippnw19971123.html (accessed on 22nd November 2012)

continue in the said region. The Conference recognized that, in order for the peaceful reunification of the Korean peninsula and for peace and security to be established in North Asian region, physicians united in the IPPNW sharing common profession are being given an opportunity to overcome the situation. This is based on their friendship and mutual understanding, and it would only worsen if left to run its course. The Conference adopted its Beijing Declaration, demanding that the US and Russia as well as other nuclear weapons states should begin negotiations towards agreeing to a treaty that will eliminate all nuclear weapons that are today placed in a state of immediate readiness. In particular, it strongly reproached the US Senate for refusing to ratify the CTBT in October 1999 and asked the US citizens to take leadership on nuclear weapons issues against their own government.[98]

The Third Conference was to have taken place in Pyongyang in North Korea in October 2001, but it was hastily suspended at the KANPP's request.[99]

The Fourth took place in 2003 in Kyoto, Japan. The Conference adopted the Kyoto Declaration and expressed strong concern that, following the 2001 9/11 attack on New York, there had been numerous indiscriminate terrorist attacks and counter military attacks causing the US Administration to uphold ever stronger unilateralism, and to clearly state in its Nuclear Posture Review (NPR) that it would not relinquish a pre-emptive nuclear strike, and called Iraq and North Korea an "Axis of Evil". As a result, Iraq was militarily attacked, led by the US and UK, and the immense damage suffered had not seen the light of

---

98 *Dai Nikai Kita Azia Chiiki Kaigi (2nd North Asia Regional Conference)* http://www.hiroshima.med.or.jp/ippnw/ippnwnitsuite/2ippnw19991016.html (accessed on 22nd November 2012)

99 *Kita Azia Chiiki Kaigi (North Asia Regional Conference)* http://www.hiroshima.med.or.jp/ippnw/ippnwnitsuite/kitaasia.html (accessed on 1st December 2012)

reconstruction even half a year after the war ended. As for North Korea, it declared its intention of developing nuclear weapons, and adopting a diplomacy of brinkmanship.[100]

The Fifth Conference also took place in Japan, at Hiroshima. The Hiroshima Declaration adopted at the Conference expressed concern that the Bush Administration referred to pre-emptive use of nuclear weapons and the barren outcome of the 2005 NPT Review Conference held in New York. It went on to point out that the fundamental problem of the NPT lay in the failure of the nuclear states to implement Article 6 of the Treaty, namely to carry out their obligation towards reducing nuclear weapons. It is worth nothing that the non-observance by nuclear states of NPT's Article 6 has been pointed out by many anti-nuclear CSOs over the years. The Kyoto Conference, encouraged by the public admission by North Korea of its possession of nuclear weapons and the reopening of the Six Party Talks, clearly stated that it would continue to do its utmost towards de-nuclearization of the Korean Peninsula in collaboration with the MP. The Conference was attended by physicians, researchers, medical students and the general public from 13 countries. The Conference also welcomed the birth of a new IPPNW branch in the Republic of Mongolia, which is a declared non-nuclear weapons state. It was decided that the Sixth Conference would be held in 2007 in Ulan Bator.[101] The Sixth Conference adopted, in addition to the customary declaration bearing the name of the city where it took place (Ulan Bator Declaration), a Declaration on Nuclear Weapons Free Zones, stating that it will work in collaboration with the UN, other CSOs and

---

[100] *Dai Yonkai Kita Azia Chiiki Kaigi (4th North Asia Regional Conference)* http://www.hiroshima.med.or.jp/ippnw/ippnwnitsuite/4ippnw2003105.html (accessed on 1st December 2012)

[101] *Dai Gokai Kita Azia Chiiki Kaigi* (5th North Asia Regional Conference) http://www.hiroshima.med.or.jp/ippnw/ippnwnitsuite/5ippnw2005821.html (accessed on 1st December 2012)

organisations to aim to achieve the following initiatives:

> "· undertaking a new Expert's Study on NWFZs in all their aspects so as to update the original 1975 UN Study. This study should examine the role and increase the effectiveness of existing NWFZs. The study should also examine the conditions and possibilities for establishing such zones in other regions, including North-East Asia, the Middle East, Central and Northern Europe, South Asia, the Gulf State region, the Southern Hemisphere, and single states for whom wider zonal arrangements are currently not feasible due to their geographic location;
>
> Convening in the next two years of an international conference of States party to NWFZs as a follow-up to the successful 2005 Mexico conference. The conference would seek to: strengthen the existing zones as well as develop support for new NWFZ initiatives, including in North-East Asia, and foster ways of coordinating and implementing action on NWFZ initiatives at the United Nations and the 2010 Nonproliferation Treaty (NPT) Review Conference;
>
> Mobilizing support for Costa Rica's initiative to have the idea of a Nuclear Weapons Convention (for the global elimination of nuclear weapons) put on the agenda for consideration at NPT Preparatory Meetings and the 2010 NPT Review Conference itself;
>
> Organizing a meeting of North-East Asian experts to discuss the possible content of the future NEA-NWFZ as well as ways and means of promoting this issue at the regional and international

level."[102]

The JPPNW made friends with the members of the KANPP at every opportunity during the North Asia Regional Conference. Also, under the inspiring leadership of the president of the Hiroshima Prefectural Medical Association, who also serves as the president of the JPPNW, the JPPNW has been providing medical support to those who were exposed to radiation while living in either Hiroshima or Nagasaki and now living on the Korean Peninsula or in countries in South America, faithful to the president's declared principle, "*Hibakusha* is a *hibakusha* wherever he or she is". People living in North Korea were excluded from this medical support due to government policy prohibiting travel to countries without diplomatic ties. The JPPNW President and officials have taken every opportunity, at the North Asia Regional conferences in Mongolia or at the IPPNW World Congress in India, to meet with representatives of the KANPP and finally realized a much awaited visit to North Korea, working through the General Association of Korean Residents in Japan. In June 2009, a JPPNW Director visited North Korea among other visiting groups. This was followed in September by a visit to North Korea by the President and Directors of the Hiroshima Prefectural Medical Association. The visitors had a meeting with the KANPP leaders and interviewed four *hibakusha*. The visitors packed a suitcase with a year's worth of internal medicine and surgery magazines purchased by the Hiroshima Prefectural Medical Association in response to the request of KANPP for recent Japanese medical books and magazines. The Japanese Government had forbidden for half a year

[102] JPPNW, *Statement on Nuclear-Weapon-Free Zones*, IPPNW 6th North Asia Regional Meeting Ulaanbaatar, Mongolia, 22th June 2007 http://www.hiroshima.med.or.jp/ippnw/ippnwnitsuite/6ippnw2007622.html (accessed on 1st December 2012)

the entry of key North Korean vessels to Japanese ports in response to the missile launch tests conducted by North Korea in July 2006. As regards the underground nuclear tests conducted in September of the same year, the Japanese Government forbade entry of all North Korean vessels.[103] Following the embargo, the University of Hiroshima Medical School made a donation of a full year's subscription of medical magazines which was learned to have been carried in a handbag by a staff member of the North Korean Association travelling to his country.[104] The JPPNW, troubled by the absence of any prospect of reopening the Six Party Talks, believes that the normalization of diplomatic relations between Japan and North Korea may contribute to building Northeast Asia's Nuclear Free Zone.

In 2002, Junichiro Koizumi, the Prime Minister of Japan, 2001-2006, visited North Korea and had a meeting with Kim Jong Il and demanded the return of a total of seventeen victims,[105] the number recognized by Japanese Government's official account of victims kidnapped by North Korea in a total of twelve cases of abduction. The North Korean government acknowledged the abduction of thirteen and agreed to return five persons but said eight were dead and explained that the remaining four claimed by the Japanese government had not set foot in the country. The real situation remains ambiguous.[106] The bilateral

---

[103] *Hiroshimaken Ishikai Sokuho No. 2083* (Report of Hiroshima Prefectural Medical Association No. 2083), 2010, pp2

[104] Ibid

[105] Headquarters for the Abduction Issue, Government of Japan, *Seifu Nintei 17 Mei Ni Kakawaru Zian* (Abduction Issue of 17 People by North Korea) http://www.rachi.go.jp/jp/ratimondai/jian.html (accessed on 21st May 2013)

[106] Ministry of Foreign Affairs Japan, Rachi Mondai No Kaiketsu: Sonota Kitachosen Tokyoku Niyoru Zinken Shingai Mondai He No Taisho Ni Kansuru Seifu No Torikumi Ni Tsuite No Hokoku (Report of Japanese Government Policy and Activities regarding Issues of Abduction and Abuse of Human Rights by North Korea)
http://www.mofa.go.jp/mofaj/press/pr/pub/pamph/pdfs/rachi_torikumi.pdf

summit meeting produced a signed Japan-North Korea Pyongyang Declaration. The said declaration confirmed the reopening of negotiations toward the normalization of Japan-North Korea relations, and that during the said negotiation the two parties would discuss matters relating to the post restoration of diplomatic relations, including that for a period agreed as appropriate by the parties, the Japanese government will provide grant aids, a low interest yen credit, humanitarian support such as economic cooperation, and that loans and credits will be provided by the Bank of International Cooperation to support North Korea's private sector economic activities. The two governments agreed to work to achieve a comprehensive resolution of nuclear issues on the Korean peninsula, and for which they will respect all related international agreements. With regard to various issues concerning security, including missiles, they will promote dialogue among related states to solve issues. The North Korean Government will, in accordance with the Declaration, extend beyond 2003 the moratorium concerning missile launch. [107] The objectives and expectations of the Japanese Government regarding the Declaration were the resolution of the issues of abduction and the North Korean nuclear weapons. While both cases were considered equal threats to Japan, nevertheless, the majority of national sentiment veered towards the resolution of the abduction cases as the priority. However, following the North Korean government's missile launch tests and nuclear tests in 2006, the sense of North Korea's nuclear threat increased around the

---

(accessed on 28th February 2014)

[107] Japan Prime Minister's Office Archives, Koizumi Sori No Enzetsu Kishakaiken Tou, Nichou Pyongyang Sengen (Prime Minister Koizumi's speech and press conference, the Japan-North Korea Pyongyang Declaration), 2002
http://www.kantei.go.jp/jp/koizumispeech/2002/09/17sengen.html (accessed on 28th February 2014)

world. In 2012, the Japan National Police Agency, responding to citizens' demand for information disclosure, announced that there were 868 persons missing and their abduction by North Korea could not be excluded.[108] In 2013 the UN Commission on Human Rights established a UN Inquiry Committee and conducted a year-long study on the North Korean Government's systematic and extensive serious cases of human rights violation including the right to food within North Korea, imprisonment facilities and torture, inhuman treatment, freedom of expression, freedom concerning life, freedom of movement, and on enforced disappearance including abduction of foreign nationals, by organizing public hearing sessions in Seoul, Tokyo, London and Washington DC and by interview over 80 victims and witnesses including Japanese abductees. As a result the final report was compiled in 2014 and demanded that urgent action be taken by the international society concerning the human rights situation in North Korea, including submission to the International Criminal Court of the extensively occurring sins against humanity by policies determined at the highest levels of North Korea.[109] As of 2014, there is no prospect of discussing the Northeast Asia Nuclear-Weapon-Free Zone Treaty (NANWFZT) at government levels. The IPPNW believes that a swift and concrete study at the levels of civil societies will provide useful reference points for the

---

[108] Tokutei Shissousha Mondai Chosaikai (Investigation Commission on Missing Japanese Probably Related to North Korea), *Keisatsu No Tokutei Shissousha Lisuto* (List of Missing People by the National Police Agency Japan'), 2012, http://www.chosa-kai.jp/121230.html (accessed on 28th February 2014)

[109] United Nations Information Centre, *Kitachosen No Zinken Ni Kansuru Kokuren Chosa Iinkai, Hokokusho O Happyo, Kohani Ni Wataru Zindo Ni Taisuru Tsumi O Shiteki* (UN Commission on DPRK's Abuse of Human Rights made the final document and indicated its broad crime against human rights), 2014, http://www.unic.or.jp/news_press/info/6912/ (accessed on 21st May 2014)

government-level operations.[110] According to the KANPP, the Cold War structural conflict remains on the Korean peninsula and it believes that the US administration has a total responsibility for stationing US troops in Korea, thereby sustaining North-South Conflict and failing to convert the Korean War Cease-fire Agreement into a Peace Agreement. Furthermore, the continuation of the Bush Administration's policy of regarding North Korea as an enemy and conducting US-Korea Joint Military Exercise covering the entire country provides North Korea with its reason not to abandon its nuclear weapons. The KANPP has a unique opinion of its own, that is to say, that a peace agreement on the Korean peninsula will be realized when political and security issues are resolved with North Korea and the US agreeing to act together under the principle of acting simultaneously, and thus removing nuclear threat which is the very source of nuclear issues of the Korean peninsula.[111] This logic implies that when North Korea totally abolishes its nuclear arms, the US too would have to do the same, which makes this an unrealistic concept at the present stage. These opinions of the KANPP are thought to represent the disposition of the North Korean government given that there appears to be de facto no freedom for civil activities in the country.

Following the Seventh Regional Conference in Hiroshima in 2009, the Eighth North Asia Regional Conference in Kathmandu in 2010 was organized jointly with the IPPNW South Asia Regional Conference. This followed the JPPNW's initiative at the Seventh Conference in inviting in addition to the members of MPPNW and KANPP, physicians and medical students from IPPNW branches in developing countries of

---

[110] *Hiroshimaken Ishikai Sokuho No. 2019* (Report of Hiroshima Prefectural Medical Association No. 2019), 2008, p1

[111] *Hiroshimaken Ishikai Sokuho No. 2018* (Report of Hiroshima Prefectural Medical Association No. 2018), 2008, p2

South Asian region and paying for their travel and accommodation expenses. At that Conference, in addition to setting deadlines for the NPT, CTBT and FMCOT, it was decided to aim for the establishment of NANWFZT. It also declared its strong support of the Hiroshima-Nagasaki Protocol which was proposed by the MP. Given the long trusting relationship between JPPNW and MP, the Conference decided to appoint Tadatoshi Akiba, Former Mayor of Hiroshima City (and the MP President) as JPPNW's honorary advisor to provide it comprehensive advice.[112] The Eight Conference in Kathmandu was participated in by members of branches from Bangladesh, China, North Korea, Finland, India, Japan, Nepal, Pakistan and Sri Lanka, and confirmed that potential threats to regional and world peace lay in the possession of nuclear weapons, abilities to develop them, expedient and temporary relations between countries, and widely dispersed differences among races that cause conflicts.[113] At both Conferences the JPPNW sponsored physicians who shared their experiences of being exposed to radioactivity in Hiroshima and Nagasaki, and poster exhibitions showing the realities of radiation damage.[114] However, it was from about that time that branches were beginning to lose steam. The MPPNW lost its leader, who relocated to Austria due to his work, and that led to its inactivity. As a result the MPPNW was not present at the Eighth Conference. Although they are still in touch with the Chapter in China, their reports regarding the names and numbers of their

---

[112] *Hiroshimaken Ishikai Sokuho No. 2112* (Report of Hiroshima Prefectural Medical Association No. 2112), 2011, p1

[113] The 8th IPPNW North and South Asia Joint Regional Conference, Kathmandu Declaration, 6th March 2011
http://www.hiroshima.med.or.jp/ippnw/ippnwnitsuite/8ippnw201036.html (accessed on 7th December 2012)

[114] *Hiroshimaken Ishikai Sokuho No. 2103* (Report of Hiroshima Prefectural Medical Association No. 2103), 2010, p3

membership are exactly the same as that of the Chinese Medical Association. It is unclear how much activity is carried out as the IPPNW China Chapter. The Chapter in the Republic of Korea is hardly active so that at the 19th IPPNW World Congress in Basil, Switzerland, 2010, it was designated as a dormant Chapter.[115] By 2012, all North Asia IPPNW Chapters, except Japan, became dormant. There is a clear need for increasing membership, recruiting medical students and leaders who are capable of managing each branch.

The 20th IPPNW World Congress took place in Hiroshima with the JPPNW in charge of its management as its Steering Committee. The JPPNW put up two major themes, namely, "Return to the origin (of Hiroshima)" and "Ensure succession to the next generation movement calling for the abolition of nuclear weapons". Since the IPPNW was established during the Cold War, with the end of the Cold War followed by an increase of regional conflicts, increasing number of branches (countries) began to focus on various themes including landmines and biological weapons, blurring their original focus. It was therefore decided to take advantage of the Congress taking place in Hiroshima to recapture the original purpose of the IPPNW activities and the slogan, "From HIROSHIMA to Future Generations" was adopted.[116] As special guests it planned to invite Barack Obama (US President), 14th Dalai Lama, Mikhail Gorbachev, the President of the World Medical Association, the President of the Japan Medical Association, the Governor of Hiroshima Prefecture, the Mayor of Hiroshima City, the Prime Minister of Japan, the Japanese Foreign Minister, the UN Secretary-General, and Kim Jong-un (Supreme Leader of the North

---

[115] Ibid

[116] Hiroshimaken Ishikai Sokuho No. 2109 (Report of Hiroshima Prefectural Medical Association No. 2109), p2

Korea).[117] Inviting Kim Jong-un was a proof on the part of JPPNW to position North Korea's nuclear issue as one of the most important ones. Among the guests invited, President of International Committee of the Red Cross, the Governor of Hiroshima Prefecture, the Mayor of Hiroshima City, President of the Japan Medical Association, and the Global Coordinator of the PNDD attended. When the JPPNW Board of Directors met ahead of the Congress at its preparatory committee meeting, the existence of a huge gap between the IPPNW Headquarters and JPPNW became apparent. While the JPPNW wished to organize the "Session on the effects on human body of radiation exposure" as a "Symposium", a name given to the Congress's core programme, the IPPNW Headquarters had designated it as an "educational lecture", a lower level event. The difference lay in the IPPNW's wish to keep all programmes of the Congress limited to the projects of its Headquarters while the JPPNW maintained that the origins of nuclear weapons abolition movement had to be the real experiences of atomic bombing of Hiroshima and Nagasaki. There was a huge gap in the understanding of the two organisations. Actually most of the IPPNW branches apart from JPPNW were mostly members of the European Committee on Radiation Risk (ECRR), which did not consider seriously actual data collected in Hiroshima and Nagasaki. Therefore, the JPPNW's views were not adopted. The session on the effects of radiation exposure on the human body" was therefore provided as an "educational lecture".[118] The ECRR is a private organisation studying and researching radiation damage mainly of Chernobyl and Fukushima nuclear power plant accidents and therefore they seem to be more strongly opposed to

---

[117] Ibid

[118] Hiroshimaken Ishikai Sokuho No. 2156 (Report of Hiroshima Prefectural Medical Association No. 2156), 2012, p4

nuclear power plants than nuclear weapons.[119] It therefore follows that the IPPNW Headquarters and the IPPNW European Affiliates are opposed to the "peaceful use of nuclear energy" as well, and are arguing strongly for a total abolition of the use of nuclear energy including nuclear weapons and nuclear power plants.[120] The JPPNW believes that anti-nuclear weapons and anti-nuclear power plant movements should be clearly separated. It asserts, therefore, that it is an extreme argument to decommission all nuclear power plants around the world just because there was a nuclear power plant accident in Fukushima.[121] The JPPNW withheld from referring to nuclear power in the outcome document of the 20th IPPNW Hiroshima Congress.

Katsuko Kataoka, the JPPNW Secretary-General, Medical Doctor, and Professor emeritus of Hiroshima University, referred to the SGI at the end of the interview for this dissertation. She said that as Japan's first organisation that spoke up against nuclear weapons, the SGI is assiduously engaged in for example, publishing many experiences of *hibakusha* as well as anti-war books. She went on to say that since the SGI is the main supporter of the Komeito, a national political party, its elected members at the national as well as at the regional levels are all committed to the abolition of nuclear weapons, and it listens carefully to the views put forward by the JPPNW. In particular, the Komeito members of the Chugoku area, including Hiroshima prefecture, visit the JPPNW headquarters to have active and serious discussions. The SGI is

---

[119] ECRR http://www.euradcom.org/ (accessed on 7th December 2012)

[120] John Loretz, *IPPNW has been a constant voice against nuclear energy*, IPPNW Peace and Health Blog, 17th March 2011
http://peaceandhealthblog.com/2011/03/17/reject-nuclear/ (accessed on 7th December 2012) IPPNW European Affiliate, Nuclear Energy and Security http://www.ippnw-europe.org/en/nuclear-energy-and-security.html (accessed on 7th December 2012)

[121] Interview with Katsuko Kataoka 2012

also helpful in disseminating her views as well as those of anti-nuclear organisations in affiliated magazines. And she stated that the JPPNW has greatly been encouraged by Daisaku Ikeda, the SGI President in his annual message - Peace Proposal as well as by the large-scale antinuclear movement. [122] Steven Leeper, the Chairman of the Hiroshima Peace Culture Foundation and the MP Secretary-General agreed to be interviewed for the purposes of this dissertation on behalf of the MP. He stated that the IPPNW is a hero among anti-nuclear CSOs, and lost no time in saying that it is the IPPNW that represents the world's anti-nuclear CSOs. [123] It was interesting to hear from the JPPNW, which de facto manages and leads IPPNW's activities, that it is encouraged by the SGI's anti-nuclear movement.

In 2010, Kataoka was invited to the High Level Expert Group Meeting, Inter Action Council's [124] subcommittee meeting. The InterAction Council as of 2014 is composed of 42 former prime ministers and presidents from 40 countries including nuclear powers such as China and the United Kingdom and provides recommendations on global issues. It adopts an annual theme for its meetings and at the end offers recommendations to leaders.[125] Present among InterAction Council members were Co-Chairman Ingvar Carlsson [126], Jean Chrétien[127], and Yasuo Fukuda[128] as well as former heads of state and

---

[122] Ibid

[123] Interview with Steven Leeper 2012

[124] InterAction Council, About Us http://www.interactioncouncil.org/about-us (accessed on 7th December 2012)
The Council was initiated in 1983 at the initiative of Takeo Fukuda, former Prime Minister of Japan, and addresses issues of peace and security, global economic revitalization, and universal ethical standard.

[125] Hiroshimaken Ishikai Sokuho No. 2090 (Report of Hiroshima Prefectural Medical Association No. 2090), Attended Inter Action Council, 25th July 2010 p1

[126] former Prime Minister of Sweden

[127] former Prime Minister of Canada

governments from five countries[129] as well as Tadatoshi Akiba, the Mayor of Hiroshima City (MP President) 1999-2011, who attended as a special guest.[130] At its High Level Expert Group Meeting, Tilman Ruff, the Co-Chairman of the IPPNW as well as experts from research institutes of eight countries[131] including those of nuclear power states, were present. With them, Randy Rudell, the Senior Political Affairs Officer of the UN Office of High Representative for Disarmament Affairs was also present.[132] Minutes and contents of the General Assembly and the High Level Expert Group Meetings are not made public, but Kataoka has reported their details, albeit in Japanese, in the JPPNW Newsletter.[133] The High Level Expert Group Meeting adopted the Hiroshima Declaration: A plea for zero nuclear weapons. The content included the prompt implementation of NPT Article 6, effectuation of CTBT and regime building and strengthening the IAEA to perfect the control of nuclear materials without any new recommendation.[134] Kataoka was shocked that there were people in favour of nuclear deterrence among those present at the High Level Expert Group Meeting. Also as a physician from Hiroshima she was not satisfied that no mention was made of the atomic bombing of Hiroshima or Nagasaki, but otherwise she found the recommendations

---

[128] former Prime Minister of Japan, and a son of Takeo Fukuda, Honorary Chairman of the InterAction Council and former Prime Minister of Japan 1976-1978

[129] Malaysia, Singapore, Republic of Korea, Jordan, and Hong Kong

[130] InterAction Council, *2010 List of Participants* http://interactioncouncil.org/2010-0 (accessed on 7th December 2012)

[131] Sweden, the US, the UK, Ireland, Japan, Australia, China, and Germany

[132] Ibid

[133] Hiroshimaken Ishikai Sokuho No. 2090 (Report of Hiroshima Prefectural Medical Association No. 2090), Attended Inter Action Council, 25th July 2010

[134] InterAction Council, *The Hiroshima Declaration: A plea for zero nuclear weapons*, publications, 19th April 2010 http://interactioncouncil.org/hiroshima-declaration-plea-zero-nuclear-weapons-0 (accessed on 7th December 2012)

appropriate.[135] At the Annual General Meeting, Yasuo Fukuda referred to the US Nuclear Umbrella saying it was important for Japan's security during the Cold War but its role is over. He has not made any statement to that effect during his term of office, nor did he promote concrete anti-nuclear policy. He is not offering any suggestion on the government's policy on nuclear weapons today. It appears that members of the InterAction Council have relaxed attitudes, having retired from their active services. The InterAction Council is not an action-oriented organisation in the fields of diplomacy or international affairs. It brings together former leaders of governments who share their experiences, exchange opinions, and release appeals. By contrast, the Elders[136] is an active organisation to which former government leaders including Jimmy Carter, Kofi Annan and the late Nelson Mandela are associated (see Chapter 5). The few recommendations the InterAction Council made were the Anti-Ballistic Missile Treaty (ABM) and the holding of the US-USSR summit meeting associated with the NPT. No action, however, was taken.[137]

(ii) Mayors for Peace (MP)

The Mayors for Peace (MP) originated in 1982 when Takeshi Araki, the Mayor of Hiroshima City (1975-1991) called for "Solidarity among cities of the world to abolish nuclear weapons" at the Second UN

---

[135] Hiroshimaken Ishikai Sokuho No. 2090 (Report of Hiroshima Prefectural Medical Association No. 2090), Attended Inter Action Council, 25th July 2010 p2

[136] The Elders: Independent Global Leaders Working Together for Peace and Human Rights http://theelders.org/ (accessed on 3rd May 2012)

[137] IAC, *Accomplishments: The Cold War Era* http://interactioncouncil.org/accomplishments (accessed on 7th December 2012)

Special Session on Disarmament held at the UN Headquarters in New York, and letters were sent from Hiroshima and Nagasaki Cities to all mayors of the world soliciting their support. The objective of the Plan is as it was when he called the mayors of the world to join forces in solidarity to pave the way for nuclear weapons abolition, "A Plan Promoting Solidarity among Cities to abolish nuclear arms" with a letter sent from Hiroshima and Nagasaki Cities to all the mayors of the world to support the initiative. The plan aims at contributing to permanent peace in the world by raising the awareness of citizens at the international level based on the experiences of Hiroshima and Nagasaki cities that have been on the receiving end of the A-bombs.

Forms of collaboration were left to each city. Collaborative cities, however, will do their best to enlarge the network by calling on other cities, work with the United Nations and begin their work on the day the document of agreement reaches the MP Office, and that Hiroshima City will serve as the window for liaison and adjustment. The cities will conduct events to contribute each in its own way to disarmament, to send messages on the abolition of nuclear weapons and all out disarmament to the UN Secretary-General and the Chairman of the UN General Assembly during the UN Week on Disarmament. The collaborative cities will exchange and share materials on peace, disarmament and security and organize a Photographic Exhibition to help citizens get to know the realities of A-bombs dropped on Hiroshima and Nagasaki.[138]

In 1985 the first Mayors' Peace General Conference was held with 67 cities from 22 countries and 33 cities from Japan and, in the following year in order to ensure that the permanency of the Conference,

---

[138] Dai 3 Kai Heiwa Shicho Kaigi Sokai Hokokusho (Report of Mayors for Peace General Conference), 1993

its secretariat was established in Hiroshima City. That is to say MP was established as an anti-nuclear CSO de factor managed by Hiroshima City. Therefore unlike other CSOs its members are not individuals but local governments in Japan and the world who support its purpose. The MP is an NGO in Advisory Status of the UN Department of Public Information (1990) and NGO in Advisory Status (Category 11) of the UN Economic and Social Council (1991).The MP has its secretariat within the Hiroshima Peace Culture Foundation (HPCF). The HPCF was established in 1967 as a bureau of Hiroshima City, and earned its status as General Foundation in 1970 and a Public Interest Foundation in 2011. The HPCF is in charge of managing the International Conference Center Hiroshima,[139] and the Hiroshima Peace Memorial Museum and the Hiroshima National Peace Memorial for the Atomic Bomb Victims located at the centre of the City's Atomic Bomb Dome that organizes exhibitions of A-bomb materials as well as collects and displays records of A-bomb victims, their names and photographs as well as organizes readings of stories of *hibakusha.*[140] Their purposes are to ensure that Hiroshima A-bomb experiences will be passed on and to collaborate with peace research institutes and related organisations from the perspective of humankind to disseminate peace ideology and promote mutual understanding and cooperation to advance world peace. That is to say, the MP and the HPCF represent the anti-nuclear departments of Hiroshima City government and are entrusted with the management of the anti-nuclear facilities constructed by the City of Hiroshima. Hiroshima Mayors serve ex officio as the President of MP

---

[139] International Conference Center Hiroshima http://www.pcf.city.hiroshima.jp/icch/english.html (20th November 2013)

[140] HPCF, About HPCF http://www.pcf.city.hiroshima.jp/hpcf/english/about/index.html (accessed on 20th November 2013)

as well as the Chairman of the Board of Directors while the HPCF serves as the MP Secretary-General.[141]

The MP today is a global anti-nuclear CSO with its membership of 5,895 cities in 158 countries (as of 1st February 2014) of which 1, 399 are from Japan. Member cities among the P5 are, 197 from the United States, 67 from Russia, 77 from the United Kingdom (including major cities such as London, Cambridge, Oxford and Glasgow, 146 from France and 7 from China (the Capitol Beijing, and major cities of Chengdu, Chongqing, Dalian and Wuhan). The seven cities of China joined the MP during the Cold War but no new entries since then. As for nuclear power states that are outside the NPT, India 17 cities including Delhi, and Pakistan 13. No city of North Korea is a member. The number of cities that join the MP is increasing every year.[142] The CSO activities on nuclear disarmament and nuclear weapons abolition inspire the hearts (emotions) of international public opinion by *hibakusha* sharing their own experiences of the atomic bombings, as opposed to merely treating them as security issues, and have reached out to local governments around the world forming a uniquely large global network. This can surely be said to be a landmark event.

Members of the MP, unlike other anti-nuclear CSOs, are local governments headed by the mayor and composed of elected representatives of the city assemblies. As such they have an advantage over other CSOs as their statements carry political legitimacy.[143]

In 2003, the MP announced the 2020 Vision Campaign stating the

---

[141] Mayors for Peace, *Heiwa Shuchokaigi Kiyaku (MR's Covenant)* http://www.mayorsforpeace.org/jp/outlines/agreement.html (accessed on 20th November 2013)

[142] Mayors for Peace, *Map Showing Member Cities* http://www.mayorsforpeace.org/english/membercity/map.html (accessed on 20th November 2013)

[143] Interview with Steven Leeper 2012

deadline by which to achieve abolition of nuclear weapons. It followed up in 2008 by making public the Hiroshima-Nagasaki Protocol charting its roadmap, and conducted a signature-collecting campaign in Japan. It set a target for the NPT Review Conference in 2010 to officially adopt the 2020 Vision Campaign. The UN Secretary-General Ban Ki-moon expressed his high expectation of the Vision.[144] The Protocol has for its pillars the rapid adoption by the P5 of Article 6 of the Protocol and the implementation of their obligation to conduct nuclear disarmament negotiation.[145] The process will involve immediate cessation of acquisition by the nuclear powers of nuclear weapons and their use. It also aimed at them starting sincere negotiations towards agreeing to a framework for nuclear weapons abolition, and to achieve by 2015 the effectuation of the NWC and to aim by 2020 to globally dismantle all nuclear weapons under strict international control.[146] In 2006, Ieper City of Belgium as a trustee city, (mayors of all trustee cities are automatically named as the MP Vice-Presidents) offered to establish an International Secretariat for the 2020 Vision Campaign, which in 2007 evolved as the 2020 Vision Campaign Association in charge of collecting and managing donations as well as planning and implementing various campaigns towards nuclear abolition.[147] As a

---

[144] United Nations, The Secretary-General, *Message to the General Conference of Mayors for Peace, Hiroshima 3rd August 2013* http://www.mayorsforpeace.org/jp/activites/meeting/8th/statements/UN_Secretary_General_en.pdf (accessed on 20th November 2013)

[145] Mayors for Peace, Protocol complementary to the Treaty on the Non-Proliferation of Nuclear Weapons for achieving a nuclear-weapon-free world by the year 2020 http://www.mayorsforpeace.org/jp/activites/others/100625_hn_giteisho/h_n_protocol.pdf (accessed on 20th November 2013)

[146] Mayors for Peace, *Hiroshima Nagasaki Protocol* http://www.2020visioncampaign.org/en/about-us/history/hiroshima-nagasaki-protocol.html (accessed on 20th November 2013)

[147] Mayors for Peace, 2020 Vision Campaign

result 1,642 cities signed in of which 1,166 were from Japan. Among the P5 the United States, Great Britain and France signed. German cities as well as many European cities signed up from the anti-nuclear group but none of the Russian and Chinese cities.[148] All signatures were presented to the Chairman of the NPT Review Conference but the Conference did not adopt it.[149] The 2020 Vision, however, was adopted as a resolution by local governments around the world including the European Parliament (EP),[150] the United States Conference of Mayors (USCM),[151] the Council of European Municipalities and Regions (CEMR),[152] the US National Conference of Black Mayors (USNCBM),[153] the United Cities and Local Governments (UCLG),[154] the Japan Association of City Mayors (JACM),[155] as well as the National Council of Japan Nuclear Free Local Authorities (NCJNFLA),[156] an international organisation.[157] However the IPPNW adopted the resolution in 2004. Its signature was a certainty since

---

http://www.mayorsforpeace.org/jp/ecbn/index.html (20th November 2013)

[148] Mayors for Peace, Hiroshima Nagasaki Giteisho Sando Shomei ZichitaiIchiran (Kaigai) (List of Foreign Cities signed to support the Hiroshima Nagasaki Protocol) http://www.mayorsforpeace.org/jp/activites/others/100625_hn_giteisho/cities_appeal.pdf (accessed on 20th November 2013)

[149] Mayors for Peace, *Hiroshima Nagasaki Giteisho (Hiroshima Nagasaki Protocol)* http://www.mayorsforpeace.org/jp/activites/others/100625_hn_giteisho/index.html (accessed on 20th November 2013)

[150] "2004", Mayors for Peace, 2020 Vision Kakuheiki Haizetsu No Tameno Kinkyukodo (Urgently Taking Action for 2020 Vision Campaign)

[151] "2004, 2006, 2007, 2008, 2009, 2010, 2011, 2012", Ibid

[152] "2006", Ibid

[153] "In 2005", Ibid

[154] "In 2007, 2010", Ibid

[155] "In 2005, 2007, 2010", Ibid

[156] "In 2004, 2007", Ibid

[157] Mayors for Peace, *2020 Vision Kakuheiki Haizetsu No Tameno Kinkyukodo (Urgently Taking Action for 2020 Vision Campaign)* http://www.mayorsforpeace.org/jp/ecbn/index.html (accessed on 20th November 2013)

IPPNW is a drafter of the NWC. The 2020 Vision Campaign continues as the MP's final objective following the 2010 NPT Review Conference. The 8th MP General Conference held in Hiroshima in 2013 formulated NWC and adopted the Hiroshima Appeal, a new Action Guideline towards the total abolition of nuclear weapons by 2020. The Appeal, in addition to its commitment to further disseminate the realities of the atomic bombings, decided that it was essential for the realization of the world without nuclear arms, to create a new community free from mutual distrust and fear of threat based on the recognition that we are all members of humankind. It pointed out that concrete policies and frameworks to promote international and regional peace and security as well as measures towards building confidence must be created in the Middle East, Northeast Asia and South Asia, where nuclear tension is rising. It declared that no time should be wasted to enlist all nations in order to strengthen initiatives in opening negotiations towards nuclear abolition, the main objective of the 2020 Vision Campaign.[158] It was further pointed out, in order to enlighten the minds of the next generation worldwide regarding the horrible realities of the Hiroshima and Nagasaki atomic bombings, efforts must be made to strengthen relationships with the United Nations, elected representatives of the people, associations of local governments, the International Committee of the Red Cross, international peace organisations as well as celebrities and organisations engaged in the fields of peace, human rights, environmental protection, culture, arts and sports.[159] The Conference resolved that such collaborative activities would be the motive power to

---

[158] Mayors for Peace, *Hiroshima Appeal,* 2013 http://www.mayorsforpeace.org/jp/activites/meeting/8th/20130805_hiroshima_appeal.pdf (accessed on 20th November 2013)
[159] Ibid

enlist international public opinion towards peace.[160] The Appeal received support from Angela Kane of the UN High Representative for Disarmament Affairs and the eight heads of state of the non-nuclear powers.[161] While the 2020 Vision Campaign listed "Disarmament and Non-Proliferation Policy of Japan", MOFA White Paper as a case of CSO activity, there is no collaboration between the Japanese government and the MP towards nuclear disarmament. Steven Leeper, the MP Secretary-General stated that the opinions of the Japanese Government and Hiroshima City are not in line regarding nuclear disarmament and non-proliferation.[162]

The MP has yet to clearly formulate practical measures or methods for realizing peace and security in the Middle East, Northeast Asia and South Asia nor ways toward building confidence. It is considered, however, that the diplomacy carried out by the MP local government members around the world will provide the foundation of this activity. Steven Leeper stated in regard to the situation of Northeast Asia, that the Japanese government should drop all conventionally given arguments concerning its territorial issues with Russia and China and to abandon all its rights to the Northern Islands and the Senkaku Islands.[163] He pointed out that it was important for the Japanese Government to show its readiness not to fight but to keep peace with all states for the realization of peace.[164] His statement is based on idealism and is in contrast to the thinking of the Japanese government (See Chapters 5 and

---

160 Ibid

161 Mayors for Peace, *Responses from the UN and national governments to the Hiroshima Appeal adopted at the 8th General Conference* http://www.mayorsforpeace.org/english/activities/meeting/8th/res_to_appeal/index.html (accessed on 20th November 2013)

162 Interview with Steven Leeper 2012

163 Ibid

164 Ibid

6). Furthermore, the Northeast Asian region has the least number of cities that are members of the MP. It is assumed that it is extremely difficult to enlarge the network even at the level of local governments due to deep rooted antagonism. On the other hand, the MP is aggressively conducting diplomacy with the nuclear states at their local government levels. The representative case is the strong collaboration with the USCM towards nuclear abolition. The USCM is a non-partisan organisation that has an affiliation of 1,399 cities each with a population in excess of 30,000. It is strengthening connections with cities by listening carefully to the needs of the cities and taking them to concerned departments of the US administration to encourage them to adopt policies to answer local needs.[165] Apparently, its sub-committee, the Standing Committee of International Affairs [SCIA] discusses international issues important to the MP member cities and constantly has close deliberations with the US Department of State and the Office of the US Trade Representative.[166] Tadayoshi Akiba, the Mayor of Hiroshima City (MP President) 1999-2011, was present at the 77th UCSM General Assembly in 2009. The MP had requested cooperation from the SCIA in advance regarding the resolution to abolish nuclear weapons by 2020.[167] As a result, the USCM adopted the resolution that it will support the MP activities, and in particular to encourage President Obama to announce the start of multilateral negotiation for nuclear abolition by 2020 at the 2010 NPT Review Conference. Also in

---

[165] The United States Conference of Mayors, *About USCM* http://www.usmayors.org/about/overview.asp (accessed on November 2013)

[166] The United States Conference of Mayors, *Legislation and Programs, International* http://usmayors.org/international/ (accessed on November 2013)

[167] Mayors for Peace, *USCM Dai 77 Kai Nenzi Sokai Heno Shusseki 2009 Nen 6 Gatsu (Attended the 77th USCM Annual Conference, June 2009)* http://www.mayorsforpeace.org/jp/gallery/2009_uscm.html (accessed on 20th November 2013)

response to Akiba's request, ten mayors signed the affiliation to the MP on the spot.[168] The 79th UCSM General Conference in 2011 adopted the resolution to request President Obama to act with leaders of other nuclear states to press for nuclear abolition by 2020, as well as request the US Congress to reduce expenditure on nuclear weapons development and to transfer the resources released to projects demanded by local governments. The USCM claimed that the Fiscal Year 2012 requesting the maximum level of budget for maintenance and improvement of nuclear warheads should be corrected at once in the face of the double digit unemployment suffered by more than 100 cities due to the worsening of the US economy resulting in mayors and local governments being forced to reduce important public services.[169] The 80th UCSM General Conference in 2012 also adopted a similar resolution,[170] and the 81st UCSM General Conference adopted the same demand as well as voiced deep regret about the lack of presence of the five UN Permanent Security Council members including the United States at the Conference: Humanitarian Impact of Nuclear Weapons (Oslo Conference) hosted by the Norwegian Government to which 127 countries were represented by their government delegates.[171]

---

[168] Ibid

[169] Mayors for Peace, Full text of a resolution in support of Mayors for Peace, Adopted at the 79th US Conference of Mayors annual meeting, Baltimore, MD, June 20 2011 http://www.mayorsforpeace.org/english/topic/2011/110712_us_conference_of_mayors/index.html (accessed on 20th November 2013)

[170] Mayors for Peace, Full text of a resolution in support of Mayors for Peace, Adopted at the 80th US Conference of Mayors annual meeting, Orlando, Florida, June 16 2012 http://www.mayorsforpeace.org/english/topic/2012/201206_us_conference_of_mayors/index.html (accessed on 21st November 2013)

[171] Mayors for Peace, Full text of a resolution in support of Mayors for Peace, Adopted at the 81st US Conference of Mayors annual meeting, Las Vegas, Nevada, June 24 2013 http://www.mayorsforpeace.org/english/topic/2013/20130624_us_conference_

While the UCSM efforts have not yet changed policies of the Obama Administration, these collaborations with local governments of the nuclear powers can be said to be unique political diplomacy carried out by the MP against the background of deadlocked negotiations between governments on nuclear weapons; and the resolutions adopted by local governments of the nuclear states are contributing to establishing stronger anti-nuclear public opinion. However, the reality on the ground is that resolutions at the local government levels do not have direct authority in determining the manufacture, dissemination and arms expansion that are issues of national security. Also, unlike other anti-nuclear CSOs, there are disadvantages that are due only to local governments. For example, Kazumi Matsui, the Mayor of Hiroshima City (2011 to present 2014) and the MP President declared on the A-bomb Day Peace Memorial Ceremony on 6th August 2013 (organized by Hiroshima City) that A-bomb and nuclear power generation were two different things. Matsui had discomfort in equating two entirely different matters, the atomic bomb aimed at killing people and the nuclear power plant for supplying energy. He did not see the point of discrediting the latter for its recent radioactive damage, just because there was not much progress seen in the anti-nuclear weapons movement. Matsui himself is not promoting the use of nuclear energy but he is seeking for the establishment of safer standards for the use of nuclear energy. However, he questions the wisdom of discontinuing its use, considering the need to ensure energy for national economy and the livelihood of the people, as well as the implications it will have on energy prices and the future energy balance including renewables. Matsui did not refer to the issues of nuclear power plants in his Peace Declaration as the Mayor of Hiroshima City both at the Atomic Day

---

of_mayors/index.html (accessed on 21st November 2013)

Peace Memorial Service on 6th August 2011 immediately following the triple disaster and in his speech the following year. Matsui took a different stance and opinion from those of Tadatoshi Akiba, who sees them in close line of thought when he said, "After the Fukushima nuclear power plant explosion many Hiroshima citizens felt that it was similar to the time when the atomic bomb was dropped on Hiroshima".[172] This conflict of views between the two mayors suggests that the policy of MP and its leader, Mayor of Hiroshima is likely to change with every election. That is to say, while they both share the main anti-nuclear objective, there can be a gap in their approaches. The same can be said of the member cities of the MP. Osaka City, the second biggest city by population (2,666,047 as of 2010)[173] in Japan joined the MP in 2009 when a liberal mayor Kunio Hiramatsu managed the city but Toru Hashimoto who replaced him in 2011 serves as a joint representative of the Japan Restoration Party, the third largest national party that supports de facto nuclear armament of Japan (as of June 2014) (see Chapter 2). Hashimoto said that "he did not know" that Osaka City was a member of the MP and said that the MP could do better in its approach to the nuclear states.[174] He added that "there was nothing wrong in an administrative branch being involved in the MP and its movement, and that he had no intention of denying Osaka city's

[172] Kamakura Kyujo No Kai (Association For Protecting Article 9 of Japanese Constitution in Kamakura City), Tadatoshi Akiba's Lecture "To Become World Without Nuclear Energy and Weapons After Great East Japan Earthquake [11th March 2011]", November 2011
http://kamakura9-jo.net/cn17/pg151.html(accessed on 21st November 2013)

[173] Osaka City Official Website, *All Population Data is from November 2010 (in Japanese)*,
http://www.city.osaka.lg.jp/toshikeikaku/cmsfiles/contents/0000014/14987/H22-11-H23-9suikei.pdf (accessed on 24th November 2013)

[174] Chugoku Newspaper, Heiwa Shicho Kaigi Kamei "Shiranai" Hashimoto Osaka Shicho (Hashimoto, Mayor of Osaka City said he does not know the City is a member of MP) 16th November 2011

involvement." However, he did go on to say, "If the objective is to abolish nuclear weapons one has to get some statements from the United States, China and Russia".[175] His statement could be presumed to mean that the only successful way for nuclear disarmament is to work on the nuclear weapons states. However, while Hashimoto basically said in 2013 that Japan must retain its national policy of the Three Antinuclear Principles, however he also stated that he would try to get the understanding of the Japanese people in the event that nuclear arms have to be brought into Japan, leaving the space for a possible review of that particular clause.[176] In that regard he explained that "it was just not possible for the US Navy's Seventh Fleet making a port call on Japan not to be in possession of nuclear weapons" and said that "as long as we are protected by the US nuclear umbrella it should be accepted.[177] In this case there was a need for it to be brought in, I will ask the people to accept it." As for the abolition of nuclear weapons, he said, "It was an ideal that can only be realized when all nations decide to abolish them" and emphasized, "That, however, was unrealistic and Japan needs to be under the US nuclear umbrella".[178] His words were problematic coming from the mayor of the city, a member of the MP. It was also a grave statement made by a representative of a national political party against the conventional policy of the Japanese government.

In this way, it is difficult to judge whether or not the member cities will sustain and share with other members the enthusiasm it had at the

---

175 Ibid

176 Chugoku Newspaper, Hikakusangensoku "Minaoshimo" Hashimotoshi "Mocikomasezu" De Genkyu (Mr. Hashimoto referred to amend the Three Antinuclear Principles) http://www.hiroshimapeacemedia.jp/mediacenter/article.php?story=20121112103358265_ja (accessed on 24th November 2013)

177 Ibid

178 Ibid

time of becoming a member due to the possibilities of newly elected mayors not necessarily sharing the same convictions. The other difficulty lies in the fact that since security policies including that of nuclear weapons are proprietary privileges of the state governments it is unknown how much member cities can influence their own government, let alone the P5 and other nuclear powers. At the Eighth MP General Conference held in Hiroshima City in 2013, it was reported that the affiliated number of cities had doubled from 2,963 cities in four years since the Seventh MP Conference. On the other hand, it was made clear that the number of active member cities including those serving as members of the board, was limited. It was therefore decided to study the possibilities of strengthening the management by creating effective networks[179] and four concrete measures were adopted. One of these was to aim at soliciting capital cities to be members since they bear enormous influence on national policies.[180] Another was to create regional groups to encourage proactive and spontaneous MP activities based on the regional features which could be carried out proactively and to make their leading members report directly to the MP Secretariat in Hiroshima City.[181] Furthermore, a decision was made to start fundraising. One suggestion was to collect 2,000 yen each year as an annual membership fee. Up to the present, activities of the MP member cities were left to the discretion of each city and the cost of activities had been borne by the member city involved. This new decision reflected the need for the member cities as a whole to support the cost

---

[179] Mayors for Peace, *Agenda item 3, Measures for strengthening Mayors for Peace's management system*, 2013 http://www.mayorsforpeace.org/english/activities/meeting/8th/Agenda3_Measures_for_strengthening_Mayors_for_Peaces_management_system.pdf (accessed on 24th November 2013)

[180] Ibid

[181] Ibid

of maintaining the MP organisation and its activities.[182] It is likely to represent the MP intention to ensure coherence of its activities.

Steven Leeper points out that the time has come for CSOs to act as a CSO alliance and not act alone. He further went on to state that since the pioneer of anti-nuclear CSO alliance, Abolition 2000 has too many differences of opinion and confrontation to be able to put together discussion and action policy, the International Campaign to Abolish Nuclear Weapons (ICAN) started at the IPPNW initiative stands as a success case.[183] The ICAN is a global campaign organisation started in 2007 under IPPNW leadership. And its Representative is Tilman Ruff, Co-Chairman of the IPPNW, Medical Doctor, and a member of the IPPNW Chapter in Australia. Its membership represents organisations in 80 countries relating to humanitarian issues, the environment, human rights, peace and development.[184] The policies of ICAN actions has been to work on national governments to begin and support negotiations on the NWC, and in order to convince and pressure them into doing so, it upholds the conviction that any form of the use of nuclear arms causes humanitarian and environmental harm, and that the prohibition of the use of nuclear weapons is as much a universal and humanitarian responsibility of the non-nuclear states.[185]The ICAN membership is divided into two groups, the CSO group working with collaborative CSO members in respective countries and the International Partners working on global anti-nuclear movement with the ICAN. International Partners include 22 organisations including The Abolition 2000, the MR,

---

182 Ibid

183 Interview with Steven Leeper 2012

184 ICAN, *Campaign overview* http://www.icanw.org/campaign/campaign-overview/ (accessed on 26th November 2013)

185 Ibid

the IPPNW and the SGI (as of 2014).[186] The ICAN has four partners in Japan including the JPPNW.[187] Its activities are mainly to enlighten people about the inhumanity and dangers of nuclear weapons. It shares with as many people possible the real stories of Hiroshima and Nagasaki *hibakusha*[188] as well as running the campaign "Don't Bank on the Bomb" campaign[189] addressed to financial institutions in nuclear power countries and others.[190]

The MP is yet to influence nuclear disarmament negotiations directly at the international level. There is, however, a need to continue to focus on how the large anti-nuclear network at the local level will further expand its political legitimacy in as many as 157 countries.

(iii) Japan Association of Lawyers Against Nuclear Arms (JALANA)

Established in 1992, an affiliate of the IALANA, the JALANA takes a legal approach to its nuclear abolition activities and seeks to establish the inhumanity and illegality of nuclear weapons based on the ICJ Advisory Opinion 1996, the NWC, and the CTBT.[191] It criticizes the

---

186 ICAN, *Partner Organisations* http://www.icanw.org/campaign/partner-organizations/ (accessed on 26th November 2013)

187 Ibid

188 ICAN, *hear the stories* http://www.icanw.org/category/hear-the-stories/ (accessed on 26th November 2013)

189 ICAN, *Don't Bank on the Bomb* http://www.dontbankonthebomb.com/ (accessed on 26th November 2013)

190 ICAN, *Parliamentary Appeal* http://www.icanw.org/projects/appeal/ (accessed on 26th November 2013)

191 Kenichi Okubo (JALANA Secretary-General, Advocate of Japan), *Kakuheiki No Ihousei No Kakuritsu No Tameni! (To Establish Illegality of Nuclear Weapons!)*, JALANA Official Website, 2007 http://www.hankaku-j.org/infomation/data/080923_02.html (accessed on 27th November 2013)

United States and other nuclear powers as representative cases for ruling with power. It also criticizes the negativity of the Japanese government towards nuclear abolition. It is extremely critical of political views and executive decision-making done in a highly political manner which ignores the rule of law. It seeks a clear legal framework leading towards nuclear abolition based on international and national laws and not by states or by political negotiation.

Its main activities consist of the presentation of legal opinion and criticizing/commenting on international and Japanese government policies, participating in informal meetings organized by the JALANA, international CSO meetings as well as sending out messages via the Internet. The JALANA is an affiliate of the IALANA but it is not established by IALANA. Its origin is a network of lawyers who provided legal remedy and support to the *hibakusha* of the atomic bombing of Hiroshima and Nagasaki. Their activities were organized and developed as the JALANA and became an affiliate of the IALANA. Japanese lawyers compose the membership of the JALANA basically but the membership has expanded to include some persons of law and scholars who are in agreement with its principles. Its membership is approximately 400 (as of 2014). The membership is the largest among the IALANA affiliates and its activities are the most energetic.[192] In comparison, the membership of the IALANA headquarters is in two digits.[193] Established in 1988 in Stockholm the IALANA developed as an international CSO with an Advisory Status with the United Nations.[194] The purposes of its activities are the abolition of nuclear arms, strengthening of international law and building of its efficient

---

[192] Interview with Kenichi Okubo, 2013

[193] Ibid

[194] IALANA Official Website, *About us*, http://en.ialana.de/about-us/ (accessed on 27th November 2013)

mechanism and legal resolution of international conflicts.[195] Its contribution to anti-nuclear activities was the drafting of the NWC. The IALANA is headquartered in Berlin, Germany and has the following affiliates: the European Office (Berlin), the Pacific Office (Wellington, New Zealand), the UN Office (New York), the South Asia Office (Colombo, Sri Lanka) and it has affiliates in 12 countries including the United States, Russia, India, and Japan.[196] The IALANA's war chest consists of membership fees of its affiliates but recently it have had few resources. The reason is that fees are paid only by the three affiliates of Germany, the United States and Japan while others are in arrears.[197] This is the reason for the JALANA to stand out among the IALANA affiliates.

The JALANA constantly sends reports of its activities to the IALANA and a Director of the JALANA serves also as a Director of the IALANA. The JALANA is present at every IALANA General Conference including the one held in Szczecin, Poland in 2011 and continues to participate in discussions with them.[198] While the IALANA concentrates its activities on nuclear arms abolition, the JALANA's activities include supporting *hibakusha*, one of which is to win for them their legal recognition as victims of atomic-bomb disease.

Judicial action concerning legal recognition of the A-bomb disease originated in 2003 when 306 complainants filed an action against the Government of Japan in 17 district courts seeking legal recognition of

---

[195] Ibid

[196] IALANA Official Website, About us, *'United States, Canada, Germany, the Netherlands, New Zealand, India '* http://en.ialana.de/about-us/ (accessed on 27th November 2013)

[197] Hankaku Horitsuka (bulletin of JALANA) No 76, Kokusai Hankaku Horitsuka Kyokai (IALANA) Rizikai Giziroku, Raina Buraun (Record of IALANA Board of Directors by Reiner Braun), p39 2013

[198] Interview with Kenichi Okubo 2013

the disease. As of 2009 the government lost 18 cases and 197 defendants were recognized as sufferers of A-bomb disease and won eligibility requirements to receive special medical allowances paid to the patients. However, there were over 7,000 cases still pending review in 2009.[199] The JALANA member lawyers who serve as agents of the complainants have made this their lifework.

The A-bomb disease refers to the disease caused by exposure to radioactivity of the A-bomb and in a condition requiring medical treatment.[200] The Ministry of Health, Labour and Welfare [MHLW] Japan recognizes as A-bomb survivors those who were within certain areas at the time of the exposure, those who entered Hiroshima and Nagasaki Cities within 2 weeks following the atomic bombing, as well as their foetuses, by issuing them A-bomb survivor medical notebooks. They number 202,000 (as of 2013). Among those the Minister of the MHLW will recognize whose chronic diseases are caused by atomic bombing and are clearly recognized in need of medical treatment as A-bomb patients. The number of persons recognized as atomic bomb patients remains at 8,552 as of 2013.[201] Patients recognized as suffering from the atomic bomb disease will receive 140,000 yen per month as special medical allowances (as of 2014).[202] The JALANA questions the correctness of the reference value given that less than 1 per cent of the 200,000 persons who experienced atomic bombing have been

---

199 Asahi Newspaper, 1st August 2009 (evening edition), p2

200 Kenichi Okubo, *Genbaku Nintei Saiban Ni Tsuite (About Trials to Certify Radiation Sickness)*, JALANA Official Website http://www.hankaku-j.org/data/jalana/002.html (accessed on 27th November 2013)

201 Ministry of Health, Labour and Welfare Japan, *Genbaku-sho Nintei (About Certifying Radiation Sickness*, http://www.mhlw.go.jp/bunya/kenkou/genbaku09/08.html (accessed on 27th November 2013)

202 Ibid

recognized as atomic bomb disease patients. The JALANA claims that many more people are suffering from cancer, leukaemia and are suffering from malfunctioning of their vital organs but the Japanese government continues to uphold its conclusion that those within a radius of two kilo metres from the epicentre would directly suffer from radioactivity and that others will have not received direct damage.[203] Even as of 2013 there were judicial cases concerning atomic bomb disease certification being fought at district courts in seven cities including Tokyo. The Japanese government's point of view regarding each disease of the defendants is that their compensation claim cannot be accepted, having checked the records of how and where they lived as well as the fact that their exposure to the environment and atomic bombing do not sustain their claim that their chronic diseases have been caused by the A-bomb.[204] The JALANA believes that the reason for the Japanese government's attitude in not actively recognizing A-bomb disease is due to its dependence on nuclear weapons.[205]

The JALANA's nuclear abolition activities focus on legislating the Three Non-Nuclear Principles in Japan (see Chapter 2), the establishment of NANWFZT in Northeast Asia and establishing the NWC worldwide.[206] Also the Japan Federation of Bar Associations (JFBA), to which all Japanese lawyers belong, thanks to the efforts of the JALANA, adopted a Declaration of a Call to Action Toward

---

203 Ibid

204 The Ministry of Justice Japan, *Genbaku-sho Nintei Sosho (Trials to Certify Radiation Sickness)*, http://www.moj.go.jp/shoumu/shoumukouhou/shoumu01_00027.html (accessed on 27th November 2013)

205 Kenichi Okubo, *Genbaku Nintei Saiban Ni Tsuite (About Trials to Certify Radiation Sickness)*, JALANA Official Website http://www.hankaku-j.org/data/jalana/002.html (accessed on 28th November 2013)

206 Interview with Kenichi Okubo, 2013

Achieving a World Without Nuclear Weapons at its 53rd Human Rights Protection Convention[207] and established in its Committee on the Constitution, the Project Team for Abolition of Nuclear Weapons.[208] Kenichi Okubo, the JALANA Secretary General serves concurrently as the Vice-Chairman of the Committee on the Constitution and the Chairman of the Project team for Abolition of Nuclear Weapons (as of 2014).

While the IALANA is not trying to enact law on the Three Non-Nuclear Principles, it is interested in and welcomes the JALANA's anti-nuclear activities.[209] The Three Non-Nuclear Principles is a national policy adopted by the Diet (parliament) of Japan (see Chapter 2); it remains to be enacted into law and as such lacks legal binding force. Collaborating with the Project Team for Abolition of Nuclear Weapons, the JFBA Committee on the Constitution, is drafting a model bill "Law prohibiting the manufacture, possession and carrying into Japan of nuclear weapons"[210] in its own right.[211] This was reflected in the 2010 official position of the JABA. It is noted that the JABA believes that legislation of the Three Non-nuclear Principles would have the power to prevent the Principles losing their substance and therefore becomeing a dead letter. It wants to prohibit Japan from manufacturing nuclear weapons and possessing them and support whatever needs to be done to prevent other countries from bringing them into the country. The JABA is contemplating the best ways and means to prohibit the

---

[207] JFBA, *Declaration of a Call to Action Toward Achieving a World Without Nuclear Weapons*, 2010 http://www.nichibenren.or.jp/en/document/statements/year/2010/20101008_4.html (accessed 28th November 2013)

[208] Hankaku Horitsuka (bulletin of JALANA) No74, p19, Spring 2013

[209] Interview with Kenichi Okubo, 2013

[210] Hankaku Horitsuka No74, p16-p18, Spring 2013

[211] Hankaku Horitsuka No77, p16-p18, Autumn 2013

passage of vessels and airplanes carrying nuclear weapons into Japan's territorial waters and air, and the kinds of measures required of governments at both national and local levels as well as business operators to ensure strict implementation of the law.[212] Realistic measures should be taken, for example to oblige the national government to demand from foreign vessels submission of non-nuclear certificates.[213] Also, regulating and controlling nuclear materials such as plutonium that can be used in nuclear weapons is challenging but must be done.[214] The JFBA contends that sufficient deliberation and study are needed in exiting from the security policy that depends on nuclear weapons of other country.[215] The JALANA believes that it was the conscious intention of the government to leave the Three Non-nuclear Principles without legal binding force and not legislate it so as to have a freehand in continuing to depend on the US nuclear umbrella as well as on the peaceful use of Nuclear energy. Therefore, the legislation of the Three Non-nuclear Principles will be a meaningful gesture by the government of Japan to demonstrate its will to quit its dependence on the US nuclear deterrence.[216] At the JALANA General Meeting on 10th November 2012, a review as well as proactive discussion took place on the proposed bill in the presence of a lawyer in charge of legislating the Three Antinuclear Principles from the Project Team for the Abolition of Nuclear Weapons. However, at the end of the meeting Okubo, the JALANA's Secretary-General, pointed out even if

---

[212] JFBA, *Declaration of a Call to Action Toward Achieving a World Without Nuclear Weapons*, 2010 http://www.nichibenren.or.jp/en/document/statements/year/2010/20101008_4.html (accessed on 28th November 2013)

[213] Ibid

[214] Ibid

[215] Ibid

[216] Hankaku Horitsuka No 77, pp12-pp13, Autumn 2013

the bill was adopted by the Project Team for Abolition of Nuclear Weapons it will be dismissed on presentation at the Committee on the Constitution of the JFBA.[217] This is due to the fact that the JFBA is an organisation with compulsory participation; therefore, it is extremely difficult to reach any consensus.[218] JFBA members come in different shades, some are also members of the JALANA and are interested in constitutional and human rights issues but there are others who are for nuclear deterrence and those who have no interest in nuclear issues. It was de facto impossible to issue a public statement that the JFBA believes that the use of nuclear weapons results in human rights infringement. [219] Also even if the JFBA officially adopted the bill it would not become law unless adopted by the Parliament of Japan. That said, however, if the JALANA, as an organisation of lawyers, drafted a proper bill the next step would be to wait for a political judgement. At that stage what becomes important is the relationship the JALANA has with the Japanese government. Here, the JALANA's stance is precisely the opposite of the JPPNW. That is to say, it maintains a strong posture leaving no room for compromise or calculation.

The JALANA's legal case is the Tokyo Atom Bomb Trial at the Tokyo District Court (1955-1963), which judged that the atomic bombing by the United States was a breach of International Law. The case was brought by three persons including Ryuichi Shimoda, a resident of Hiroshima, who started a judicial action against the government of Japan demanding compensation for damage due to atomic bombing and to prevent a violation of international law by the United States. In 1963, the Tokyo District Court ruled as follows.

---

[217] Interview with Kenichi Okubo 2013

[218] Ibid

[219] Ibid

"The atomic bombing of Hiroshima and Nagasaki by the US forces, infringes on the international law that demands (that action be taken) for military purposes. And since the atomic bomb is an inhuman weapon, (the use of it) violates the basic principles of International Law that unnecessary affliction should not be incurred in war.

・However, unless recognized by specific convention, it is only the state that has the rights of international law. The hibakusha (those who have been atom bombed) has no other way but to seek remedy for their rights under the national law.

・The court of Japan cannot adjudicate on the US government.

・US law does not seek damages caused as a result of illegal action taken by public servants discharging their duties.

・All told, hibakusha do not have rights in international law or domestic law. Even if the plenipotentiary group abandons rights in the Peace Treaty with Japan, it will have no effect on hibakusha.

・Needless to say hibakusha should have sufficient redress but that is not the duty of the court. We cannot but lament the poverty of politics."

(Tokyo District Court Judgement 7th December 1963.

Toshimasa Koseki the Chief Judge, Yoshiko Mitsubushi Judge, Akira Takakuwa Judge)[220]

(Translated by Fujiko Hara)

---

220 Hankaku Horitsuka No 76, pp10-pp11, Summer 2013
Nihon Hidankyo (Japan Confederation of A-and H-Bomb Suffers Organisations), T*okyo Genbaku Saiban (Tokyo Trial on Dropping Atomic Bombs)*
http://www.ne.jp/asahi/hidankyo/nihon/rn_page/menu_page/side_menu_page/saiban_sosyou/tokyosaiban.htm (accessed on 28th November 2013)

This judgement made during the Cold War, 33 years prior to the ICJ Advisory Opinion 1966, was the world's first legal recognition of the illegality of the use of nuclear weapons and was an epoch making feat legally, and in terms of the history of the court and anti-nuclear action. As was stated in the judgement, however, the case was beyond the jurisdiction of a district court and its judgement had neither the legal binding power nor viability. Also it was clearly stated that it was a political issue.

In 2006, the JALANA released a plan for a new trial, accusing the US of dropping atomic bombs, with all *hibakusha* from Hiroshima and Nagasaki as complainants and the US Administration as the accused and aimed to officially file it in 2007.[221] It aimed at creating a case of penal punishment for the users of nuclear weapons considering that failure of the US government to take responsibility for the atomic bombing of 1945 is the cause that supports the increase of nuclear powers and provides facile support for their argument that nuclear weapons may be used for the purposes of national defence.[222] In reality the jurisdiction of the Japanese court is hardly to be compared with the courts of other governments including the US administration. Moreover, it is said that US courts will not take up cases involving the conduct of US armed forces in foreign countries. In the first place the US army's military actions will not come under judicial scrutiny.[223] The JALANA understands this but it considered meaningful the act of bringing the issue before the court and for the courts in Japan and the US to record and hold in safekeeping the letters of complaint clearly stating that the

---

[221] JALANA, *Shin Genbaku Saiban Koso (Plan of New Trial Accusing Dropping Atomic Bombs by the United States) by Kenichi Okubo*, 20th August 2006 http://www.hankaku-j.org/data/hoka/004.html (accessed on 28th November 2013)

[222] Ibid

[223] Ibid

atomic bombing is the worst holocaust and genocide.[224] This is the JALANA's own view. *Hibakusha* and many anti-nuclear CSOs could be sympathetic to it, but atomic bombing is very different to the holocaust and its genocide. Genocide aims to eradicate a specific group of people (race, religious group, etc) just like ethnic cleansing. But the US's aim of atomic bombing on Japan was not to exterminate Japanese citizens.

In 2010, the Japan NGO Network for Nuclear Weapons Abolition (JNNNWA)[225] was initiated as a place of communication among Japan's main anti-nuclear CSOs. Its purpose was to create a framework for the de-legitimization of nuclear weapons including the NWC, so as to reduce the role of nuclear arms in national security policies, create new measures for nuclear non-proliferation for civic use of nuclear power, and the building of a regional nuclear-free peace system in Northeast Asia.[226] The JNNNWA emerged from the time of a series of Preparatory Sessions for the NPT Review Conferences since 1995 and about the time of the Oslo Conference: Humanitarian Impact of Nuclear Weapons in 2013 organized by the Ministry of Norwegian Foreign Affairs. At that time, representatives of the Japanese anti-nuclear CSOs met, and organized symposia mainly in Tokyo as well as at the Oslo Conference Report Meeting where the JALANA, the SGI and representatives of anti-nuclear CSOs based in Tokyo came together. Basically they all shared a common objective, that of nuclear abolition. Their approaches were different, however, and this new organisation of JNNNWA provided them the opportunities to freely discuss their activities, share their policies as well as recognize and respect different

---

[224] Ibid

[225] Japan NGO Network for Nuclear Weapons Abolition [JNNNWA] http://nuclearabolitionjpn.wordpress.com/ (19th August 2013)

[226] Ibid, *Purpose* http://nuclearabolitionjpn.wordpress.com/about/ (accessed on 19th August 2013)

approaches taken by each organisation. JNNNWA provided them with a gathering with high degrees of freedom.[227] Of the five JNNNWA directors one serves as JALANA's director.[228] The purpose of inaugurating the JNNNWA was to have free exchange of views with the MOFA. JNNNWA's member anti-nuclear CSOs share common JNNNWA's member anti-nuclear CSOs all sharing a common wish that the government of the only country that experienced atomic bombing would take action in support of nuclear abolition.[229] Since its inception the JNNNWA has held three meetings at the MOFA with officials in charge (as of 2014).[230] The relevant minutes have not been made public, but the outlines of the NGO questions and the Foreign Ministry's responses are uploaded in the official websites of both the MOFA and the JNNNWA. The first meeting took place on 21st November 2012 at which views were exchanged on the Joint Declaration concerning the inhumanity of nuclear weapons at the First Committee of the UN General Assembly as well as regarding the Conference: Humanitarian Impact of Nuclear Weapons in 2013 (Oslo Conference). The second was on 1st July 2013 at which views were exchanged on nuclear disarmament and non-proliferation. The third meeting was on 7th February 2013 at which views were exchanged with the Japan Nuclear Regulation Authority regarding spent fuel issues. Regarding nuclear disarmament, the first meeting covered the opinions of both sides. At

---

227 Kazuhiro Tobisawa's Memo to Record Statements of Each Attendee, Oslo Conference Follow-up Meeting, which was held by Japan NGO Network for Nuclear Weapons Abolition at Meiji Gakuin University, Tokyo, 19th March 2013

228 JNNNWA, *Purpose* http://nuclearabolitionjpn.wordpress.com/about/

229 Interview with Kenichi Okubo 2013

230 JNNNWA, *Gaimusho tono Iken Kokankai (meetings with MOFA, Nuclear Regulatory Agency, and Nuclear Regulatory Committee)* http://nuclearabolitionjpn.wordpress.com/?s=%E6%84%8F%E8%A6%8B%E4%BA%A4%E6%8F%9B%E4%BC%9A (accessed on 29th November 2013)

the meeting ten NGOs were represented including the JALANA and the SGI and the Ministry was represented by seven persons; the Vice-Minister, the Assistant Vice-Minister in charge of Disarmament, Non-Proliferation and Science Department, the Director of Arms Control and Disarmament Division (ACDD), the Senior Officer of ACDD, the Special Assistant to the Director of ACDD, and an Officer of ACDD. The outline of the views and questions submitted by NGOs prior to the meeting included criticism of the refusal of the Japanese government to sign the Joint Declaration on Humanitarian Aspects of Nuclear Disarmament and its reasons. There was a firm agreement of the government to be represented at the Oslo Conference and to include in the official delegation *hibakusha*, representatives of their associations, as well as medical specialists on atomic bomb diseases recommended by the NGOs. Also included in the questions was how would the government reflect the outcome of the Oslo Conference in its policies, for example, translation into Japanese of the materials relating to the inhumanity of nuclear weapons. Also a question was asked of the MOFA regarding its plan on how the Oslo conference would be related to the Foreign Ministers of the Non-Proliferation and Disarmament Initiatives (NPDI) Hiroshima Conference (2014). And finally the NGO side asked if it were possible for the Ministry to collaborate with the NGOs and the *hibakusha* organisations.[231] The MOFA responded to these questions regarding its refusal to sign the Joint Declaration at the First Committee of the UN General Assembly as well as the opinion of the government regarding the inhumanity of nuclear weapons, and said

---

[231] JNNNWA, Kokurensokai Daiichi Iinkai Oyobi Raishun No Osuro Kaigi Ni *Kansuru Sitsumonsho (Written Inquiry to Foreign Minister on the UN 1st Committee Resolution and Oslo Conference)*, 19th November 2012 http://nuclearabolitionjpn.files.wordpress.com/2012/11/20121119_ngoquestions.pdf (accessed on 29th November 2013)

that it had already answered the question asked by a Komeito member of parliament during a session of the Diet. The government of Japan shares the sufferings of the victims of the Atomic bombing in Hiroshima and Nagasaki and agrees that nuclear weapons are inhuman weapons, but the greater concern of the government is to find ways of preventing the use of nuclear weapons. According to MOFA, there are two ways of avoiding their use, de-legitimization of nuclear weapons and dependence on the nuclear deterrence of the US nuclear umbrella.[232] However, it responded, even if the Japanese government supported the de-legitimization of nuclear weapons, there was no guarantee that they would not be deployed, moreover, no international organisation existed that would clamp down on their illegal use.[233] Herein lies the fundamental need for establishing international statute. For example, even if the NPT is strengthened, or the NWC is effective, at present there is no way to penalize violating contracting states. Even if a case of violation was notified to the UN Security Council, there have not been sanctions that would force a violating state to abandon its nuclear weapons. Assuming that de-legitimization of nuclear weapons was written into law, if a state illegally possessed nuclear weapons, there is no guarantee that the state would never use the weapon. [234] The criterion of the judgment of the government is "can it unfailingly protect the citizens under present uncertainties?". Kenichi Okubo, the JALANA Secretary-General had a counterargument.

---

[232] JNNNWA, *Kakuheiki No Higohoka O Meguri Gaimusho To Ikenkoukankai O Okonaimashita* (JNNNWC and MOFA held a meeting for discussion how to make use of nuclear weapons illegal), 22nd November 2012 https://nuclearabolitionjpn.wordpress.com/2012/11/22/mofaroundtable_report20121121/ (accessed on 29th November 2013)
[233] Ibid
[234] Ibid

> "This is a fundamental issue. Certainly, there are no penalties for breaching international laws. But how would the guilty state be seen and treated by the international community? It could not be positive ones. That can be understood as the penalty for breaching international laws."
> (Kenichi Okubo's answers to this writer's question at the Oslo Conference Follow-up Meeting, which was held by the Japan NGO Network for Nuclear Weapons Abolitio at Meiji Gakuin University, Tokyo, 19th March 2013)[235]
> (Translated by Fujiko Hara)

On this question MOFA said that the realistic approach towards nuclear disarmament would be centred on diplomatic negotiations and contended that remaining under the US nuclear umbrella is the general consensus.[236] The point here was the Japanese government's reply that the nuclear weapons issues should be resolved basically by diplomatic means. The reasons for the Japanese government's conventional dependence on the US nuclear umbrella come from the instability of the situation in Northeast Asia. If so, rather than continuing with diplomatic efforts to remain under the US nuclear umbrella, making good use of diplomacy to resolve regional issues is more likely to lead to fundamental solutions. In fact, the US's extended deterrence including its nuclear umbrella is established by the National Defence Programme Outline of the Japanese government and is established as the cornerstone of the government's diplomacy and defence with over half a century since the conclusion of the Security Treaty with the USA. It can be said the government is neglectful of making other diplomatic efforts.

---

[235] Kenichi Okubo's Answer to Kazuhiro Tobisawa, the Follow-up of Oslo Conference, JNNNWA at Meiji Gakuin University in Tokyo, 19th March 2013

[236] Ibid

Regarding the recent territorial and historical perception issues, the Japanese government is prompted by the US Administration to solve them peacefully (see Chapter 5).

At the Oslo Conference (4th and 5th March 2013) P5 were absent and the Japanese government delegation was limited to only four persons. Regarding the absence of the P5, Keinichi Okubo, the JALANA Secretary-General made the following remarks from a lawyer's point of view.

> "None of the P5 sent government representatives to the Oslo Conference. If government representatives were to be present, international public opinion would be quick to point out that the P5s also recognized the inhumanity of the nuclear weapons. And if this would trigger establishment of norms concerning the inhumanity of nuclear weapons, the P5s will be constrained in deploying political and diplomatic negotiations with the strength of a nuclear power. They are against recognizing the inhumanity of nuclear weapons because they are afraid of that."
> (Kenichi Okubo's answer to this author [Kazuhiro Tobisawa]'s question, the Follow-up of the Oslo Conference, which was held by the JNNNWA at Meiji Gakuin University, Tokyo, 27th March 2013)
> (Translated by Fujiko Hara)

At the beginning the Japanese government had no plan of inviting *hibakusha* to join its delegation to the Oslo Conference but at the request of the organisation of *hibakusha* and the CSOs, it finally agreed to share two of the four participation slots given to Japan. A representative of the *hibakusha* and Masao Tomonaga, the Head of the

Japanese Red Cross Nagasaki Genbaku Hospital who is knowledgeable about the atom-bomb disease were to join the delegation. The Japanese government asked the two civilians to pay for their travel and accommodation expenses.[237] The presence of the Japanese delegation at the Oslo Conference was given an extremely cold reception due to its refusal to sign the Joint Declaration on the Inhumanity of Nuclear Weapons at the First Committee of the UN General Assembly, even though it represented the only country that suffered from the A-bomb.[238] The Anti-nuclear CSO group had organized a two-day Civil Society Forum (2nd and 3rd March 2013) organized by the ICAN prior to the Oslo Conference. The Forum had four panel discussions with the attendance of experts and government officials such as Patricia Lewis, the Co-Chairman of the IPPNW and a member of the Chatham House in the UK,[239] Gry Larson, the Vice Minister of Foreign affairs Norway and had good discussion concerning the effects of the use of nuclear weapons from various angles as well as on the significance of the Oslo Conference.[240] Actor Martin Sheen also participated and talk shows took place. All in all, the entire Forum had the participation of approximately 500 persons, 130 organisations from 60 countries. There

---

[237] Kazuhiro Tobisawa's Memo to Record Statements of Each Attendee, *Statement by Terumi Tanaka (Secretary-General, Japan Confederation of A and H bomb Suffers Organisations)*, Oslo Conference Follow-up Meeting, which was held by Japan NGO Network for Nuclear Weapons Abolition at Meiji Gakuin University, Tokyo, 19th March 2013

[238] Chugoku Shimbun (Chugoku Newspaper), Hiroshima Peace Media Center, Interview with Terumi Tanaka, head of the Japan Confederation of A-and H-Bombs Suffers Organizations, on nuclear disarmament conference in Oslo, 18th March 2013

[239] Chatham House, Experts, Dr. Patricia Lewis, Research Director of International Security http://www.chathamhouse.org/about-us/directory/182053 (accessed on 29th November 2013)

[240] ICAN, *ICAN Civil Society Forum*
http://www.icanw.org/campaign-news/norway/oslo-civil-society-forum/ (accessed on 29th November 2013)

were 33 speakers including a *hibakusha* from Hiroshima.[241] Steven Leeper represented the MP from Japan, and the MP booth was set within the Forum premises, MP pamphlets were distributed, and sought support for the 2020 Vision Campaign as well as membership to the MP.[242] The JALANA was also represented and Kenichi Okubo used an opportunity to speak and called out his five points: "Remember Hiroshima and Nagasaki", "Let's expedite the Nuclear Weapons Convention!" "Let's reduce the danger of the use of nuclear weapons!", "Let's get nuclear powers to live up to their responsibilities of nuclear disarmament!" and "Lets together build a world without nuclear weapons and war!"[243] The SGI jointly with the ICAN organized a large anti-nuclear exhibition: "Everything You Treasure – For a World Free From Nuclear Weapons".[244] The exhibition was first presented in 2012 at the 20th IPPNW World Congress.

The JALANA as a member of the JNNNWA, or the JALANA alone have on occasions discussed the issue with the government of Japan, but the government seems to have no intention of giving up relying on nuclear deterrence so that there seems no chance of it changing its stance. In fact, the JALANA is asked by people in charge in the government to tell them if there is a way other than depending on the

---

241 ICAN, *Report : ICAN Civil Society Forum 2013* http://goodbyenukes.wordpress.com/ (accessed on 29th November 2013)

242 HPCF Heiwa Bunka (Japanese Newsletters) No. 83, *Noruwe Osuro De Kaisai Sareta Shiminshaki Foramu Heno Shusseki (Attended to a Civil Society Forum in Oslo, Norway)* http://www.pcf.city.hiroshima.jp/hpcf/heiwabunka/pcj183/Japanese/02J.html (accessed on 29th November 2013)

243 Kenichi Okubo, *Oslo Kaigi (Oslo conference)*, Hankaku Horitsuka (bulletin of JALANA) No 76, p24-p25, Summer 2013

244 People's Decade for Nuclear Abolition (SGI's special website for nuclear weapons abolition), *Exhibition Tour, SGI Participates in Oslo Conference on Humanitarian Impact of Nuclear Weapons*, 2013 http://www.peoplesdecade.org/decade/exhibition/eyt/2013/130305.html (accessed on 29th November 2013)

US nuclear umbrella.[245]

On the other hand, as regards the NANWFZT, the JALANA sees North Korea's nuclear issue as a direct threat in the Northeast Asian region and maintains its own points of view.[246] That is to say, it believes that North Korea's nuclear development is in response to the US Administration's hostile view of it and that is causing it to conduct brinkmanship diplomacy. The JALANA asserts that the international community should respect North Korea's conventional views and accept them as the will of the government of the sovereign state of North Korea; including its view that US nuclear weapons threaten the sovereignty of North Korea, its criticism against the unwarranted privilege P5 enjoy within the NPT regime, its criticism against Big Power superiority and Big Power centred schemes, and its view that the Korean War has not yet terminated.[247] His theory is that labelling North Korea as a 'rogue state' or 'terrorism supporting state' and for Japan, its neighbour, to seek shelter under the US nuclear umbrella itself is the cause of incitement. Therefore, the JALANA strongly believes that the US Administration's policy of hostility against North Korea has to be changed.[248] The JALANA's assertion contains criticism against the inequality of the NPT regime that allows the P5 alone to legally possess

---

245 Interview with Kenichi Okubo 2013

246 Kenichi Okubo, *Kitachosen no Kakubuso Kyoka o Kaerutameni (To Stop Escalation of North Korean Nuclear Armament)*, JALANA 2009 http://www.hankaku-j.org/data/hoka/007.html (accessed on 1st December 2013)

247 Ibid

248 Kenichi Okubo, Kakuhaizetsu Joyaku Soki Zitsugen No Tame Ni – Kokusai Minshu Horitsukyokai Hanoi Taikai De No Zimukyokucho Speech (To Make the Nuclear Weapons Conventions to Force Immediately – Speech by JALANA's Secretary-General at the Conference of International Association of Democratic Lawyers [IADL] in Hanoi), JALANA Official Website, 2009 http://www.hankaku-j.org/infomation/data/090619.html (accessed on 1st December 2013)

nuclear arms, and the big power arrogance of the permanent members of the UN Security Council.[249] It believes that the fundamental cause of nuclear proliferation goes back to the P5 race for nuclear development and the nuclear deterrence theory that began from the Cold War period. It calls on the P5 to respect the principles of the United Nations of equal rights for big and small states and non-interference in internal affairs, and to stop the policy of the big revolver and change their attitude to conducting dialogue.[250]

Regarding denuclearization of North Korea, the JALANA believes there is but one possibility. Japanese lawyers are starting to support the North Koreans who were Japanese nationals during the war and who were exposed to atomic bombing while living in Hiroshima and Nagasaki and returned to their homeland following the end of Second World War. The aim is to begin a judicial action to win them recognition as atom bomb victims and to explain to the North Korean government the realities of atomic bombing. The JALANA as of 2014 does not have a clear action plan.[251]

As regards Japan-China relations, on the Senkaku Islands that Japan controls and over which China claims sovereignty, Kenichi Okubo is clear that this is a territorial issue. Though the Japanese government continues to deny the existence of territorial issue over the islands, Okubo believes that it should referred to the International Court of Justice and have it resolved judicially rather than leaving it to become a military flash point between the two countries (see Chapter 5).[252]

---

[249] Kenichi Okubo, *Kitachosen no Kakubuso Kyoka o Kaerutameni (To Stop Escalation of North Korean Nuclear Armament)*, JALANA 2009 http://www.hankaku-j.org/data/hoka/007.html (accessed on 1st December 2013)

[250] Ibid

[251] Interview with Kenichi Okubo 2013

[252] Ibid

The JALANA whose starting point is supporting victims of Atomic bombing, is forcefully raising its voice against maintaining the existing nuclear power plants, their new developments, and immediate decommissioning of all nuclear power plants in Japan since the 2011 nuclear power plant explosion in Fukushima (Tokyo Electric Power Co. Ltd.) following the East Japan triple disaster. It has increased exchanges with IALANA affiliates to share opinions on nuclear power plant decommissioning. For example, in 2012 the JALANA invited the President and the Secretary-General and a member of the German Association of Lawyers Against Nuclear Arms (GALANA) to Japan and organized an informal meeting to learn from the German government's experience of deciding to quit nuclear power energy as the will of the nation.[253] At present (2014) most of JALANA's activities are devoted to supporting nuclear power plant abolition programmes.

(iv) Soka Gakkai International (SGI)

The Soka Gakkai International (SGI), is an international extension of the Soka Gakkai (Japan), a Buddhist lay organisation embracing the Doctrine of the Buddhist monk Nichiren 1222-1282, established in 1930 in Japan and dedicated to the development of peace, culture and education based on Buddhist teachings. The SGI was established on 26 January 1975, unanimously, at the International Buddhist League that took place in Guam, with the representatives of Soka Gakkai members of various countries. Soka means 'creating values'; Gakkai means 'learned society'. To begin with, in 1930, it was called the Soka Kyoiku Gakkai (Soka Educational Society). This had much to do with the Soka

---

[253] Hankaku Horitsuka (bulletin of JALANA), Datsu Genpatsu O Kimeta Doitsu No Keiken Ni Manabu (Learning German experience which has determined to abolish nuclear reactors),2012, p33-p37

Gakkai's first president, Tsunesaburo Makiguchi. He was a geologist and the president of a Tokyo school. His disciple Josei Toda (then the Soka Gakkai's Secretary General) would become the second president following the end of the war. Toda was a mathematics teacher at the same school. The Soka Gakkai Japan started as a gathering of schoolteachers who professed Nichiren Buddhism. The SGI, as of 2014, has 12 million plus members in 192 countries. Its commitment is to respect diverse races, occupations and customs, create value in every sort of situation, so that each member can contribute to his/her family, friends and communities, and to conduct initiatives on peace, culture and education on a global basis.[254] The SGI organisation in each country aims to contribute to peace and development of each community and is uniquely involved in activities to meet its needs and priorities, on global issues; however, the SGI actively also collaborates with international NGOs and UN organisations. Committed to tolerance and pluralism, including religious pluralism, the SGI is involved in inter-religious dialogue for building human solidarity for the resolution of issues concerning humanity.[255] The SGI calls these activities, Humanism in Action.

The commitment to globalism transcending all national borders, including Japanese, is borne out of the philosophy of the Buddhist monk Nichiren (see Chapter 4) in the 13th century as well as out of the Soka Gakkai's experience of being oppressed by the Japanese Military Government during the Second World War. During the War, the Japanese Military Government established Shinto as the State religion and forced the Japanese people to follow its practices. It had intended to establish a national regime with the emperor, the head Shinto priest and

---

[254] Soka net, *SGI No Gaiyo (Overview of SGI),* http://www.sokanet.jp/sgi/gaiyo.html (accessed on 17th October 2013)
[255] Ibid

living god, as an absolute monarch. This was a ploy of the Military Government to abuse religion in order to establish a nationalistic totalitarian state to control the people.

The Nichiren Shoshu, a group of monks of Nichiren Buddhism to which the Soka Gakkai belonged, ordered Makiguchi in 1943 to worship the State Shinto amulet. Makiguchi refused. As a result the Special High Police of the Military Government arrested Makiguchi on account of Lèse Majesty and for violating the Public Order Act. He was jailed with Toda. Next year Makiguchi died in prison from malnutrition and old age. The Soka Gakkai (Japan) with a membership of about 3,000 was almost paralyzed. Freed at the end of the war, Toda rebuilt the Soka Gakkai with his disciple Daisaku Ikeda, the Soka Gakkai's Third President and current SGI President, who had joined the Soka Gakkai in 1947. In 1952 the organisation became an independent religious corporation and towards the end of the 1950s its membership had grown to include 750,000 households. Of all the many schools of Nichiren Buddhism, it was only Makiguchi and Toda who refused to worship the State Shinto amulet. All schools of Nichiren Buddhism had succumbed to the religious control of the Japanese Military Government. Under the oppression of Japanese militarism, it was Makiguchi and Toda who remained committed to freedom of religion and Nichiren Buddhism. These commitments provide the foundation of the SGI's anti-war and human rights movements.

In 1991, the Soka Gakkai won its independence from the Nichiren Shoshu. In fact the Nichiren Shoshu expelled the Soka Gakkai on account of Ikeda proposing that Beethoven's Symphony No.9 be sung at the meeting scheduled on 16 November 1990, accusing him of going against the Nichiren tenet, something that is probably unthinkable today.[256] The Nichiren Shoshu has not joined the anti-nuclear movement nor CSO activities that the SGI is involved in. Today, its monotheistic thinking is closed and not compatible with the religious pluralism of the Soka Gakkai.

In December 1945, under the occupation policy of the General Headquarters, the Supreme Commander for the Allied Powers (GHQ) provided the Shinto Directive for the Japanese government to enact laws to ensure establishment of religious freedom. It was only after the occupation by the GHQ that basic human rights including the freedom of religion were enshrined in Japan. And it was only after Ikeda became the SGI President that the anti-nuclear activities began, which are today one of the major pillar of the SGI's peace activities. It all started when Josei Toda, in 1957, came out with the Declaration Calling for the Abolition of Nuclear Weapons[257] before 50,000 Soka Gakkai Youth Division members in Japan. In the Declaration Toda defined nuclear weapons as an absolute evil that threatens the very survival of humankind and the worst kind of weapon that denies the dignity of life (see Chapter 4). However, due to illness Toda passed away the following year.

Ikeda had established practical anti-nuclear activities as part of the SGI. Ikeda did this, starting in 1960, by conducting private diplomacy, travelling to 54 countries, and by initiating talks on world peace and creating cultural and educational exchanges. He also conducted dialogues with national leaders, cultural, educational scholars, and from

---

[256] Association of Youthful Priests Dedicated to the Reformation of Nichiren Shoshu, *Dai Ku Kanki No Uta Ha Gedo Raisan (Singing the Beethoven's 9th Symphony is Praising Non-Buddhist Teachings)*, 16th December 1990 http://www.nichiren.com/jp/organ/organ02/org02_2.html (accessed on 4th May 2012)

[257] Josei Toda, *Declaration Calling for the Abolition of Nuclear Weapons*, http://www.joseitoda.org/vision/declaration (accessed on 9th January 2010)

1975 published an Annual Peace Proposal which has become the basis of today's SGI movement against nuclear weapons (see Chapter 4, 5 and 6).

The SGI, unlike the JPPNW, the MP, and the JALANA, is not a professional group dealing with nuclear weapons and security. It is ordinary citizens, regardless of whether they are SGI members, or their occupation or their nationality, who engage in anti-nuclear activities inside and outside Japan. The anti-nuclear CSOs base their activities on holding exhibitions, organizing collection of signatures, publications, and conducting public opinion polls.[258] Their purposes were to change the mind sets of national political leaders including those in nuclear weapons states; to build solidarity among the CSOs, United Nations and national governments; to record real experiences of the wars, including the dropping of the atom bombs, and to pass them on to the young people who will be the bearers of tomorrow's anti-war and anti-nuclear movements. The national SGIs, including Japan, hold monthly meetings in various regions in small groups of ten to discuss not only Buddhism but also the anti-nuclear as well as environmental issues that the SGI promotes. These meetings provide open spaces for non-SGI members to join freely and discuss social issues as well as current events.

The SGI also believes that the United Nations should be a parliament of humankind and adopts a UN centric approach. Ikeda's Annual Peace Proposals contain various propositions for strengthening the UN system, also including his lecture entitled 'Leonardo's Universal Vision and the Parliament of Humanity[259] that he delivered in 1994 at

---

[258] Hirotsugu Terasaki, Chairman of Soka Gakkai Peace Committee, Shimin No Koe Koso Rekishi Kaiten No Gendoryoku (Voice of Ordinary People is Motive Force to Transform History), Seikyo Newspaper 16th November 2010 p2

[259] Daisaku Ikeda, *Leonardo's Universal Vision and the Parliament of Humanity, 1994*,

the University of Bologna, Italy.

In 1981, the SGI was given associate status at the UN Department of Public Information and the UN High Commissioner for Refugees. Then in 1983, a similar status at the UN Economic and Social Council was granted, and in 1997 status that allows the consultative presence as a NGO followed.[260]

The SGI's activities as an anti-nuclear NGO entered full scale mode in the 1990s.[261] The specific features of the SGI anti-nuclear activities as an NGO are that it always cooperates and collaborates with other anti-nuclear CSOs, the United Nations, national governments and regional municipalities. For example, although the SGI is totally responsible for creating panels and managing exhibitions, in most cases the SGI more or less at all times puts the names of collaborators before their own. The way the SGI goes about carrying out anti-nuclear activities on their own, shows that most of the time it believes building solidarity among collaborators is more important than advertising itself.

The SGI created its first anti-nuclear exhibition in 1982 and continues to go around the world as of 2014, dating names and contents to fit the times. The very first exhibition was called Exhibition 'Nuclear Arms: Threat to Our World (ENATOW)' and was exhibited from 1982 to 1988.[262] The Exhibition covered three themes, 'Overview of the

---

http://www.daisakuikeda.org/sub/resources/works/lect/lect-05.html (accessed on 9th January 2010)

260 Soka Gakkai International, *NGO Activity Report, Introduction*, SGI Office of Public Information 2009 p3

261 Interview with Hirotsugu Terasaki and Kimiaki Kawai of Soka Gakkai Peace Committee, 2010

262 UN, SGI, Hiroshima City, and Nagasaki City, *Review of Exhibition: Nuclear Arms: Threat to Our World*, Part 1 p5

The first ENATOW took place from 3 June to 3 July 1982 at the UNDPI, jointly organised by the SGI, and Hiroshima City and Nagasaki City in the Public Robby of the UN Headquarters in New York. Javier Perez De Cuellar, the UN Secretary-General 1982-1991, and 200, 000 people visited. The

nuclear damage of Hiroshima and Nagasaki', 'Nuclear Weapons today', and 'Disarmament and Development'. Photographs of the aftermath of atomic bombings in Hiroshima and Nagasaki, goods that survived, as well as an assumed damage expected in New York and Tokyo with a 1 mega ton nuclear bomb, accompanied with scientific figures and percentages.[263] Anti-nuclear exhibitions were held also by the JPPNW, the MP and the JALANA and other anti-nuclear CSOs but the SGI exhibitions stand out for their magnitude as well as excelling in drawing in speakers who were top leaders of political, cultural and social worlds. They were held in communist and socialist countries including Beijing and Moscow[264] notwithstanding the Cold War. Each exhibition was co-sponsored by government organisations in the host country (see Chapter 5 and 6). Javier Perez de Cuellar pointed out that the most significant point of the exhibition was that it was held in Moscow during the Cold War period.

"…The exhibits have demonstrably reflected the strenuous efforts the United Nations has been making since its earliest years in trying to halt the nuclear arms race. The holding of this exhibit in Moscow is especially significant at a time when the Soviet Union and the United States of America are engaged in negotiations that offer hope of real and highly significant reductions in nuclear weapons. It will, I am sure, be the deepest wish of every visitor to this exhibition that these

---

opening ceremony had as guest speakers, Yasushi Akashi (UN Undersecretary-General), Takeshi Araki (Mayor of Hiroshima City, and Founder and Chairman of the MP later), and Ustinov (UN Undersecretary-General for Political and Security Council Affairs).
The exhibition also took place in 39 cities in 24 countries by 1988, and was visited by 1,670,900 persons.

[263] Ibid, Part 5 p1-p5

[264] Belgrade (1985), Beijing (1986) and Moscow (1987)

negotiations will succeed and open the way to complete nuclear disarmament. This is the necessary course toward which every display in this exhibit points. To eliminate the threat of global destruction is also the course demanded by the human conscience."

(Javier Pérez de Cuéllar, Moscow, 1987)[265]

All through the Cold War years, China and the USSR developed nuclear weapons as part of their national defence policy. There were hardly any diplomatic relations with Japan because she belonged politically to the West. It was a period of serious political tension, and the fact that exhibitions could be held in the capitals of both countries had much to do with individual relations of trust that Ikeda had nurtured through his Annual Peace Proposals and private diplomacy (see Chapter 5 and 6).

In the post-Cold War period of 1996 to 2003, the Exhibition 'Nuclear Arms: Threat to Humanity' (ENATH) was organized in Costa Rica and other South American countries,[266] which support the anti-nuclear agenda and nuclear abolition. The Costa Rican Government submitted a draft NWC to the UN General Assembly, while South American countries have ratified the Treaty of Nuclear-Free-Zones in South America, well known as the Treaty of Tlaterco 1968. The SGI's

---

[265] UN, SGI, Hiroshima City, and Nagasaki City, *Review of Exhibition: Nuclear Arms: Threat to Our World*, Part 1 p2

[266] Ibid

Costa Rica (1996), Argentina (1997), Uruguay (1997), Peru (1998), Venezuela (1999), Argentina again (at National University of Comahue, 1999), Bolivia (2000), Mexico (2003).

In Costa Rica, it was co-sponsored by the Office of the President's wife, the Arias Peace Foundation, established by former President Oscar Arias, Lanacion Co., Ltd., a major newspaper company and the SGI in capital, San José. With the participation at the opening of the President and the First Lady, Oscar Arias (former President), Minister of Foreign Affair, Minister of Welfare, Minister of Culture, Youth and Sports, and Minister of Information.

exhibition was recognised as a national public event or national cultural event in these countries.[267]

In 1997, the SGI established the SGI UN Liaison Offices (SGIUNLO) in New York and Geneva and, as of 2014, it has the SGIUNLO in all three UN cities including Vienna. The objectives are to strengthen alliances with the UN and other CSOs, so as to draw together all opinions and to reflect them as much as possible in global decision making. The operations of each Office, while different in details reflecting features of each UN city, are based on nuclear abolition, human rights education and resolving environmental issues that the SGI promotes. The SGIUNLO in New York, for example, is engaged in peace and security as a counterpart of the First Committee of the UN General Assembly. At the Third Session of the Preparatory Committee for the 2010 NPT Review Conference in New York, with the support of the ICAN, a workshop entitled, "Nuclear Abolition and Human Security" was held with seven *hibakusha* invited from Hiroshima and Nagasaki to share their experiences with over four hundred New Yorkers.[268]

Among the UN- related NGO alliances, the biggest civil society counterpart to the UN is the Conference of NGO (CoNGO). Its membership of 3,000 NGOs, including the SGI, has committees, sub-committees and working groups in each UN city that participates in the UN decision-making process. The CoNGO in New York has the

---

[267] Seikyo Newspaper 13th April 1997
Exhibitions were held in other regions as well under co-sponsorship of presidential office, national and city governments. In Argentina, for example, Uruguay and Peru, the exhibition was recognised as national public event and in Argentina the Presidential Office and Cultural Agency had recognised it as national cultural event.

[268] Interview with Hiro Sakurai of SGI UN Liaison Office in New York, 2010
Soka Gakkai, Soka Gakkai Annual Report 2009, Activities of Peace, Culture, and Education, 4 NGO Katsudo (NGO Activities), 2009 p30

Committee on Disarmament, Peace and Security[269] that includes nuclear disarmament and the Representative of the SGIUNLO in New York serves as its president. The Committee in tandem with the 2010 NPT Review Conference organized a Workshop "Depleted Uranium Weapons- A Continuing Challenge in Working Towards a Ban".[270] Each NGO has a strong emotional attitude of not collaborating unless its own principles and opinion are accepted. Among CoNGOs there are active committees as well as stagnating ones, depending on the leadership of their presidents' among them, The Committee on Disarmament, Peace and Security is quite active and has its own official website apart from the CoNGO site. The SGIUNLO in New York is committed to being a coordinator, encouraging member NGOs to continue to participate in discussion rather than taking leadership as the president. This attitude is based on Buddhist training that one should listen before stating one's own views. At times, meetings come to an end listening patiently to what others have to say before it makes its own views known. The CoNGO in Geneva has a sub-committee, the NGO Committee on Disarmament of which the SGI and the International Peace Bureau were members from its inception. The CoNGO in Vienna also has the NGO Committee on Peace, specializing also on disarmament. There are no special rules regarding the roles of CoNGO and relationships.

On the other hand, Geneva had been the centre of inter-governmental disarmament diplomacy, such as the meeting

---

[269] Committee on Disarmament, Peace and Security of CoNGO http://disarm.igc.org/ (accessed on 14th July 2011)

[270] NGOCDPS, *"Deleted Uranium Weapons – A Continuing Challenge in Working Toward a Ban"* http://disarm.igc.org/index.php?view=article&id=351%3Adepleted-uranium-weapons-a-continuing-challenge-in-working-toward-a-ban&option=com_content&Itemid=77 (accessed on 3rd November 2011)

between Ronald Reagan and Mikhail Gorbachev during the Cold War, and the Geneva Conference on Disarmament, as well as the centre of CSO activities on disarmament. However, deliberations at the Geneva Conference on Disarmament had stagnated for some time, and in its place, there have been increased activities at the Office of UN High Commissioner for Human rights and the Office of UN High Commissioner for Refugees.

As a result, the nuclear disarmament CSO community moved to the US. Up until about 2009, NGOs involved in disarmament activities were limited to the SGI and the International Peace Bureau; but since Obama's Prague speech, the Geneva Conference on Disarmament has received renewed attention so that ICAN and the Nuclear Age Peace Foundation and other anti-nuclear CSO and NGO alliances have opened offices in Geneva. However, Geneva is the centre for continued human rights activities so that SGIUNLO in Geneva has human rights education as its main undertaking but it also plays a coordinating role as a long-acting NGO in Geneva, in assisting them in their dealings with the UN Office in Geneva and with fellow NGOs. The SGI also participated from the beginning in the Geneva Forum organized by the UN Institute for Disarmament Research and which has been engaged in all sorts of disarmament activities since the time of its establishment. The Geneva Forum is distinct from the CoNGO and is a highly diplomatic organisation to which ambassadors and heads of academic institutions belong, as well as the Graduate Institute of International Studies, University of Geneva, with which the SGI has friendly relations. Rebecca Johnson, the Co-Chair of the ICAN, however, is also a participant. According to the SGIUNLO in Geneva, the SGI never engages in governmental diplomacy and political bargaining, its presence is merely to update new information regarding disarmament.[271] In this way, the SGI clearly separates its CSO and political roles concerning nuclear disarmament. Political decision-making belongs to the role of the government while that of CSOs is to form anti-nuclear public opinion in order to create a favourable environment for a decision to abolish nuclear weapons. This is Ikeda's attitude, as already evident in his private diplomacy with China and the USSR (see Chapter 5 and 6).

The SGI has also the challenge of keeping its activities very active. Many anti-nuclear CSOs in Japan seriously suffer stagnation in their activities, mainly due to aging of the *hibakusha*, the fading memories of nuclear bombing as well as the shortage of successors willing to take on the mission. However, it may be that the SGI has succeeded in nurturing a young generation to be responsible for anti-nuclear activities by involving members of the Soka Gakkai Youth Peace Committee (Japan) and the SGI-UK Youth Peace Committee as well as members of the SGI Youth Division members to plan and manage anti-nuclear exhibitions and signature-collecting campaigns. The starting point can be traced back to Toda bequeathing Ikeda and others his instruction to carry on nuclear abolition activities. It is in line with the spirit of Buddhism, 'Oneness of Mentor and Disciple' [272] that disciples will carry on to achieve the wish of their mentor. This is a thought that enables enterprises and activities to perpetuate; at the same time it is a wisdom that prompts young people to act spontaneously and is applicable as well to all organisations and systems. It can be enormously effective in promoting activities that require long-term commitment across generations.

---

[271] Interview with Kazunari Fujii 2011

[272] SGI, *The Oneness of Mentor and Disciple*, http://www.sgi.org/buddhism/buddhist-concepts/the-oneness-of-mentor-and-disciple.html (accessed on 3rd November 2011)

As one of the examples of the anti-nuclear movement by the SGI Youth Division, the SGI-UK Youth Peace Committee in response to requests received from some universities and schools[273] in the UK, jointly organized the Exhibition: From a Culture of Violence to Culture of Peace: Transforming the Human Spirit' (EFCVCPTHS. see Chapter 4).[274] The activities of the SGI-UK Youth Peace Committee had been carried out spontaneously based on Ikeda's Nuclear Abolition Proposal 2009 entitled 'Building Global Solidarity Toward Nuclear Abolition',[275] with the objective of building strong public solidarity towards nuclear abolition'.[276]

On the international scale, at the Soka Gakkai General meeting held in 1971 in Japan, Ikeda called for action for world peace: "there has never been a stronger will for a movement by the public awakened to the rights of their survival". In response, the Soka Gakkai Youth Division (Japan) began and achieved its "Ten Million Signature Collection Campaign" that started from Hiroshima in 1973. In 1975, Ikeda delivered the collected signatures when he met Kurt Josef Waldheim, the UN Secretary-General 1972-1981 at the UN

---

[273] School of Orental and African Studies (SOAS), University of London (2010), Roehampton University (2011), and the St Bernard's Catholic Grammar School (2011)
SGI, *Peace and Disarmament: "Transferring the Human Spirit" Shown at Roehampton University, UK*, Jan 24 2011
http://www.sgi.org/news/peace/peace2011/transforming-the-human-spirit-shown-at-roehampton-university-uk.html (accessed on 3rd November 2011)

[274] SGI-UK, Youth Peace Committee,
http://www.sgi-uk.org/peace/youth-peace-committee (accessed on 3rd November 2011)

[275] Daisaku Ikeda, President of SGI, *Nuclear Abolition Proposal 2009: Building Global Solidarity Toward Nuclear Abolition*,
http://www.daisakuikeda.org/assets/files/disarm_p2009.pdf (accessed on 3rd November 2011)

[276] Ibid

Headquarters.[277] In 1997, Ikeda collaborated with Abolition 2000 and collected 13 million signatures in three months and presented them to David Krieger, a key person in Abolition 2000 and the President of the Nuclear Peace Foundation. The signatures were duly submitted to the UN Office in Geneva.[278]

The SGI designed Hiroshima and Nagasaki cities that were atom-bombed as the bases for promoting peace.[279] It adopted the 'Hiroshima Resolution' to protect the rights for life in 1973, at the 1st Regional General Meeting of the Soka Gakkai Youth Division in the Chugoku Region, which includes Hiroshima Prefecture. The anti-nuclear campaign culminated in the establishment of the Soka Gakkai Hiroshima Peace Committee that would take on the collection and publication of individual experiences of *hibakusha*. It organized the Hiroshima Course, inviting prominent personalities including Frederik Willem de Klerk, former President of South Africa and Kazumi Matsui, the Mayor of Hiroshima City (MP President). A total of 141 such courses had been held as of 2011.

The collection of *hibakushas*' experiences was published as "Fly high butterflies of HIROSHIMA: messages from HIBAKUCHI".[280] The book is a valuable collection of first hand experiences of *hibakusha* who had all these years hidden the fact that they had been victims for fear of not finding employment, as it was known that some had been fired after their secrets became known. The book was published in 2003

---

277 Hiroshima Soka Gakkai Official Website, *Peace Wave from Hiroshima ~1979 (in Japanese)*, http://www.hiroshima-soka.jp/ayumi/ayumi_1.html (28th November 2012)

278 Ibid 1990~

279 Interview with Daisaku Shiode and Toru Hidaka of the Soka Gakkai Hiroshima Peace Committee 2012

280 Soka Gakkai Youth Peace Committee, *Mae! HIROSHIMA No Chocho: Hibakuchi Kara No Message*, Daisan Bunmeisha 2003

with an opening message from David Krieger.

The Soka Gakkai Hiroshima Peace Committee, starting in 1995, continues to undertake a survey of students' awareness and commitment to peace covering five prefectures of the Chugoku Area. In 2011 the survey was conducted on various university campuses from 16 May to 3 July, distributing 3,000 sheets of questions and had 77 per cent replies, with the breakdown, male 56 per cent and female 44 per cent. To the question; "Do you think that nuclear weapons may be used in the conflicts and wars in the future?", 86 per cent answered in the positive. Also to the question, "Do you think nuclear abolition is possible?" 57 per cent, which was the greatest number answered, "While nuclear abolition is impossible, disarmament is possible". This was followed by 18 per cent of the students who thought, "Even nuclear disarmament was not possible". To the question, "Do you think there can be a movement towards nuclear abolition by debating the issue?", 54 per cent replied positively.[281] In the same survey conducted in 2013, 63 per cent of students answered, "nuclear weapons must not be used under any circumstance". This number showed decline for three consecutive years. (In 2010 the figure was 72%). Twenty-nine per cent of the students supported the idea, "Nuclear weapons can be used as the last resort for self-defence". This represented an 8% increase from 2010. Forty-eight per cent responded, "Dropping atomic bombs on Hiroshima and Nagasaki by the US is unforgivable." For three years running, the ratio was below half.[282] The results of the survey were transmitted by

---

[281] Hiroshima Soka Gakkai News Vol. 13, Dai16kai Gakusei Heiwa Ishiki Chosa (16th Survey of Students on Awareness of Peace), 2012 p23-p24

[282] Chugoku News Paper, Kakuheiki Mitomenai 63% Soka Gakkai Gakusei Chosa (tt 'Research by Soka Gakkai Students Division: Only 63% said 'Using Atomic Bombs to Hiroshima and Nagasaki is not Acceptable"), 24th August 2013
http://www.hiroshimapeacemedia.jp/mediacenter/article.php?story=201308281

the worldwide press including Reuters, to the effect that even people of Hiroshima who had been subjected to A-bomb injuries had fading memories, as well as that there was a slow increase in the support of the use of nuclear arms as the last resort.[283]

The SGI Youth Division regularly conducts awareness surveys on nuclear weapons, targeting the younger generation ranging from 15 to 45 years-old. The other survey conducted from December 2012 to March 2013 covered nine countries (Japan, the United States, the United Kingdom, Italy, Australia, South Korea, Brazil, Malaysia, and Mexico) and received 2,840 responses. These showed that 91.2 per cent of young people believed 'nuclear weapons were inhumane'. But when asked to name the countries that own nuclear weapons, only 72 % named the US, 55.5% Russia, North Korea, 42.3%, and China, 42.1%. The UK, France, India, Pakistan and Israel were mentioned by less than 20%, revealing that they had an extremely low-level perception of the realities concerning the possession of nuclear arms. The results of the survey were announced on April 2013 at the UN Office in Geneva during the Second Session of the Preparatory Committee for the NPT Review Conference[284]. Also at the 2013 JNNNWA Symposium, the SGI spent all of its allocated time for this purpose.[285]

It can be said that the SGI survey report hit a blind spot of the activities of the many anti-nuclear CSOs. That is to say, that most of the anti-nuclear CSOs had focused on activities among the experts and took

---

04735439_ja (accessed on 30th September 2013)

283 Hiroshima Soka Gakkai News Vol. 13, Dai16kai Gakusei Heiwa Ishiki Chosa (16th Survey of Students on Awareness of Peace), 2012 pp3-p24

284 The People's Decade for Nuclear Abolition, *Survey: International Survey by SGI Youth Shows 91%Consider Nuclear Weapons Inhumane*, 2013 http://www.peoplesdecade.org/decade/survey/2013/130424.html (accessed on 2nd November 2013)

285 JNNNW Symposium, which received Tilman Ruff the Co-Chairman of the ICAN, at Meiji Gakuin University in Tokyo on 12th May

for granted that people were against nuclear weapons development and their use without any room for dissent. In order to establish a major anti-nuclear international sentiment that most anti-nuclear CSOs hope for, they would have to take in the majority of the younger generation who have little feeling for what threats nuclear weapons represent. It can even be pointed out that pursuing self-satisfying activities based merely on theories resulted in the weakening of the existing CSOs, for example, in their shortage of successor activists and the unsuccessful continuation of their activities.

The SGI established an English website exclusively dedicated to sharing survey results and the contents of its activities were named, 'the People's Decade for Nuclear Abolition',[286] in addition to its official website. There are only a few Japanese anti-nuclear CSOs that have official English websites. The MP has an English page which translates all entries on its Japanese official website and this is a major reason for the MP to enjoy worldwide linkage. Neither the JPPNW nor the JALANA have websites in English, so while they come under the IPPNW and IALANA, their messages are limited to their domestic activities.

The Komeito, a political party that Ikeda established in 1964, distinct from the SGI, is also promoting nuclear abolition. The Komeito was established to represent the masses at a time when political parties were limited to those sponsored and supported by big business or capitalists, labour unions and communists. Ideologically, it takes a middle way approach, and its party platform commits it to the peace and welfare of the people. In that sense the Komeito is the first political party established by an anti-nuclear CSO. While the Soka Gakkai

[286] People's Decade for Nuclear Abolition http://www.peoplesdecade.org/ (accessed on 2nd November 2013)

(Japan) is its supporting body, it never had Ikeda as its party head or an official. It is managed as an entirely different, independent party from the Soka Gakkai (Japan) or the SGI. From its establishment in 1964 through the Cold War period, the Komeito was an opposition party, and in terms of nuclear disarmament it approached it as a global issue and demanded the government and the cabinet adopt independent and original policies towards easing of tensions in Northeast Asia.[287] The Japanese government, however, did not deploy a unique diplomacy, regardless of those of the US government or Western nations. On the other hand, there was a unique case in which Japan was able to undertake successful diplomacy. That was the case in which the Komeito was able to build a bridge between the Japanese and Chinese governments responding to a request from Ikeda whose initiative had enabled a negotiation to take place towards normalization of diplomatic relations (see Chapter 4). Following the end of the Cold War, the Komeito has participated as a coalition partner of the Liberal Democratic Party (see Chapter 2) continuing to work at reflecting opinions and suggestions of anti-nuclear CSOs in regard to the government's decision making.

In 2010, the Komeito shared its ultimate objective regarding anti-nuclear activities with the SGI-- the bringing into effect the NWC. The Komeito issued its new peace policy 'Let's become a most humane country'. The policy included holding an international conference at the

---

[287] Kokkai Toshokan (National Diet Library), Kokkai Kaigiroku Kensaku Sisutem (Search System of Minutes of the Diet), *Takehisa Tsuji's Query to Prime Minister Eisaku Sato at the Plenary Session of the House of Councillors 26th November 1964*, (Komeito's first query at the Diet), only in Japanese http://kokkai.ndl.go.jp/cgi-bin/KENSAKU/swk_dispdoc.cgi?SESSION=8922&SAVED_RID=1&PAGE=0&POS=0&TOTAL=0&SRV_ID=3&DOC_ID=12629&DPAGE=1&DTOTAL=17&DPOS=17&SORT_DIR=1&SORT_TYPE=0&MODE=1&DMY=11524 (accessed on 8th August 2010)

Japanese government's initiative, to invite national political leaders and representative citizens to find ways of building a collaborative system; and to revise the Rome Statute of the International Criminal Court (ICC) to identify the use and threat of the use of nuclear weapons as war crimes.[288] As its practical step, it declared five points to be followed: to realize President Obama's visit to Hiroshima, Nagasaki and Okinawa, steadfastly holding to the Three Anti-nuclear Principles and to declare no-possession of nuclear weapons, to organize a 'nuclear abolition summit' in 2015 (the seventieth year since the atomic bombs were dropped) with national leaders, to establish nuclear-free zones by the members of the Six Party Talks, and to take concrete initiatives towards the bringing into effect of the NWC.[289] It also clearly stated that the Japan-US Alliance was the cornerstone of Japan's diplomatic and defence policies.[290] This can be conjectured in that Japan is relying on the US army stationed in the country to avoid holding its own independent military power, and to prevent Japan's re-militarization including nuclear armament. One can say this is a natural position for the Komeito, which has maintained its support for the important role of Article 9 of the Japanese Constitution in building the country's post war peace and prosperity.[291] The Japan-US Alliance is usually understood to allow Japan to depend on the US nuclear umbrella, but the Komeito proposes a Japan-US Alliance, which does not depend on nuclear deterrence. This assertion aims at reducing the role of nuclear weapons

---

[288] New Komeito Official Website, *Yamaguchi Vision 2010 (in Japanese)* https://www.komei.or.jp/policy/policy/vision.html (accessed on 25th September 2011)

[289] Ibid

[290] Ibid

[291] New Komeito, Kenpo 9 Jo Kenzi Subeki (We should keep Article 9 of the Constitution), 15th March 2013 https://www.komei.or.jp/news/detail/20130315_10593 (accessed on 11th April 2013)

possessed around the world. That is to say, nuclear weapons states appear to believe that nuclear possession will deter nuclear attack from others. After all, it is not clear what each weapons state has in mind, which renders nuclear deterrence meaningless in the event of accidental attacks from North Korea or future threats of nuclear terrorists.[292] They contend that the only way to ensure the peace and security of each nation is to abolish nuclear weapons altogether.[293]

Also, the KCPANW is searching for every possible approach, and considers the Nagasaki Hiroshima Process as a realistic approach to nuclear abolition.[294] According to KCPNA, there are no Japanese politicians who can honestly talk or exchange views with politicians of nuclear weapons states, starting with the US. And this is one of the reasons why the Japanese government is reluctant to take the initiative.[295] The KCPNA believes that the Japanese anti-nuclear CSOs have important roles to play and considers that through exchanges between Japanese and US CSOs, the Japanese government's message may be communicated to the US government. It further believes that the CSOs can play a role in lobbying national governments.[296] The KCPNA also actively maintains communication with the chief Japanese CSOs and invites representatives of the main CSOs to join when the KCPNA receives a report from Japan's Foreign Ministry representative. For example, in 2010 when the Japanese government and the Australian government announced their Joint Statement, the KCPNA organized a meeting with the person in charge from MOFA and invited the representatives of the main anti-nuclear CSOs. CSO representatives

---

292 Interview with Masayoshi Hamada, Chairman of the KCPNA and Member of the House of Councillors (Former Vice-Foreign Minister Japan) 2010

293 Ibid

294 Ibid

295 Ibid

296 Ibid

requested MOFA to clarify the phrase 'reducing the role of nuclear weapons' contained in the Japan-US Joint Declaration[297] released at the time of US President Obama's visit to Japan in November 2009, realization of 'negative Security Assurance' and the bringing into effect of the NWC under Japan's leadership.[298]

Summary:

The four anti-nuclear CSOs in Japan are highly motivated and have strong international connections, but the JPPNW and the JALANA have been struggling with decline of their chapter memberships in other countries and the dilemma between the issues of nuclear power and nuclear weapons. The MP has been becoming a leading organisation on the global stage of nuclear disarmament, and is the only organisation which has political legitimacy at the level of local politics. However, there is serious difficulty of sustainable activities if new mayors of MP member cities are negative or do not mind about nuclear disarmament. The SGI has the longest history and the largest scale of activities against nuclear weapons compared with the other three Japanese anti-nuclear CSOs. The other CSOs represented by the JPPNW admitted that they have been greatly encouraged by Ikeda and the SGI's ant-nuclear activities. In Chapter 4, this dissertation will clarify the SGI's basic philosophy against nuclear weapons, which has developed sustainable and influential activities.

---

[297] Office of the Press Secretary, the White House, *Remarks by President Barack Obama at Suntory Hall, Tokyo, Japan*, 14th November 2009 http://www.whitehouse.gov/the-press-office/remarks-president-barack-obama-suntory-hall (accessed on 27th May 2010)

[298] New Komeito Official Website, *Kakuhaizetsu No Ridoyakuni (Komeito Leads to Promote Nuclear Abolition)*, 20th February 2010 https://www.komei.or.jp/news/detail/20100220_496 (accessed on 11th April 2013)

PART 3: Case Study: the Work and Career of Daisaku Ikeda

Chapter 4: Daisaku Ikeda and the SGI: Philosophical Basis for Rejecting Nuclear Weapons

This chapter focuses on Daisaku Ikeda for a number of reasons. He is a very skilful private diplomat, and his organisation, the SGI, has a great size and scale of network and activities in the world together with a strong religious conviction. Also, Ikeda has been prepared to go into politics and even created a political party in Japan. Thus he has a very unique background.

Ikeda has been suggesting concrete ways of achieving nuclear abolition through the Annual Peace Proposal he has continued to publish since 1975 as well as in many papers in which he analyses the social and political situation of the times. During the Cold War he also made propositions including the holding of the US-Soviet summit meeting; and when the Cold War period ended, he called for the strengthening of civic societies and proposed a nuclear abolition summit of heads of states and governments.

This chapter focuses on Ikeda's philosophical basis, in particular during the Cold War period. An analysis will be made of his thoughts to enable a comparative analysis with other, including opposing, views. Ikeda's anti-nuclear philosophy is based on the dignity of life, its methodological process is deduction, and he conducts his private diplomacy as low politics centred on cultural and educational exchange.

The Toda Declaration 1957 was recognized and appreciated by other major anti-nuclear CSOs as it was Japan's first declaration demanding abolition of nuclear weapons. [1] Regarding the Toda Declaration Ikeda notes that the use of nuclear weapons itself is a serious challenge to the dignity of life and right of humanity for its survival.

> "On September 8, 1957, Josei Toda, second president of Soka Gakkai, made his proclamation against the use of nuclear weapons. Believing firmly that any threat to humanity's right to survival is diabolic, satanic and monstrous, he declared the use of nuclear weapons to be absolutely evil and entrusted the Young Men's and Young Women's divisions (of Soka Gakkai) with the task of carrying out an antinuclear campaign. Mr. Toda considered the use of nuclear weapons diabolic in that it takes life and criticized attempts to justify the possession of nuclear weapons from the fundamental Buddhist standpoint. "
> (Ikeda's Annual Peace Proposal "Spreading The Brilliance of Peace Toward the Century of the People"1987)[2]

Ikeda's basic philosophy of nuclear abolition is based on Nichiren Buddhism which, in turn, is based on Mahayana Buddhism as well as being influenced by the history of oppression against Soka Gakkai (Japan) under the militarist government of Japan and his own experience of war. It is therefore, based on his utmost commitment to protect the dignity of human life and to deny actions that suppress them. Ikeda shares his conviction, based on Buddhist philosophy, that the dignity of life is a universal value that should not be changed or reduced due to political, economic or social pressures.

---

[1] Interview with Katuko Kataoka, Secretary-General of JPPNW, 2012

[2] Daisaku Ikeda, *Annual Peace Proposal 1987*, p22-p23, * this copy was provided by the SGI Peace Committee

"Dignity of life is a universal principle that shapes our activities and attitudes, not just what we individually feel as a result of individual propensities and experience. If that is not so, then due to one's life experience and individual propensities, one may recognize the dignity of certain people and things but sacrifice the lives of others for the very same reason. If we are to tolerate this we will deny expectations on the principle of the dignity of life"[3]

(Translated by Fujiko Hara)

Ikeda had declared three points as the SGI's basic policies, of which creating a social movement for nuclear abolition is one.

"- SGI and the Peace-making Role of Nongovernmental Organizations -

On the occasion of this tenth anniversary, I should like to reiterate some of the basic policies of SGI.

1, As good citizens, the members of Soka Gakkai International resolve to contribute to the prosperity of our respective societies and countries, while respecting their individual cultures, customs, and laws.

2, The members of Soka Gakkai International resolve to aim for the realization of eternal peace and the prosperity of humanistic culture and education, based on the Buddhism of Nichiren Daishonin, which clearly defines the dignity of human life.

3, The members of Soka Gakkai International resolve to

---

[3] Daisaku Ikeda, Ikeda Daisaku Zenshu Dai 1 Kan (1st Volume of the Complete Works of Daisaku Ikeda), Seikyo Newspaper 1988, p473-p474

contribute to the happiness of humankind and the prosperity of the world, while strongly denying war and violence of any kind; to support the spirit of the Charter of the United Nations; and to make positive steps toward cooperating with its endeavour to keep world peace, with the abolition of nuclear weapons and the realization of a warless as the supreme purpose.

The Realization of the goal of a warless world demands uniting the masses of the whole globe. To contribute to its achievement, with the cooperation of the United Nations and the cities of Hiroshima and Nagasaki, since 1982 the Soka Gakkai Youth division has been sponsoring an exhibition entitled "Nuclear Arms: Threat to Our World", in the hope of consolidating the will of all people to oppose nuclear war and work for the abolition of nuclear weapons"[4]

Ikeda did establish a political party in Japan but the Soka Gakkai (Japan) and the SGI have no intention of being involved in politics. Out of respect for their cultural mores and the law, it does not conduct missionary work in China and other countries. At all times he keeps his distance from political interests. After his experience of oppression during the Second World War he became convinced that political power can become insane. This may well be the reason for his cautious approach to political power. Also, by keeping his distance from politics he believes that he can be free of compromise in his CSO activities.

Ikeda: The nuclear age is shaking the raison d'etre of the absolute

[4] Daisaku Ikeda, New Waves of Peace Toward the Twenty-first Century: A Proposal Commemorating the Tenth Soka Gakkai International Day (Annual Peace Proposal 1985), January 26, 1985, p221-p222 (this English copy was provided by the SGI Peace Committee)

sovereign states...that is to say, I feel strongly that the nation-state system the world has known since the 17th century is shaken....

Norman Cousins: I too agree with that. States too have their own rights. For example, nation states may have the rights, for moral obligation such as in order to protect its people, to allow some people to be sacrificed. But states or their administrators certainly do not have the right to allow conditions for the continuation of life to be exposed as the target of attack. Nuclear war is not a war limited to the hostile states involved. Nuclear war destroys nature's balance of life that enables continuation of life.

Ikeda: Naturally, we cannot unilaterally treat sovereign states as all bad. As I have already stated, the emergence of nation states is in a sense a result of the process of a need to play "defensive" and "autonomous" roles. I do not think it is right to deny the historical facts. However, one must not overlook the fact that sovereign states inevitably do have a "spell of power", which by nature may end in ruling people oppressively for its purpose. Strident progress of science and technology has brought about destructive power of arms and their increasing lethality has increased to a grotesque level the danger of sovereign states that have such tendencies. The situation has become unavoidable for Gorbachev, the Soviet President to say that "New Thinking" should be introduced in diplomacy to give priority to human values rather than class-oriented values[5]

(Translated by Fujiko Hara)

This thinking is different from other CSOs that radically criticize the state, and opens the door for communication with political

[5] Daisaku Ikeda and Norman Cousins, Sekai Shimin No Taiwa (Dialogue Between Citizens of the World), Seikyo Newspaper 2000, p239-p240
It was originally published in 1991 (only in Japanese)

organisations such as the state and international organisations (see Chapter 2 and 3). The SGI's peace movement is based on realism and dialogue,[6] and it is conducted with understanding that nuclear disarmament must finally depend on political will and political decisions. However, in his view, national governments, including Japan, are delaying the progress of nuclear disarmament due to national interests or even reversing it. In the face of this history, he is conducting private diplomacy outside the sphere of inter-governmental diplomacy, attempting to ease political tension that restrains efforts at disarmament (see Chapter 5 and 6).

In a sense he is trying to provide an ideal model of a CSO's role in the field of security, by recognizing the different dimensions that CSOs have compared to political activities, and to exercise power with a realistic sense of balance. This can be playing the role of the sail of a ship, that is to say, CSO thinking and activities are expected to create a balance. This can be playing the role of the sail of a ship, that is to say, CSO thinking and activities are expected to create a balance - so that the political steering house will not make a mistake.

> "Some may think the SGI is a religious organisation with the purpose of advancing into the political world for after all the Soka Gakkai is the main body responsible for establishing the Komei Political Association (predecessor of the Komeito). The entry into the political circles was our choice to open a new way given the chaotic political situation of Japan. There is not need for other countries to emulate it. Members of the SGI will become involved in politics it will be a huge negative in carrying out religious activities. In addition, the other religious

[6] Interview with the Soka Gakkai Hiroshima Peace Committee 2012

organisations and political parties in Japan will take pains to point out the relationship with the SGI and politics and invite unnecessary vigilance in foreign countries. It is therefore important to make it clear that we have no intention to be involved in politics overseas. Above all, it is important to have people understand that the Soka Gakkai is not at all a religion for Japanese people alone, that it is a global religion for the whole of humankind…Buddhism teaches us that unless it differs from the principles of Buddhism one should obey local customs and mannerisms of the times. I wish that the SGI members in various countries will take this to heart, be part of the local society and be involved in realizing the prosperity and happiness of the people"[7]
(Translated by Fujiko Hara)

"…Life is the foremost of all treasures. It is expounded that even the treasures of the entire major world system cannot equal the value of one's body and life. Even the treasures that fill the major world system are no substitute for life…"
(Hakumai Ippyo Gosho [Gift of Rice], which was written in 1280 in Japanese, The Writings of Nichiren Daishonin)[8]

It is a feature of Nichiren Buddhism, that, unlike religions that seek peace of mind, it seeks to practise its principles in contemporary society. At a time when concepts of democracy, world peace and human rights were absent in the feudal society of Japan, Nichiren advised three times

---

[7] Daisaku Ikeda, Shin Ningen Kakumei 7 (New Human Revolution' Vol. 7), Seikyo Newspaper 2004, p272-p273
[8] Nichiren, Gift of Rice [Hakumai Ippyo Gosho], the Writings of Nichiren Daishonin Volume I, Soka Gakkai 1999, p1125 (English)

(1260, 1271, 1274) the de facto supreme leader of Japan Tokiyori Hojo (1227-1263) and his successor Tokimune Hojo (1251-1284) and others that they should change their attitude and he continued to be persecuted for saying this. His main message was to tell the leaders of Japan to give first priority in thinking about the people. And he also maintained that anyone who wishes peace and security must first wish the same for the whole world.

> "…If you care anything about your personal security, you should first of all pray for order and tranquillity throughout the four quarters of the land, should you not?…"[9]

Nichiren also wrote in a letter to one of his disciples "A king sees his people as his parents,"[10] in other words respect and cherish the masses as one's own parents. His assertions were accused by the military (samurai) government of the time of being a way to control the country as well as to criticize existing religious organisations and temples that were connected with political powers of the time. As a result, Nichiren who had not violated any law suffered from relentless persecution and was twice exiled (to the Izu islands from 1261 -1263 and the Sado islands (1271- 1274). The military arm of the military government burned his hermitage which was heavily damaged (1264) and a death penalty was declared (1271). Nichiren, however refused to change his assertion or his attitude.

In particular, Nichiren's first teachings in 1260 were considered the

---

[9] Nichiren, On Establishing the Correct Teaching for the Peace of the Land (Rissho Ankokuron), the Writings of Nichiren Daishonin Volume I, Soka Gakkai 1999, p24 (English)

[10] Nichiren, Offerings in the Snow [Ueno dono gohenji], the Writings of Nichiren Daishonin Volume II, Soka Gakkai 1999, p809 (English)

most important in his lifetime.[11] That was that he had sent Tokiyori Hojo his admonitions called "*Rissho Ankokuron (On Establishing the Correct Teaching for the Peace of the Land*". It takes the form of a story in which Nichiren assumes the role of host and entertains his guest, Hojo. The two lament the chaotic situation of their times and the extraordinary environmental calamities. The guest asks ten questions while the host answers nine. It is not a one way communication but a mutual dialogue, where the importance of dialogue in resolving issues is stressed. Ikeda's private diplomacy takes after Nichiren's attitude and attempts to build friendly relations based on mutual understanding through dialogue. However, in 13th century Japan, Tokiyori Hojo ignored Nichiren's warning and deported him to small islands. While Nichiren's admonition was not heeded by the government of the day, his untiring attitude and philosophy were bequeathed to and implemented by Makiguchi, Toda, and Ikeda in the 20th century. In this sense, it seems only inevitable that Ikeda as a -Buddhist would act strongly to oppose nuclear arms that threaten dignity of life.

In 1944 Makiguchi, the Soka Gakkai's First President, who had been arrested by the former Japanese military government, felt that was the moment he must address the government.[12] When he had been investigated by the Special High Police he denied that the emperor was a living god, stating that he was an ordinary person who could make mistakes. Those words were direct criticism of the military government

[11] Soka Gakkai, Daihyo Teki Na Gosho: Rissho Ankokuron (the Most Major Writing of Nichiren "Rissho Ankokuron [On Establishing the Correct Teaching for the Peace of the Land]"), http://www.sokanet.jp/kaiin/kisokyogaku/gosho/01.html (accessed on 16th july 2011)

[12] Soka Net, Soka Gakkai Ni Tsuite (About Soka Gakkai), Shodai Kaicho Makiguchi Tsunesaburo (tt 'First President Tsunesaburo Makiguchi'), http://www.sokanet.jp/info/president/makiguchi.html (accessed on 16th July 2011)

that was controlling the state through the State Shinto.

> "...The Emperor is also an ordinary person, he studied at the Peer's school (where members of the imperial family studied from preschool to higher education, while ordinary people were also accepted but a big number of aristocratic children studied there). The emperor studied how to be an emperor. His Majesty the Emperor is not above making mistakes. In the first year of Meiji, Yamaoka Tesshuu (man in charge of the Emperor's education at the time) apparently offered a great deal of advice pointing out mistakes..."[13]
> (Translated by Fujiko Hara)

Makiguchi also explained the Nichiren Buddhist philosophy and the Soka Gakkai objective talking about the dignity of life, that people are all equal and that unless the world become peaceful, individual happiness will not be realized.

> "The purpose (of the Soka Gakkai) was through living out the teachings of Buddha, establish truly happy lives for each individual and at the same time with the Buddhist philosophy that teaches dignity of life, will bring eternal peace, rich culture and create human-centred education and thereby contribute to the development of humankind....The great religious leader Nichiren said that if anyone wants to enjoy happiness the first thing to do is to pray for the happiness of others around one",

---

[13] Supervised by Koichi Miyata and Edited by Daisanbunmei-Sha, Inc, Makiguchi Tsunsaburo Gokuchu No Tatakai – Zinmon Chosho To Gokuchu Shokan O Yomu (Fighting of Tsunesaburo Makiguchi in Prison – The Records of Interrogations and His Letters in Prison), Daisanbunmei-Sha 2000, p132

stating that individual happiness cannot be had without the peace and stability of the world. In that sense the Soka Gakkai aims at not just individual happiness but is working towards the emergence of society that has true peace and happiness"[14] (Translated by Fujiko Hara)

The meaning of any suggestion made to a king is to challenge leaders of the country to put right wrongs and make clear what justice means and to correct what is not just. Today when people are the sovereigns, it means enlightening not just the leadership but also more pervasively ordinary citizens.[15] This is precisely the reason why the SGI aims at building anti-nuclear international public opinion through grass roots activities.

On the other hand, Susumu Nishibe, former Professor at the University of Tokyo (Socioeconomics) opposes anti-nuclear ideology based on giving priority on life from the standpoint of promoting nuclear armament. Nishibe questions, "Is there no value beyond life?" He believes that putting human life above all other values is not an absolute belief but was forged following the defeat in a war that resulted in a great number of deaths.[16] He believed that respect for human life is not a goal in itself but a necessity in living one's life.[17]

---

[14] SOKAnet 、 Gairon (Outline), http://www.sokanet.jp/info/gaiyo.html (accessed on 6th January 2010)

[15] SOKAnet, Nichiren Daishonin No Goshogai: Rissho Ankoku Ron To Hounan (Life of Nichiren: "On Establishing the Correct Teaching for the Peace of the Land" and Religious Persecution), http://www.sokanet.jp/kaiin/kisokyogaku/nichiren/03.html (accessed on 16th July 2011)

[16] Susumu Nishibe, *Kakubuso Ron (Theory of Nuclear Armament)*, Kodansha 2007, p82-p83

[17] Iibid

"Life is a means. If one were to make the means the primary value then the purpose of living becomes secondary. As a result one would do away with 'self-respect and self-reliance 'in order to ensure one's 'safety and survival'. While there are many types of nihilism, to put life as of the foremost importance, it abandons from the beginning genuine interest in the human spirit. One may say that is the worst kind of nihilism. Without dealing with the hollowness and distortion of our spirit that followed the defeat of the war it is shameful for us to talk about children's education. This is the worst kind of the feeling of meaninglessness leading to a thought "if only my life is guaranteed people and the country will have bliss." This is nothing but the end of progressivism. The idea of giving priority to life may be called 'value denying value'. Such cancerous cells are propagating in the depths of human consciousness. That is why all they can do is to place a label of 'inhumane weapons' on weapons of mass destruction and do nothing but shake with fear. It is this sort of trend that is spreading throughout our contemporary world. It is also unmistakable that the link between our thinking 'give life priority' and 'fear of nuclear weapons' is most prominent in this archipelago (Japan)"[18]

(Translated by Fujiko Hara)

Nishibe's theory suggests that peace should be regarded simply as 'a state of the absence of war. 'Since the theory of nuclear deterrence is born out of the 'balance of fear', it is a necessary evil for the realization of peace. Also, he complains that while Japan should have a much

[18] Ibid

greater sense of crisis against the nuclear weapons of the US, Russia and China, it remains noncommittal because of its nihilistic defence of the dignity of life.

> "If respect for life is nihilism itself, nihilism must certainly be permeating in nuclear fear. That is to say, are we not trapped in a most strange and peculiar psychology of having no fear of the tens of thousands of nuclear weapons that the US and Russia have and a few hundreds bombs China possesses. That must certainly be fear only in name without any content. The Japanese have taken it on for themselves to establish throughout the archipelago an ideology of fear of nuclear weapons from the imaginary fear that they now have. Their efforts are seen in symbolic posts put out by municipalities in front of railway stations throughout the country to declare "A Non-nuclear Peace City'. That is to say, one cannot even recognize the simple message that nuclear deterrence means preventing nuclear war through nuclear armament. that nuclear deterrence means "preventing nuclear war through nuclear deterrence'. Quite apart from the issue of the effectiveness of nuclear deterrence, people do not even get the message that the purpose of nuclear deterrence is to bring about peace. Since the Japanese people look away from this reasonable point, there is really no defence if we are teased that nihilism for the Japanese applies only to their spirit. Altogether the meaning of 'peace' is becoming ambiguous in Japan. That is to say, the meaning of 'peace' can never be positively defined. Peace is only understood negatively, that is to say, 'a state of absence of war.' As people can drown in the Pacific Ocean, peace can often 'make people suffer boredom

> and impatience, sink into languor and spend time being jealous'. They are not only in danger of such lethargy but it is not too much to say that people in Japan are suffering from the social pathology of peace."[19]
> (Translated by Fujiko Hara)

Nishibe's logic may be said to be an amalgamation of philosophies most Japanese have on nuclear armament. Behind their logic lies the spiritual rehabilitation of Japan. They go back as far as criticizing the Allied Powers occupation of Japan.

> "Following the end of the Great Asia War (Pacific War) all the Japanese, including the leftists and rightists all welcomed the coming of peace. What I would like to say is simply that while it is fine to welcome the end of the war, why do we have to rejoice and happily welcome "peace made by the Occupying forces for the occupying forces (to suppress us)". It was clearly a peace forced on us. If that is the case, the peace must certainly contain 'enmity', given that it was a total war fought on both sides 'without rules of war' . The other party certainly must have their righteousness, we (Japan) too fought for our (Japanese) just cause. That was why there was on our part a certain amount of enmity against the suppression (peace). Is this not what we call history." [20]
> (Translated by Fujiko Hara)

While this dissertation does not attempt to look at the rights and

---

[19] Ibid p84-p86

[20] Ibid p87-p88

wrongs of the occupation policies of the Allied Powers, it can at least be said, that the occupation policy enabled the Japanese citizens to realize basic human rights for the first time. Also historically speaking, wars could not easily be defined as a dualism between good and evil. Nishibe's criticism could well be said to express the deep rift between political realism and liberalism. Therein lies Japan's nationalistic thinking. And that leads to thinking that the nation comes before all else, that people exist because the state exists. This type of thinking can be said to have originated in the Japanese thoughts that led to nationalism and totalitarianism prior to the end of the Second World War. That is to say, the discourse towards Japan's nuclear armament is not new thinking in response to the global issues today of nuclear proliferation and the changes of the times, rather it is to revive nationalism and for the purpose of dealing politically, diplomatically and militarily with the nuclear powers of China and Russia, and most likely also in order to include the US, Japan too ought to adopt nuclear deterrence. Also, Japan asserts that since each state has different righteous causes, it is only natural that they come into conflict as in other phases of history.

Ikeda advocates overall pluralism including religious pluralism and argues in favour of the need to exert efforts to find commonalities as human beings going beyond differences of race, state and habits. In terms of religion, it is a clear negation of religious exclusivities, such as religion for a single country, a single race and religions that denounce different things and heresies, religion that binds human freedom and rights by exercising religious precepts in seclusion. Obsession against differences often found in the sub-consciousness is not limited to religion but can too often be seen in conflicts between races and states. Lecturing on "Mahayana Buddhism and Twenty-First Century"[21] at

[21] Daisaku Ikeda, *Mahayana Buddhism and Twenty-First Century*, Ikeda

Harvard University in 1993, Ikeda spoke of the Buddhist view that the natural world including humankind exists in interdependent relations and his deductive vision.

> “Buddhism uses the term "dependent origination" (Japanese. engi) to describe symbiotic relations. Nothing--no one--exists in isolation. Each individual existence functions to bring into being the environment which in turn sustains all other existences. All things, mutually supportive and related, form a living cosmos, what modem philosophy might term a semantic whole. This is the conceptual framework through which Mahayana Buddhism views the natural universe. Speaking through Faust, Goethe gives voice to a similar vision. 'All weaves one fabric; all things give/Power unto all to work and live." The poet, whose insights now strike us for their remarkable affinity to Buddhism, was criticized by his young friend Eckermann as "lacking confirmation of his presentiments."The intervening years have offered a steadily swelling chorus of affirmation for the prescience of Goethe's, and Buddhism's, deductive vision.”[22]

Christopher S. Queen, Lecturer in Extension of Harvard University, was of the opinion that Ikeda’s lecture was a response to Samuel P. Huntington’s challenge to the world written in his essay, Clash of Civilizations.

> “President (Ikeda)’s vision was in itself a significant answer to

---

Center for Peace, Learning, and Dialogue (based in Boston, USA) http://www.ikedacenter.org/20th-anniversary/founding-lecture (accessed on 16th July 2011)

[22] Ibid

the challenge Professor Huntington put to the world. In fact, Professor Huntington, in his later years invited scholars of world's religions and attempted to rethink his thoughts. Professor Huntington invited scholars of world's religions and attempted to rethink his thoughts. He revisited not just closeness of religions that become factors of "Clash of Civilization" but also attempted to shed light on religious universal wisdom that could be the source of building a "Great Land of Togetherness". I believe that the SGI President's lecture has given rise to new thinking to change the Professor's thinking."[23]
(Translated by Fujiko Hara)

Joseph Nye, former Dean of the John F. Kennedy School of Government at Harvard University, US Assistant Secretary of State under Jimmy Carter 1977-1979, Chairman of the US National Intelligence Council 1993-1994, and advisor to the Obama Administration, who was a commentator at Ikeda's lecture, took note of Ikeda who said there are no other times other than when deep and inner self-discipline and self-control are required in people's mind at a time when there is confusion is caused between peoples of different culture when they clash. Nye emphasized the need for intelligent control of one's feelings and a grasp of situation when attempting to resolve peacefully serious political situations.

"…Franklin Roosevelt and George H.W. Bush had excellent qualities in common, namely to own both the intelligence to control emotions and intelligence to grasp situations. It is my

[23] Christopher S. Queen, Bunmei Wo "Shototsu" Kara "Kyosei" He To Hiraku Eichi (Wisdom to transfer civilization from 'clash' to 'co-exist'), Seikyo Newspaper 16th September 2012, p3

understanding that pursuit of emotional control and spontaneous motivation expounded by Buddhism are deeply connected with the ancient Greek philosophy including that of Aristotle's. To become a fine leader it is important to know oneself, and deepen ways to control one's desires and cravings. While there may be differences in Oriental and Occidental traditions, I think wisdom born from them has deep similarities...I support President Ikeda's opinion, because there is a deep connection with what I strongly insisted in my book about "intelligence that can have a good grasp of the situation. Whether it is a domestic matter or international one, groups of people have insistent cultures. Within a group there are special small groups with culture and specific attitudes. In order to take the leadership, one must have the ability to grasp the situation of cultural 'differences', more so, in a diverse international community. Therefore, unless cultural 'differences' are sensitively recognized and coped with, conflicts will develop. If one wants to avoid conflicts and clashes, then there is a need to deepen one's understanding of different cultures. As President Ikeda emphasizes, leaders must nurture their own inner self-discipline that leads to and sensitively copes with the situation, and manages one's emotions."[24]

(Translated by Fujiko Hara)

For example, during the Cold War in Japan, anti-communism became a majority sentiment and the government was not able to keep a

---

[24] Joseph Nye, Intabyu Shincho "Daitoryo No Lida-Sip To Amerika No Zidai No Souzo" O Megutte (Interview regarding his new book "Presidential Leadership and the Creation of the American Era"), Seikyo Newspaper, 1st January 2014, p6

cool political and diplomatic judgement in relation to China and Russia. The Japanese government failed to grasp a future situation in which China with its national power due to its enormous population would have a presence in the international community that cannot be denied. Therefore it could not grasp the timing to start diplomatic relations towards normalization of relations. In contrast, the US Administration sent Henry Kissinger, (then) the Assistant to the President for National Security Affairs secretly to China in 1971 followed by a lightening visit from Richard Nixon in 1972. The US did not share its China policy with its ally Japan. This was aimed at checking the USSR through the US-China rapprochement based on the political theory "My Enemy's Enemy is My Friend". It underscores flexible and cool judgement of the international situation by the US beyond ideological emotion of anticommunism. Japan's government diplomacy lacked those attributes. As a result of which until Ikeda took the initiative towards normalization of relations with China, Japan was isolated as far as diplomatic relations in Northeast Asia were concerned (see Chapter 4). On the other hand, Ikeda's private diplomacy was not highly political, it was low politics, not being prisoner to anti-communistic emotions in Japan at the time or delegating communism to anti-religious ideology. Rather he realized that by reconciling Japan-China and Japan-Russia relations, it could lower the threat of a new war in which the use of nuclear weapons could be assumed. In this sense he had the power of grasping the situation beyond that of the Japanese government at the time.

Ikeda, starting from the 1960s, began building cross cultural understanding and mutual trust. Ikeda's dialogue with other knowledgeable persons did not always produce agreement on all points. He believed in the merit of having dialogue and saw values in finding areas where they could come to agree and understand. The worst thing to be feared for him was the discontinuation of dialogue and exchange among civilizations. His first dialogue with intellectuals outside Japan was with Richard Coudenhove-Kalergi in 1967. It began with Coudenhove-Kalergi proposing a meeting with Ikeda on his visit to Japan.[25] At their 1972 dialogue, they agreed on most views such as that national power rested not in the military but in culture, and that building friendly relations with China held a key to world peace. And they referred also to nuclear disarmament.

Coudenhove-Kalergi is known to have liberal ideas going beyond the sovereignty of nations, such as his belief in Pan-Europeanism and/or the concept of creating a World Federation, and held a realistic perspective regarding nuclear issues and the future of Japan. According to him, abolition of nuclear arms was difficult, even if a Nuclear Abolition Convention were to be established, and it would be a challenge to realistically abolish nuclear weapons. He cited the case of totalitarian countries in which nuclear development was more easily done in secret through news censorship. The only exception was the establishment of an organisation that can force states to comply and in which all military power on earth would be concentrated. He believed too that it was not realistically possible at this point[26]. Even if so-called international law were to become universal, the absence of an institution to penalize offenders was a similar challenge faced by contemporary

---

[25] Hidenori Tozawa (Professor of Graduate School of Law, Tohoku University), *Coudenhove-Kalergi To Soka Gakkai (Coudenhove-Kalergi and Soka Gakkai'),* RCK Forum http://www.law.tohoku.ac.jp/~tozawa/RCK%20HP/RCKjap3.htm (accessed on 24th December 2012)

[26] Daisaku Ikeda, Ikeda Daisaku Zenshu 102 (The Complete Works of Daisaku Ikeda volume 102), Bunmei Nishi To Higashi (Civilisations: West and East' dialogue with Richard Coudenhove-Kalergi), Seikyo Newspaper 2003, p70

* the original book of its dialogue was published by Sankei Newspaper in 1972 (only available in Japanese)

society.

According to Ikeda, the cardinal point for world's leaders concerning nuclear disarmament was the fear they had of 'enemy countries'. What they should be afraid of was the destructive power of the weapons. Ikeda therefore believed that since it was only Japan that knows this from its experience, Japan is in a position to take the leadership in establishing world peace in unique ways.[27] He also believed that in considering Asian solidarity, the issue of nationalism could not be avoided. In fact, nationalism in a broad sense that encompasses the whole of Asia has not yet been developed. However, nationalism in the narrow sense, he pointed out, was causing conflicts between states.[28] Rather than doing away with nationalism, what was needed was to develop a higher order solidarity to a level of global community and global citizenship. He believed that the reality of international politics had not reached that level yet.[29]

Coudenhove-Kalergi pointed out that given the present Japanese government's foreign policy catering blindly to US wishes, not much can be expected in the way of initiating a dialogue. As for reasons he said that as long as Japan followed the US and was unable to recognize China, Japan could do nothing internationally to promote dialogue.[30] Also, he predicted that no nuclear weapons would be used in war because nation states already knew that nuclear war meant a mass suicide involving their own countries. That said, should a nuclear war occur, he emphasized that Japan should at least seek protection from one of the nuclear weapon states. According to his analysis of the international situation, states without nuclear weapons would require

---

[27] Ibid, p71
[28] Ibid, p95
[29] Ibid, p96
[30] Ibid, p87

protection by nuclear states, and the US-Japan Security Treaty functioned in favour of Japan. However, under his liberal thinking, he asserted that Japan should in the future go beyond differences of ideology and regimes and play a role in promoting friendly political and economic relations with all countries, and keep its absolute neutrality by not being party to one or the other camps. By so doing, Japan would be able to maintain its peace, as well as actively contribute to world peace and furthermore play a role in stopping what was then the greatest threat from happening, by which was meant a Third World War. And if and when an unlikely war would start, Japan could stay out of it and maintain its neutrality. [31] Further, because Japan in its Peace Constitution prohibits maintaining military force, there was a need to keep military capacity for its defence and maintain armed neutrality. Neutrality should not be modelled after the Swiss model but follow Belgium. He further proposed that Japan's strategic system, should have in place a neutrality security pact with three states, the US, the USSR and China. If and when one of the three states invaded Japan the remaining two neutrality partners would support Japan. [32] Ikeda however did not accept his thoughts.

Ikeda: This is indeed a very difficult issue, isn't it. Suppose that one state invaded Japan and with nuclear arms, it is given that we will receive destructive damage. And in the unlikely event of three countries entering the war, even if we can keep independence at least in form, I would rather think we would not be able to substantially recover as a state. I believe that Japan should actively seek to realize a peaceful world without

[31] Ibid, p74

[32] Ibid, p83-p84

wars, and a world without national boundaries.[33]
(Translated by Fujiko Hara)

The remarks made by the two people, both having experienced the Second World War, realistically showed fear that the Third World War involving super powers could develop into using nuclear weapons. On that premise, the two agreed on the principle that the world must continue to live in co-existential harmony. Coudenhove-Kalergi spelled out his belief that the progress of science and technology have made distances short between nations so that in the end the world would be forced to aspire to live in co-existence. Ikeda, however, was not sure that the progress of science and technology could be a necessary condition for co-existence but whether it could be a sufficient condition, he was not sure. Certainly, the world has distance - wise become nearer, but that implied - no compulsion for states to come to a compromise. Co-existence based on deterrence was one underpinned by fear, and could not be called an ideal state for co-existence. As for realistically promoting peace, he believed the key lay in overcoming ideological differences. For that purpose there was a need for an ideological foundation, and only when it combines with science and technological conditions, can it provide sufficient condition for co-existence. And the ideology that exceeds one of conflict has to be a philosophy that can sublimate science and technology to human dimensions. Coudenhove-Kalegi replied that the avoidance of the Third World War was made only possible through some spiritual movement that could transcend all conflicts, be it that of race, religion, ideology and nationality, and by thoroughly confirming the importance of

[33] Ibid, p84

co-existence and mutual trust. [34] Ikeda asserted that a for spiritual movement to act as an ideological condition to sublimate inter-state conflicts, there must be more than efforts made on a case by case basis to maintain friendly peaceful relations. There was an additional, need to build internationalism beyond state egoism, in other words, a universal spirit for global citizens.[35]

Further, Ikeda defined 'peace' as a state in which dignity of life has preference over everything else, in other words, a situation in which life will not be sacrificed for whatever reason.[36] On the other hand, Coudenhove-Kalergi asserted that apart from a war of aggression, defensive wars are not necessarily considered immoral, that international politics should devote all strengths to stamp out all wars of aggression by distinguishing types of acts of war.[37]

Ikeda's way of reasoning does not follow a Western inductive approach that attempts to derive universal norms and laws by compiling individual and specific examples, By contrast, his is a Buddhist and Oriental deductive approach that attempts to derive individual as well as specific conclusions from the universal hypothesis. That is to say, his is an approach that starts out by defining 'all human beings belong to the same planetary race', therefore, 'they must live together'. Or to establish 'respect for life' as a universal value, and then to clear obstacles found in the process of reaching it. This is a process of counting backwards and is called the deductive approach. Ikeda also saw the need for a deductive approach in diplomacy, and advocated such a deductive diplomacy (see Chapter 5 and 6). His private diplomacy, therefore, had from the first the objective of developing

[34] Ibid, p94
[35] Ibid, p94-p95
[36] Ibid, p168
[37] Ibid, p169

friendly relations with China and the Soviet Union. Practically it meant overcoming differences and distinctions at various dimensions and to try and find commonalities and point of similarities.[38] An inductive approach, on the other hand, considers national interests and gains and looks for parts that can be a compromise; as a result of multiple negotiations, a peaceful solution may result, or depending on terms, lead to decisive conflicts. Both outcomes are assumed.

In 1974, André Malraux, a French novelist, art theorist, Minister of Information 1945-1946, and Minister for Cultural Affairs 1959-1969 under Charles de Gaulle, visited Japan for the Mona Lisa exhibition as the French Government's special envoy, and asked for a meeting with Ikeda.[39] Later in 1976 the dialogue between the two was published. They discussed Japan-French art and culture but also nuclear issues and the role of the UN. Malraux was a man of culture, who during the Second World War fought Germany under the Nazis as a member of the resistance and after the war served as Minister of Cultural Affairs and had the opportunity as well to interview JFK, Jawaharlal Nehru and Mao Zedong. He was also a politician who represented France, a nuclear weapons state, as a member of parliament.

During the early part of their dialogue, Malraux stated conclusively that a nuclear war was totally a fantasy. Already then leaders of the US and the Soviet Union had a hotline between them. Malraux explained that the need for the hotline was a result of a research conducted by physicists of the two countries under Truman and Stalin. It was agreed that if more than ten powerful nuclear bombs in their possession were

---

[38] Daisaku Ikeda and Norman Cousins, Sekai Shimin No Taiwa (Dialogue Between Citizens of the World), Seikyo Newspaper 2000, p78
It was originally published in 1991

[39] Seikyo Newspaper, SGI Kaicho No Taiwaroku No. 27 André Malraux (SGI President's Record of Dialogue No. 27: André Malraux), 26th February 2014, p3

detonated due to their chain reaction there was a danger that the whole earth would be annihilated. Ikeda stated that the 1945 atomic bombing of Japan should not be left as a Japanese experience alone, but should be considered a precious experience of humankind. He went on to tell Malraux that many Japanese have adoration and reverence towards France's culture and arts, but the French possession of nuclear arms was hurting that goodwill and urged Malraux to work to stop nuclear testing. Malraux in turn replied that the only way to avoid nuclear war and nuclear arms race was to monitor the number of nuclear arms of each country and to reduce them, and that it was not important to stop nuclear tests. According to Malraux, from his meeting with John F. Kennedy, he believed that the US is not thinking of a total abandonment of their nuclear strategy. Since the US and USSR both keep nuclear weapons against the potential power of the other, under such circumstances abandoning nuclear weapons is not part of any nuclear weapons country's thinking. Ikeda pointed out in response, the absence of an independent body to monitor nuclear weapons, and the possibility of their use as a result of accidental political conflict. That means the only way to wipe out the threat of nuclear weapons is their total abandonment and that applies today when nuclear threats can come from non-state actors.

Malraux believed that talks and discussions for nuclear abolition are needed but treaties and agreements are in the end not that important. Somewhat improbably, he went on to say that treaties are regarded as important in Europe when civilization does not evolve as was the case from Napoleonic times to 1914, but there is no criticality in establishing them at a time when the situation has changed.[40] As for Ikeda, while

[40] Daisaku Ikeda and André Malraux, *Ningen Kaumei To Ningen No Joken (Changes within: Human Revolution and Human Condition)*, Seikyo Newspaper 1981, p106

the process towards nuclear abolition is taking place in various localities with discussions and social movements, he believed that there was a need for an ideology that would establish the importance of the dignity of life. While today this was left to the consciences of scientists involved in nuclear development and the politicians control nuclear weapons, he believed the abolition of nuclear weapons would catch on once a broader range of people became convinced of the dignity of life. As for a concrete plan, he would hold summit meetings of top leaders on nuclear abolition. All will start from coming to the table for discussion, this was a simple but solid principle and when talks begin to take effect, history will undergo a huge change. Returning to Malraux's words, Ikeda told him what was important was not the formal treaties and agreements but the contents of the talks. The important thing would be to see whether mutual understandings and mutual trusts were beginning to develop, and then the nuclear issue could be the very first challenge humankind should resolve.

Ikeda believed that it was mutual distrust that creates the political tension that might lead states to develop nuclear weapons. In his dialogue with Malraux, Ikeda shared his experiences of visiting China and the Soviet Union in 1974, the year before, when Alexei Kosygin, the USSR Prime Minister stressed the urgent importance of resolving nuclear disarmament, (see Chapter 6), and that ordinary people in both China and the Soviet Union wanted peace (see Chapter 5 and 6); further, in his meetings with the leaders of the two countries, he was able to feel human touch and trust even in his first meetings with them. Including those experiences, Ikeda pointed out that continuous inter-state conflicts have roots in their historical rivalries, which form respective prejudices that impede mutual understandings. The way to resolving them is to

* it was originally published in 1976 (only in Japanese)

have exchanges between peoples, which could take educational, academic as well as cultural forms. He further pointed out that the key was to promote exchanges between young generations of people who have less inclination to be involved in past conflicts.[41]

> **Ikeda**: Military power is used when a military super power wishes to push through its logics, while cultural exchange would depend on what people on the receiving side absorbs. That is to say while military force destroys, culture has creation at its base. Contemporary wars, especially nuclear wars would lead to a total destruction of culture. Wars are projections of human narrow-mindedness and intolerance while culture is an expression of the richness of human life. Given the essence of human life, the two are incompatible. There is but one choice. I believe deeply in the need for culture to envelope power. That is to say, I believe that 'distrust' and 'hostilities' apt to be created by politics must be converted to 'trust' and 'understanding' by the original light of culture.[42]
> (Translated by Fujiko Hara)

Ikeda also believed that culture has a role to encourage political and economic exchanges, and even when there were political conflicts and interruption of economic exchange as long as cultural exchange continues they can be put back right.

> **Ikeda**: Assuming that a ship represented politics and economy, then the sea on which the ship sails is the ties between peoples.

---

[41] Ibid, p77-p78

[42] Ibid, p89

> At times the ship may be wrecked but as long as there is sea, comings and goings will continue. Culture, education and peaceful exchange are, therefore, the right that will build eternal friendship.[43]
> (Translated by Fujiko Hara)

In 1975, having completed his visit to China and the Soviet, Ikeda had his first meeting with Henry Kissinger in Washington. Since then, the two men have met several times. A collection of their dialogues and letters were published (in Japanese) covering as friends would, broad topics including their respective thoughts on life to nuclear abolition, relations with China and the USSR.[44] Both shared their positions on saying no to nuclear weapons, to rapport with China and on their preference to refer to historical and philosophical analysis on matters at hand. The two men agreed that a fundamental change in the way of thinking was needed in resolving nuclear issues.

Since starting to write from a young age on matters of international issues, Kissinger realized that nuclear weapons had brought qualitative change to human history.[45] For in the past, states undertook wars in order to avoid situations worse than war, but nuclear weapons have the power to destroy mankind and could invite the worst possible

---

[43] Hiroyasu Kobayashi (President of Min-On Concert Association, Japan), Chugoku To No Bunka Koryu: the Min-On Concert Association, Ikeda Daisaku To Nichu Yuko No Ayumi (Cultural Exchange with China: Min On Concert Association, Daisaku Ikeda's Track for Japan-Chinese Friendship), People's Daily Overseas Edition Japan Monthly 2012, p60

[44] Seikyo Newspaper, Soka Gakkai No Hi Kinen Tokushu (Special Edition of Soka Gakkai Memorial Day), 4th May 2014, p2

[45] Daisaku Ikeda and Henry Kissinger, *Heiwa To Zinsei To Tetsugaku O Kataru (Philosophy of Human Peace)*, Seikyo Newspaper 2008, p137
It was originally published in 1987

outcome.[46] However, he believes there is a certain dilemma in that thinking. That is, if one gave an impression of fearing nuclear war as the worst, it will give those who believed in the worst kind of brutal violent revolution, a chance to blackmail with nuclear weapons.[47] This category of persons would be likely to include terrorists, dictatorial despotic states and totalitarian states. With that recognition, Kissinger stressed that all people and countries should avoid blackmail using nuclear wars and nuclear weapons. However, the difficulty of nuclear weapons is that no amount of negotiations could go beyond symbolic meanings, so that he cannot win over the temptation to say, "Let me make suggestions that would not lead to changing what we have today".[48] According to Kissinger, the decisive aspect of nuclear disarmament negotiation is the conclusion of an agreement that would bring about real difference. Just reducing the number of nuclear warheads would remain as mere symbolic change, since the remaining number of nuclear warheads would be sufficient to kill off the human race many times over.[49] He pointed out that the kind of agreement that can bring real change was one that would lead to finding solutions to reduce the danger of nuclear war. While there are many who intone opposition to nuclear war, they have violent feelings but too many lack the practical means to realizing their objective[50] Ikeda found empathy with Baruch Spinoza's (1632-1677) words, "Peace is not an absence of war, it is a virtue, a state of mind, a disposition for benevolence, confidence, justice" and interpreted that phrase to mean building a cultural situation within the human spirit is the key to starting a journey

---

[46] Ibid, p137-p138
[47] Ibid, p138
[48] Ibid
[49] Ibid
[50] Ibid

to peace.[51]

> **Ikeda** : I believe there is a big reason why the issue of war and peace should be dealt as human issues, and not solely as questions of military and political systems. One could say that wars start in the minds of man, a tragedy that we act, rather than a disaster that befalls on us.[52]
> (Translated by Fujiko Hara)

He went on to say that recent military strategic thinking with nuclear war at its apex viewed human beings as 'objects' and calculates how they could be efficiently killed based on extremely inhuman logic of how human life can be damaged or extinguished. He saw this in the way people involved calculated mutual assured destruction by first use of nuclear weapons.[53] Ikeda also asserted that a feature of modern civilization would be said to be that science and politics earned a predominant place among various human activities and at the base of it all was a thinking that attempted to vertically divide our world into subjective and objective spheres, with humans attempting to control the objective world.[54] As a result liberated human competence expanded its sphere of discretion incomparably compared to previous times. This is what the world sees in today's mega science and mega political systems.[55] Ikeda, however, sees that this kind of civilization is now at a dead end; by contrast, the objective world is now dominating human beings, and deepening the darkness of distrust and conflict, an aspect of

---

[51] Ibid, p140
[52] Ibid
[53] Ibid
[54] Ibid, p140-p141
[55] Ibid, p141-p142

modern history in which human beings are ruled by the objective world. In that sense, people see a page of modern history in which human beings are intimidated by nuclear weapons and subordinated by science, military and political clout. A systematic change requires a fundamental conversion of thinking.[56] Kissinger agreed and added that the desire to maintain peace is not found in destroying the present system but we must be convinced that the solution will be found in the present system.[57] This can be said to be a denial of systemic change likely to accompany radical and violent means, but it was necessary to press on a needed action to build a framework of disarmament while improving the existing system. Kissinger also took note of Japan, which has a peace constitution, and had renounced the right of belligerency, as to what impact it could have on the international society, against the ever-increasing mutual dependency of the global economy.[58] At the same time, however, Kissinger pointed to a line of thinking that historically speaking there is no reason why an economic power does not become a military power.[59] To which Ikeda responded, that the actual situation of political power was important. It must not remain simply a tool for bargaining at the table of international power politics that would just be an extension of the old regime. Japan must have a firm ideal as a peace-loving nation and its political power should be maximized by employing its economic and cultural strengths.[60]

In 1987, Ikeda and Norman Cousins, an American political journalist, author, and adjunct professor in medical sciences at University of California Los Angeles, met twice at Soka University of

---

[56] Ibid, p142
[57] Ibid, p142-p143
[58] Ibid, p169
[59] Ibid, p168
[60] Ibid, p168

America in Los Angeles established by Ikeda. A collection of their dialogues was published in Japan in 1991. During the 1990s, Cousins as a special envoy of JFK had the experience of sitting at the nuclear disarmament talks between JFK and Nikita Khrushchev,[61] and as a liberal promoter of nuclear disarmament movement criticized the US dropping of nuclear bombs on Japan;[62] he also pursued a role as political leader in advancing nuclear disarmament as well as in raising the anti-nuclear public opinion,[63] and maintained a strong desire to advance a peace movement.[64] Also from 1960 to 1990 he presided over the Dartmouth Conferences that took place in New Hampshire to which the US and the Soviet intellectuals were invited to discuss US-Soviet relations and international peace, promoting unofficial dialogue between the two powers during the Cold War period. The participants were limited to the non-governmental representatives of the two countries,[65] but the Ford Foundation and the Kettering Foundation on the US side and the Soviet Peace Committee and the Institute for U.S. and Canadian Studies supported the Conferences financially as well.[66] The significance of the Conference was that it nurtured individual

---

[61] Interviewed by Harry Kreisler, *The Quest for Peace: Conversation with Norman Cousins <Kennedy and Khrushchev>*, 12 September 1984 http://globetrotter.berkeley.edu/conversations/Cousins/cousins3.html (accessed on 11th August 2012)

[62] Ibid, <*The Dropping of the Atomic Bomb*> http://globetrotter.berkeley.edu/conversations/Cousins/cousins1.html (accessed on 11th August 2012)

[63] Ibid, <*Political Leaders and Public Opinion*> http://globetrotter.berkeley.edu/conversations/Cousins/cousins2.html (accessed on 11th August 2012)

[64] Ibid, <*The Peace Movement*> http://globetrotter.berkeley.edu/conversations/Cousins/cousins4.html (accessed on 11th August 2012)

[65] Richard Felix Star, *Foreign Policies of the Soviet Union*, Hoover Press 1991, p87

[66] Ruud van Dijk, *Encyclopedia of the Cold War*, Taylor & Francis 2008, p645

friendships and mutual understanding, and through participants the US and Soviet governments had the opportunities to learn about the honest understandings and opinions of private citizens. The Conference played a role in continuing mutual communication for thirty years through civilian exchange in spite of the officially closed doors of communication.

In their dialogue Ikeda and Cousins agreed on the need to enlighten the world about the Japanese experience of nuclear bombing, to ensure a central place for the United Nations, the need to change the existing views of states, and to overcome evil aspects of states and also of the need for peace education. But this dissertation mainly analyses their dialogue about 'summit meetings and civilian diplomacy'.[67] At least Ikeda himself was aware of the importance of direct meetings between top national leaders, when he made public in 1968 his opinion regarding the need to normalize Japan-China relations. In his Annual Peace Proposal which he began from 1975, he kept calling for a US-Soviet summit meeting. The Summit meeting took place in 1985. In his dialogue with Cousins, Ikeda expressed his expectation that the face-to-face meeting of the top leaders would not only have a direct impact on policies but most importantly, that it would provide the opportunity to dispel the deeply rooted distrust between the US and the Soviet Union.[68] He pointed out that in the nuclear age, the top national leaders must unavoidably think of the future of their countries simultaneously with the fate of humankind. That is to say, there was a need to change the way he thought from being the face of a state to a leader representing humankind. With regard to diplomatic relations, he

---

[67] Daisaku Ikeda and Norman Cousins, Sekai Shimin No Taiwa (Dialogue Between Citizens of the World), Seikyo Newspaper 2000, p121-p154
It was originally published in 1991

[68] Ibid, p125

maintained that while diplomat-centred foreign relations are important, there was a need to have exchanges not involving state representatives and there was a need to have exchanges concerning matters beyond representing states and protecting national interests.[69] Cousins responded by advocating organizing a world conference of sages to find solutions for global security issues. This may have been inspired by his experience of the Dartmouth Conferences.

> **Cousins** : In the past, there was a request to organize summit meetings only when the world found itself in severe difficulties. There was also a general feeling that if we can get the most powerful persons to sit around the same table the foundation for everlasting peace could be strengthened. Today, however, it is not enough to have meetings of persons of high status alone. It is not enough unless we can have the top thinkers together to hold the meeting. The peace we are searching for is not that cheap to be found by someone who will go into the mountains and learn some magic. The indispensable peace we long for today is what we find by realizing lofty ideals and purposes. A letter of credence inviting participants must not just be pretentious with ribbons, but must accompany honest statements and objectives. It would be simply difficult unless we have the wisdom to create new ways of living in all countries so that humankind will be able to continue to live on earth.[70]
> (Translated by Fujiko Hara)

While approving the holding of a kind of world conference of sages,

---

[69] Ibid, p132

[70] Ibid, p131-p132

Ikeda pointed out that, given the need to be freed from limitation and spells of national interests, exchanges of people through various civil sector diplomacies in areas of academia, art, sports and to a certain extent, commercial transactions and tourism, would have greater impact on diplomacy by emphasizing people rather than states.

> **Ikeda** : Even today when logics of states dominate our life, we see often, in spite of some political twists and turns, unmovable trust and friendship flowering among scholars, artists, and sports athletes. In Japan too we often talk about "People to People Diplomacy.[71]
>
> (Translated by Fujiko Hara)

Cousins expounded on the need to bring together intellectuals to grope for solutions beyond summit meetings, while Ikeda urged a bottom-up approach promoting people-to-people exchange at the grass roots. From the nuclear disarmament perspective, there is a need for an enlightenment campaign using plain words to enlist the general public. Many of the powerful CSOs are groups of experts, so that the expansion of their activities is somewhat limited (see Chapter 2).

Ikeda's thoughts and ways of thinking constitute the basis today of the anti-nuclear movements of the SGI. The SGI Peace Committee has a new perspective - that the nuclear weapons issue is also one of logic.[72] They understand that nuclear issues can only be resolved with the full involvement of the government and all involved persons including the CSOs. The Committee also believes that one of their roles is to assist governments, including the Japanese; rather than judging their attitudes

---

[71] Ibid, p133

[72] Interview with Kimiaki Kawai of the SGI Peace Committee 2013

by their one-off statements and formal opinions instead carefully examine their hidden logic and look for room for negotiation and help put together a logical basis. For example, the Japanese government recognized the inhumane aspects of nuclear weapons but it continued to refuse to sign the United Nations Joint Statement on that subject, considering the Japan-US Alliance and potential threats from neighbouring countries (see Chapter 2). The SGI Peace Committee thought that it should first value the fact that it recognized nuclear weapons as inhumane weapons. And it praised the presence of the Japanese government representative at the 2013 Oslo Conference in spite of its failure to sign. The SGI Peace Committee believes one of CSO's role is to encourage government representatives to continue to be present. According to the SGI Peace Committee, in promoting nuclear disarmament movement what should be feared is jumping from one logic to another. Many anti-nuclear CSOs have defined nuclear weapons as being sharply against morality and ethics. If that were the case the US and other nuclear weapons states have been violating ethics and humanity for more than half a century. There was no way the nuclear weapons states would accept that logic because it would then be tantamount to accepting they were wrong. The SGI Peace Committee believes it must also avoid nuclear powers turning defiant and spurring on nuclear development saying it has nothing to do with ethics or morality. They believe in the need to place good logic on top of another, in other words they feel that an inclusive perspective rather than confrontation is important. At the 2013 Oslo Conference they paid attention to the statement of the Egyptian Government representative as charting a realistic roadmap to nuclear abolition.

"...The Treaty on the Non-Proliferation of nuclear weapons

could be **a vehicle** to achieve nuclear disarmament as long as nuclear weapon States fulfilled their obligations under Article VI of the Treaty and started negotiating in good faith on nuclear disarmament, and the universality of the Treaty was achieved…"[73]

The SGI Peace Committee believes that nuclear issues should not be discussed exclusively within an ethical framework, and that the discussion should even transcend the security framework, to be able to simply state that nuclear weapons are prohibited in the legal framework of international laws and must therefore be abolished. It believes that this kind of simple legal framework would be something that all concerned parties would be able to accept.[74]

The SGI Peace Committee has held separate meetings with the Arms Control Department Division of the MOFA and has built trusting relations by explaining their logic and sharing the SGI's perspective. This collaborative attitude led to the presence of the Japanese Ambassador to Bahrain on behalf of the Japanese government at the SGI's Anti-nuclear Exhibition in that country.

From 2007 to 2011, the Exhibition: From a Culture of Violence to Culture of Peace: Transforming the Human Spirit' (EFCVCPTHS) [75]

---

[73] Delegate of Egypt, *Conference on Disarmament Discusses Nuclear Disarmament, News & Media UNOG*, 5 March 2013 http://www.unog.ch/80256EDD006B9C2E/%28httpNewsByYear_en%29/CA654DA3242244FAC1257B250067B11F?OpenDocument (accessed on 3rd April 2013)

[74] Interview with Kimiaki Kawai of the SGI Peace Committee 2013

[75] Material provided by SGI (about the EFCVCPTHS) in Japanese
The exhibition was held in over 220 cities in 28 countries, in eight languages (English, Spanish, Chinese, Japanese, Thai, Nepali, Italian and German). Furthermore, there are plans to translate it into more six languages as of 2011 (Portuguese, Finnish, Dutch, Icelandic, Serbian and Macedonian)

was organised. The feature of these presentations is that they are not only supported by UN organisations and government agencies, but they are also co-sponsored by a CSO and NGO alliance including ICAN. The exhibition is based on the proposal Ikeda made in his Annual Peace Proposal 2006, that in order to break through the stagnation of the nuclear disarmament negotiations and activities, for the next decade up to 2016, there should be 'Ten Years of Action' in which the United Nations and NGOs will collaborate to promote nuclear abolition. This was an attempt to break the stagnation at the civilian level, recognising that even during the post-Cold War era there were no international conferences deliberating on nuclear disarmament as was also the case with the UN Special Session on Disarmament. The Weapons of Mass Destruction Commission that the Swedish Government launched had proposed international conferences for disarmament but it had not reached the point of successfully building solidarity for nuclear disarmament.[76] The objective of SGI was to involve other CSOs, not just government organisations, to create a big anti-nuclear global flow.

Special mention should be made regarding the EFCVCPTHS, that it was held in 2013 in Bahrain (an Islamic country)'s capital, Manama (Al Manamah).[77] Tension had increased in the Middle East because of the

---

[76] WMDC
http://www.un.org/disarmament/education/wmdcommission/index.html
(accessed on 19th May 2011)
WMDC Report, *Recommendation 26, etc, Weapons of Terror - Freeing the World of Nuclear, Biological and Chemical Arms,* 2006
http://www.isn.ethz.ch/Digital-Library/Publications/Detail/?ord588=grp2&ots591=0C54E3B3-1E9C-BE1E-2C24-A6A8C7060233&lng=en&id=26614
(accessed on 19th May 2011)

[77] The exhibition was held under the co-sponsorship of the SGI, the ICAN, the Bahrain Center for Strategic International and Energy Studies known as the DERASAT, the UN Information Centre, for the Gulf Countries, and the Inter Press Service (IPS) and with H.E. Shaikh Khalid bin Ahmed bin Mohammed Al Khalifa, the Foreign Minister of Bahrain as the Patron.

conflict between Iran and the US government over suspicion of Iran's nuclear development. At the 2010 NPT Review Conference it was agreed that an international conference should be held towards building a nuclear free Middle East but it has yet to materialize (as of 2014). The Opening Ceremony of the Bahrain National Museum was graced by the Patron as well as diplomatic corps of eighteen countries and regions, including Shigeki Sumi, the Japanese Ambassador to Bahrain as well as dignitaries from the UN agencies.[78]

At the Ceremony, the Foreign Minister of Bahrain criticized the nuclear test conducted a month earlier by the North Korean government (February 2013), and proposed that the responsibility imposed by the UN Security Council resolution be implemented as a statement from the Kingdom of Bahrain. He also urged the Iranian government to comply with the resolutions of the UN Security Council resolution and the IAEA Board of Directors, and to make responsible decisions leading towards peacefully and diplomatically resolving the nuclear issue. The Exhibition provided a place for the government to urge nuclear disarmament diplomatically.[79]

The SGI Peace Committee was responsible for planning and operating the exhibition. The same committee visited the Bahraini Embassy in Japan to explain the plan and received endorsement.[80] Since going through third parties such as politicians and political parties would complicate matters, the SGI undertakes to contact governments

---

DERASAT http://www.derasat.org.bh/ (accessed on 19th May 2011)

[78] Seikyo Shimbun Newspaper 18th March 2013 (in Japanese)
Also, the press conference preceding the event was attended by representatives of co-sponsoring organisations including the Executive Director of SGI Peace Committee, and guests, including the Vice-Minister of Foreign Affairs, Bahrain, Shigeki Sumi (Japanese Ambassador to Bahrain), and Peter Grohmann, the Resident Representative of the UN Development Programme.

[79] Ibid

[80] Interview with Kimiaki Kawai of SGI Peace Committee, 2013

or embassies directly to explain and to negotiate.[81] The SGI also directly visited the DNPSD of the MOFA to invite the Japanese Ambassador to Bahrain to the opening of the exhibition; he accepted.[82] The SGI has successfully developed trusting relations with the DNPSD of the MOFA through logical dialogue and by following Ikeda's ways of doing things.

Ikeda has actively promoted dialogues between civilizations and religions and had exchanges with the Simon Wiesenthal Center, a Jewish human rights organisation, as well as with Martin Luther King Jr. International Chapel at Morehouse College. He has co-authored a book on 'Spirit of India – Buddhism and Hinduism' with Ved P. Nanda, Professor of the University of Denver (USA)[83] as well as inviting an Iranian, Majid Tehranian, Professor of Harvard University as the first Director of the Toda Institute for Global Peace and Policy Research, a research institute based in Hawaii.

The SGI also has strong links with the United States, the biggest nuclear weapons state in the world. In April 2014, the SGI conducted an interfaith symposium entitled "Making a Difference: Faith Communities and the Humanitarian Consequences of Nuclear Weapons"[84] at the United States Institute of Peace in Washington DC. This symposium was intended to follow up on the Conference: Humanitarian Impact of Nuclear Weapons (Oslo Conference 2013) and its second conference held in Mexico in February 2014[85]. Also, this symposium was organized

---

[81] Ibid

[82] Ibid

[83] Daisaku Ikeda and Ved Prakash Nanda, *The Spirit of India – Buddhism and Hinduism*, The Institute of Oriental Philosophy 2005 (published only in Japanese)

[84] Participants to the Symposium included one hundred religious, academic and NGO representatives from Muslim, Christian and Jewish faiths.

[85] Ministry of Foreign Affairs Mexico, *Second Conference on the Humanitarian Impact of Nuclear Weapons 2014*,

at the same time as the Third Session of the Preparatory Committee for the 2015 NPT Review Conference (28th April-9th May in New York)[86] and provided the opportunity to deliver the voice of civil society to its deliberation.[87]

The SGI explained that it organized the symposium based on Ikeda's statement that 'building a world without nuclear arms is not just removing their threat, but a challenge for citizens to open the way to an era based on peace and co-existence'.[88] The symposium candidly pointed out that there was a lack of uniform strategy to achieve a world without nuclear arms, whether to press forward the present situation or maintain it, or to go for legal prohibition or take a step by step approach.[89] It made the roles of the state and the civic society clear by stating that if it was the role of the states to build a clear route towards nuclear abolition then it is the role of civil society to arouse international public opinion in support.[90] The symposium adopted the Joint Statement of US Religious Committees on the Humanitarian Consequences of Nuclear Weapons,[91] and it was presented by hand by

---

http://www.sre.gob.mx/en/index.php/humanimpact-nayarit-2014 (accessed on 21st August 2014)

[86] United Nations Office for Disarmament Affairs, Third Session of the Preparatory Committee for the 2015 Review Conference of the Parties to the Treaty on the Non-Proliferation of Nuclear Weapons (NPT) 28April-9 May 2014, http://www.un.org/disarmament/WMD/Nuclear/NPT2015/PrepCom2014/index.shtml (accessed on 21st August 2014)

[87] Seikyo Newspaper, Beikoku De Kakuhaizetsu Heno Shukyokan Kaigi (SGI held an interfaith symposium in the United States to abolish nuclear weapons), 1st May 2014

[88] Ibid

[89] Ibid

[90] Ibid

[91] SGI, Joint Statement of US Religious Committees on the Humanitarian Consequences of Nuclear Weapons – Making a Difference: Faith Communities and the Humanitarian Impact of Nuclear Weapons, 24th April 2014 http://www.sgi.org/assets/pdf/Joint-Faith-Statement-Antinukes.pdf (accessed

the representative of the SGI Peace Committee to Enrique Roman Morey[92], the Chairman of the Third Session of the Preparatory Committee for the 2015 NPT Review Conference and Angela Kane, the UN High Representative for Disarmament Affairs.[93]

Keynote lectures were also given by three high level professionals[94] on nuclear weapons and arms control in the United States including Anita Friedt, the US Principal Deputy Assistant Secretary of State for Nuclear and Strategic Policy. The symposium provided a place of dialogue between persons in charge of the nuclear strategy of the US administration and civil society. Friedt represented the Obama Administration at the symposium.[95] On this, Kent E. Calder of Johns Hopkins University[96] commented, "the attendance of a high level person in charge of the nuclear strategy from the US Department of State is evidence that the US administration is attaching importance to the event. Under President Ikeda, the SGI is playing a major role in achieving peace and stability in the world".[97]

---

on 21st August 2014)
This was signed by religious leaders of the fourteen organisations including the SGI

92 The Peruvian Ambassador to the United Nations

93 Seikyo Newspaper, SGI Amerika Homondan Kakuheiki Haizetsu O Motomeru Kyodoseimei O NPT Saikento Kaigi No Junbi Iinkai Gicho Ni Teisyutsu (tt 'The SGI Visiting Group to the United States submitted the Joint Statement calling for nuclear abolition to the Chairman of the Preparatory Committee of the NPT Review Conference'), 5th May 2014

94 Andrew Kanter (former Director of the Physicians for Social Responsibility), Daryl Kimball (Executive Director of the Arms Control Association), and Anita Friedt

95 SGI, *Press Release: US Faith Group Unite to Call for Nuclear Weapons Abolition, Stressing Devastating Humanitarian Impact*, 25th April 2014 http://www.sgi.org/news/press-releases/press-release-2014/us-faiths-call-for-nuclear-weapons-abolition.html (accessed on 27th April 2014)

96 Director of the Edwin O. Reischauer Center for East Asian Studies, Johns Hopkins University

97 Seikyo Newspaper, Beikoku De Kakuhaizetsu Eno Shukyokan Kaigi (SGI held an interfaith symposium in the United States to abolish nuclear weapons),

It could be surmised that Barack Obama had an eye on Ikeda's thoughts and action from the time of his inauguration, if not earlier. He invited Ikeda to his inauguration in 2009, which was duly attended by the representative of the SGI-USA.[98] Also, when Obama visited Japan the same year and spoke in Tokyo on the US Asian Policy, the White House sent Ikeda an invitation; the honour fell on the representative of the Soka Gakkai (Japan) who presented a congratulatory message from Ikeda to President Obama to James P. Zumwalt of the US Embassy.[99] Obama's nuclear abolition policy and doctrine are supported by former US officials in charge of US foreign and military policies such as Henry Kissinger who had sent the Wall Street Journal his articles on nuclear abolition, and others who are known to have supra-partisan support as witnessed by their being part of discussion that takes place in the Oval Office in the White House.[100]

John F. Kennedy (JFK)[101] asked to meet Ikeda in November 1962, immediately after the Cuban Missile Crisis.[102] Ikeda had established in

---

1st May 2014

98 Seikyo Newspaper, Oabama Daitoryo Ga Shunin: SGI Kaicho Ga Keishuku No Message (Mr. Obama became the new US President, and the SGI President sent his message for cerebration to Mr. Obama), 22nd January 2009

99 Deputy Chief of Mission of the US Embassy in Tokyo 2008-2009 and Deputy Assistant Secretary of State for East Asia and Pacific Policy 2011-2012 Seikyo Online, Obama Daitoryo Enzetsu Ni SGI Kaicho O Shotai: Harada Kaicho Ga Dairi Shusseki (The SGI President was invited to the President Obama's Speech, and President Harada of the Soka Gakkai Japan attended instead), 15th November 2009
http://www.seikyoonline.jp/news/headline/2009/11/1186692_2447.html (accessed on 2nd February 2011)

100 Reuters, Kissinger, Shultz back Obama to push eliminate nuclear arms, 20th May 2009
http://blogs.reuters.com/talesfromthetrail/2009/05/19/kissinger-shultz-back-obama-push-to-eliminate-nuclear-arms/ (accessed on 16th January 2010)

101 US President 1961-1963

102 "Ikeda Daisaku No Kiseki" Hensan Iinkai (The Editing Committee of the "Daisaku Ikeda's Track), Ikeda Daisaku No Kiseki III: Heiwa To Bunka No Daijo (The Daisaku Ikeda's Track III: The Great Castle for Promoting Peace

1961, the *Komei Siji Renmei* (Komei Political League) the predecessor of the Komeito, and by the following year it had grown to become the third biggest political party at the House of Councillors (Upper House of the Japanese Diet). JFK had just averted the Cuban Missile Crisis and was conscious of the northeast Asian situation, another centre of East West confrontation. Ikeda surmised that JFK wished to directly confirm whether the fast rising Soka Gakkai (Japan) and the Komeito were anti-communist or tolerated it[103]. The main purpose of Ikeda's meeting with JFK was to convey to him the contents of the Declaration Calling for the Abolition of Nuclear weapons 1957 and to ask him to open the way for nuclear abolition through the direct meeting of the heads of the US and the Soviet Union from the perspective of human beings beyond the care of nation-states.[104] The meeting did not happen due to the opposition of the ruling political party of Japan. The ruling party interrupted the proposed meeting between JFK and Ikeda, a civilian. Since Prime Minister Hayato Ikeda (1960-1962) had a brief courtesy meeting with JFK on 22 June 1962 during the Japan-US Summit,[105] no Japanese person had met JFK.

In August 1963, JFK signed with the USSR and the United Kingdom the first Partial Test Ban Treaty, and was assassinated in November of the same year, so the meeting with Ikeda did not take place. Ikeda, however, met with Edward Kennedy, JFK's younger

---

and Culture), Ushio Co., Ltd. 2008 p244

103 Ibid p245

104 Seikyo Newspaper, SGI Kaicho No Taiwaroku: Dai 23 Kai – Edward Kennedy, Amerika Join Giin (the 23rd Record of the SGI President's Dialogue with Leaders and People: Edward Kennedy, US Senator), 23rd December 2013 p3

105 "Ikeda Daisaku No Kiseki" Hensan Iinkai (The Editing Committee of the "Daisaku Ikeda's Track"), Ikeda Daisaku No Kiseki III: Heiwa To Bunka No Daijo (The Daisaku Ikeda's Track III: The Great Castle for Promoting Peace and Culture), Ushio Co., Ltd. 2008 p244-p245

brother, and developed friendly relations. In January 1978, Edward Kennedy visited Japan with his family including JFK's daughter Caroline, the US Ambassador to Japan from 2013 to the present (as of 2014).

On 11 January Edward Kennedy visited the Hiroshima Peace Memorial Museum and gave a lecture on "Peace and Nuclear Disarmament".[106] On 12 January, the following day, he met with Ikeda in Tokyo and the two discussed nuclear issues and the need for relaxing tensions with China and the USSR. Edward Kennedy's stay in Tokyo was limited to two nights and three days, it was therefore singularly exceptional for him to have talks with a civilian.

> **Ikeda**: Abolition of nuclear weapons must be undertaken as an issue of the whole humanity.
>
> **E. Kennedy**: That is exactly so. What my brother John called for in his inaugural speech was the promotion of a treaty to ban nuclear tests, since that call for nuclear disarmament is a concrete path for non-proliferation of nuclear weapons. In my speech in Hiroshima yesterday I called for the abolition of nuclear weapons. I urged in my speech that this was the initiative that Japan and the US together should be taking on. The joint objective for Japan and the US means it is the joint objective of the whole humanity. (Here, citing examples of racial discrimination and the bogging down of the war in Vietnam, he said that that the fundamental power that will push

---

106 Hiroshima Heiwa Media Center of Chugoku Shimbun (Hiroshima Peace Media Center of the Chugoku Newspaper), *Hiroshima No Kiroku 1978 1Gatsu (The Records of Hiroshima in January 1978)*, http://www.hiroshimapeacemedia.jp/mediacenter/article.php?story=20100628120059236_ja (accessed on 18th November 2012)

forward stalemated political reality lay in morality.) Politics without morality was powerless. The reason I wanted to see the president (Ikeda) was due to my interest in morality.

Ikeda: The leaders and people of the Soviet Union are all human beings. The leaders and people of China are also the same human beings. I believe based on that understanding, we should arouse international public opinion to the fact that 'humankind is a single community'. I wish you would challenge the cause with a clear understanding that we are all members of a single human community.

E. Kennedy: I believe that for people to have mutual understanding and respect, one must start acting as a fellow human being and encourage spirits to seek rapport. I endorse your thoughts, President Ikeda. We must return to being a human person. Go back to being a human person.'[107]

(Translated by Fujiko Hara)

Edward Kennedy had just visited China to search ways for normalizing diplomatic relations between the US and China. The following year, 1982, the US and China normalized their relations. In 1982, Edward Kennedy sent Ikeda his book *'Freeze! How We Can Help Prevent Nuclear War (Bantam Books 1982)'*. He also sent a congratulatory telegram when the SGI-USA East Territory held a general meeting in 2007 at the John F. Kennedy Center for the Performing Arts, Washington D.C.[108] Obama appointed Caroline

---

[107] Seikyo Newspaper, SGI Kaicho No Taiwaroku: Dai 23 Kai – Edward Kennedy, Amerika Join Giin (the 23rd Record of the SGI President's Dialogue with Leaders and People: Edward Kennedy, US Senator), 23rd December 2013 p3

[108] Ibid

Kennedy as the US Ambassador to Japan in 2013. She said in her acceptance speech at the US Senate Commission on Foreign Relations that it all began with her visit to Japan in 1978.

"I can think of no country in which I would rather serve than Japan. I first visited in 1978 with my Uncle, Senator Kennedy, and was deeply affected by our visit to Hiroshima".

(Statement by Ms. Caroline Kennedy, Nominee for U.S. Ambassador to Japan, Senate Foreign Relations Committee, September 19, 2013)[109]

Obama, therefore, can be said to have strong interests in Ikeda through Kissinger, Edward Kennedy and other acquaintances, and Ikeda's anti-nuclear movement and private diplomacy, as well as nuclear abolition activities of the SGI.

Finding commonalities with parties that profess different ideas and perspectives and collaboratively take on the issues at hand, are examples of Ikeda's perspective based on Buddhism and what he practised in his private diplomacy (see Chapter 4 and 5). According to Ikeda, the key to thinking beyond 'differences' lies in looking for similarities rather than differences.

Cousins : I heard and saw many things in different places. As one travels around the world, one will find people living in mud huts and those who live in bamboo dwellings. Similarly, in

---

[109] The United States Senate Committee on Foreign Relations, *Statement by Ms. Caroline Kennedy, Nominee for U.S. Ambassador to Japan, Senate Foreign Relations Committee*, September 19, 2013, p3 http://www.foreign.senate.gov/imo/media/doc/Kennedy_Testimony.pdf (accessed on 17th October 2013)

music some people prefer five musical scales while others prefer twelve. Or take vegetarians, for example, some have become vegetarians for religious reasons while others for their own preferences.... I was educated sufficiently about these differences. The only thing I regret is that I did not learn about the absence of any significance in these differences. The absence of significance should be taught but I regret that it was not. Differences among humans are so slight that there is really no meaning to point it out. However, education I received did not stop to say how similar we all are. Perhaps because similarities were so simple a fact. Among the simple truths, and the most simple truth is that humankind represents a single community that shares life and death.

Ikeda : Professor, you just told me that a simple truth' is important. I believe that means to think with "people' at the starting point, rather than states and races. There are people yearning for peace and freedom in states that are under different political systems and ideologies. That is the role of high religions, inter alia, that of Buddhist teachings. In this regard, Mahayana Buddhism offers a well-tried traditional way of thinking, going above various differences to find commonalities.... That is to say, the spirit of Buddhism summarized in the Lotus Sutra teaches us of the dignity of life of all living creatures the value of which must never be violated. Seen from this premise it is only to be expected that it will lead to an absolute equality without any differences or obstacles among people.[110]

---

[110] Daisaku Ikeda and Norman Cousins, Sekai Shimin No Taiwa (Dialogue Between Citizens of the World), Seikyo Newspaper 2000, p76-p79
It was originally published in 1991

On that point one can say that the SGI is contributing towards ensuring that the Japanese government does not retract from the nuclear disarmament policy as well as in establish a collaborative setup among the CSOs. With regard to establishing international rules regarding nuclear abolition which the SGI peace Committee aims at, the challenge is how to make it meaningful in the face of the lack of an organisation able to sanction and take measures against violators, as pointed out by Coudenhove Kalergi and Malraux.

Ikeda has consistently stated that cultural exchanges and person-to-person dialogue are the key to mitigating conflicts and supporting inter-state diplomatic relations. He believes it is a direct way to move nuclear disarmament forward in the world. To demonstrate this, this dissertation will now analyse Ikeda's private diplomacy with China and the USSR during the Cold War in Chapter 5 and 6.

Chapter 5: Ikeda and China

In 2009, in an article entitled "A world without nuclear weapons," Thomas C. Schelling[1] expressed strong doubt as to whether a world without nuclear weapons was truly desirable.[2] His theory is premised on the argument that the abolition of nuclear weapons would not eliminate nuclear threats, and would only result in creating further tension in the world. In the world without nuclear weapons envisaged by Schelling, countries with a past history and know-how in producing nuclear weapons such as the P5, Israel and North Korea, would resume weapons production, which would lead to a world where full-readiness for the deployment of these weapons could be planned and executed at any time. He also warned that we would see a world where such countries would secure methods of emergency communications, engage in repeated practical training and, under a state of high alert, establish targets for pre-emptive attacks on nuclear facilities of other countries.

At that point, he claimed, there was a danger that all crises would turn into nuclear crises, and all wars develop into nuclear wars. For example, he warned that there is a possibility that countries which initially acquired even a small stockpile of nuclear weapons will force their will on other countries and make pre-emptive strikes, resulting in a world where there were increasing triggers for pre-emptive strikes, which would ultimately increase tension in the world. While affirming a theory of nuclear deterrence, he pointed out that in the past 60 odd years,

---

[1] American economist (2005 Novel Memorial Prize in Economic Sciences, shared with Robert Aumann). Professor of Foreign Policy, National Security, Nuclear Strategy and Arms Control at the School of Public Policy at University of Maryland, College Park.

[2] Thomas C. Schelling, *A world without nuclear weapons?*, On the Global Nuclear Future Vol. 1, American Academy of Arts & Sciences, Fall 2009 https://www.amacad.org/content/publications/pubContent.aspx?d=945 (accessed on 27th June 2015)

nuclear weapons have not been used in any war involving nuclear weapon states.[3] The reason Schelling gives for this is that the use of nuclear weapons is deplored throughout the world, and he concludes that a taboo on the use of nuclear weapons has already been widely established, to the extent that this taboo applies to Indian-Pakistani hostilities and conditions surrounding Israel.[4]

In this way, Schelling's logic indicates that the simple eradication of nuclear weapons will not result in putting an end to political tensions or conflicts among countries and international society. In other words, political tension and conflict trigger nuclear issues. Therefore, the weapons issue, including the nuclear issue, will always be a secondary issue and a secondary factor. Underlying the development of nuclear issues exist fundamental problems such as religious or ideological confrontation, territorial disputes or resource acquisition, where negotiation and compromise among countries are difficult.

The problem of the use and development of weapons arises from the desire of countries to maintain an advantageous position amid negotiation processes and political tension that have been preceded by some kind of political problem or conflict. Therefore, the reason nuclear issues arise time and again is due to the existence of an existing problem. In other words, these nuclear issues do not suddenly erupt at the outset. Therefore, to resolve nuclear issues, it is essential to eliminate the underlying fundamental tensions, that is, find a pathway or

---

[3] Schelling mentioned about the warfare: US vs. North Korea (Korean War), US vs. China, US vs. Viet Cong, US vs. North Vietnam, US vs. Iraq twice, US vs. Taliban in Afghanistan, Israel vs. Syria and Egypt, UK vs. Argentina, and USSR vs. Afghanistan
Thomas C. Schelling, *A world without nuclear weapons?*, On the Global Nuclear Future Vol. 1, American Academy of Arts & Sciences, Fall 2009 https://www.amacad.org/content/publications/pubContent.aspx?d=945 (accessed on 27th June 2015)

[4] Ibid

breakthrough to the resolution of these tensions. Thus, it cannot be simply said with certainty that harmonious relations will develop among countries at loggerheads with each other if achievement of nuclear abolition is possible.

One typical example is Indo-Pakistan relations. Underlying the conflict between these two countries were religious confrontations between Hindus and Muslims. As these escalated, the Two-Nation Theory,[5] proposed by the Muslim side, claimed that even if as a people they were ethnically of the same lineage, they could not coexist due to religious differences, and thus the two states of India and Pakistan came about. Since it is difficult to simply geographically divide the two, serious Indo-Pakistan Wars[6] on four occasions developed into a nuclear arms race over border areas where both Hindu and Muslim residents live together in mixed areas. For example, the issue as to which country owned the princely state of Kashmir, located in the territory of both India and Pakistan, was the trigger of the Indo-Pakistan War of 1947. The Maharaja of Kashmir at the time was Hari Singh, who was a Hindu, but 80% of the country was Muslim, and Singh, who was forced to decide whether Kashmir belonged to India or Pakistan, decided that it belonged to India. The Pakistani government and the Muslims in Kashmir vehemently opposed the decision, whereupon the Indian government dispatched troops to aid Singh, causing a dispute to erupt. The dispute over Kashmir continues to this day (as of 2015).

These political tensions became the cause of the nuclear arms race of the two countries. Furthermore, from the 1950s onwards, India became locked in confrontations with Pakistan and China over national

---

[5] This theory was introduced by the All-India Muslim League led by Muhamad Ali Jinnah at the Lahore Resolution 1940 to divide India to two distinct nations.

[6] In 1947, 1965, 1971 and 1999 (Kargil War)

borders. The armies of both India and China became involved in armed conflict over the eastern border of Kashmir in September 1959 and this developed into large-scale military combat in 1962. China possesses nuclear arms, which had been legitimized by the NPT, and this placed India in a difficult predicament. Although China's conflicts with both the Soviet Union and the United States encouraged its nuclear development, it cannot be denied that actions such as China's deployment of troops in areas adjacent to India's borders have escalated tension. When the Sino-Soviet split developed in the 1960s, the USSR threw its support behind India while China gave its support to Pakistan, further intensifying tensions. When Pakistan was subsequently defeated in the Indo-Pakistani War of 1971, East Pakistan was separated and became the independent state of Bangladesh, driving Pakistan into a precarious situation. This situation is believed to be an underlying reason for Pakistan's possession of nuclear arms.[7]

In May 1974, India became the sixth nuclear weapon state in the world when it conducted an underground nuclear test and announced that it had nuclear capability. India's possession of nuclear capability caused the balance in Indo-Pakistan relations to deteriorate, with Pakistan being placed in a unilaterally disadvantageous position against India. Several days after India's underground nuclear test in May 1998, Pakistan also conducted a nuclear test and became the seventh nuclear weapon state in the world. Both India and Pakistan oppose the NPT, which recognizes only the legitimacy of the P5 as nuclear weapon states, and have not become members. The conflicts between these two

---

[7] Mari Izuyama & Shinichi Ogawa, Nuclear Policies of India and Pakistan, Bulletin Vol 5 of the National Institute for Defence Studies Japan (Ministry of Defence Japan), August 2002 pp44 http://www.nids.go.jp/publication/kiyo/pdf/bulletin_j5-1_3.pdf (accessed on 1st July 2015)

countries today encourage the threat of terrorism. Forces believed to be Islamic extremists have been behind many terrorist threats as well as shooting incidents and bombings, including a hotel in Mumbai, India where foreigners stay, as well as railway stations, claiming the lives of 174 people including 34 foreigners and causing many injuries (Mumbai Terror Attacks 2008).[8]

The three nuclear weapon states of India, Pakistan and China are directly involved in these territorial disputes, and the abolition of nuclear weapons by even one of these states would result in an upset in the balance of power. Furthermore, at the root of the conflict between India and Pakistan is an ethnic conflict due to differences in religion and, therefore, it would be difficult to achieve nuclear abolition unless both territorial disputes and religious/ideological problems are resolved.

On the other hand, the logic that the use of nuclear weapons is a taboo, another assertion of Schelling, and therefore will not become a reality is a view that can only be described as wishful thinking. There is a possibility that political leaders will emerge who will view the threat of nuclear terrorism or nuclear weapons as a tool for achieving their country's national interests or to threaten other countries. For example, Russian President Vladimir Putin revealed that he considered deploying nuclear weapons during the crisis in the Ukraine and Crimea in 2014.[9] His assertion was that Crimea was historically Russian territory, and the international media in countries around the world reported his declaration of deployment of nuclear weapons. Furthermore, Putin indicated that he would deploy 40 new intercontinental ballistic missiles

---

[8] BBC News, *Surviving Mumbai gunman convinced over attacks*, 3 May 2010 http://news.bbc.co.uk/2/hi/south_asia/8657642.stm (accessed on 1st July 2015)

[9] BBC News, *Ukraine conflict: Putin 'was ready for nuclear alert'*, 15th March 2015 http://www.bbc.com/news/world-europe-31899680 (accessed on 1st July 2015)

with nuclear weapons, which put the brakes on various North Atlantic Treaty Organization (NATO) countries opposing the independence of Crimea.[10] NATO Secretary General Jens Stoltenberg described this approach as a routine ploy of Russia, indicating that there were no grounds for the deployment of these missiles.[11] In view of recent low oil prices and Western economic sanctions, Steven Pifer[12] expresses doubt as to whether Russia actually has the financial means to deploy new nuclear arms. Pifer, however, also claimed around 2010 that many NATO countries doubted the United States would continue its deployment of weapons in Europe and whether they were necessary, but that those voices were no longer listened to following Putin's announcement about the deployment of nuclear weapons.[13] In other words, he suggests the view that US nuclear weapons should continue to be deployed in Europe is one held by the majority of the NATO countries.[14] Pifer also believes that Putin does not view nuclear weapons simply as a means of deterrence but as a method of intimidation and force, and indicates that this attitude represents a new threat.[15] In the history of nuclear development up until now, there was a

---

[10] BBC News, *Putin: Russia to boost nuclear arsenal with 40 missiles*, 16th June 2015 http://www.bbc.com/news/world-33151125 (accessed on 1st July 2015)

[11] (Stoltenberg said) "(The statement from Mr. Putin) was confirming pattern and behaviour of Russia over a period of time; we have seen Russia is investing more in defence in general and its nuclear capability in particular. This nuclear sabre-ratting of Russia is unjustified, it's destabilising and it's dangerous"
Ibid

[12] Director, Arms Control and Non-Proliferation Initiatives of the Brookings

[13] Steven Pifer, *Putin's nuclear saber-rattling: What is he compensating for?*, the Brookings 17th June 2015
http://www.brookings.edu/blogs/order-from-chaos/posts/2015/06/17-putin-nuclear-saber-rattling-pifer (accessed on 1st July 2015)

[14] Ibid

[15] (Pifer said) "…more alarmingly, the Russian President may see nuclear weapons not just as tools of deterrence, but as tools of coercion. That would be

basic assumption that the production and deployment of nuclear weapons were entirely means of deterrence but Putin's case is an example whereby there is a possibility that nuclear weapons will become a method for changing territorial borders or conditions or the political climate.

Josei Toda, the second president of Soka Gakkai, in 1957 stated that the desire to use nuclear weapons came from a karma of evil that lies latent deep within the human spirit and, under the influence of this karma, human beings attempt to control and dominate others by means of fear and threats rather than dialogue and cooperation.[16] As a Buddhist philosopher, Toda used the word "evil" and described the deep psyche of human beings who, as the possessors of the most powerful weapons, come to want to use these to fulfill their own desires. In the process, he says, they forget the human value of humility and cease to listen to arbitration or the opinions of others.

In regard to territorial disputes between Japan and other countries, China claims territorial rights in the Senkaku Islands, which is the territory of Japan. This issue will be discussed later. An example of a significant territorial dispute involving Japan, which triggered an arms race, is a conflict encompassing seven countries[17] including China over territorial rights in the South China Sea. After the end of the Second World War, Japan relinquished its territorial rights in the South China Sea, and because it subsequently did not reaffirm its ownership, the seven countries in the surrounding area have continued to dispute

---

new and potentially dangerous"
Ibid

[16] Josei Toda, *Declaration Calling for the Abolition of Nuclear Weapons*, Josei Toda Website Committee http://www.joseitoda.org/vision/declaration (accessed on 1st July 2015)

[17] China, Philippines, Vietnam, Indonesia, Taiwan, Brunei and Malaysia

territorial rights of the Spratly Islands and other territories.[18] This marine area is an expansive exclusive economic zone (EEZ), is rich in marine resources, and is also a strategic zone, and therefore intermittent military clashes are ongoing.

In the Battle of the Paracel Islands in 1974, China defeated Vietnam and occupied the Paracel Islands. In 1988, China again defeated Vietnam in the Johnson South Reef Skirmish and took over part of the Spratly Islands. Both China and Taiwan claim all territory of the South China Sea, while Vietnam, the Philippines, Malaysia and Indonesia all claim territorial rights in part. There is no indication of an end to China's hard line, which is backed by military might. In 2014, the Philippines Ministry of Foreign Affairs disclosed photographic evidence of China's building of artificial islands through landfill of reefs within territory of the Philippines on the Spratly Islands and protested to China that it was violating international law.[19] China, which claims rights to all territory of the South China Sea, responded by saying that it was free to do whatever it wanted to do within its own territory.[20]

The heads of state of various countries including the United States and Japan criticized China at international conferences and other forums, stating that they did not recognize its alteration of existing boundaries. [21] The Japanese government criticized China's advance in marine areas,

---

[18] Article 2 of The Treaty of Peace with Japan
[19] The Nikkei (Newspaper) 15th May 2014, The Philippines, Chugoku No Minami Sina Kai Umetate Shashin Kokai (The Philippines exposed photos that China making reclaimed land in the South China Sea) http://www.nikkei.com/article/DGXNASGM1502R_V10C14A5FF1000/ (accessed on 3rd July 2015)
[20] Ibid
[21] The IISS Shangri-La Dialogue: 13th Asia Security Summmit
MOFA, The 13th IISS Asian Security Summit – The Shangri-La Dialogue – Keynote Address by Shinzo ABE, Prime Minister, Japan "Peace and prosperity in Asia, forevermore, Japan for the rule of law, Asia for the rule of law, And the rule of law for all of us", 30th May 2014

and while strengthening its financial assistance to Pacific nations (see Chapter 1), also strengthened its military alliances. In April 2014, Japan revised the Three Principles on Arms Exports prohibiting the export of arms manufactured in Japan and the international joint development of arms, and under strict provisions established the Three Principles on Transfer of Defence Equipment and Technology which allows these.[22] Moreover, the Japanese government made an agreement with the government of the Philippines to strengthen cooperation in defence and to conduct joint training. [23]

Furthermore, the Japanese government provided six patrol boats for Vietnam's marine police and agreed to further strengthen cooperation with the Vietnamese government in the area of marine security in both the East China Sea and the South China Sea. [24]The United States government, which was without extra capacity due to reduction in its military capability and its engagement in the war on terrorism, welcomed this action of Japan's. In a Reuters interview in January 2015,

---

http://www.mofa.go.jp/fp/nsp/page4e_000086.html (accessed on 3rd July 2015)
U.S Department of Defense, *Secretary of Defense Speech, IISS Shangri-La Dialogue,* 31st May 2015
http://www.defense.gov/speeches/speech.aspx?speechid=1857 (accessed on 3rd July 2015)

[22] MOFA, *The Three Principles on Transfer of Defence Equipment and Technology*, 1st April 2014 http://www.mofa.go.jp/press/release/press22e_000010.html (accessed on 3rd July 2015)

[52] Reuters, Nihon Ga Tsuyomeru Minami Sina Kai He No Gunziteki Kanyo Chugoku Kensei No Nerai (Japan strengthens its military collaboration in the South China Sea, it aims to contain China), 16th March 2015, http://jp.reuters.com/article/marketsNews/idJPL4N0WE1YA20150316 (accessed on 4th July 2015)

[24] The Nikkei (newspaper) 1st August 2014, Seifu, Vietnam Ni Senpaku 6Seki Kyoyo Gaisho Kaidan De (Japanese government agreed to give 6 boats to Vietnam at the meeting between the Japanese and Vietnam government) http://www.nikkei.com/article/DGXLASDE01004_R00C14A8PP8000/ (accessed on 4th July 2015)

Robert L. Thomas, Commander of the US Seventh Fleet, expressed US expectations of Japan by saying it was only logical that in the future Japan's Self Defence Forces would be active in the South China Sea. [25]In its explanation of comments made by Japanese government sources, Reuters also reported that, while there was no formal written memorandum among the countries, the United States, Japan and Australia had common security policies to assist Southeast Asian countries in establishing security. [26]

At the same time, Iskander Rehman[27] analyses the true intention of China's hard line in the South China Sea by saying that China wants to secure the ocean area as an area for deploying nuclear submarines connected to its strategic nuclear submarine bases.[28] Based on the analyses of various Chinese observers and naval strategists, he has drawn the conclusion that China's strategy in the South China Sea is to hold in check and deter the influence of the United States and other allies deployed in the Indian Ocean and the Pacific Ocean, which it believes is closing in on its own country. [29]

> "Pointing to the US's extended network of allies in the Indo-Pacific region, and to their own relative isolation, Chinese

---

[25] Reuters, Nihon Ga Tsuyomeru Minami Sina Kai He No Gunziteki Kanyo Chugoku Kensei No Nerai (Japan strengthens its military collaboration in the South China Sea, it aims to contain China), 16th March 2015, http://jp.reuters.com/article/marketsNews/idJPL4N0WE1YA20150316 (accessed on 4th July 2015)

[26] Ibid

[27] Associate of Nuclear Policy Program, Carnegie Endowment for International Peace

[28] Iskander Rehman, *Dragon in a Bathtub: Chinese Nuclear Submarines and the South China Sea*, Carnegie Endowment for International Peace, 9th March 2013 http://carnegieendowment.org/2013/03/09/dragon-in-bathtub-chinese-nuclear-submarines-and-south-china-sea (accessed on 4th July 2015)

[29] Ibid

> strategists fear that Beijing's growing navy could be ensnared within the first island chain-a region which they describe as stretching from Japan all the way to the Indonesian archipelago. Applying this maritime siege mentality to naval planning; they fret that the US Navy could locate and neutralize their fledgling undersea deterrent in the very first phases of conflict, before it even manages to slip through the chinks of the first island chain."[30]

From the above analyses, it can be said that political tensions lead to arms races, which are further exacerbated by more tension. Daisaku Ikeda, who developed his own private diplomacy, contends that serious mutual distrust is at the root of political tensions, and indicates that even if these tensions cannot be completely resolved, it is important to maintain constant exchanges between diplomatic channels and people to ensure that they do not escalate into an arms race or catastrophic military clashes including further nuclear development.

One point noted by Wendy Sherman, US Undersecretary of State for Political Affairs, in regard to the rise of China and regional political tension in Northeast Asia, was China's exploitation of feelings of victimization among East Asian countries including China and South Korea, which previously experienced colonial occupation by Japan. Sherman indicated that China encourages these feelings as a form of political manipulation.

> "Of course, it is not hard for a political leader anywhere to earn cheap applause by vilifying a former enemy... (She added after pointing to various disagreements that relate to Japan's colonial

---

[30] Ibid

past) But such provocations produce paralysis, not progress".[31]

Sherman indicates that this construct of Japan as the victimizer and its former colonies including China and the Korean Peninsula as the victims has been politically exploited and has escalated current regional political tensions. The relevance of this factor and China's advances into ocean waters as well as territorial disputes in recent years cannot be clearly or directly confirmed. Furthermore, if there were just reason to claim territorial rights, China could take the matter before the International Court of Justice (ICJ) as a way of reaching peaceful settlement of territorial disputes. However, despite the Japanese government's indication that it is prepared to actively take these territorial disputes before the ICJ, the Chinese government has never even once done so (as of 2015).

Furthermore, the 2015 NPT Review Conference was unable to have its final document ratified and the conference ended in failure. The reason for this was China's vehement opposition to the inclusion in the document of one sentence advocating that many people, including political leaders, visit the atomic bomb areas of Hiroshima and Nagasaki to understand the cruel reality of the use of atomic weapons. China contended that this inclusion was a strategy on the part of Japan to emphasize that it too was a victim of the Second World War. [32]The

---

[31] Financial Times (FT), *US diplomat angers Seoul with comments on regional tension, 2nd March 2015* http://www.ft.com/cms/s/0/9e78bf88-c0b8-11e4-9949-00144feab7de.html#axzz3hDLvigMt (accessed on 21st July 2015)

[32] United Nations, *2015 Review Conference of the Parties to the Treaty on the Non-Proliferation of Nuclear Weapons (NPT)*, 27th April to 22nd May 2015 http://www.un.org/en/conf/npt/2015/index.shtml (accessed on 21st July 2015)
Kyodo News, *Japan to keep urging world leaders to visit Hiroshima and Nagasaki*, 25th May 2015
https://english.kyodonews.jp/news/2015/05/354521.html (accessed on 21st July

final draft included a significant amount of other important text relating to the NPT review, and China's reaction can only be seen as quite extreme. Under the laws of war (also known as international humanitarian law), the indiscriminate killing of people using bombs is unlawful. [33]

The lives of many Japanese people who were not soldiers were indiscriminately sacrificed due to the dropping of the atomic bombs, and therefore these *hibakusha* victims must also be classified as war victims. In this context, Japan too is a victim of war. It is only fair to at least recognise this and apply the same legal criteria. When judgment is made on the basis of political assertions and arguments, there is a strong possibility that biased views and distorted facts will develop. The fact that the 2015 NPT Review Conference became the venue for a Sino-Japanese political game rather than a venue for debate over nuclear disarmament was a step backwards in time and can be considered a major setback in the NPT debate. Japan's aggression and colonization of China and the Korean Peninsula are historical facts that both the United States government and the Japanese government acknowledge, and both countries criticize Japanese militarism and totalitarianism before and during the Second World War.

At the UN General Assembly in the autumn of 2015, the Japanese government aims to have a three-point resolution adopted which encourages political leaders and young people of countries around the world to visit the atomic bomb sites, stresses that nuclear weapons are inhumane and catastrophic, and indelibly engraves on the memory of the world the tragedies of Hiroshima and Nagasaki. [34]The objective of

---

2015)

[33] Protection of Civilian Populations Against Bombing From the Air in Case of War, League of Nations, September 30, 1938

[34] The Nikkei, Kaku Gunshuku Kokuren Ketsugi Mezasu (Nuclear

the NPT Review Conference is to have the final document unanimously adopted in principle; but UN resolutions are ratified by majority vote and, therefore, even if China and other countries oppose the resolution, there is a possibility it will be ratified.

The four Japanese anti-nuclear CSOs are ideologically premised on humanitarianism and make no reference to emotional, ideological or political confrontation including political manipulation. First of all, in their activities they make no distinction between the Japanese and people of other countries. The JPPNW treats nuclear issues as a health problem affecting all of humanity. It also affirms that SGI is a worldwide multinational religion, that JALANA will attempt to assist atomic bomb victims in North Korea, which has no diplomatic relations with Japan, and that MPs of Japan should relinquish all territories (of Japan) under dispute (see Chapter 3). From the perspective of conservatives who give priority to Japan's national interests, this stance will appear to be in opposition to national interests, and may be interpreted as siding with China and South Korea. Of course, the claims of MPs will not result in a realistic compromise proposal or smooth resolution measures.

In the 1960s and 1970s, Daisaku Ikeda asserted that mutual distrust was at the root of the Sino-Japanese and Russo-Japanese conflict. Irrespective of the period, all governments adopt unilateral, emotional and political strategies that place their countries first, and the Chinese and Japanese governments are no exception. The final resolution of conflicts between states requires negotiation between their governments, and in that respect CSOs do not have the techniques for intervening. What concerned Ikeda at the time was not only the almost complete absence of diplomatic channels but also the escalating animosity of

---

Disarmament : Aiming to Reach an UN Resolution) 26th July 2015, pp2

countries toward each other based on preconceived notions, which could result in a catastrophic ending that is nuclear war. The private diplomacy advocated by Ikeda could be called 'public preventive diplomacy', a combination of both public diplomacy and preventive diplomacy.

Public diplomacy is a government activity undertaken with the understanding that it is important to appeal not only to the governments of partner countries but also to the citizens of the home country to achieve the objectives of government foreign policy. [35]Rather than diplomacy initiated by the government, public diplomacy is driven by the power of the people through organizations such as CSOs, and promotes understanding of one's own country by eliminating mutual ignorance, prejudice and misunderstandings through interaction among people with a view to enhancing the country's image and sense of affinity. Public diplomacy is also more flexible and active than government diplomacy, and there is an expectation that it will steadily eliminate feelings of resentment and conflict. [36] Moreover, public diplomacy takes on a strong civilian tone, avoiding government and territorial disputes by instead focusing on areas of cultural exchanges, among others, and there is a strong possibility there will be interchanges where people's sincere feelings are communicated.

---

[35] Kazutaka Hisada, Public Diplomacy To Bunka Hasshin Kyoten: Nihon To Kankoku No Hikaku O Chushin Ni (Public Diplomacy and Basis of Culture Creation: Comparison between Japan and South Korea), No 180 Bulletin of Society of Humanities 2013, Kawagawa University (Japan)
http://human.kanagawa-u.ac.jp/gakkai/publ/pdf/no180/18004.pdf (accessed on 2nd August 2015)

[36] Record China, Nichukan Ha "Higashi Asia Kokyo Gaiko Kyodotai" No Kakuritu O:
Seifu O Koeta Minkan No Chikara De Ittai To Naru (Japan, China and South Korea should create an "East Asian Public Diplomacy Community": Unify with Private Powers over Governments), 2nd August 2013
http://www.recordchina.co.jp/a75035.html (accessed on 2nd August 2015)

For example, Japanese animated films, which have spread to countries all around the world, have enhanced positive feelings about Japan and an interest in Japan among people who have never travelled to Japan or know little about political conditions in Japan. This is one form of public diplomacy. This is also called cultural diplomacy or soft power diplomacy. [37]

On the other hand, preventative diplomacy encompasses activities aimed at resolving an already existing conflict before it develops into a dispute or, if a dispute does develop, activities to keep it from proliferating.[38] This generally takes the form of mediation, conciliation or negotiation. In the past, organizations such as the United Nations complemented this diplomacy with preventative disarmament by collecting and disposing of weapons, such as guns that were the main cause of disputes in countries[39] with conflict zones or political instability. [40] Therefore, public diplomacy and preventative diplomacy are led by the United Nations or governments but Ikeda advocated private diplomacy from beginning to end. This is one difference with the conventional definition of 'diplomacy'.

Ikeda's private diplomacy promoted frank dialogue that was not based on diplomatic language or social etiquette between Japan and China and Japan and the USSR in efforts to have an impact on preventing a worsening in relations. This impact also meant reducing

---

[37] Kazutaka Hisada, Public Diplomacy To Bunka Hasshin Kyoten: Nihon To Kankoku No Hikaku O Chushin Ni (Public Diplomacy and Basis of Culture Creation: Comparison between Japan and South Korea), No 180 Bulletin of Society of Humanities 2013, Kawagawa University (Japan)
http://human.kanagawa-u.ac.jp/gakkai/publ/pdf/no180/18004.pdf (accessed on 2nd August 2015)

[38] UN Information Centre, Funso Yobo (Preventing Disputes)
http://www.unic.or.jp/activities/peace_security/conflict_prevention/ (accessed on 2nd August 2015)

[39] Ibid. El Salvador, Liberia, Sierra Leone and East Timor

[40] Ibid

the possibility of the use of nuclear weapons. In Sino-Japanese relations, he engaged in activities to raise awareness regarding nuclear disarmament at the public sector level and to create the groundwork for diplomatic normalization in 1972. In Japanese-USSR relations, in an environment where a peace treaty had not yet been signed, he engaged in activities to raise public awareness of nuclear disarmament from the USSR's top leaders to general civilians. Moreover, he promoted a closer relationship with Japan through cultural exchanges, continued to engage in frank dialogue, and achieved direct dialogue between the Soviet government, the Japanese government and MOFA.

The Japanese government is passive on nuclear disarmament today, due to the instability of Northeast Asia. That is to say, Japan considers this a serious threat, because Russia, China and North Korea, countries with which Japan has diplomatic issues, are all nuclear weapons states, and this instability is possibly serious enough to provoke Japan to become nuclear also (See Chapters 2 and 3). Terumasa Nakanishi, Professor emeritus in International Politics, Kyoto University, Japan, is of the opinion that if and when North Korea, a nuclear weapons state, is unified with the Republic of Korea, unified Korea will be a nuclear state, which leaves Japan the only country without nuclear weapons in the Northeast Asian region. He believes that Japan will then find itself in an extremely precarious situation, and the only measure left for Japan to take is nuclear deterrence. He also believes that the threat from Chinese nuclear weapons is the greatest threat for Japan.[41]

> "A realistic solution does not come from an unaccountable number of spirit-consoling services organized in Japan for the

---

[41] Terumasa Nakanishi, Nippon Kaubuso No Ronten (Arguing Point of Japanese Nuclear Armament), PHP Kenkyujo 2006, p25

victims of atomic bombings, or numerous anti-nuclear gatherings held globally. "Deterrence" is the only way of resolving nuclear issues that threaten human lives and national survival. The priority for Japan today is to engage in serious debates on the matter and come to an unshakable conclusion[42]. ...North Korean, as well as Russian nuclear weapons are based on modern technology comparable to that of the US and there are signs of a rapid upgrading. The most urgent threat is "Nuclear China", as we witness its tough stance against Japan in the East China Sea and the unprecedented efforts at expanding its conventional as well as nuclear capacities".[43]
(Translated by Fujiko Hara)

The East China Sea issue concerns rights over a gas field in the area claimed both by the Governments of Japan and China, and the territorial rights forcefully claimed by the PRC and Taiwan over the Senkaku Islands effectively controlled by Japan. The area has attracted the interest of the countries in the surrounding area since the Economic Commission for Asia and the Far East conducted a survey in 1968 and found the East China Sea contains large-scale oil and gas fields.[44] In 2004, China without prior notice to Japan started a full-scale gas field development[45]. The gas field in question is located within the EEZ of

---

42 Ibid

43 Ibid, p39

44 Kyoko Hamagawa, Chosa To Joho: Issue Brief No 547: Higashi Shina Kai Ni Okeru Nicchu Kyokai Kakutei Mondai (Research and Information: Issue Brief No 547: Issue of the Line of Demarcation between Japan and China in East China Sea), Section of Diplomacy and Defence, National Diet Library of Japan, 16th June 2006, p1
http://www.ndl.go.jp/jp/diet/publication/issue/0547.pdf (accessed on 28th April 2013)

45 Ibid

the two countries. Japan claims that the boundary should be at the median line between Japan and China based on the United Nations Law of the Sea (UNCLOS) established in 1982 and its related rules, while the Chinese government claims, based on the 1958 Treaty on Continental Shelf[46] it should be the Okinawa Trough which lies at the end of its continental shelf.[47] With regard to the territorial issue of the Senkaku Islands, the government of Japan which effectively controls them claims absence of territorial issues and explains the situation in 12 languages including Chinese on the official website of the MOFA.[48] On 7 September 2010, when a Chinese fishing boat invaded the Senkaku Islands sea area, the Japan Coast Guard (JCG) ordered its departure as unlawful. The Chinese fishing boat continued its operation but when leaving the area collided with two JCG boats and damaged them. The JCG arrested the captain and the crew on grounds of sabotaging JCG official duties. When it was made clear that Japan intended to start a legal process in Japan, the Chinese government decided that it would stop the comings and goings of its cabinet member level representatives to Japan, thereby stopping negotiations on increasing the number of air routes, postponing coal-related meetings and scaling down of the visit to Japan of Chinese tourist groups on the same day.[49] The Japanese side,

---

[46] Ibid, p4

[47] MOFA, Higashi Shina Kai Ni Okeru Shigenkaihatsu Ni Kansuru Wagakuni No Hoteki Tachiba (Our Country's Legal Standpoint regarding the Issue of Developing Natural Resources in East China Sea), November 2008 http://www.mofa.go.jp/mofaj/area/china/higashi_shina/tachiba.html (accessed on 8th December 2013)

[48] MOFA, *Japanese Territory: Senkaku Islands*, http://www.mofa.go.jp/region/asia-paci/senkaku/index.html (accessed on 8th December 2013)

[49] Jeremy Page and Norihiko Shirouzu, *Toyota Faces Fine in China at Sensitive Time for Ties*, The Wall Street Journal, 20th September 2010, http://online.wsj.com/news/articles/SB10001424052748703399404575505601971499626?mg=reno64-wsj&url=http%3A%2F%2Fonline.wsj.com%2Farticle

including its communist party, reacted against the measures announced by the Chinese government, pointing out that the Senkaku Islands were historically as well as under international law are Japanese territories.[50] Since then there have been frequent anti-Japanese demonstrations in China.[51]

With regard to the Senkaku Islands, the 1972 Blue Book of MOFA explained that Japan had conducted studies of the area on repeated occasions starting in 1885, and in spite of them being uninhabited. Recognizing after thorough research that no evidence was found that the Qing Dynasty had ruled over them, accordingly, in 1895 by cabinet decision they were incorporated into Japan.[52] Also, they are not included in the territories that should be abandoned, such as the erstwhile former colonial lands. Article 3 reveals that they were placed under US governance by the occupation policy, and returned to Japan by the Okinawa Reversion Agreement of 1971.[53]

The US government expressed its desire for a peaceful resolution of the Senkaku Islands issue through dialogue, but according to its conventional understanding, clearly stated that the said islands were within the applicable scope under the US-Japan Security Treaty, therefore recognizing them as Japanese territories.

"**President Obama**: We stand together in calling for disputes in

---

%2FSB10001424052748703399404575505601971499626.html (accessed on 8th December 2013)

[50] Japanese Communist Party, *Shimbun Akahata (Newspaper the Red)*, 20th September 2010

[51] The Epoch Time (English Edition), *Behind China's Anti-Japan Protests, the Hand of Officials*, 19th September 2012 http://www.theepochtimes.com/n2/china-news/behind-chinas-anti-japan-protests-the-hand-of-officials-292859.html (accessed on 8th December 2013)

[52] MOFA, Gaiko Seisho 1972 (Diplomatic Blue Book 1972), 8th March 1972, p507-p508

[53] Ibid

the region, including maritime issues, to be resolved peacefully through dialogue. We share a commitment to fundamental principles such as freedom of navigation and respect for international law. And let me reiterate that our treaty commitment to Japan's security is absolute, and Article 5 covers all territories under Japan's administration, including Senkaku Islands"[54]

The Chinese Foreign Ministry criticized Obama's statement at its press conference on 23 April 2014.[55] The Chinese Foreign Ministry press officer announced that the Chinese Government regarded the islands as its own territory, and strongly opposed the application of the US-Japan Security Treaty over them, urging the US not to intervene in the territorial issues between Japan and China.[56] China also underlined that the US-Japan Security Treaty was a bilateral agreement signed during the Cold War period, and should not affect China's sovereignty and its legal rights and interests.[57]

Zhou Enlai in his talks with the Komeito delegation visiting Beijing to pave the way for the normalization of Japan-China relations as well as during his negotiation with Kakuei Tanaka, the Prime Minister of Japan 1972-1974, for the normalization of bilateral relations had clearly stated that he would not refer to the issue of the Senkaku Islands.

---

[54] The White House (Office of the Press Secretary), *Joint Press Conference with President Obama and Prime Minister Abe of Japan (at Akasaka Palace in Tokyo, Japan)*, 24th April 2014 http://www.whitehouse.gov/the-press-office/2014/04/24/joint-press-conference-president-obama-and-prime-minister-abe-japan (accessed on 12th May 2014)

[55] Irib World Service, *Chugoku, Amerika Daitoryo No Senkaku Hatsugen Ni Hanpatsu (China Offended US President's Speech Regarding Senkaku Islands)*, 24th April 2014 http://japanese.irib.ir/news/latest-news/item/44769 (accessed on 12th May 2014)

[56] Ibid

[57] Ibid

Prime Minister Zhou: There is no need to refer to the Senkaku Islands. I had not taken (any interest) in them but the historians are making it an issue due to the oil question. In Japan too, Kiyoshi Inoue (Japanese historian) has an earnest interest. There is no need to seriously regard this issue[58]

Prime Minister Tanaka: What are your thoughts on the Senkaku Islands? There are people coming to me with suggestions."

Prime Minister Zhou: I have no wish to talk about the Senkaku Islands issue this time. It is not good to talk about it. It became an issue because there is oil there. If there is no oil, neither Taiwan nor the US will make an issue out of them. Following the normalization of relations within how many months should we exchange our ambassadors?"

Foreign Minister Ohira (Japan): We will make the necessary arrangements as soon as possible but I cannot say within how many months in our joint statement...[59]

(Translated by Fujiko Hara)

Zhou's thoughts were that the Senkaku Islands issue had roots in competition for acquisition of resources and therefore should not be made a political issue and impede normalization of relations between China and Japan. The Japanese Foreign Ministry, however, in its document prepared regarding the Senkaku Islands issue in March 2013,

[58] MOFA, Dai 2 Kai Takeiri Yoshikatsu Shu Onrai Kaidan Kiroku (Record of 2nd Meeting between Yoshikatsu Takeiri and Zhou Enlai) on 28th July 1972

[59] MOFA, Tanaka Sori Shu Onrai Sori Kaidan Kiroku (Record of Meeting between Prime Minister Tanaka and Prime Minister Zhou Enlai) between 25th and 28th September 1972

asserted that there was no fact of agreeing with the Chinese side to mothball the Senkaku Islands issue or to keep it opaque since Tanaka had not given a clear response to Zhou's remarks.[60]

In the 2000s, Japan began to see China increasingly as a threat due to the Senkaku islands issue and that of the gas fields in the East China Sea. At the centre of the threat lies China's nuclear weapon. As a neighbour, Japan naturally comes within its reach. As a result, there are increasingly opinions expressed in Japan that it needs to go nuclear, and criticism of the US administration for its passive attitude in seeking a peaceful resolution of the matter.

> "As China strengthens its economic and military powers.... it is questionable if the US administration would attempt to 'protect' Japan from the Chinese Communist Party's arrogant policy against Japan. That is because the US-China military balance will (is likely to?) shift in favour of China....' "In our contemporary world, it is only states with nuclear weapons that have true influence in the international community. Non-nuclear states cannot have true right of speech. The US, China, North Korea and Russia all of which are nuclear armed know this only too well"[61]
>
> (Translated by Fujiko Hara)

On 11 September 2012, the Japanese government bought the Senkaku Islands from the landowner (a Japanese national) for

---

[60] MOFA, *Senkaku Shoto Ni Tsuite (About Senkaku Islands)*, March 2013, p10 http://www.mofa.go.jp/mofaj/area/senkaku/pdfs/senkaku.pdf (accessed on 5th June 2013)

[61] Kan Ito (Japanese right wing political analyst), Chugoku No Kakusenryoku Ni Nihon Ha Kuppuku Suru (Japan will be Grovel before Chinese Nuclear Arms), Shogakkan Shinsho 2011, p204-p205

2,050,000,000 yen, 'nationalizing the islands". The Chinese government violently opposed the deed and since then no Japan-China summit meeting has taken place to date.[62] From the Chinese government's point of view, the act of nationalizing the islands shifted the conflict from Chinese government vs. Japanese landowner to a fully-fledged conflict between the states, Chinese government versus Japanese government. True, this action has enabled the Japanese government to promptly exercise its authority to protect the islands militarily if and when an emergency situation arises. Seen from the Japanese government's point of view, the Senkaku Islands do not pose any territorial issue and since it was altogether a domestic issue there was no need for it to consider the will of the Chinese side. On 26 December 2013, when Shinzo Abe, the Japanese Prime Minister 2006-2007 and 2012 – as of 2015, paid his respects to the Yasukuni Shrine where Class A war criminals of the Second World War are enshrined, the Chinese government reacted vehemently condemning the Japanese government for not learning historical lessons from its war of aggression. Since then there has been no exchange between the governments to date in 2014.[63]

The new Chinese President Xi Jinping took office in 2012, but no Japanese prime minister, members of parliament or high officials of the government were able to have talks with him until the summit meeting between Xi and Japanese Prime Minister Shinzo Abe on 10th November 2014 at the conference of APEC (Asia-Pacific Economic

---

[62] MOFA, *Nicchu Shuno Kaidan (Japan-China Top-Level Meeting)*, 13th May 2012 http://www.mofa.go.jp/mofaj/area/jck/summit2012/jc_gaiyo.html (12th May 2014)

[63] Stephen Harner, *After Yasukuni, China Closes The Door On Abe: Why Is He Smiling*, Forbes 1st February 2014 http://www.forbes.com/sites/stephenharner/2014/01/02/after-yasukuni-china-closes-the-door-on-abe-why-is-he-smiling/ (accessed on 12th May 2014)

Cooperation).[64] The summit meeting was regarded as a start to recovering the bilateral diplomatic relationship between Xi and Abe. But they could not come up with any definite ideas for solutions for the issues such as over the Senkaku Islands.

Between 2012 and 2014, a number of attempts have been made by pro-Chinese members of parliament to conduct parliamentary diplomacy. Masahiko Komura[65] requested the Chinese Government for a visit to Beijing in April 2013 and to have talks with Xi Jinping but to no avail and gave up the idea.[66] Komura did visit China in May 2014[67] and had a meeting with Zhang Dejiang.[68] The two men agreed on the need for improving bilateral relations but remained confrontational regarding the history of the Senkaku Islands. They were not able to come to an agreement in charting a road map to a summit meeting. Both

---

64 MOFA, *Japan-China Relations: Japan-China Summit Meeting*, 10th November 2014 http://www.mofa.go.jp/a_o/c_m1/cn/page4e_000151.html (accessed on 14th November 2014)

65 Vice-President of the Liberal Democratic Part 2012-as of 2014, Member of the House of Representatives 1980-as of 2014, Former Minister of Foreign Affairs 1998-1999 and 2007-2008, Minister of Defence 2007, Minister of Justice 2000-2001, and Minister of Economic Planning Agency 1994-1995, the second person in the hierarchy of the ruling parties and the Chair of the Japan-China Friendship Parliamentarians Union, Japan

66 Sankei Newspaper, Nicchugiren Hochu O Chushi Chukinpei Shuseki Menkai Medo Tatazu (The Japan-China Friendship Parliamentarian's Union Gave Up To Visit China Because They Could Not Arrange Meeting With Xi Jinping), 22nd April 2013
http://sankei.jp.msn.com/politics/news/130422/stt13042214000002-n1.htm (accessed on 12th May 2014)

67 Sankei Newspaper, Nicchugiren No Komura Shi Cho Shi To Senkaku Rekishi De Hageshii Oshu Nicchu Shuno Kaidan No Michisuji Miezu (Mr. Komura of the Japan-China Friendship Parliamentrian's Union and Mr. Zhang Traded Barbs Over History and Senkaku Islands), 6th May 2014
http://sankei.jp.msn.com/politics/news/140506/plc14050608000003-n1.htm 12th May 2014

68 Chairman of the Standing Committee of the National People's Congress 2013-as of 2014 and former Deputy Prime Minister 2008-2013, China

men had heated exchanges especially over the Senkaku Islands issue.[69]

> **Komura** : My people think that China is attempting to change the status quo by force.
> **Zhang**: They (Senkaku islands) are China's indigenous territories and cannot absolutely give in.
> **Komura** : Rather than making unilateral statements, we should make efforts to realize a summit meeting[70]
> (Translated by Fujiko Hara)

On the other hand, the Komeito, a coalition partner of the Abe cabinet, made its sixth visit to China as a party on January 2013, and had talks with Xi Jinping in the Great Hall of the People on 25 January, the first among Japanese political circles.[71] The Komeito, however, regards this parliamentary diplomacy as one between the Komeito and the Communist Party of China and therefore the meeting was not with the Chinese Head of State but with the Secretary General of the Communist Party of China.[72] There are two possibilities about this meeting, whether the Komeito refrained from having talks with Xi Jinping as China's head of state or whether the Chinese side was willing to have an exchange between political parties with Xi Jinping as Secretary General of the Chinese Communist Party. Both possibilities exist.

At the meeting with Xi Jinping the Komeito presented him with Prime Minister Abe's personal letter.[73] They both agreed to promote

---

[69] Ibid

[70] Ibid

[71] Komei Newspaper, To Hochudan Shu Kinpei Soshoki To Kaidan (The Komeito's Group to Visit China Met Xi Jinping), 26th January 2013, p1

[72] Ibid

[73] Ibid

bilateral strategic mutual relationships from 'a broad perspective'.[74] The Komeito also brought up the question of the Senkaku Islands issue and the realization of a Japan-China summit meeting.[75] According to the report announced by the Komeito the dialogue between the two went as follows.

On the issue of the Senkaku Islands:

Xi: While our standpoints and views differ, we should resolve the issue by controlling it with dialogue and deliberation.

The Komeito: While it is a fact that we come from different standpoints, diplomatic issues will definitely be resolved through dialogue and dealing cooling with each other.

Xi : Squarely facing the issue will lead us to the future. I would like you to learn from the lessons of the past and prudently deal with the issue.

The Komeito : It is important to address the issue based on our shared understanding and pass it on to the future generation…Improving our relations in a big way through economic activities, academia, cultural and personal exchanges will lead to stable relations.

On Summit Talks:

The Komeito : In order to solve a difficult situation, we believe it is important that our politicians and leaders engage in dialogue. Prime Minister Abe looks forward to having a Japan-China summit meeting. We would appreciate it if you would work to deepen human and trusting relations between our prime minister and Secretary General Xi Jinping.

---

[74] Ibid

[75] Ibid

Xi : I take seriously your suggestion for high-level exchanges between leaders of our countries and will have it seriously studied. Dialogues between leaders have special roles to play and it is important to create a positive atmosphere.[76]

(Translated by Fujiko Hara)

During its four days stay in Beijing from 22 to 25 January that year, the Komeito had meetings with various strata of the Chinese government and China-Japan related organisations. They included Wang Jiarui[77], Yang Jiechi[78], Tang Jiaxuan.[79] The Komeito focused on building dialogue based on the broader issues of Japan-China relations rather than focusing on the individual issues of the Senkaku Islands as well as promoting bilateral exchange in the fields of culture, art and education.

This approach is based on Ikeda's proposition in normalizing Japan-China relations and his deductive diplomacy. That the Komeito was able to have talks with Xi and leaders of other strata is due to the party's founder, Ikeda having built friendly relationships with the four generations of top leaders, Zhou Enlai, Deng Xiao Ping, Jing Zemin, and Hu Jintao. A deductive approach based on the whole situation is a replay of Ikeda's initiatives in the 70s and the private diplomacy with the USSR in the 90s successfully leading to the first Japan-China Summit meeting in 1972 and the first visit to Japan by Gorbachev, the USSR leader in 1991 (see Chapter 6). In both cases private diplomacy succeeded where the government of Japan's diplomacy failed to deliver.

---

[76] Ibid

[77] Head of International Department of the Central Committee of the Communist Party of China

[78] Foreign Minister of the People's Republic of China

[79] President of the China-Japan Friendship Association, and Former Minister of Foreign Affairs of the People's Republic of China 1998-2003

The Komeito parliamentary diplomacy too realized talks with Xi which neither the government or other parliamentarian diplomacy could do. That said, disputes emanating from competition for resources will require substantially long period and patient dialogue and negotiation between the two governments. What is important is not to interrupt the diplomatic channel. When governmental negotiations are troublesome, diplomacy by political parties and parliamentarians as well as dialogue and exchanges between civic organisations become crucial. Issues of competing for resources and territorial issues have a great possibility of military collision since neither side will give in. The cardinal point of diplomatic strength is to avoid collision and lead to resolution.

Since China is a nuclear weapons country, other anti-nuclear CSOs also have strong interests in the Senkaku Islands issue. The JALANA is determined that military resolution should be avoided in every instance and for reason that it asserted that the Japanese government should accept the Senkaku Islands as a territorial issue and resolve it together with the Chinese government under International Law (see Chapter 4). The MP asserted that the Japanese government should renounce the territorial rights of the Senkaku Islands, show an attitude of non-contest and appeal to the world that Japan is an absolute state for peace (see Chapter 4). Both claims run against the official view of the government. It is, however, common to all anti-nuclear CSOs that Japan should absolutely avoid conflict with China, a nuclear weapons state.

Effective governmental diplomatic efforts maintain channels for diplomacy where they can continue dialogue at a low temperature even when they are involved in conflictual situation. This was made clear in Kissinger's visit to China in 1971 and Nixon's in 1972. In contrast throughout the Cold War period, the Japanese government was very passive in building diplomatic channels with rival states. Since the 13

May 2012 Japan-China-Korea summit meeting held in Beijing, no new Japan-China summit meeting has taken place until November 2014[80]. There was no improvement in Japan-China relations, deemed the worst relations since the end of Second World War.[81] By its very nature there should be opportunities for the heads of the two governments to engage in direct intercourse or at least greetings on some occasions such as international conferences. There was a need, however, for a forward-looking dialogue to resolve issues between the two states.

Through successful experiences of Ikeda's private diplomacy, one can say that CSO activities that involve cultural exchanges, without national or strategic interests, can play effective roles in linking diplomatic channels between contesting states. Henry Kissinger and Ikeda pointed out that diplomacy should have realistic viewpoints and always keep open diplomatic channels for constant communication with negotiating partners.

> **Kissinger** : The art of diplomacy is to find interests that both sides can accept, or when interests differ, to find ways to make them correspond. This is not easily achieved with sufficient number of discussions. It has been my conviction that to have successful diplomatic achievement it is essential to understand the negotiating party's psychology, culture and motives. Not only that one should have interests to truly understand the other. If one were to think that represents the technique, you are wrong. Successful diplomats, some criticize saying that they only say

---

[80] Prime Minister Shinzo Abe and President Xi Jinping met at a conference of Asia-Pacific Economic Cooperation in Beijing on 10th November 2014

[81] Stephen Harner, *After Yasukuni, China Closes The Door On Abe: Why Is He Smiling*, Forbes 1st February 2014 http://www.forbes.com/sites/stephenharner/2014/01/02/after-yasukuni-china-closes-the-door-on-abe-why-is-he-smiling/

things the other wants to hear. That is wrong. Distinguished diplomats manage to adjust when a rival has contrasting views. In diplomacy one meets the same person many times over. That means one may successfully deceive the other once but one would forever lose his trust. Even when agreement is made, if it goes against the interest of one's own country, no state will abide by it.

Ikeda : From that sense, I offer my respects to your Excellency for contributing to world peace through bold and honest diplomacy without having fixed ideas. In any case, dialogue is the right way, be it at the individual or state levels, to bring peace and stability to our communities. Communities lacking in dialogue eventually result in endless mistrust, suspicion, bitterness and fear, just as a pool of water will stagnate if there are no outlets. We must not forget that feelings will eventually become idées fixes and will only increase if left to linger. I believe that the only way to break out from such blind alleys is to have honest and courageous dialogue. But of course dialogue does not always guarantee a favorable outcome. However, just as backwater is cleaned up by running water we must continue to move and talk. A breakthrough should come from such efforts[82]

(Translated by Fujiko Hara)

Ikeda's Chinese independent diplomacy became public on 8 September 1968 when, at the 11th Soka Gakkai Student Division Meeting that took place at Tokyo's Nihon University Hall, he made a

---

[82] Daisaku Ikeda and Henry Kissinger, *Heiwa To Zinsei To Tetsugaku O Kataru (Philosophy of Human Peace)*, Seikyo Newspaper 2008, p165-p166
It was originally published in 1987

five point recommendation towards normalizing Japan-Chinese relations, before more than ten thousand members of the Student Division and the media. The points were: 'recognition of the Beijing government', 'direct negotiation by heads of governments (toward normalization of diplomatic relations), 'approval of China's UN affiliation', 'expanding economic and cultural exchanges', and 'destruction of the 'Yoshida Letter' intended to restrain Japan-China trade'.[83] His reasons for this proposition were that there could not be peace and stability in Asia without Japan normalizing relations with China, which had then a population of 700 million.[84] Also, he made public the propositions on 8 September, the same day as the Toda Declaration of 1957, with the determination to prevent China-Soviet confrontation in which probable use of nuclear weapons could be assumed, given that China succeeded in its first nuclear bomb test in 1964.

> "...here I would like to refer to Japan-China issues. There may be many who think discussing the issue of China is not appropriate at this time. From our principles of globalism and world citizenship the Chinese issue must be addressed first and foremost. As a Japanese person and as a youth who wishes for a peaceful future I would like to think together with you over these matters. I am certainly not a worshiper of communism. All

---

[83] People's Daily Overseas Edition Japan Monthly, Ikeda Daisaku To Nicchu Yuko No Ayumi: Nicchu Kokou Seijouka 40 Shunen Kinen (Daisaku Ikeda and History of Japan-China Friendship: The 40th Anniversary of Diplomatic Normalization between Japan and China), 2012, p5

[84] Hirotomo Teranishi (Professor of Soka University), Ikeda Daisaku No Ningen Shugi Gaiko (Daisaku Ikeda's Diplomacy for Humanism: Example of His First Visit to China and the USSR in 1974), Soka Kyoiku Dai 3 Go (Soka Education No 3), p9

I want to do is to convey to you that under the present circumstances of international community, we must make friends with all countries for the peace of the world and not just in Asia. In today's nuclear age it is not an exaggeration to say that whether we can save humankind from annihilation depends on whether we can build friendship across national boundaries. I would like you to know that the reason I refer to the China issue is simply because of my thoughts on this very point. Without the resolution of this issue we cannot truly say that the war has ended. The Japanese government's position that the peace issue has been settled by the Peace Treaty signed in 1952 between Japan and the Nationalist Government in Taiwan is just an abstract idea ignoring the presence of 700 million people on the continent. Normalization of diplomatic relations will only become meaningful when peoples of two countries understand each other, enjoy exchanges and contribute to bringing about world peace. Issues between Japan and China are complex and cannot be resolved without mutual understanding and deep trust, and above all without shared wish for peace. Perfunctory diplomacy of the past and the so-called Western style inductive approach of first resolving small issues in order to finally arrive at restoration of diplomatic relations will result in failure after tremendous efforts. I believe that a better way lies in starting from a larger view, a basic line agreed between prime minister and chief executive of the two countries and to follow up to resolve detailed issues. I would like to assert here that a deductive method is the straight way to resolving problems. I am confident that they will eventually see the light if the leaders of Japan and China will persevere to conduct forward-looking

negotiations over and over again…"[85]
(Translated by Fujiko Hara)

At the time of establishing the Komeito in 1964 Ikeda proposed that the party should promote normalization of Japan-China relations as its foreign policy.[86] Therefore, Ikeda's 1968 proposition, made as the representative of the Soka Gakkai (Japan) with approximately ten million members, then had a huge impact not just in Japan but in China as well. At the same time, it provoked demonstrations and blackmailing tactics from numerous anti-Chinese right wing organisations in Japan.[87] The contents of Ikeda's proposition were immediately wired to Beijing by a correspondent of the Guang Ming Daily and presented to Zhou Enlai, the Chinese Prime Minister.[88] Zhou was close to Mao Zedong and was knowledgeable about Japan, having studied at a number of Japanese universities from 1917 to 1919. It was revealed by the US government's secret diplomatic documents made public in 1995 that, immediately following Ikeda's proposition, Japan's MOFA leaders from Nobuhiko Ushiba, the then administrative vice minister of Foreign Affairs strongly criticized the Ikeda proposition. He said to the US Ambassador in Japan as well as the US military commanders in Japan during the Japan-US security consultation meeting[89] that it was

---

[85] People's Daily Overseas Edition Japan Monthly, Ikeda Daisaku To Nicchu Yuko No Ayumi: Nicchu Kokou Seijouka 40 Shunen Kinen (Daisaku Ikeda and History of Japan-China Friendship: The 40th Anniversary of Diplomatic Normalization between Japan and China), 2012, p18

[86] Ibid

[87] Hirotomo Teranishi (Professor of Soka University), Ikeda Daisaku No Ningen Shugi Gaiko (Daisaku Ikeda's Diplomacy for Humanism: Example of His First Visit to China and the USSR in 1974), Soka Kyoiku Dai 3 Go (Soka Education Volume 3), p9

[88] Seikyo Newspaper, 11th September 2012, p3

[89] Sankei Newspaper, Soka Gakkai No Minkan Gaiko O Kenen: Gaimusho Bei Ni Hyomei 68 (Ministry of Foreign Affairs Japan Expressed Serious Concern

obstructing Japan's China diplomacy. The reasons for the criticism were that Ikeda gave the Chinese government "a grossly wrong expectation" by referring among others to a prompt setting up of a Japan-China summit meeting towards normalization of diplomatic relations and China's accession to the United Nations.[90] The criticism made by MOFA's top leader was not made public in Japan, apparently for reasons that the Ministry did not see any real opportunity for the normalization of relations at the time. In 1968 China was going through a Cultural Revolution with the Mao Zedong group arresting Liu Shaoqi and other government leaders and the proposition seemed unrealistic.[91] This criticism revealed that the Japanese Foreign Ministry considered diplomacy and security its exclusive prerogative. For this reason one can safely contend that there was hardly any collaboration with CSOs including the SGI with regard to government diplomacy in the Northeast Asian region at that time.

From the end of the Second World War, the Japanese government collaborating with the government of the US, its ally, recognized Taiwan as the sole government of China and regarded the People's Republic of China consistently as "a China issue" in its annual Diplomatic Blue Book, continuing to regard it with enmity. With regard to the China-India border conflict of 1962, the Japanese government declared its support of the government of India.

> "Prime Minister Hayato Ikeda, in his letter to Jawaharlal Nehru, the prime minister of India wrote, it is exceedingly regrettable that Communist China has turned to a large scale military

---

about the Soka Gakkai's Private Diplomacy in Meeting with the US Government, 1968), 16th February 1995

90 Ibid

91 Ibid

operation as regards the issue (China-India national border incident), and went on to express his deep sympathy for what India experienced and in the name of the government of Japan and its people declared every support will be given to the efforts of the Indian government in its effort to resolve the issue based on international justice".

(Diplomatic Blue Book, 1963)[92]

(Translated by Fujiko Hara)

During China-Soviet confrontation in the 1960s China became politically and diplomatically isolated from both camps. In its official statement the Chinese government explained that the Partial Test Ban Treaty of 1963 and the US's hostile policy against China were responsible for China's nuclear armament.

"The Chinese government has consistently asserted the total prohibition of nuclear weapons and complete abolition. If these assertions had been realized China would have had no need to develop nuclear weapons. However, our assertion met an obstinate resistance from American imperialism. All along the Chinese government has been pointing out the following. The Partial Test Ban Treaty signed by the US, UK and the Soviet Union in Moscow in July 1962 is a gross trickery that ridicules peoples of the world. The treaty strengthens the nuclear monopoly of the three major nuclear weapons states and aims to

---

[92] MOFA, Dai 3 Sho: Waga Kuni To Kakkoku Tono Shomondai – Azia Nishi Azia O Nozoku (Issues between Our State and Other States – Asia except West Asia), Gaiko Seisho (Diplomatic Blue Book), 1963 http://www.mofa.go.jp/mofaj/gaiko/bluebook/1963/s38-3-5.htm#2 (accessed on 12th May 2014)

bind the hands and legs of all other peace loving states."
(Chinese government statement on nuclear weapons test. 16 October 1964)[93]
(Translated by Fujiko Hara)

While one cannot absolutely acknowledge the veracity of the statement of the Chinese government, it can be conjectured that one of the major reasons for its decision to choose nuclear armament was its recognition that its national strength could not rank alongside the US and the Soviet Union as well as its isolation in the Northeast Asia where political tension was rising. At present in 2015, the Chinese government is committed to non-first use of nuclear weapons but it has not made public the number in their possession.[94] It cannot be denied that this invites unwanted speculation due to an inability to eradicate Chinese nuclear threats. According to Japanese diplomatic documents a small number of academics, politicians and businessmen were trying individually to develop friendly relations and search for possibilities for normalization of diplomatic relations through communication with Zhou Enlai and other government officials. These never developed into a major movement.

Professor Oyama : Countries of the East, particularly China and Japan should have closer relations given our historical and geographic factors.

---

[93] Kajima Institute of International Peace, Nippon Gaiko Shuyo Bunsho Nenpyo 2 (Diplomatic Archives and Chronological Table of Japan' volume 2), Hara Shobo 1984, p525-p527

[94] People's Daily Online, Gaiko Bu: "Chugoku Ha Kaku Danto 250 Patsu Hoyu" To No Hokoku Ni Tsuite (Ministry of Foreign Affairs China: "About the Report that China is possessing 250 Nuclear Warheads"), 4 January 2013 http://j.people.com.cn/94474/8269873.html (accessed on 17th December 2013)

Prime Minister Zhou : We would like to recover normal relationships with countries of the world, and in particular with Japan. However, as long as Japan continues to be a tool of the US to invade China and Eastern countries, and continues to regard the People's Republic of China and the Chinese people with hostility, and continues to maintain so-called diplomatic relations with surviving bandits of Chiang Kaishek. Japan will increasingly become a factor of instability in the Pacific and impede the possibility of concluding a peace treaty between Japan and New China and establish normal diplomatic relations.
Professor Oyama : I believe there are no qualms about having cultural and economic exchanges between our peoples even when diplomatic relations are yet to be established.
Prime Minister Zhou : That's right. We welcome representatives of Japanese people to visit my country, while at the same time I hope that our people can also send delegations to Japan. Today, however, American imperialism and Japanese reactionaries are blocking developments of China-Japan friendly relations. Both the present governments of Japan and the US are openly implementing the US government's so-called embargo and doing the best to impede development of trade between China and Japan as well as our cultural exchanges. For these reasons peoples of our countries must struggle hard together to defeat those impediments.
Dialogue by Prime Minister Zhou Enlai of China and Professor Ikuo Oyama (Political Science, Waseda University, Japan. 28 September 1953)[95]

---

[95] Kajima Institute of International Peace, Nippon Gaiko Shuyo Bunsho Nenpyo 1 (Diplomatic Archives and Chronological Table of Japan' volume 1), Hara Shobo 1983, p569-p570

(Translated by Fujiko Hara)

On 5 March 1964 the Japanese government announced that, while it would not build a formal diplomatic relations, it would separate political and economic relations and recognize having economic relations with China.[96] This made those in favour of building friendly relations with China expect that trade centred economic exchanges would develop into friendly relations in the first half of the 1960s. Kenzo Matsumura,[97] who was one of the few pro-Chinese politicians in the Liberal Democratic Party Japan travelled to China and had talks with Zhou in Beijing on 16, 17, and 19 September 1962 and agreed that normalization of bilateral relations including political and economic relations was desirable.[98] Accordingly, a 1962 Memorandum on Japan China Long Term Comprehensive Trade was exchanged and a semi-governmental, semi-private trade system was established with liaison offices established in both countries using government guaranteed loans.[99] While a total export-import trading of

Edited by the China Affairs Bureau of MOFA, Nicchu Kankei Kihon Shiryoshu 1949-1969 (Basic Document Collection in Relation between Japan and China 1949-1969), the Kazankai Foundation 1970, p50-p52

[96] Ibid, p231

[97] Member of the House of Representatives 1928-1969, Adviser ot the Party, Former Minister of Welfare 1945, Minister of Agriculture and Forestry 1945-1946, and Minister of Education 1955

[98] Edited by the China Affairs Bureau of MOFA, Matsumura Kenzo Ziminto Komon To Shuonrai Chugoku Sori To No Kaidan Ni Kansuru Memo 1962 Nen 9 Gatsu 19 Nichi (Memorandum about Meeting between Kenzo Matsumura, Advisor to the Liberal Democratic Party Japan, and Zhou Enlai, the Chinese Prime Minister 19th September 1962), Nicchu Kankei Kihon Shiryoshu 1949-1969 (Basic Document Collection in Relation between Japan and China 1949-1969), the Kazankai Foundation 1970, pp214

[99] Edited by the China Affairs Bureau of MOFA, Nicchu Kankei Kihon Shiryoshu 1949-1969 (Basic Document Collection in Relation between Japan and China 1949-1969), the Kazankai Foundation 1970, p215-p216

approximately £36,000,000 per annum was hoped for,[100] it accounted for about half of total Japan-China trade at the peak. This was called 'LT Trade'[101] taking the first letter of Liao Chengzhi, the Chairman of Asia-Africa Solidarity Committee of China, and Japanese representative, Tatsunosuke Takasaki.[102] LT Trade was one of few Japan-China economic and diplomatic routes at the time and was expected to have promoted exchange among trading and business people, but was not able to encourage political and public opinion towards normalization of diplomatic relations. Liao was born and grew up in Japan and spoke the language fluently and was representative of those knowledgeable about Japan on the Chinese side. He assumed chairmanship when the China-Japan Friendship Association was established in 1963. As an external Association established by the government of China, it was intended to develop friendly relations with Japan in political, economic, cultural, science and technology and social fields.[103]

In the early 1960s Tatsunosuke Takasaki in his meeting with Zhou Enlai referred to the Soka Gakkai; and during the first half of the 1960s Zhou instructed persons in charge of Japan in the Chinese government to investigate the Soka Gakkai. The People's Daily of China interviewed Ieshige Akioka, who was the Beijing correspondent of the major Japanese newspaper Asahi Shimbun and who knew Zhou, in 2012 to write down the situation at the time.

---

[100] Ibid

[101] Edited by the China Affairs Bureau of MOFA, Nicchu Kankei Kihon Shiryoshu 1949-1969 (Basic Document Collection in Relation between Japan and China 1949-1969), the Kazankai Foundation 1970, p215-p216

[102] a businessman, Member of the House of Representatives 1955-1964, Minister of Economic Planning Agency 1955-1956, Minister of Internationa Trade and Industry 1958-1959, and Director-General of Science and Technology Agency 1959, Japan

[103] China-Japan Friendship Association http://211.144.130.250/index.php?m=content&c=index&a=show&catid=9&id=1433 (accessed on 19th January 2013)

Question: What was the reaction of the Japanese correspondents in Beijing concerning Ikeda's 1968 proposition?
Akioka: I have not talked with other correspondents but I realized that the move made by the Soka Gakkai, a big organisation, would be a force towards Japan-China normalization. I knew that Prime Minister Zhou was studying the Soka Gakkai. He was checking how big an impact it has in Japan.
Question: Why do you think Prime Minister Zhou shows a serious interest in the Soka Gakkai?
Akioka : At the time, what China was most interested in was whether or not Japan would be able to open diplomatic relations with China independently of the US. Nothing could come of it if Japan was crushed under US pressure. That was why I think he was interested in the real power of the Soka Gakkai.
Question: On 5 December 1974, Prime Minister Zhou who was not well met Mr. Ikeda, but that was during the middle of the Cultural Revolution. Why do you think he met with the leader of a Japanese religious organisation at that time?
Akioka: I am sure the Gang of Four was angry. Prime Minister Zhou was considerate of the situation of other people. He is not the kind of a person who would unilaterally push things to the other person. He would listen to what the other person had to say and looked for points they could agree on. I believe it was because Prime Minister Zhou judged that Mr. Ikeda had contributed to recovering diplomatic relations. Prime Minister Zhou knew that the Soka Gakkai initiative was not for its own interest. I believe Prime Minister Zhou was watching the Soka

Gakkai and Mr. Ikeda right through Mr. Ikeda's (1968) proposition to his meeting (in 1974)[104]
(Translated by Fujiko Hara)

In September 1963, Tatsunosuke Takasaki met Ikeda and recommended that he visit China and talk with Zhou. Sawako Ariyoshi, a novelist, a Christian and pro-Chinese was in China in May 1966 and was asked to carry Zhou's message inviting Ikeda to visit China when she met Zhou in Beijing. Ariyoshi on her return delivered the message to Ikeda. In March 1970, Kenzo Matsumura was inspired by Ikeda's 1968 proposition and visited Ikeda proposing that the two to travel to China together. Ikeda believed that normalization of diplomatic relations was a political matter that was best resolved at the political level and proposed that the Komeito visit to China.

Ikeda : I thank you for your offer but I am a religious person and the Soka Gakkai is a Buddhist organisation Normalization of diplomatic relations can only be successful at the political level. Therefore, I will ask the Komeito which I had established to accompany you.
Matsumura : I will tell Prime Minister Zhou everything about President Ikeda and the Komeito[105]
(Translated by Fujiko Hara)

---

[104] People's Daily Overseas Edition Japan Monthly, Ikeda Daisaku To Nicchu Yuko No Ayumi: Nicchu Kokou Seijouka 40 Shunen Kinen (Daisaku Ikeda and History of Japan-China Friendship: The 40th Anniversary of Diplomatic Normalization between Japan and China), 2012, p34-p35
[105] Zhou Enlai School of Government, Nankai University (China), Edited by Kazuteru Saionji, *Shu Onrai To Ikeda Daisaku (Zhou Enlai and Daisaku Ikeda)*, Asahi Sonorama 2002 (in Japanese), p118

Ikeda was aware that religion and politics are from different dimensions. Civic organisations and civilians who lack political legitimacy do not have the legal qualification to be directly involved in political decision-making. Problem solving of political matters would have to be done in the final analysis by the government and political parties.

In the month that followed (April 1970), Zhou met Matsumura in Beijing and asked Matsumura to convey his message that he strongly welcomed Mr. Ikeda's visit to China. In July 1972, the Komeito made its first visit to China, met Zhou Enlai and compiled a report on China's claim (assertion).[106] And on returning, the visiting party shared the report with Kakuei Tanaka, the Japanese Prime Minister. Now understanding what the government of China had in mind, the Japanese government decided to start negotiations towards the normalization of relations with China. At that time, Richard Nixon's visit to China in 1972 had resulted in closer US-China diplomatic relations, diplomatically isolating Japan, who continued to follow an anti-China stance in the Northeast Asian region. Two months after the Komeito's visit to China, Kakuei Tanaka went to China in September 1972 and met Zhou Enlai and other members of the Chinese government and negotiated for the normalization of bilateral relations.[107] It was during

---

[106] MOFA, Dai 1 Kai Takeiri Yoshikatsu Shu Onrai Kaidan Kiroku (Record of Meetings between Yoshikatsu Takeiri of Komeito and Zhou Enlai No1), 27th July 1972
Ministry of Foreign Affairs Japan, Dai 2 Kai Takeiri Yoshikatsu Shu Onrai Kaidan Kiroku (Record of Meetings between Yoshikatsu Takeiri of Komeito and Zhou Enlai No2), 28th July 1972
MOFA, Dai 3 Kai Takeiri Yoshikatsu Shu Onrai Kaidan Kiroku (Record of Meetings between Yoshikatsu Takeiri of Komeito and Zhou Enlai No3), 29th July 1972

[107] MOFA, Tanaka Sori Shu Onrai Sori Kaidan Kiroku (Record of Meetings between Prime Minister Tanaka and Prime Minister Zhou), 25th – 28th September 1972

Tanaka's visit to China that normalization of Japan-China diplomatic relations was announced in the Joint Declaration. Nixon's visit to China in 1972 left Japan out of the diplomatic loop but it was able to restore relations with China ahead of the US. It was not until 1978 that the US was able to normalize its relations with China.

Although Japan-China diplomatic relations were restored, there was no change in the nuclear threat in the Northeast Asian Region as long as confrontation between China and the Soviet Union remained. Between Japan and China, in 1978 a treaty of friendship was signed when no peace treaty had existed. Between Japan and the Soviet Union diplomatic relations had been normalized in 1956 but the signing of the Peace Treaty had been postponed, and it remains unsigned. (see Chapter 6).

Ikeda visited China ten times[108] between 1974 and 1997. The main thrust of his visits was always cultural, artistic and educational exchanges, but he also met with political leaders and discussed nuclear issues. His first visit was in 1974 from 30 May to 15 June at the invitation of the China-Japan Friendship Association. Most of Ikeda's visits overseas were in response to invitations from cultural and educational organisations of the host countries and were always aimed at promoting private diplomacy through cultural exchanges. During his first visit to China his schedule centred on educational and cultural exchanges consisting of his visit to Beijing University and to high, middle and primary schools. On 6 June, however, he had talks with Li Xiannian, the Deputy Prime Minister of China 1954-1980, and its President 1983-1988.[109] Zhou Enlai was too ill; therefore Li

---

[108] *1974 (twice), 1975, 1978, 1980, 1986, 1990, 1992, 1994, 1997,* The People's Daily Overseas Edition Japan Monthly 2012, p50-p51

[109] Zhou Enlai School of Government, Nankai University (China), Edited by Kazuteru Saionji, *Shu Onrai To Ikeda Daisaku (Zhou Enlai and Daisaku Ikeda)*,

represented him in meeting Ikeda. At the time of Ikeda's second visit to China in December 1972, at Zhou's strong wish, Ikeda met him at the hospital where Zhou was. At the meeting with Li in June 1974, the two exchanged views on many matters: the Treaty of Peace and Friendship between Japan and the People's Republic of China, freedom under a socialist society, the policy of the great powers, the Five Principles of Peaceful Coexistence (Pancha Si-la) agreed between Zhou and Nehru of India in 1954, prevention of bureaucratization, the United Nations, the Socialist Camp and nuclear weapons. In particular, Ikeda strongly wished for the conclusion of the Treaty of Peace and Friendship between Japan and the People's Republic of China; this is clearly stated in Ikeda's book and also from the study of the Zhou Enlai School of Government, at Nankai University, China. Its specific contents, however, are not made clear.[110] Also, Ikeda wrote in his book that during his visit to Beijing's No. 35 Middle High School on 3 June he saw students digging air-raid shelters in preparation for a USSR attack. He was terrified, recalling that he too had dug similar air-raid shelters during the Second World War. He realized that China today was Japan yesteryears and so he gave himself the greatest task of communicating this fact to the USSR to avoid China-Soviet confrontation.[111]

After completing his first visit to China, Ikeda went on his way to the USSR in September 1974, three months later. He met with Alexei Kosygin, the USSR Prime Minister and extracted the promise that "the USSR will not launch an attack on China". Again, three months later he made his second visit to China in December 1974 and passed on those words to the Chinese leadership including Zhou Enlai and Deng Xiao

---

Asahi Sonorama 2002, p73

[110] Ibid, p73

[111] Daisaku Ikeda, Shin Ningen Kakumei 20 (New Human Revolution volume 20), Seikyo Newspaper 2011, p71-p72

Ping (see Chapter 5). Ikeda played the role of building communication that had been extinct between the two countries.

Ikeda's meeting with Li Xiannian on 6 June 1974 was long, lasting over 2 hours and 15 minutes. They covered four delicate topics such as socialism and human freedom, organisation and bureaucracy, nuclear weapons and peace in Asia, and China's thoughts on world peace.[112] China's policy of non-first use of nuclear weapons remains the basic nuclear policy of China to this day in 2015. The Chinese government believes that the nuclear issue started with US-Soviet confrontation and therefore the two countries should take the first steps towards nuclear abolition. Following this meeting Ikeda met with the Japanese press and made public the contents of the meeting.[113] The Asahi Shimbun in its evening paper on 7 June quoted Premier Li as saying; "even with the advance of socialism China will co-exist peacefully with Japan and Europe.[114] One can point out that the role of private diplomacy is to draw out honest words that cannot be clearly stated and to make them public as free agents.

At Ikeda and Hu Yaobang's meeting on 6 June 1984, they discussed nuclear abolition and Hu agreed to the SGI organizing an anti-nuclear exhibition: "Nuclear Arms: Threat to Our World" in China. During their discussion, Ikeda referred to Zhao Ziyang Prime Minister of China 1980-1987 proposing nuclear disarmament in Paris, saying that the SGI too was promoting nuclear abolition and asked what roadmap the Chinese Government had in achieving nuclear abolition.[115] Yaobang answered, "We are strongly for disarmament. The two super powers

---

112 Seikyo Newspaper, 28th June 2010, pp3 (provided by Soka Gakkai Office of International Affairs)

113 Ibid

114 Ibid

115 Seikyo Newspaper, 7th June 1984, p1 (this copy was provided by Soka Gakkai Office of International Affairs)

must take the lead in reducing arms. In particular nuclear arms must be reduced and abolished. Even if they cannot be abolished they should be reduced. In this regard too you (the SGI) have done a big job. Answering Ikeda's further question regarding China's concrete vision for nuclear abolition, he explained, "The two countries (the US and the Soviet) have no ears to listen to us. What we can say is limited. Because we cannot even manage our airspace," he said jokingly explaining the difficulty of achieving nuclear abolition.[116] Ikeda proposed that the SGI relocate the anti-nuclear exhibition then circulating at UN Headquarters in New York and Geneva and set it up in Beijing, to which Yaobang responded positively right on the spot. It was agreed that the contents and other details would be studied for the opening of the exhibition with persons involved.[117] It is conjectured that Yaobang had no second thoughts because the Chinese government's position was for nuclear abolition. Also when the SGI anti-nuclear exhibition was held in Moscow (1988) the Soviet Government was of the opinion that the basic problems of nuclear armament rested with the US, which after all was the world's first country to develop and deploy the weapons. One may say that both China and the Soviet governments used the occasion strategically to appeal to the world that they were peaceful countries in approving the holding of the exhibition (the Soka Gakkai Office of International Affairs has provided its private opinion regarding the Moscow exhibition, for the purpose of this thesis, which is referred to in Chapter 6). In any case, there were no anti-nuclear exhibitions before and after this one, either in Moscow or in Beijing, which were bigger in scale or that enjoyed the rare permission of the two communist governments.

---

[116] Ibid

[117] Ibid

The SGI production, "Nuclear Arms: Threat to Our World" was exhibited in the Chinese Revolution Museum in Tienanmen Square in Beijing from 21 to 30 October 1986 co-sponsored by the UN Public Relations Bureau and Soka Gakkai, with the support of the Chinese Peoples Foreign Friendship Association, China-Japan Friendship Association, UN International Year of Peace/ China Organizing Committee, Chinese National China Women's Federation, and the UN Association of China. The exhibition had the full support of the Chinese government who put up a huge signboard at the entrance of the Exhibition. Li Peng, former Vice-Prime Minister of China 1983-1987, and many high officials of the government visited the exhibition, while the Ambassador from the Soviet Union as well as other ambassadors stationed in China attended and from Japan Hitoshi Motojima Mayor of Nagasaki and Sato Miyanaga Chairman of the Hiroshima City Council attended on behalf of its mayor. A total of 70,000 people attended the exhibition. The opening ceremony was covered by special correspondents from every media in Japan, while the People's Daily and China's central national television station also covered the occasion for domestic consumption. 1986 happened to be the UN International Year of Peace and the Chinese government had established an International Year of Peace Chinese Organizing Committee in support. The Committee also was one of the supporting organisations of the anti-nuclear exhibition.

The exhibition was made possible, due to the deep trusting relations Ikeda had with the Chinese government. The government of China tends to be extremely nervous about ideologies that are opposed, or even if not opposed, different from government's policies as witnessed by the Tiananmen incident. This was a trend seen in the communist sphere at the time. No organisation that was not trusted could ever have had the opportunity to conduct a large-scale anti-nuclear exhibition in the capital of a country developing nuclear weapons. It may be said that the Chinese government must have understood that Ikeda's anti-nuclear ideology and the SGI anti-nuclear exhibition were not harmful to it. In fact the contents of the exhibition was neither pro-Western nor pro-Eastern. Rather than condemning nuclear weapons states it appealed to the people to recognize the threat of nuclear weapons themselves. Studying the history of the anti-nuclear movement, it is clear that the movement attacks nuclear weapons states. They tend to demand governments of nuclear states reduce or abolish their nuclear weapons, in other words to change their policies. As a result governments of nuclear weapons states would make every effort to justify themselves and would lose the original essential attempt at abolishing nuclear weapons altogether. Governments around the world negotiating with the Chinese government cannot put aside the threat of Chinese nuclear weapons during their diplomatic negotiations, especially those relating to national security negotiations between governments, despite the fact that the Chinese have made a declaration of non-first use. In that sense no nuclear weapons state has legitimate reasons for it alone to possess them. It might well be thought that this amounted to a self-righteous excuse. The SGI anti-nuclear exhibition focused on the threats of nuclear weapons and tried to expand the circle of empathy for the abolition of nuclear weapons. Today it is beginning to be recognized that global issues must be dealt with cooperatively whatever the differences of ideology and methodology. In this sense the SGI anti-nuclear movement had prescience. Trusting relations between Ikeda and the Chinese government were mainly established over a lengthy period of cultural, artistic and educational exchanges. Such exchanges covered a broad sphere. For example, the Min-On Concert

Association (Tokyo, Japan) established by Ikeda in 1963 has sponsored thirty public performances by twenty-three organisations as of 2012, starting with sponsoring the Chinese Beijing Art Group in Japan in September 1975.[118]

Also, the Tokyo Fuji Art Museum (Tokyo, Japan) established by Ikeda in 1983 has sponsored fourteen China- related exhibitions between 1985 and 2012. And they include introducing Japanese and Western arts to China, as well as organizing exhibitions of photographs by Robert Capa, which are collections of the Tokyo Fuji Art Museum Ikea founded in Tokyo, and their relationships with China. That is to say, it is not just a one-way introduction of Chinese arts to Japan but it includes those aimed at deepening mutual understanding.[119] The Museum eagerly introduces Japanese and Chinese objects of art to Europe. For example, "Maki-e Lacquer & Oriental Ceramics" (co-sponsored by the Austrian Royal Silver Museum and the Tokyo Fuji Art Museum) with the support of Austrian Ministry of Art planned to introduce Japanese and Chinese arts to Austria, and were seen by nearly 100,000 people.[120]

As far as educational exchange was concerned, Soka University Ikeda founded in 1975 was the first to receive six Chinese students paid for by the state.[121] And Ikeda himself became their guarantor. One of the six, Cheng Yonghua, after graduating from Soka University returned

---

[118] People's Daily Overseas Edition Japan Monthly, Ikeda Daisaku To Nicchu Yuko No Ayumi: Nicchu Kokou Seijouka 40 Shunen Kinen (Daisaku Ikeda and History of Japan-China Friendship: The 40th Anniversary of Diplomatic Normalization between Japan and China), 2012, p76

[119] Ibid

[120] Tokyo Fuji Art Museum, *Tenran Kai Shosai: Maki-e Lacquer & Oriental Ceramics*
http://www.fujibi.or.jp/exhibitions/profile-of-exhibitions.html?exhibit_id=2199709181 (accessed on 18th April 2014)

[121] Ibid, p52

to China and joined the Chinese Foreign Ministry. In 1977 he was assigned to the Chinese Embassy in Japan, then he was promoted to Deputy Asian Bureau, and in 2003 returned to Japan as Minister in the Chinese Embassy, then served as China's ambassador in Malaysia in 2006 and Chinese ambassador in Korea in 2008. And from 2010 to as of 2015 he is the Chinese Ambassador in Japan. Cheng remains faithful to conventional Chinese government's policies. When interviewed in 2012 by Japanese media he candidly stated that on the Senkaku Islands issue, "it had been agreed to shelve the issue by the two sides at the Japan-China negotiation for normalization of diplomatic relations. If that agreement to shelve the issue were to be lost, there is a danger that China and Japan will lose peaceful days forever.[122] He made a visit to the Nagasaki Atomic Bomb Museum (in Nagasaki) on 18 December 2010 and offered flowers at ground zero as the Chinese Ambassador in Japan. He stated at the time, referring to the nuclear weapons of China, that China declares non-first use and would not use nuclear bombs in non-nuclear weapons countries and regions.[123] As of September 2012, Soka University has mutual student exchange programmes with forty Chinese universities under academic exchange programmes.[124] It is likely that the Chinese overseas students have been affected by Ikeda's ideology of peace including promoting China-Japan friendship and

---

[122] Chiyako Sato, *Interview with Cheng Yonghua*, Mainichi Newspaper 17th September 2012 (in Japanese)

[123] The Nagasaki Shimbun, Chunichi Chugoku Taishi Ga Bakushinchi De Kenka "Rekishi Kyokun Ni Heiwa Kosei He" (Chinese Ambassador to Japan Offered Flowers at the Hypocentre: To Transmit the Historic Lesson to Posterity), 19th December 2010 http://www.nagasaki-np.co.jp/news/peace/2010/12/19124557.shtml (accessed on 27th March 2011)

[124] People's Daily Overseas Edition Japan Monthly, Ikeda Daisaku To Nicchu Yuko No Ayumi: Nicchu Kokou Seijouka 40 Shunen Kinen (Daisaku Ikeda and History of Japan-China Friendship: The 40th Anniversary of Diplomatic Normalization between Japan and China), 2012, p53

building of harmonious societies and anti-nuclear weapons. From 1989 to 2012, 111 of Ikeda's books were translated into the Chinese language and published.[125] And the Chinese are studying Ikeda's philosophy. As of 2012, there are twenty-six universities and research institutions, including Daisaku Ikeda Study Group at the Beijing University established in 2001, and the establishment in 2009 of the Daisaku Ikeda Research Centre at the Shanghai Normal University. Their research themes cover "Harmonized Society and Harmonized World", "Cultural Diversity and Harmonized World" and "Peace and Education", all of them focusing on Ikeda's thoughts on humanism and pluralism.[126] Also, as of 2012, Ikeda has received honorary degrees from China's 117 universities extolling Ikeda's contribution to Japan-China friendship, international peace and education, including Professor Emeritus from the Beijing University in 1984, and the same from the Tsinghua University in 2010.[127] It was due to the results of these exchanges that the Soka Gakkai was able to organize in Beijing an anti-nuclear exhibition, with the Chinese government recognizing its importance. This is evidence that the low politics of culture, arts and education have an impact on nuclear disarmament which otherwise belongs to the realm of high politics.

Ikeda's private diplomacy with China has thus been very influential in mitigating strains in the relationship between Japan and China, which were neighbours but seriously confronted each other and were on the point of rupture in diplomatic relations.

In contrast to Ikeda's private diplomacy, there is an organisation called the Elders[128] which also deploys private diplomacy at the global

---

[125] Ibid, p74-p75

[126] Ibid, p64

[127] Ibid, p68-p69

[128] The Elders: Independent Global Leaders Working Together for Peace and

level in resolving international human rights issues and conflicts between states and for peace building. This dissertation analyses their private diplomacy about the Israeli-Palestinian conflict. The organisation was initiated in 2007 at the appeal of Nelson Mandela. As of 2014, Kofi Annan serves as its Chair with Gro Harlem Brundtland[129] as Deputy Chair. The organisation is composed of thirteen members including former heads of state, Jimmy Carter, Mary Robinson[130], Gracia Machel[131] and Lakhdar Brahimi[132]. They represent fighters for women's rights, human rights, education, peacekeeping, and include post conflict resolution experts. Their motto is to undertake independent activities not fettered by the interests of specific states or governments.[133] They focus on Climate Change, the Iranian nuclear issue, the Israeli-Palestinian issue, establishment of women's rights and Myanmar issues. They conduct regular meetings twice a year and are engaged in resolution of problems through dialogue by visiting concerned countries on specific issues.

Among the activities of the Elders, their Israel Palestinian initiatives may be compared with Ikeda's private diplomacy with China. Japan-China relations and the Middle East issue have commonalities, in that both experience a state of war in adjacent regions with the resultant mutual distrust and conflict that they cannot give up. Among the activities of the Elders, the Middle East issue is the gravest (as of the

---

Human Rights http://www.theelders.org/ (accessed on 13th October 2013)

[129] first woman Prime Minister of Norway

[130] first woman President of Ireland and former UN High Commissioner for Human Rights

[131] an international advocate for women's and children's rights; former freedom fighter and first Educational Minister of Mozambique

[132] former Algerian freedom fighter, Foreign Minister, conflict mediator, and UN diplomat

[133] The Elders, *What do the Elders stand for?* http://www.theelders.org/about (accessed on 13th October 2013)

present in 2015), and they have visited the region in continuous years, 2009, 2010 and 2011, and actively undertaken activities. They summarize information received on the spot as well as providing their analysis in reports and sharing them internationally on their website.

The basic stance of the activities of the Elders is to prompt parties concerned to solve their problems on their own initiative and for the Elders not to become involved directly in decision-making or even participate as subjects in that process. They also maintain neutrality and independence, not taking one or other side. For example, with regard to the Middle East issue, their activities prompt both the Palestinian Authority and the Israeli government to work together for solutions. Specifically, they will visit leading figures of both governments and citizens playing out grass-root peace movement activity and encouraging them to come to mutual understanding through dialogue and communication. The activities include building bridges between citizens and decision-makers so as to reflect the voice of the ordinary people in policy decisions.[134] The Elders state that their activities reflect neither typical social movements mobilizing citizens in great numbers nor charitable organisations raising money for their activities[135]. Their activities prompting dialogue for mutual understanding between states and peoples resemble Ikeda and the SGI activities but are different in that the Elders do not become parties involved.

A delegation of the Elders[136] visited Israel and the West Bank in 2009. They held talks with youth representatives, non-violence activists,

---

[134] Ibid, How Do They Work?

[135] Ibid, How Can I Support The Elders' Work?

[136] The Elders, *On the delegation: Ela Bhatt, Gro Harlem Brundtland, Fernando Henrique Cardoso, Jimmy Carter, Mary Robinson and Desmond Tutu.* http://theelders.org/israel-palestine/elders-work (accessed on 13th October 2013)

womens' organisations, human rights specialists, UN staff as well as officials of the Israeli government and the Palestine Authority. The Elders explained that the premise of prompting both governments to build peace has to be that citizens in both regions are in agreement with the process, hence their efforts at talking with citizens.[137] The visitors felt that many citizens in both areas have developed distrust of their own government as well as the political process itself after experiencing repeated failings of the peace process and ensuing military conflict. The Elders felt that continual failure of the peace process was due to the government negotiators of both sides becoming disconnected from time to time and losing communication, and -felt that greater diplomatic efforts should be made to bring government leaders of both sides closely connected to each other[138]. Also in their meetings with civil society leaders and business leaders in both regions they found that most welcomed the US government support for the peace process but also realized that the J. Street and other conservative Jewish organisations in the US lobbying against the peace process were major obstacles to peace. Therefore, the Elders' delegation wrote to President Obama during their stay in the Middle East asking him to promptly undertake the peace process and to continue to work to have the walls surrounding Gaza removed.[139] However, one cannot say as of today in 2015 that the US government is undertaking an epoch-making initiative, while the Middle East situation is clearly worsening. The Elders prepared a report for 2009 that showed their support for the Palestinian Authority's plan for achieving statehood in the future.

---

[137] The Elders Report 2009, p9 http://www.theelders.org/docs/middle-east/People-and-Peace-in-the-Middle-East.pdf (accessed on 13th October 2013)

[138] Ibid, pp11

[139] Ibid, pp12

The Elders paid keen attention to mutual reconciliation developed through economic relations between the two regions. The Elders called it "economic peace" and pointed out that it was essential to the peace-building process. Specifically, from early 2009, the government of Israel had, though very gradually, allowed Arabs living in Israel access to markets of the West Bank. The Elders placed great expectations on deepening relationships between the two regions in the West Bank.[140] Building peace through economic connection is a different approach to the SGI and it was a unique viewpoint contributed by a group of former political leaders. In the Japan-China relations following the Second World War, politicians and business people of the two countries tried to sustain bilateral exchange through trade, albeit, with difficulty. That is to say that "economic friendship" is an important factor in linking regions mired in conflicts but that there is no conclusive evidence that 'economic peace" can be realized. Total Japan-China trade in the first half of 2014 stood at $168,359,000,000 (export: $77,995,180,000, import: $90,354,100,000), with the Chinese share of the total Japanese trade being 20.1%, for the first time overtaking the US share of 18.4%.[141] Even so, Japan-China relations are considered to be at their worst in history, and economic exchange is unlikely to drastically change the situation. The world's media tended to report on the seriousness of the Palestine-Israeli conflict and impressed on world opinion that after the Israeli government erected walls around Gaza the two areas were completely separated. It seemed that there was no room for any negotiation. However, the Elders were able to impress on international society that there are exchanges between citizens of

---

[140] Ibid, p14

[141] Japan External Trade Organization, *Kisha Happyo (Press Release)*, 19th August 2014 http://www.jetro.go.jp/news/releases/20140819742-news (accessed on 21st September 2014)

both regions, albeit small. This was an important feat brought about by the private sector.

The Elders' visit to the Middle East in 2010 included stopovers in Egypt, Jordan and Syria among others. They made clear their support for the Palestine Authority pointing out that no peace process would go forward as long as Israel continued to rule Palestinian land.[142] They also criticized the denial of Arab identity in East Jerusalem as a major factor impeding the peace process, directing similar criticism at neighbouring Arab nations.[143] That is to say, the Elders claim that Arab countries should give greater support to the Palestinian Authority. On the other hand, the Elders also endorse the existence of Israel. The Elders believe that the citizens of Israel in their hearts wish for a peaceful coexistence with their neighbours and confirm that it is their natural right to have a state in which they can live in peace. The Elders wrote that their report on the visit to the Middle East in 2010 should not be interpreted as anti-Israel.[144] To summarize the report, the Israeli government should stop ruling the Palestinian region, but Israel also must have guaranteed statehood, also that there is a need for a peace process that ensures both sides coexist together. In their meetings with the political leaders of Egypt and other Arab countries, Arab leaders have cited the need for an international mediation, particularly, the need for an initiative from the US government.[145] However, they have strong reservations as to how much the US government can take the diplomatic

---

142 The Elders, "A Just and Secure Peace for All: Report of The Elders' visit to Egypt, Gaza, Israel, Jordan, Syria, and the West Bank 15-22 October 2010" , p1
http://www.theelders.org/docs/middle-east/The_Elders_Middle_East_Trip_Report-October-2010.pdf (accessed on 13th October 2013)

143 Ibid, p2

144 Ibid

145 Ibid, p4

initiative, given that its relations with Israel are much deeper than those with Palestine.[146]

Jimmy Carter and the Elders' delegation visiting Israel and Palestine in 2012 met Simon Peres, the Israeli President, and Mahmoud Abbas, of the Palestinian Authority (President of the State of Palestine) to propose that there can be no realization of peace in the region except to find a two state solution.[147] As of 2015 no such compromise has been proposed. The Elders' approach is an ideal form of grassroots peace movement, for they have had direct contacts and information exchanges with heads of states, representatives of economic communities and civic societies. Since Jimmy Carter and other former political leaders from Western and industrialized countries are members of The Elders they can get directly in touch with present leaders of the US and other major countries. This is a huge advantage for any civic movement, but they have not reached a point to have their outcomes evaluated. Since the SGI has a history of half a century of peace movement we will have to wait another 50 years to compare with the outcomes of The Elders' diplomacy. At present, its activities stop at interfering but not intervening to resolve issues through assisting governments.

Reports of the Elders' visit to the Middle East show that the Elders have the key to influencing the US administration, as the importance of its initiative in the Peace Process by the Administration is recognized by the general public as well as their leaders in the Israeli and Palestinian regions. The Elders believe in the need for high level diplomatic efforts in order to continue the dialogue towards the peace process. That means it could seek an opportunity on behalf of the US administration, to play an arbitrary role in carrying the process forward. CSOs will need to be

---

[146] Ibid

[147] The Elders, Press Release, 22 October 2012

involved as main actors in global issues by assisting political decision-makings without being effected by political interests.

Chapter 6: Ikeda and the USSR

In 1956 Japan normalized its diplomatic relations with the USSR. Originally, establishing a bilateral peace treaty was envisioned at the same time, but the Northern Territories that the Soviets attacked and occupied (even after the Japanese surrender), having unilaterally broken the Soviet-Japanese Neutrality Pact of 1941, remained an insoluble issue. The northern most territories Japan wants to have returned became an enormous obstacle on which both sides failed to concede, leaving the issue under continuous deliberation after the normalization. Japan did invade China and neighbouring states, but in the case of the USSR Japan has been invaded.

> Article 1: Both Contracting Parties undertake to maintain peaceful and friendly relations between them and mutually respect the territorial integrity and inviolability of the other Contracting Party.
> Article 2: Should one of the Contracting Parties become the object of hostilities on the part of one or several third powers, the other Contracting Party will observe neutrality throughout the duration of the conflict.
> (Soviet-Japanese Neutrality Pact 1941)[1]
> (Translated by Fujiko Hara)

As the consequence of thc Japan-Soviet war during the Second World War, 600,000 Japanese military personnel were sent to Siberia, where approximately ten per cent of them died. The USSR unilaterally incorporated the Northern Territories in February 1946, and forcefully evacuated approximately 17,000 Japanese from the islands. The

[1] MOFA, the Soviet-Japanese Neutrality Pact, 13th April 1941

Japanese government held that the Northern Territories, unlike the issues with the Senkaku Islands, were a territorial issue between Japan and the Soviet Union.

> Article 9
> The USSR and Japan have agreed to continue, after the establishment of normal diplomatic relations between them, negotiations for the conclusion of a peace treaty. Hereby, the USSR, in response to the desires of Japan and taking into consideration the interest of the Japanese state, agrees to hand over to Japan the Habomai and the Shikotan Islands, provided that the actual changing over to Japan of these islands will be carried out after the conclusion of a peace treaty".
> (Soviet-Japanese Joint Declaration. 19 October 1956)[2]
> (Translated by Fujiko Hara)

Since then, due to the Northern Territories' Issue no Peace Treaty has been signed with Russia as of 2015. No USSR leader had visited Japan until Gorbachev in 1991 due more to political tension caused by territorial issues rather than ideological confrontation.

The Japanese government continues at all times to pick the Northern Territories' Issue as its priority for discussion. This is a typical case of the inductive diplomatic approach of the Japanese government in achieving the big objective of signing a peace treaty through repeated deliberations.

Ivan Kovalenko, the Director of Japan Section, International Affairs Division of the Communist Party of the USSR, feared that the existing

---

[2] Kajima Institute of International Peace, Nippon Gaiko Shuyo Bunsho Nenpyo 1 (Diplomatic Archives and Chronological Table of Japan' volume 1), Hara Shobo 1983, p784-p786

power balance between the US, USSR, China and Japan would shift leaving the Soviet Union isolated as a result of Richard Nixon's visit to China in 1972, and the ensuing normalization of China—Japan relations.[3] He regarded Ikeda with alarm for having had a hand in achieving the normalization and so he began investigating the Soka Gakkai.[4] Kovalenko had originally enrolled in the Faculty of Oriental Studies at the Far Eastern Federal University of Vladivostok to study Japan. After graduation he served in the military and was involved in the psychological operation in the Battle of Khalkhin Gol, 1939. Following the Second World War, he served as the editor-in-chief of Nippon Shimbun (Japanese Newspaper) for the Japanese prisoners interned in Siberia, responsible for brainwashing the Japanese prisoners to turn pro-Soviet and he served as the Japan agent responsible for Soviet policy regarding Japan. He suspected Ikeda of being pro-China and against the USSR.[5]

In December 1973, under Soviet guidance, A. L. Jarocinnki, a member of the Academy of Sciences of the USSR and M.P. Kim, a historian and its associate member, visited Ikeda at the Soka University he established in Tokyo in 1971. This was a visit made to a Japanese educational organisation by members of the Soviet Academy of Sciences at a time when Japan-Soviet political exchange was difficult. Ikeda was prepared for their visit and asked them to convey the following message to Alexei Kosygin, the USSR Prime Minister (1964-1980): 'The establishment of a United Nations for Education', 'establishment of a cultural exchange association between Japanese and Soviet students', 'establishment of an Oriental Philosophy Faculty in

[3] Editing Committee of the "Ikeda Daisaku No Kiseki", *Ikeda Daisaku No Kiseki (Track of Daisaku Ikeda volume 2)*, Ushio Shuppansha 2007, p138

[4] Ibid, p139

[5] Ibid

Moscow State University', an 'Academic Exchange Agreement with Soka University', 'establishment of a Food United Nations (for the resolution of food issues), and the 'freezing of nuclear tests'.[6] Jarocinnki replied that they were wonderful suggestions but since they were not experts, earnestly asked Ikeda to visit Moscow.[7] This was the first invitation Ikeda received from the USSR.

On 8 September 1974, at the invitation of Moscow State University, Ikeda set foot for the first time in the USSR. The date, 8 September, was the day when Josei Toda issued the Declaration Calling for the Abolition of Nuclear Weapons in 1957. It is clear that Ikeda visited the USSR with the Declaration in mind and with the determination to achieve nuclear abolition. Coincidentally, Ikeda's Recommendation on Normalization of Japan-China Relations made in 1968 was on that very date, 8 September. (see Chapter 4). At the time of Ikeda's visit to the USSR there was no doubt that the Academy of Sciences and Moscow State University were following directions of the Soviet government and the Communist Party. The USSR embassies in various countries served as the bases of their intelligence. It is assumed the same for China at the time. In fact, Ikeda's invitation came from the Moscow State University after some unsuccessful decision-making between the Central Committee, Communist Party of the USSR and the Ministry of Foreign Affairs of the USSR as to which should host the visitor.[8] Kovelenko had much to do with the decision. This can be confirmed from his following report to the Central Committee of the Communist Party.

"1, Mr. Ikeda is a leader of Japan's largest 10 million-member

---

6 Ibid

7 Ibid

8 Ibid

Buddhist Organisation.

2, The Soka Gakkai has a big mass media.

3, We cannot be disinterested to knowing how the Soka Gakkai evaluates the USSR foreign policy.

4, Mr. Ikeda's views are in concert with us as regards co-existence of the US and USSR"[9]

(Translated by Fujiko Hara)

The reference made in item 2 to 'a huge mass media' is the Soka Gakkai's bulletin, Seikyo Newspaper. As of 2014 it has a nominal subscription of 5.5 million.[10] For these reasons Kovalenko considered the invitation to be issued from Moscow State University in order to dilute any political appearance.[11] Kovalenko also arranged Ikeda's meeting with Kosygin. What he had in mind was that a top level meeting between Kosygin and Ikeda would foreclose any criticism by members of the Communist Party Central Committee, as was usually the case. Kovalenko recalled the situation at the time in 1994.

"It was learned that at first the leaders of the Soviet Communist Party did not welcome the visit of President Ikeda of the Soka Gakkai to the Soviet Union. This was because the leadership did not have the correct information concerning the Soka Gakkai. The Party's Central Committee had a long discussion concerning the Soka Gakkai and President Ikeda. There were arguments particularly at the party's international department. Some maintained that no appropriate information was available

---

[9] Ibid

[10] Seikyo Online, *Goaisatsu (Greeting)*, http://www.seikyoonline.jp/seikyo/ (accessed on 1st December 2013)

[11] Ibid

about the character of the Soka Gakkai and President Ikeda. The invitation could wait until we made further studies. The majority was of the opinion that the invitation should wait until after studies had been made about the objectives of the Soka Gakkai, the personality of President Ikeda as well as their social orientations. I was the only member of the International Department who did not go along with the opinion of the majority. I was consistent that President Ikeda must visit the Soviet Union and maintained that he should have top-level meetings and receive a national welcome. In the end my opinion won and the party bureaucrats were defeated. A special decision was made that he would have a national welcome. It was also decided that the Ikeda-Kosygin meeting should take place at the Kremlin Palace. However, it was decided that the invitation would be issued not from the Party Central, but from the Moscow State University after weighing up another candidate, the Federation of Foreign Cultural Exchange Organisations. At the meeting with Premier Kosygin, President Ikeda who was the Chief of the visiting delegation, shared his thoughts on politics and philosophy as well as the activities of Soka Gakkai that had a membership in excess of ten million. Kosygin was surprised at this and lost no time in stating that contacts between Soka Gakkai and the Soviet social organisations could build productive and cooperative relations that could contribute to meaningful Soviet-Japan relations".[12]
(Translated by Fujiko Hara)

---

[12] Ivan Kovalenko, *Daibyaku Renge volume 11* (appeared in Japanese), November 1994

During his ten-day stay in the USSR, Ikeda held talks with a number of top leaders[13] in education, culture, and politics including Mikhail Sholokhnov (Nobel Laureate 1965). Ikeda's central topic was nuclear disarmament and avoidance of China-Soviet confrontation. Kosygin gave Ikeda his word that he was not thinking of isolating China.

> "**Ikeda**: China is concerned about the Soviet's approach to it.
> **Kosygin**. The Soviet Union has no intention of either attacking China or isolating it.
> **Ikeda**: Can I pass on to Chinese leaders what you told me?
> **Kosygin**: Certainly".[14]
> (Translated by Fujiko Hara)

Without giving details, Ikeda sent the Japanese media his recollections of their dialogue appraising Kosygin's words on nuclear abolition on which he spent most of the time.

> "On the last day of my stay in the Soviet Union, I had an opportunity to have a dialogue with Prime Minister Kosygin. It took about an hour and a half, and I expressed my convictions

---

[13] Ikeda met: the President of Moscow State University, the Minister in charge of Middle and High School Education (Minister for Secondary Education), the First Deputy Minister of Culture, the Chairman of the USSR Supreme National Conference, the Deputy Governor of the Academy of Sciences, the First Mayor of Moscow, the Chairman of the USSR Federation of Foreign Cultural Exchange Organisations, the Mayor of Leningrad, the Deputy President of Leningrad University, and the President of the Theologian Academy.

[14] Takayuki Nakazawa, Gorubathofu To Ikeda Daisaku (Gorbachev and Daisaku Ikeda), Kadokawa Shoten 2004, p61-p62
Zhou Enlai School of Government, Nankai University (China), Edited by Kazuteru Saionji, *Shu Onrai To Ikeda Daisaku (Zhou Enlai and Daisaku Ikeda)*, Asahi Sonorama 2002, p285

regarding nuclear issues. Prime Minister (Kosygin) stated clearly that the Soviet Union had no intention of using nuclear weapons and that it was seriously considering their total abandonment through due process. He was not thinking of isolating China. I make it a point to accept things said by people of responsibility. Perhaps he shared his innermost feelings because I was a civilian and not a politician. I also confirmed in China its strong decision and will towards total abolition of nuclear weapons. It seems to me that all mankind share that wish. I asked myself how could the wishes be bridged. There is no other way than for the top leaders of the world to come together to continue patiently to talk about the matter. At the same time the key lies in having a civilian exchange on a broad front".[15]

(Translated by Fujiko Hara)

Kovalenko explained that Kosygin instructed him to maintain close relations with Ikeda after the dialogue.[16] According to the Soka Gakkai Office of International Affairs, it appears that details of Ikeda's talks conducted in 1974 and 1975 were not recorded and talks seemed to have taken place within a limited time and were conducted with unpractised interpreter(s), with one side asking a question and the other answering it (often incorporating his own ideas and principles).[17] However, it seems that the positions are clearly expressed through what Ikeda made public through the media and also his own writings.[18]

---

[15] Tokyo Shimbun (Tokyo Newspaper), 25th September 1974

[16] Ivan Kovalenko, *Daibyaku Renge volume 11*, November 1994

[17] The Soka Gakkai Office of International Affairs provided to this dissertation its views on Ikeda and Kosygin's talks for the purposes of this dissertation with a proviso that it was strictly a view of the Office.

[18] The information provided by the Soka Gakkai and this represents their

In 1979, Ikeda published an article in the Japanese media entitled, "*Chikuseki Sareta Fuukaku Prime Minister Kosygin (A cultivated man, Prime Minister Kosygin)*" concerning the talks he had with the Premier in 1974 and 75.

> "The last two meetings I had with Prime Minister Kosygin exceeded two hours and during that time he was consistent in his conviction regarding nuclear disarmament. In fact it was stronger during our second meeting. I recall Kosygin saying with passion, "There are enough nuclear arms to destroy the whole world. There is no guarantee that something horrible will not happen with someone like Hitler appearing. Sooner or later, there is no doubt that humankind will decide on nuclear disarmament"[19]
>
> (Translated by Fujiko Hara)

Vladimir Tropin, who then was the Vice President of Moscow State University, wrote in his book, written in Japanese, "*Seishin No Shiruku Rodo Wo Motomete (In Search of A Spiritual Silk Road)*"[20] referring to Ikeda's written contribution to the media wrote, "*Kosygin is a realist politician who clearly recognized that nuclear deterrence would not totally save the world from nuclear destruction*".[21]

Ikeda visited Beijing in December 1974, three months after his visit to the Soviet Union and informed Zhou Enlai and Deng Xiao Ping about what Kosygin had said. It could be surmised that this was important

---

views

[19] Daisaku Ikeda, Sunday Mainichi (a magazine of Mainichi Newspaper), 11 February 1979

[20] Daisaku Ikeda, Seishin No Shiruku Rodo Wo Motomete (In Search of a Spiritual Silk Road), Ushio Shuppansha 2010

[21] Remark, Soka Gakkai Office of International Affairs

information for the Chinese at a time of aggravated Chinese-Soviet relations. A month later, in December 1974, Ikeda met with Henry Kissinger, at the Office of the Secretary at the US Department of State in Washington. While what they discussed was not made public, but it can be assumed that Ikeda told Kissinger about his visits to China and the USSR as well as his cherished opinion regarding nuclear disarmament and peace. These would have been valuable information to the US regarding the then situation concerning China and the USSR. As for the Japanese government, without Ikeda's initiative Japan would have been left behind diplomatically when the US made a sudden visit to China bypassing Japan. Kissinger entrusted Ikeda with an apology to the Government of Japan for his discourtesy due to the need (of the US Administration) to keep the visit a diplomatic secret.[22] Ikeda after his return to Japan communicated the message to Eisaku Sato, the Prime Minister (1964-1972). Sato is said to have shown his relief saying that those words had saved the honour of the Japanese government.[23] The significance of Ikeda's private diplomacy during 1974 and 75 was that it involved bringing together the four countries, the US, the USSR, China and Japan. It may be assumed that his main contribution during this time was in easing Chinese-Soviet conflicts but his communication with the US at the same period had great diplomatic significance. The US Administration is likely to have been closely watching the easing of diplomatic relations between Japan, China and the USSR without being involved. Ikeda's timely visit to the US may have saved the US Administration from nurturing unnecessary conjecture and misunderstandings. The Japanese people came to learn of this later when Kissinger, in a book he co-authored with Ikeda, described US

[22] Ushio Shuppansha, *Ushio (Monthly Magazine)*, November 2007, pp110

[23] Ibid

diplomacy vis-à-vis China in relation to its domestic situation.

> "**Kissinger:** Secret diplomacy is not always a magic pill but there are times when open diplomacy is not possible. The US's China diplomacy is a case in point. Without secrete diplomacy the object of American diplomacy was not likely to have happened. China then was a mystery for most Americans. President Nixon and his advisors did not understand too well how China would respond to the US's proposal for a public negotiation.
>
> **Ikeda:** I understand you.
>
> **Kissinger**: Also there was a powerful political force that was dead against normalization of relations with China in any form. There would have been a fierce domestic outcry had the Administration proceeded to negotiate without knowing Beijing's possible reaction. It could easily have had worse repercussions than at the time of the Vietnam War. The Administration had to check China's possible response and there was no way but sending a secret envoy. It was because there were absolutely no diplomatic relations then. All messages were communicated through an intermediary. And naturally they were extremely short. This was a typical case of secret diplomacy playing an essential role in establishing the first contact.
>
> **Ikeda**: I see.
>
> **Kissinger**: President Nixon only made it public after knowing that the secret diplomacy had succeeded in contacting China. This was how the US-China diplomatic relations came to be publicly carried out. Naturally, there were sacrifices paid for this secret diplomacy. That is to say, we made some close friends

suffer discomfort, particularly Japan's outstanding Prime Minister Sato. The US could have attentively let Prime Minister Sato know before President Nixon made public my visit to Beijing. Since that time, I continue to regret the way we failed to let Japan know.

Ikeda: These are precious words coming from you in person. I am sure readers in Japan share my thoughts that they are important words"[24]

(Translated by Fujiko Hara)

Ikeda's visit to the USSR was taken up on the cover pages of Japan's mainstream media. According to their reports Ikeda had proposed, during his dialogue with Kosygin, visits to Japan of Kosygin, Brezhnev and Podgorny, the three Soviet leaders.[25] Kosygin responded, "A visit to Japan is on our schedule. Brezhnev, the Secretary General says he would also like to visit." However, he stated, "The time is not ripe for the leader of the USSR to visit Japan. We wish a visit to the USSR this year of the Foreign Minister for the purpose of negotiating a peace treaty.[26] Kiichi Miyazawa, Japanese Foreign Minister 1974-1976 and Prime Minister 1991-1993, did visit the USSR mid- January 1975 and conducted the third negotiation for the Japan-Soviet Peace Treaty with Andrei Gromyko, the USSR Foreign Minister. No peace treaty was signed even with the Brezhnev government and neither was Kosygin's visit to Japan realized. Gromyko did make his third visit to Japan in 1976 following his first visit in 1966 but no conspicuous improvement

---

[24] Daisaku Ikeda and Henry Kissinger, *Heiwa To Zinsei To Tetsugaku O Kataru (Philosophy of Human Peace)*, Seikyo Newspaper 2008, p163-p164 It was originally published in 1987

[25] Takayuki Nakazawa, Gorubathofu To Ikeda Daisaku (Gorbachev and Daisaku Ikeda), Kadokawa Shoten 2004, p67

[26] Ibid

was made in bilateral diplomatic relations.

Since then Ikeda visited the Soviet Union in 1975 to have his second dialogue with Kosygin. He went again in 1981 to talk with Nikolai Tikhonov, in 1987 to have his second talk with Tikhonov and on 27 July 1990 to have a dialogue with Mikhail Gorbachev.[27] During his meeting in 1981 with Nikolai Tikhonov, the Chairman of the Council of Ministers 1980-1985, Ikeda proposed a summit meeting between the US, China, Japan and the Soviet Union. Ikeda believed that humankind wished for the earliest possible US-USSR summit meeting to take place not in Washington or Moscow but some third place such as Switzerland but at that time no summit leader was willing to go along with his views.[28] The Soviet invasion of Afghanistan in 1979 was globally criticized and the 1980 Moscow Olympic Games that took place a year before Ikeda's meeting with Tikhonov was boycotted by nearly fifty countries including the US, Japan and China. While the whole world vehemently criticized the USSR, Ikeda visited the country in 1981 for cultural exchanges. The group consisted of over 200 members including the Soka Gakkai fifes and drums and the Soka University chorus who were welcomed warmly and got to know many Soviet citizens and students,[29] and also held an exhibition of Japanese dolls (traditional crafts) to introduce Japanese culture and arts.[30] Ikeda must have believed that at times when political tension is the highest it is important to bring peoples together though cultural exchange and for the leaders to talk with each other.

February 1990's version of "*Warera no Hoppou-ryodo (Our Northern Territories)*" published by MOFA'S Ministerial Secretariat

---

[27] Ibid, p79-p80

[28] Ibid

[29] Ibid, p68

[30] Ibid

Public Relations for domestic purposes, listed Soka Gakkai President Ikeda's visits to the USSR in 1974 and 1975 [31] twice in its Chronological Table of Japan-Soviet Relations following the Normalization of Relations. This shows that the MOFA too had to recognize the importance of Ikeda's visit to the USSR. However, Ikeda's visit to the Soviet Union is deleted from the 2013 version of the same "*Warera no Hoppou-ryodo (Our Northern Territories)*". Further, there is no description of exchanges conducted by other civilian organisations with the Soviet Union or Russia. This is proof that the government does not recognize the significance of civilian diplomacy due to its strong belief that negotiation between states remains the sole prerogative of government diplomacy.

The Government of Japan remained persistent in its attitude to the Northern Territories Issue so that fierce exchanges continued between Japan and the Soviet Union. The exchanges that took place in 1970 between Haruki Mori, the Vice-Minister for Foreign Affairs Japan and A.P. Okonishnikov, the USSR Chargé d'Affairs ad interim to Japan spells out clearly the assertions of both parties regarding the Northern Territories Issue.[32] A long quotation follows below as it was important in clarifying the essence of the issue. Comparing these views it was clear that there is a marked difference on the Northern Territories Issue between the Japanese and Soviet governments. The Japanese government gives this issue the greatest priority in bilateral relations and as the most important issue, it assumes no compromise in diplomatic negotiations. Without the resolution of this issue, it will not negotiate regarding a peace treaty. The government of the Soviet Union on the other hand regards the Return of the Northern Territories

---

[31] Ibid

[32] See Appendix (Statements)

Campaign conducted by the Japanese government and political publicity as hostile activities against the Soviet Union, and not a territorial issue. It appears it cannot understand why "an individual issue" should be an obstacle to having negotiations on the most important inter-states issue such as concluding a peace treaty.

Rigidity between the two camps of East and West gradually began to loosen as Mikhail Gorbachev assumed the Soviet leadership in 1985 His "New Thinking" in diplomacy and his powerful support for nuclear disarmament opened a dialogue with the Western countries, and it also brought about a great change in the situation of Northeast Asia. In his inauguration speech as the Soviet Communist Party Secretary General on 11 March 1985, he clearly stated his intention of improving China-Soviet relations. He met with Li Peng, Vice Prime Minister of China 1983-1987 in Moscow and communicated the intention of the Soviet government to seek improvements in Chinese-Soviet relations.[33] In May 1989, Gorbachev visited China, providing an opportunity for improving China-Soviet relations. Also, on 30 September 1990 at lightning speed he established relations with the Republic of Korea which was politically in the Western camp. Gorbachev did not visit Seoul, however.

With regard to nuclear disarmament, Gorbachev released on 25 January 1986 a public statement in the name of the Soviet Secretary General that he would aim for the total abolition of nuclear weapons by the 21st century.[34] He stated that the 20th century presented humankind with nuclear energy but this enormous benefit could well become a

---

[33] Takayuki Nakazawa, Gorubathofu To Ikeda Daisaku (Gorbachev and Daisaku Ikeda), Kadokawa Shoten 2004, p190-p191

[34] George Shultz, *[Document Type: Commentary] Cold War: Reykjavik (Reagan-Gorbachev) Summit (Shultz memoirs)*, Margaret Thatcher Foundation, 12th October 1986 http://www.margaretthatcher.org/document/110620 (accessed on ast December 2013)

means of destruction, and asked us whether we can rationally resolve the antithesis. Specifically, he posited that the development of space weapons would be an extremely dangerous act. For these reasons it was more rational to start by abolishing nuclear weapons.[35] Since Gorbachev repeatedly used the term "rationally" in his declaration it can be interpreted that he was espousing nuclear abolition from a moral point. At that time, however, countries in the Western camp, including the government of Japan merely registered this declaration as propaganda.[36] By contrast, on 27 January of the same year Ikeda sent an article to Novosti Press Agency in support of Gorbachev's statement including his wishes, opposition to militarization of space, dependence on 'faith in deterrence' rooted in mutual distrust can only result in an arms race contrary to advancing negotiation for disarmament, and that the US-Soviet Summit meeting should work to dispel mutual distrust.[37] The Novosti Press Agency was established in 1941 as the Soviet Information Bureau and reorganized in 1961 as a press agency. Since it can be seen as the substantial information bureau for the Soviet government one can assume that Ikeda's message had surely reached the Soviet leadership.

The US-Soviet summit meeting between Gorbachev and Ronald Regan in 1986 in Reykjavik, Iceland and the signing of the 1987 Intermediate Range Nuclear Forces Treaty are both famous events. In the month following the Reykjavik Summit, Gorbachev visited India on 27 November 1987 and with Rajiv Gandhi, the Prime Minister of India 1984-1989 jointly declared "the Delhi Declaration on the Principles of a

---

[35] Takayuki Nakazawa, Gorubathofu To Ikeda Daisaku (Gorbachev and Daisaku Ikeda), Kadokawa Shoten 2004, p205-p206

[36] Ibid

[37] Ibid, p207

Nuclear Weapons Free and Non-Violent World".[38] The Declaration established ten items, including; making peaceful co-existence the universal norm of international relations, recognizing human life has the highest value, making non-violence the foundation of activities of human community, and uniting under the common principles of disarmament and development regardless of religion and race. With regard to nuclear disarmament, the need was recognized for establishing agreements on six items, including: total nuclear abolition by the end of the 20th century, suspension of deploying nuclear weapons in space, total prohibition of nuclear tests, prohibition of development and manufacture of new WMDs, prohibition of the use and stockpiling of chemical weapons, and reducing the levels of conventional weapons and military force. Nuclear abolition referred to in the Declaration reflects Mahatma Gandhi's spirit of non-violence, and as such it shows Gorbachev opening to a sense of morality and spirituality in addition to his merely political approach to the subject. This ideology belongs neither to Marxism nor Leninism; it is Gorbachev's manifestation of his personal feelings beyond political bargaining of nuclear weapons reduction aimed at relaxation of cold war tension.

In his Vladivostok speech on 28 July 1986 Gorbachev spoke in favour of Japan's Three Non-Nuclear Principles and the Peace Constitution but pointed out that the country that should show leadership in advancing nuclear disarmament and peace was not doing so because it was under the US military umbrella. His declaration read as an indirect comment aimed at the US but it can also be understood to voice his regret that Japan as the only country that was bombed with

---

[38], Nivedita Das Kundu, *Celebrating the 25th Anniversary of the Delhi Declaration, Russia & India Report*, 25 November 2011 http://in.rbth.com/articles/2011/11/25/celebrating_the_25th_anniversary_of_the_delhi_declaration_13302.html (accessed on 7th June 2012)

nuclear weapons had an important mission to bring about world peace but was not able to do so.

> "We support a change to having better relations with Japan as it has become a country with first class significance. The country that was the first victim of the US nuclear weapons has in a short period made a great advance in the fields of industry, trade, education, science and technology to receive our admiration. The enviable outcome that Japan enjoys is not due merely to the concentration, discipline and energy of the people of Japan but the Three Non-Nuclear Principles on which its foreign policy is publicly built. However, attention must be paid to the recent reality that these principles along with the Peace article of the Japanese Constitution increasingly markedly ignored…Since the latter half of the 1970s, the US has enlarged its military power in the Pacific and under the pressure of the US, three military states of Washington, Tokyo and Seoul are in the process of being formed. … Of the three nuclear weapons states of this region, two states, China and the Soviet Union have the obligation of non-first use of nuclear weapons, however the US deploys nuclear weapons delivery systems and nuclear warheads on the Korean peninsula, which is one of the regions' critical areas, and deployed on Japanese territory nuclear weapons delivery vehicles"[39]
> (Translated by Fujiko Hara)

Starting on 25 May 1987 the SGI produced an anti-nuclear

[39] MOFA, Diplomatic Blue Book No. 31, 1987, p403-p404

exhibition, "Nuclear Arms: Threat to Our World" [40], which took place at Moscow City Allied Artists Hall on Kuznetsky Most Street in the heart of Moscow. [41] According to the Soka Gakkai Office of International Affairs, a great deal of complex effort went into the preparation of the exhibition. Unfortunately, no materials survive from which to learn of the efforts concerned.[42] There was a statement from the First Deputy Chairman of the Soviet Supreme Council, Piotr Demichev who was present at the opening of the exhibition: "This is totally in line with our present aim of nuclear abolition". He implied that the Soviet government was aware that the exhibition was in line with Gorbachev's policy of nuclear abolition. According to the Soka Gakkai Office of International Affairs, the Soviet government has consistently said, "We do not wish war. Ours is a country that aims for peace" and that it was forced to possess nuclear weapons because the US does. The Soviet people whom Ikeda met all without exception expressed the same thoughts. On the other hand, it may be said that cooperating in the opening of the anti-nuclear exhibition provided the Soviet government with a political opportunity to be able to profess that it was a peaceful country. On this question the SGI had a different view recognizing, namely, that it was generally accepted at the time in the world of international politics that the Soviet Union was for disarmament since Praslaf Davinic, a Soviet national, was the head of

[40] * List of SGI's Anti-Nuclear Exhibitions, which the SGI Peace Committee made and provided for this thesis

[41] Under the co-sponsorship of the UN Disarmament Bureau, UN Public Relations Bureau, Soviet Peace Protection Committee and the SGI. Also, supporting organisations included the Soviet Ministry of High and Middle Special Education, the Soviet Foreign Friendship Cultural Exchange Association, the Soviet Women's Committee, Soviet National Youth Committee, Hiroshima City and Nagsaki City. Seventy thousand people visited the exhibition.

[42] * Soka Gakkai Office of International Affairs provided their remarks with copies of materials to this thesis

the World Disarmament Campaign Office of the UN Disarmament Bureau. Davinic was involved as well in the opening of the anti-nuclear exhibition. Compared with the same exhibition in China the difference was that in Moscow the UN Disarmament Bureau was listed among the collaborating organisations. If this proved to be a case of sheer political utility, according to the Soka Gakkai Office of International Affairs, Ikeda had no qualms about being used. He intended to do his best above and beyond the expectation of the Soviets, and inspire them by showing the real current of peace. In his opening speech at the Exhibition, he challenged the audience to agree that they all have an anti-nuclear obligation.

> "Japan is the one and only country on which nuclear bombs were dropped. I believe personally that as a Japanese person, a pacifist and as a Buddhist I have the obligation, the mission, responsibility and the right to share throughout the world our harrowing and cruel experiences."
> (Ikeda's Speech at the Opening Ceremony, Moscow)
> (Translated by Fujiko Hara)

The exhibition displayed valuables for the first time, and a panel at the exhibition explained in detail the cause and effect of nuclear war, including epidemic diseases, leukaemia and starvation.[43] No content of the exhibition was changed because it was displayed in the Soviet Union. In fact, it had more things to exhibit including assumed radiation exposure if and when a nuclear bomb is dropped on Moscow, the history of the US-USSR disarmament negotiations, and even expected climatic changes of the planet engulfed in a 'nuclear winter'. There was

---

[43] Seikyo Newspaper, 27th May 1987, p1

even a panel encouraging peaceful use of military budgets.[44] The initiator of the IPPNW Benard Lown was also a welcome guest and in his meeting with Ikeda shared his thoughts after viewing the exhibition, saying that citizens' diplomacy or something of that kind was needed to initiate a movement for nuclear abolition.

> " ....You know, the problem is that the facts (of atomic bombings and devastation caused) are forgotten by all except the Japanese people...in that sense it is of great significance that the exhibition has been shown around the world. One can never overemphasize the importance of educating humankind. In fact TIME (magazine) referring to the Dialogue between President Ikeda and Professor Arnold J. Toynbee wrote, "The passion of the SGI President has created an anti-war united forces of people to people". I believe this is really an important point. In the end, unless we engage people there will be no political change. The IPPNW too aims at reaching out to make people participate. The key is how we will change their mindsets. It is not enough for doctors to give their patients medicine to restore their health. The role of doctors is to help patients change their way of life. Doctors must help patients understand what will really help them. In that sense, unless we have hundreds of people embark on new diplomacy we will not be able to really resolve global issues"[45]
> (Translated by Fujiko Hara)

At the time Gorbachev was out of the country, visiting Romania.

---

[44] Ibid

[45] Bernard Lown, Seikyo Newspaper, 27th May 1987

Ikeda attended the opening ceremony of his anti-nuclear exhibition and on the following day, 26 May 1987, met Nikolai Ryzhkov, Soviet Prime Minister at the Kremlin for one hour and twenty minutes.[46] Ryzhkov gave Ikeda Gorbachev's message welcoming him to the Soviet Union and praised the SGI's peace activities. The rest of the time was spent with Ikeda raising six questions and Ryzhkov answering them. Those were nuclear disarmament and peace, Japan-Soviet relations and role of Japan in the Asia and Pacific region, prospects of the USSR-US summit meeting, participation at the Seoul Olympic Games, the agenda of the Soviet Communist Party Central Committee General Meeting in June of that year (1987) and expectations for the youth who will be shouldering the next generation. Valentina Tereshkova, the Chair, Soviet Foreign Friendship Cultural Exchange Association, Ivan Kovalenko, Head of the Soviet Foreign Ministry were also at the meeting. From Ryzhkov's statements that were made public, one senses a somewhat cautious attitude towards the SGI from the position of a communist state that denies religion, but one can feel a sense of trust for allowing the anti-nuclear exhibition to take place.

> "This time, SGI President Ikeda visited the Soviet Union with a noble mission, the Exhibition, "Threat of Nuclear Weapons to our World". … the significance of this event is not limited to the exhibition itself, but in bringing the message against nuclear weapons. It is most important and most necessary. The exhibition theme and that it is taking place is most timely and is received with great welcome, and we are satisfied. … To be honest, it is not all that difficult to understand, and identify with the philosophy of the Soka Gakkai. This is because we are

[46] Seikyo Newspaper, 28th May 1987, p1

unbelievers. However, in our relations as humans and also with regard to international activities, there are great meanings in studying the thinking and philosophy of the Soka Gakkai. I have not read all the SGI President Ikeda's Annual Peace Proposals but that is what I feel. I read his words in this book (collection of Annual Peace Proposals) that he wishes "to work to achieve peace for all humankind". While it is difficult to evaluate his standing with this single sentence, but I believe it speaks of the essence of the activities of the Soka Gakkai and of its President."

On disarmament issues:

Today, simply the number of missiles should not affect humankind. It's because humankind can be destroyed even with one tenth or one hundredth of the missiles we already have. What is truly needed now, is a new approach and philosophy for our humankind to survive. What we need is a new approach to relations between states. This is the very thinking that lies at the basis of the comprehensive disarmament proposal made by Secretary General Gorbachev since last year. It was also the basis of his statement at the International Forum that took place in Moscow early this year. We must consider the tragedies of Hiroshima and Nagasaki, give thought to the positions of the victimized Japanese people and to exert efforts so that this terrible disaster will not be repeated. As the only atom-bombed country Japan must become a country that will sound a huge warning to all humankind. If nuclear war takes place today, the disastrous scene will be a thousand times that of Hiroshima and

Nagasaki."[47]

(Translated by Fujiko Hara)

These statements of Ryzhkov can be said to have consistency with Gorbachev's diplomatic philosophy, "New Thinking". With regard to Japan-Soviet relations, he recognizes the important role and presence of Japan in the Asia Pacific region, and emphasized that the Soviet Union should build good neighbourly relations including economic cooperation with its geographic neighbour Japan. He did not, however, fail to put in his conditions with regard to Japan-US relations and the Northern Territories Issue.

> "Soviet- Japan relations including economic issues, while not satisfactory at present, are important from the perspective of all mankind. Japan could not be disinterested in the nature of its neighbouring countries. For this reason, we must build the basis for co-existence. We have no intention of giving a warning as regards Japan-US relations. I do not believe the Japan-US linkage necessarily hinders normalization of the Soviet-Japan relations. Recently, there are intensified Japan-US economic relations, what it teaches us is that a propensity to have special relations with a single country is not wise in international relations. I believe that Japan needs comprehensive friendly relations. As regards Soviet-Japanese relations, there are issues regarding Shibomai, Hakotan, Kunashiri, and Etorofu (the Northern Territorial Issue). What is important there is whether there is a political will to see progress in Soviet-Japan

[47] Ibid

relations."[48]

(Translated by Fujiko Hara)

In December 1987, immediately following the signing of the Intermediate Range Nuclear Forces Treaty, the Gorbachev Government sent a special envoy, A. L. Adamishin, the Soviet Foreign Minister, to Japan to provide an ex post facto explanation. Adamishin presented the explanation to the government of Japan as well as visiting Ikeda to explain the contents of the Treaty[49]. This would indicate that the Gorbachev Government considered Ikeda at least as important as the government of Japan as regards his nuclear policy.

The Japanese government failed to grasp the overall situation following the easing of East-West tensions by continuing to set their priority on the single issue of the northern territories. As the Soviet-Western nations relations improved, the Japanese government made it its top foreign policy priority to realize the historic first ever visit to Japan of the Soviet leader and to open a way for drastic improvement of bilateral relations towards normalization.[50] With that in mind the Japanese government held seven meetings between the Japanese-Soviet foreign ministers after the January 1986 visit to Japan of Eduard Shevardnadze, the Minister of Foreign Affairs of the Soviet Union (1985-1990).[51] Also, starting with Shevardnadze's second visit to Japan in 1988, there were seven meetings of the Peace Treaty

---

[48] Ibid

[49] Takayuki Nakazawa, Gorubathofu To Ikeda Daisaku (Gorbachev and Daisaku Ikeda), Kadokawa Shoten 2004, p218

[50] Ministry of Foreign Affairs Japan, *Diplomatic Blue Book 1991*, http://www.mofa.go.jp/mofaj/gaiko/bluebook/1991/h03-4-4.htm (accessed on 20th March 2010)

[51] Ibid

working group.[52] In May 1989, the Japanese government proposed, while working on the priority issue of a peace treaty that included the 'territorial issues', to expand overall Japanese-Soviet relations including other areas.[53] The other area meant economic assistance in particular. Japan welcomed an economic mission from the Soviet Union, which was suffering from a fiscal crisis at the time, shared Japan's know-how in economic development and, as part of the humanitarian assistance, provided 2.6 billion yen worth of medical devices to the area suffering from the Chernobyl nuclear power plant disaster and a 1 billion yen worth grant in food and medical goods as well as 100 million dollars credit in food for the purposes of humanitarian assistance.[54] It was clear that they were provided with the objective of gaining an immediate return of the Northern territories. The Soviet Government, suffering from a fiscal crisis, naturally accepted the support but the road map concerning the progress of negotiations of a peace treaty and resolution of the Northern Territories Issue remained obscure.

In July 1990, the Japanese Government dispatched to the Soviet Union, Yoshio Sakurauchi, the Speaker of the House of Representatives of Japan to finalize agreement on Gorbachev's visit to Japan. On 25 July Sakurauchi and the Japanese government mission met Gorbachev, but the visiting group demanded an immediate return of the Northern Territories from the start, Gorbachev saying angrily, 'We can call them our Southern Territories' and cut short the meeting.[55] The meeting lasted seven minutes. Masaru Sato, former chief analyst of the Intelligence and Analysis Service, the MOFA, reckoned the seven

---

[52] Ibid

[53] Ibid

[54] Ibid

[55] Masaru Sato, Kokka No Zibaku (Self-Locking of State), Fusosha 2010, p118

minute meeting was reduced to about three and half minutes because of the need for interpretation, that means a mere 1 minute 45 seconds per person.[56] Sato is a top expert in Japanese-Soviet and Japanese-Russian relations. He is a Christian, with an academic degree in Theology from the Doshisha University. During his post-graduate years he studied in Prague. After his graduation he wished to study the Czech Protestant theologian Josef Hromadka. However, since Hromadka was anti Soviet, Sato feared that as a citizen of Japan he would be refused entry into the Czech Republic, which was then in the Soviet sphere of influence, so he decided to join the MOFA hoping that he would not be refused entry. Sato joined the MOFA in 1985 and in the following year, he studied English and Russian at the Defence School of Languages, Beaconsfield, UK and joined the language department of Moscow State University in 1987. He was a staff member at the Japanese Embassy to the USSR (later Russia) from 1988 to 1995. When Gorbachev was apprehended in the August 1991 coup d'état, he was in charge of communication with the MOFA with regard to Gorbachev's fate. From 1998 to 2006 when he retired from the Foreign Service he remained central to Japan's Soviet and Russian diplomacy.

Two days later, on 27 July 1990, Gorbachev held talks with Ikeda. The talks took 1 hour and 30 minutes.[57] It was customary in those days for the Soviet government to decide prior to meeting with its President, how much time would be allowed, whether 10, 15 or 30 minutes, and communicate this to prospective visitors.[58] The time allocated was 1

---

[56] Masaru Sato, Ikeda SGI Kaicho No Minkan Gaiko Ga Hatasu Igi (The Meaning of Private Diplomacy by SGI President Ikeda), Magazine Ushio, Ushio Shuppansha, November 2007, p206

[57] Daisaku Ikeda, Daido O Ayumu: Watashi No Zinsei Kiroku 3 (Taking Moral Principles: My Records of Life' Vol.3), Mainichi Newspaper Co. Ltd., 2002, p36

[58] Ibid

hour and 30 minutes. In the talks, Gorbachev replied to Ikeda's request for his visit to Japan, "Sometime around cherry blossoms the next year". In other words Gorbachev told Ikeda that he would visit Japan in the spring of 1991. It is well known that indeed the visit was made in April of 1991. On 28 July, the day after their meeting, the Japanese media including the main newspapers reported on the first page the meeting between Ikeda and Gorbachev and Gorbachev's intention to visit Japan.

Sato explained the meaning of the talks held between Ikeda and Gorbachev. According to him, the Soviet Government was prepared to announce the intention of Gorbachev's visit to Japan during his talks with Sakurauchi but that was changed to the talks with Ikeda. Ikeda referred to the talks in his own notes (memorandum).

> "I had some homework for the talks. This is because the situation was very fluid whether or not the President's visit to Japan would be realized. Two days before my visit, negotiations with the Japanese Parliamentary delegation were not successful and the question of his visit to Japan had been returned to a blank sheet. … I said, "We want you to come with your lady Raisa during the most beautiful season, in spring when cherry blossoms are out or in autumn when our maples are in full colour". When I told him that we greatly awaited his visit, the President said: "Up to now there were just too many stereotyped dialogues. If we start to walk in collaboration, things will be resolved eventually. It will do no good to continue to refer to "preconditions" or "final warnings". I said to him, "I believe now is the chance for you to visit Japan." He expressed himself definitely and said. "I will definitely realize my visit to Japan. It is not normal not to have dialogue with Japan. If possible I

would like to visit Japan in the spring." In this way, the historical visit to Japan by the highest leader of the Soviet Union became a reality."
(Ikeda's memorandum 2002)[59]
(Translated by Fujiko Hara)

According to Sato, there was no overstatement in the memorandum. This was the moment when the Japanese government's Soviet diplomacy depended on Ikeda.[60] He went on to say that Ikeda who did not refer to the Northern Territories Issue, was the best person as far as the Soviet Government was concerned.[61] In fact, the MOFA fearing a possible breakdown of Sakurauchi's talks with Gorbachev the resultant failure of Gorbachev's visit to Japan would lead to a collapse of bilateral relations, urgently asked Ikeda to request Gorbachev to visit Japan in their meeting.[62] Ikeda accepted the request saying that he "will act as a man of culture because that is what he is".[63] Sato took note of Ikeda's comments that he would act as a man of culture, and said that Ikeda was able to contribute to Japan's national interest because as a man of culture he kept a certain distance from politics.[64] Sato says it is true that with threats from terrorism and conflicts with communist countries it is difficult to find compromises among countries but it is cultural and educational exchanges that can provide answers.[65] The

---

[59] Ibid, p48-p49,
[60] Masaru Sato, *Kokka No Zibaku (Self-Locking of State)*, Fusosha 2010, pp118-pp119
[61] Ibid, p119
[62] Masaru Sato, Ikeda SGI Kaicho No Minkan Gaiko Ga Hatasu Igi (The Meaning of Private Diplomacy by SGI President Ikeda), Magazine Ushio, Ushio Shuppansha, November 2007, p206
[63] Ibid
[64] Ibid
[65] Ibid, p205

following are his thoughts on the subject.

> "President Ikeda and the Soka Gakkai have steadily promoted international exchanges in many ways including through the Soka Universities…the (Japanese) diplomats have not been able to make good use of the networks created by President Ikeda and the Soka Gakkai. Even today the diplomats fail to read signals sent from abroad…The Soka Gakkai enjoys a solid presence in Japan as a religious, social and cultural organisation with a network encompassing the elites and the grass roots. No diplomacy can ignore these facts" (Masaru Sato 2007)[66]
> (Translated by Fujiko Hara)

Ikeda and Gorbachev's meeting is evidence of how citizens' multiple and steady cultural exchanges at the grass roots level can provide the key to relaxing tension between states. It is not a sufficient explanation for Sato to point out that the Soviet government communicated Gorbachev's visit to Japan because Ikeda did not refer to the Northern Territories Issue. The meeting was made possible due to educational and cultural factors. Present at the meeting were Gorbachev's government staff and advisors including Chingiz Aitmatov, a writer and member of the Soviet Presidential Conference (Advisory Board), Anatoli A. Lgunov, President of Moscow State University, Gennadii Yagozin, Chairman, Soviet State Education Council, Anatoly Chernyaev, a Principal Foreign Policy Advisor to President Gorbachev, Karen Brutents, the First Deputy Chief of the International Department of the Central Committee, the Communist Party of the USSR, Dunaev,

---

[66] Ibid

Editorial Committee member of Novosti Press Agency.[67] They were supporters of Gorbachev's "New Thinking" and Perestroika and the brains central to Gorbachev's Government.

Ikeda published with Logunov their dialogue entitled, "The Third Rainbow Bridge" in 1987 in Japanese. It was translated and published in Russian in 1998, and in Chinese in 1990. The dialogue covered the authors sharing their common thoughts on peace and education coming from different regimes and religious views. At the time he met and talked with Gorbachev, Ikeda was preparing for the joint publication of a Dialogue with Aitmatov, "Ode to the Grand Spirit".[68] The book was published in Japanese in 1991, in German in 1992 and in Russian in 1994. The dialogue covered poetry and literature. Ikeda also had a dialogue with Yagozin when he was the Minister in charge of Soviet High and Middle School Education. Ikeda was a long-standing friend of Dunaev since his first visit to the Soviet Union in 1975.[69] Also, Gorbachev had graduated from Moscow State University from which Ikeda received an honorary Doctorate in 1975, when Logunov was President of the University. Since Moscow State University and Soka University have academic exchange agreements with an active exchange of students, Ikeda's meeting with Gorbachev was a friendly one unlike a formal courtesy call. It is reasonable to suggest that the degree of trusting relations was different from the outset between the soil of private diplomacy based on cultural and educational exchange which Ikeda had nurtured over fifteen years, and that of government diplomacy. Also the Soviet side regarded Ikeda not as a political

---

[67] Takayuki Nakazawa, Gorubathofu To Ikeda Daisaku (Gorbachev and Daisaku Ikeda), Kadokawa Shoten 2004, p247

[68] Daisaku Ikeda, Daido O Ayumu: Watashi No Zinsei Kiroku 3 (Taking Moral Principles: My Records of Life' Vo.3), Mainichi Newspaper Co. Ltd., 2002, p40

[69] Ibid, p41

phenomenon but as a cultural person from the beginning.[70]

As of 2015, nineteen universities of the Soviet Union and Russia have bestowed on Ikeda honorary degrees. After the Cold War Gorbachev and Ikeda jointly published "Moral Lessons of the Twentieth Century" in Japanese in 1996 and in eleven languages including English in 2005, covering their thoughts on life and philosophy. Political diplomacy tends to end when issues are discussed and overcome. Cultural exchanges, however, continue at the citizens' level with further exchanges of personnel and information. Cultural relations are apt to continue behind the scenes even when political relations cease. In that sense cultural relations could be said to be firmer than their political relative. In this case, Gorbachev's choice to communicate an important decision of the Soviet Union to Ikeda rather than to a representative of the Japanese government underscores that cultural exchange can at times represent high politics. Gorbachev's April 1991 visit to Japan signified the end of the Cold War in Northeast Asia as it was the first visit to the region by the Soviet Union's supreme leader.

When the Russian Government took over after the collapse of the Soviet Union, it conferred on Ikeda the Order of Friendship in 2008 in recognition of his contribution to the development of relations between the Russian Federation and Japan. Sponsors were Gorbachev, Sergay Baburin, the Vice-Speaker of the State Duma, Zinaida Dragunkina, Member of the Federation Council, Viktor Sadovnichy, the Rector of Moscow State University, Aitmatov and Aleksaner Serebrov, a Soviet Cosmonaut.[71] Ikeda had published his dialogue with Sadovnichy,

---

[70] Seikyo Newspaper, Message from Gorbachev for 40th Anniversary of Ikeda's Visit the USSR, 8th September 2014, p1
(Gorbachev wrote) President Ikeda is a philosopher having a keen intellect, a humanist, and a man of letters"

[71] Seikyo Online, Rosia Kokka Ga Jokun O Kettei Ikeda SGI Kaicho Ni Yuko Kunsho (Russian Government decided to confer its Order of Friendship to SGI

"Beyond the Century: Dialogue on Education and Society"[72] in 2002, "The Cosmos, Earth and Human Beings" with Serabrov in 2004"[73] sharing his thoughts on education, peace and Japan-Russian Friendship. All Russian editions were published by Moscow State University Press and Ikeda's dialogue with Sadovnichy was published as one of the projects of the 250th anniversary of Moscow State University.[74] Ikeda's books without exception cover his own fields, peace, culture, education, religion, philosophy and life. This does not change even when he is engaged in dialogue with politicians or business people. His dialogue with Gorbachev did not stray from his conviction so that they talked not about political issues but about philosophy and life. One can assume he is committed to achieve mutual understanding through power of culture and dialogue.

Sadovnichy was a member of The Conference of Japanese-Russian High-Level Expert Group on three occasions from 2003 to 2005. The Conference was proposed in June 2003 by Japanese Prime Minister Junichiro Koizumi to strengthen Japan-Russian relations over the medium to long term and was established by agreement at the Japan-Russia Summit Meeting with Russian President Vladimir Putin

---

President Ikeda), 1st February 2008
http://www.seikyoonline.jp/news/headline/2008/02/1185504_2144.html
(accessed on 19th March 2010)

72 * Japanese edition 1: *"Atarashiki Jinrui-wo, Atarashiki Sekai-wo"*, Ushio Shuppansha Co., Ltd., Tokyo, 2002
Japanese edition 2: *"Gaku-wa Hikari"*, Ushio Shuppansha Co., Ltd., Tokyo, 2004
Russian edition, Moscow State University Press, 2005
Chinese edition (orthodox), Cheng Yin Culture enterprise Co., Ltd., Taipei, 2006

73 * Japanese edition, Ushio Shuppansha Co., Ltd., Tokyo, 2004
Russian edition, Moscow State University Press, 2006

74 Soka Gakkai, Toward an Era of Human Empowerment: Books on Buddhism and Humanity, 2007, p18

on 20 October the same year[75]. The members included representative politicians, business people, journalists, scholars and sports athletes of the two countries with seven each from Japan and Russia.[76] The first meeting in 2004 addressed five points including general issues of Japanese-Russian relations, territorial issues, the possibility of cooperation in the field of security, cooperation in the field of economics and personnel exchange.[77] And as the conferences proceeded, with the second in February 2005 and the third in March 2006, concrete issues that had to be resolved became clear. Furthermore, at the suggestion of the Japanese-Russian High Level Conference, a Japanese-Russian Junior Parliamentarians Conference was initiated and met twice up to 2005. Starting at the second conference, three key points for promoting Japanese-Russian relations were identified. They

---

[75] MOFA, Nichiro Kenzin Kaigi Dai 1 Kai Kaigo Kekka Gaiyo (Result Summary: The 1st Conference of Japanese-Russian High-Level Expert Group), 14th April 2004 http://www.mofa.go.jp/mofaj/area/russia/kenjin01_gai.html (accessed on 4th February 2010)

[76] * Japanese side: Yoshiro Mori (Former Prime Minister * Co-Chair of this Conference), Hiroshi Okuda (Chairman of Toyota Motor, President of Japan Business Federation), Nobuo Shimotomai (Professor in Modern Russian Politics, Hosei University, Tokyo), Tasuku Takagaki (Advisor of Tokyo Mitsubishi UFJ Bank, President of Japan Association for Trade with Russia), Yasuhiro Tase (Columnist of Nihon Keizai Shimbun, a Japanese Newspaper), Akihiko Tanaka (Professor in International Politics, University of Tokyo), Yasuhiro Yamashita (Professor of Tokai University, Member of Board of Directors of International Judo Federation, Member of Board of Directors of All-Japan Judo Federation)
Russian side: Yuri Luzhkov (Mayor of Moscow City * Co-Chair of this Conference), Sergey Bogdanchikov (President of Rosneft), Georgy Boos (Vice-Speaker of State Duma Lower House), Evgeny Velikov (President of Kurchatov Institute), Arkady Volsky (Founder and Head of Russian Union of Industrialists and Entrepreneurs [RSPP]), Viktor Sadovinichy (Rector of Moscow State University), Valentina Tereshkova (Cosmonaut, Chair of Russian Association of International Cooperation)

[77] MOFA, Nichiro Kenzin Kaigi Dai 1 Kai Kaigo Kekka Gaiyo (Result Summary: The 1st Conference of Japanese-Russian High-Level Expert Group), 14th April 2004 http://www.mofa.go.jp/mofaj/area/russia/kenjin01_gai.html

were political, economic and educational. To date the Japanese government's Soviet/Russian diplomacy was focused heavily on the political field, namely the Northern Territories Issue and the establishment of a Peace Treaty and also the economy, such as providing economic support and conducting economic exchanges. Focusing on the field of education was a new agenda. At the second conference it was clearly stated that 'the most important conditions' required in building a true bilateral partnership rested on deeper mutual understanding and trust among citizens of Japan and Russia as well as fostering good mutual relationships; and that it was the people to people exchange between the two countries that will play a big role in achieving that objective.[78] Specifically, six recommendations were presented to the leaders of the two countries: simplification of visa issuance; promoting tourism with support from both government and private sectors; youth exchange between Japanese studying the Russian language and Russians studying Japanese; organizing Japan-Russian student sporting events; promoting exchange of journalists to encourage correct and positive information delivery; and ensuring the success of the 150th anniversary events of the Treaty of Commerce and Navigation between Japan and Russia (Treaty of Shimoda) 1855.[79] The third conference confirmed the need for strengthening the six items. It is noted that on the Northern Territories, which is the main political issue, the conference went no further than vaguely stating that it was important to find solutions acceptable to both parties. At the same time, a very clear opinion was expressed suggesting the need for wisdom in

---

[78] MOFA, Nichiro Kenzin Kaigi Dai 2 Kai Kaigo: Nichiro Shinzidai Ni Mukete (The 2nd Conference of Japanese-Russian High-Level Expert Group: Toward A New Era of Japanese-Russian Relationship), 2nd February 2005 http://www.mofa.go.jp/mofaj/area/russia/kenjin02_b3.html (accessed on 4th February 2010)

[79] Ibid

preparing a more favourable context.[80] However, that was the last meeting of the Conference of Japanese-Russian High-Level Expert Group, demonstrating the difficulty of resolving the issue.

In the end, the chances of resolving the issue will be determined by the decisions of the two governments reflecting the political climate of the times. However, civilian activities in promoting mutual understanding by Ikeda and the Japanese-Russian High Level Expert Group have an enormous role to play in continuing dialogue and avoiding any deterioration of relations or worse. The attempt at initiating the Japanese-Russian High Level Expert Group was a good start, but that it could not continue has much to do with it being sponsored by governments, and therefore, discussions remained within political and national interests. While the need was recognized for educational and people-to-people exchanges, they have not developed to a level that encourage participation of ordinary people. Actions beyond political interests and dialogue and honest assertions on things that matter are likely to be the strength of CSO activities. The four anti-nuclear organisations referred to earlier (see Chapter 3) are successful in carrying out exchanges in countries or regions that have lost relations with the Japanese government. They have been successful in having positive exchanges and enjoying positive outcomes beyond the political framework. It is in actions carried out beyond a political framework that can assist governments and find ways of resolving political issues. For those reasons, CSO activities are essential for resolving global issues. Relations between governments and CSOs are best when each plays its unique role. Governments should not treat

---

[80] MOFA, Nichiro Kenzin Kaigi Dai 3 Kai Kaigo Kekka Gaiyo (Result Summary: The 3rd Conference of Japanese-Russian High-Level Expert Group), 27th March 2006 http://www.mofa.go.jp/mofaj/area/russia/kenjin03_gai.html (4th February 2010)

civilians and CSOs as their subordinates, as pawns in game of chess. It is thought ideal and best for each to complement each other and collaborate in resolving matters of common interest.

There is another kind of private intervention in diplomacy which is a good case study for comparison with Ikeda's private diplomacy. Examples of resolving global political issues through cultural activities can be seen in the campaign of Bob Geldof, an Irish born Rock musician who engaged in saving Africa from famine. There was also Bono and other Rock and Pop singers from England and Ireland, who were inspired by the BBC's 1984 broadcast on Ethiopian hunger, who organised a charity project by top musicians "Band Aid". Organizers, Geldof and Midge Ure produced a record called "*Do They Know It's Christmas?*", which was released in December 1984. It was a commercial hit and collected 8 million pounds sterling which they provided as aid to relieve famine.[81] This event made Geldof's activities recognized the world over. His activities did not stop at raising funds but won recognition in his relief of Africa's famine crisis by a broad community of ordinary people and voters and contributed to the awareness and formation of global public opinion. It is a successful case of realizing the creation of public opinion, which is a key objective of citizen's activities. This success led to a further success when in July 1985, 180 plus artists gathered from around the world to support a Charity Concert "Live Aid", which mobilized an audience of over 180,000, with simultaneous broadcasting of the event in 84 countries, culminating in historically the biggest charity concert. Geldof continues his activities.

His activities with Band Aid and Live Aid influenced Margaret

---

[81] BOBGELDOF.COM, *Live Aid*, http://www.bobgeldof.com/content.asp?section=31 (accessed on 17th October 2013)

Thatcher government's support policies for overseas developing countries. In September 1986, Timothy Raison, Minister for Overseas Development resigned. Raison's resignation and Thatcher's response did not refer to British public opinion concerning African famine, but it coincided with the time when Geldof's activities had aroused public opinion. It can be that the minister's resignation was the result of the need for the UK government to rethink its conventional attitude.[82] It might be added that Geldof was made an honorary Knight Commander of the Order of the British Empire by Queen Elizabeth II.

In the 2000s, Geldof assisted the British government, as a citizen, on its poverty policy as well as its support of developing countries. At the 31st G8 Summit (6 to 8 July 2005) that took place in Gleneagles Hotel in Scotland (known as the Gleneagles Summit), Tony Blair the Prime Minister of the host country and Chair adopted Aid to Africa and debt cancellation as a main theme. Blair also advocated actively involving not just governments but also civil society of the main countries. Geldof responded to the call, organizing with Paul McCartney, Madonna, Stevie Wonder and Pink Floyd, the world's top artists charity concerts in eight cities, London, Tokyo, Philadelphia, Paris, Rome, Berlin, Toronto and Moscow on 2nd July, ahead of the Summit with a single theme "Make Poverty History". This was the greatest concert in history that mobilized a two million plus audience. This was assessed as an important case that elevated the role of music from entertainment to diplomacy, completely sharing diplomatic objectives and successfully communicating the messages by reaching out to ordinary people.[83]

---

[82] CatholicHerald.co.uk, *Geldof attacked Howe*, originally printed in the 6th June 1989 http://archive.catholicherald.co.uk/article/6th-june-1986/3/geldof-attacks-howe (accessed on 4th February 2010)

[83] Jiji Press, Gaiko (Diplomacy", a journal) Vol. 18, Kantaro Oguri: Ongaku To Gaiko (Music and Diplomacy), p118, March 2013

This was a case of giving full play to the unique qualities of civilians in assisting the British government, an ideal form of CSO activities. The Summit agreed to increase international support to African countries suffering from poverty, to 25 billion dollars by 2010, doubling the support given in 2004. Geldof was given full marks and immediately following his concert, he was nominated as a 2006 Nobel Peace Laureate.[84]

Geldof's activities made an immeasurable impact in inspiring public opinion in major industrial countries. However, how much this has changed the poverty issue on the ground in Africa remains unclear. There is no knowledge of what impact this had on the policies of Ethiopian as well as other African governments. Geldof did send funds raised by charity activities and the 31st G8 Summit also decided to send relief funds, but there is no way of knowing whether they were all used totally for fighting poverty. Needless to say, not much monitoring can be done, since giving strict instructions concerning the use of funds will involve intervening in internal affairs. Fund assistance does have pitfalls. There is a need to find better ways of giving support, such as ensuring exclusive use for poverty alleviation. In that sense, Geldof's activities remain simply an intervention in much needed poverty alleviation.

The SGI appears to avoid campaigns which just send support money. It started its activities in 1973 by raising relief funds for refugees from Vietnam. With the support of the Office of the United Nations High Commissioner for Refugees (UNHCR) it has by 2000 conducted twenty-one campaigns for refugee relief and collected a total of 1.4 billion yen.[85] That was not all, for twenty years beginning 1982, it

---

[84] BBC News, *Geldof nominated for Nobel Prize*, 6th July 2005 http://news.bbc.co.uk/2/hi/entertainment/4657627.stm (accessed on 17th October 2013)

[85] SokaNet, *Zindo Shien (Humanitarian Aid)*,

conducted exhibitions publicizing the issues refugees faced and showing the way to solving them. Also beginning in 1980 it dispatched inspection teams fourteen times to refugee camps to check the health and livelihood of refugees in collaboration with the staff supporting them on the ground to provide necessary support. The SGI also provided support in Cambodia for its first democratic election in 1992 following the long civil war. At the time the United Nations Transitional Authority in Cambodia (UNTAC) was planning the first democratic election and there was a need to educate citizens, for whom voting was new and a radio station was established for informing the public.[86]

Inspiring public opinion through Internet devices and SNS does provide strong motivation for changing political systems, as witnessed by the Arab Spring. The power of public opinion is the power of the voters and is one of the most effective means to change policies. However, public opinion stirred by arousing emotions can contain aspects of violence, as in the case of the French Revolution in the 18th century, which came to be considered the world's first effective violent revolution in achieving change in the political system. On the other hand, public opinion inspired by arousing emotions is likely to be a momentary arousal. The more critical the political issue, the more there is a need for a painstakingly worked out long-term action. A case in point is the anti-nuclear CSO movement, which has a history of some seventy years since the dropping of atom bombs on Japan in 1945. This is not something that can be resolved in one generation. Poverty in African countries too has a long history with deep roots. There is a need, therefore, for painstaking attention to detail including examining the situation on the ground, dispatching medical staff and experts, at the

---

http://www.sokanet.jp/hbk/heiwa.html (accessed on 17th October 2013)

[86] Ibid

same time as providing much-needed funds. There are also possibilities of Geldof inspired experts and citizens working in Africa on their own to eradicate hunger, but this has not yet reached the stage for evaluation.

PART 4: Conclusion

Conclusion

The purpose of this study has been to analyse the nuclear policy of the government of Japan, the sole atomic-bombed nation, clarify the effects Japanese anti-nuclear CSOs have, and to examine more closely some aspects of nuclear disarmament initiatives that have been pursued in Japan, particularly the work and career of Daisaku Ikeda.

The government's nuclear policy was examined in detail. Conventionally it was a three-prong policy consisting of nuclear disarmament, non-proliferation and the peaceful use of nuclear power. National security was added as the fourth, and this commands the highest priority today. As the government of the only atom-bombed nation, it is expected to be forcefully assertive in the cause of nuclear abolition. It has not been able to take on a leadership role, however, for two reasons. The first is that its national security depends on an extended nuclear deterrence, arising from being protected under the US nuclear umbrella. Secondly, it has difficult relations with neighbouring China and Russia, both nuclear weapons states. Furthermore, the northeast region of Asia is a crucible of nuclear weapons with the presence of the largest number of nuclear states and this situation contributes to the passivity of the Japanese government in promoting nuclear disarmament. An examination of these realities has established that nuclear disarmament is a complex diplomatic issue fermented by multifaceted mutual distrust, political tension, and historical as well as national conflicts and cannot be resolved by focusing solely on nuclear weapons.

The Non-Nuclear Three Principles are enshrined as Japanese national policy but they have not been legislated into law, thus have no binding effect. Moreover, haunted by its past of committing aggression in China and neighbouring countries, as well as bound by the legacy of the Cold War, Japan is under sustained political and diplomatic duress with China and Russia. It is self-evident that the graver the issues, the greater the threat Japan feels from those countries' nuclear weapons. Furthermore, the military alliance Japan has with the US since the end of Second World War places its national security under the US nuclear umbrella. The dilemma of being the victim of the atomic bombings, and having to depend on another country for its national security leaves Japan passive towards total abolition and instead promoting a step-by-step reduction of nuclear arms, calling for their eventual elimination. The government has yet to develop a plausible process and a time frame for reaching the goal. On the other hand, deteriorating relations with China and Russia since early 2000 is giving some conservatives, as well as like-minded members of parliament, the opportunity to raise voices in favour of Japan's nuclear armament.

As the Second World War generation ages and declines in number, memories of the atomic bombings are fading away and with it the so-called 'nuclear allergy'. Today's young generation has no qualms about possessing nuclear weapons, and even believes their country should re-arm as it is surrounded by unfriendly nuclear-weapons states. Unable to call loudly for the abolition of nuclear arms, the government of Japan has its hands tied. Herein lies the challenge of Japanese anti-nuclear CSOs, namely, to find ways to pass on the anti-nuclear legacy to the future generation, especially at a time when their activities are beginning to wane as time passes. The anti-nuclear CSOs in Japan are forcefully demanding total abolition of nuclear weapons and are harshly critical of the government for its passive stance in opting for a gradual disarmament, as well as for its dependence on the US nuclear umbrella for national security. The CSOs and the government are polarized over nuclear policy.

This study focuses on the comparative analysis of the activities of the country's four representative anti-nuclear CSOs and analyses their relationships with the government. The four organisations respectively occupy distinct, professional domains and have strong bases and relationships with the international community in driving their activities. Most of the Japanese anti-nuclear activities have their origin in the aftermath of the atomic bombing of 1945 and are successfully supporting A-bomb victims. For example, the JPPNW provides medical support to the victims, while the JALANA acts as legal agents for the victims in winning on their behalf government certification enabling them to receive medical care as A-bomb disease patients. The SGI conducted personal interviews with the victims, collected their testimonies and published them as a record for posterity. The mission of the MP, which is managed by the A-bombed cities of Hiroshima and Nagasaki, is to disseminate information within Japan and to the wider world, about the enormous damage nuclear weapons cause and to rally support against their future use.

The Japanese anti-nuclear CSOs are most active today among their counterparts. For example, the JPPNW, which began as a Japanese branch of the IPPNW, a Nobel laureate for its anti-nuclear activities, is today the core organisation that financially supports the IPPNW but also its branches worldwide. The JALANA also contributes today as the largest branch of the IALANA by sharing on-the-ground knowledge and experience needed for successful activities.

The point at issue is whether or not the damage inflicted by atom bombs will remain solely the experience of Japan and the Japanese people or whether it has a universal value that could be adopted as a global standard for nuclear abolition. There are anti-nuclear CSOs around the world including Japan that point, from scientific perspectives, to the danger of using nuclear energy for electric power generation, treating nuclear energy and nuclear weapons within the same category. Some of these CSOs even assert that the abolition of all nuclear materials is crucial, placing priority on abolishing nuclear power development over abolition of nuclear weapons. Clearly they cannot have real experiences of atomic bombing at the centre of their activities, and it is also clear that not all CSOs have common objectives, but rather, in fact, that they have different motivations.

In today's post-Cold War period, there are two possible cases in which the development, possession and use of nuclear weapons could become an issue. One such situation could be created as a result of an escalating political tension that halts all levels of exchange and communication between states that are involved. The other would be when nuclear weapons fall into the hands of terrorists. In the first case, CSOs can attempt to resolve complex racial, cultural, religious, and social customs and competition for resources, by promoting civilian exchanges. As for the latter, the only way to prevent nuclear arms from falling into the hands of terrorists is to ensure complete abolition of nuclear weapons from the world. To that end, NPT Review Conferences have to be strengthened by convincing as many states as possible to respect what has been agreed to. At the same time, efforts must be multiplied to establish a firm, international public opinion against nuclear weapons by emphasising their anti-humanitarian aspects and to have resolutions adopted to that affect at international conferences that have political legitimacy. To make this a reality, a platform should be prepared to encourage support and participation of nuclear weapons states as well as states protected under a nuclear umbrella. On that point, the problem will not be resolved by unilaterally criticizing nuclear weapons states or states protected under nuclear deterrence. The only way to prevent the threat of nuclear weapons falling into the hands of terrorists is, to put it in extreme terms, to abolish all nuclear weapons from the world.

Beginning in the year 2000, Henry Kissinger and other leaders in US foreign relations and defence policies called for de-nuclearization and US President Obama's Prague speech was intended as a warning against the threat from terrorists. There was no regret expressed for dropping atomic bombs on Japan or apologies for the victims, there were only plain warnings concerning national security. In reality, negotiations on nuclear disarmament remain deadlocked among nuclear weapons states, and with states outside the NPT regime illegally possessing nuclear arms, in particular, North Korea, and there is no roadmap for resolving this. Furthermore, the US Administration remains unable to define a concrete process for nuclear abolition.

It goes without saying that nuclear disarmament can only be achieved by political decision-making. It is not possible for the CSOs to participate directly in that process as they remain beyond the pale of politics. All four organisations, however, are not satisfied with the Japanese government's passive involvement in the issue and strongly believe that the government representing the only nuclear bombed country should take the initiative in the international drive for nuclear disarmament. Each CSO has a different relationship with the government. The JALANA has no hesitation in criticizing the passive attitude of the Japanese government and urges it to drop its convenient calculation and forcefully lead international anti-nuclear forces. The MP, though representing local governments, takes a different stance on the national government's nuclear disarmament policy. The MP conducts its own international anti-nuclear campaign, formulates its own action plan for abolition, and pursues diplomatic relations with fellow local governments. The IPPNW and the SGI each conduct their own unique activities compared to other CSOs but understand the merit of deepening collaboration with the government, recognizing that without its involvement the goal of nuclear abolition cannot be achieved. In the post-Cold War era, many of the anti-nuclear CSOs, including the four organisations, adopted as their objectives the establishment of an international covenant for nuclear abolition. The question is whether such an international law has the necessary efficacy and binding power. Basically, international laws have binding powers only over contracting states. Therefore, many states including the P5 need to sign and ratify an anti-nuclear weapons treaty (or treaties) in order for total elimination of nuclear weapons. As regards nuclear disarmament, the NWC has the support of anti-nuclear CSOs as well as states committed to nuclear abolition.

However, for the Convention to be effective it would have to include the P5. Since the P5 are members of the UN Security Council, it is unlikely that other nuclear-weapon states would have the temerity to violate the Convention. It follows that nuclear disarmament efforts should be aimed directly at the P5. When threats from non-state actors are envisioned today, it must be clearly established that nation states are the main decision-makers in the post-Cold War global world.

The JALANA and other CSOs are pursuing a number of ways to encourage decision making by the Japanese government. The JALANA, as an organisation of lawyers, is pursuing jointly with the JFBA to legislate into law the Three Non-Nuclear Principles. A model law has been drafted but a way has not been found for it be presented to the parliament and adopted by an act of parliament. The JALANA's parent organisation is famous for having successfully drafted the NWC into law, but that was made possible with the collaboration of the government of Costa Rica. Drafting a law by a CSO alone is far from having it adopted by the legislature into law. Needless to say, the JALANA is justified in asserting that the Three Non-Nuclear Principles should be written into law. The government has no excuse for its lack of commitment about nuclear disarmament due to its neglect over time to have the important national policy written into law. Understandably, it may find it difficult to act more forcefully on the international stage but it has all the power and reasons at home to enact nuclear disarmament law. It is far easier than having to negotiate disarmament with nuclear weapons states. This is, however, the job of the legislature, and it is not realistically possible for CSOs to undertake what is the duty of the decision-makers.

Given that national security poses the greatest obstacle to achieving nuclear disarmament, focus was placed on private diplomacies conducted by anti-nuclear CSOs as a key to resolving the bottleneck. Beginning in the year 2000, the JPPNW has been developing cordial relations with the North Korean branch of the IPPNW by presenting it with much needed medical books. And through the good offices of the KANPP it is accessing the North Korean government, with which the Japanese government has no diplomatic relations, trying to establish a foothold in building a Northeast Asian Nuclear Free Zone.

The JALANA does not have its own unique private diplomacy, but it has a plan to initiate exchanges with North Korea through supporting citizens who were exposed to the atomic bombing in 1945 while in Japan and who returned to their country at the end of the war. The MP has an on-going diplomatic relationship with its counterparts at the local government level. It has succeeded in increasing the number of its affiliates even in nuclear weapons states including the US, and has collaborated with the US Mayors' Association in submitting a letter to the Obama Administration advising nuclear abolition. The efforts of the three organisations concerning their private diplomacies and attempts at building exchange channels remain extremely limited and concrete outcomes are yet to be had. In fact, these efforts are still in infancy and have not yet reached a level of evaluation. Many of Japan's CSOs, including the JPPNW and JALANA, lack young members who are willing and able to take up these issues, due to dilution of the memories of atomic bombing. It is therefore, not clear if their private diplomacy will continue to expand. Against this background, this thesis focuses on SGI President Daisaku Ikeda's private diplomacy and his anti-nuclear activities during the cold war period. Having started in 1957, the SGI is a pioneer of anti-nuclear CSOs engaged in comprehensive nuclear disarmament activities over half a century consistently with a political decision-making perspective and in collaboration with other CSOs. The activities originate in the Nichiren Buddhist philosophy of the 13th century as well as in the ideology founded on the dignity of life based on the oppression against the SGI from the Japanese militarists during the Second World War. These represent a slightly different point of view from other Japanese anti-nuclear CSOs. The SGI's anti-nuclear activities are based on realism and dialogue as developed by its President Daisaku Ikeda. His unique approach was to conduct private diplomacy through cultural exchange aimed at building peace, including nuclear abolition, with countries such as China, the Soviet Union and the United States even during the cold war. Such diplomatic efforts included roving anti-nuclear exhibitions produced by the SGI and taken to countries including China and the USSR and other communist states in collaboration with the UN and other CSOs. The governments of

China and the USSR have continued since then to claim they were developing nuclear weapons solely for the purposes of self-defence.

When the governments of the two countries actually allowed and even supported the SGI anti-nuclear exhibition to take place, these were significant events that turned into reality what might have been their mere verbal commitment for nuclear disarmament. There is however, no way to know what political will and intentions lay in the background.

Ikeda was also conscious from the beginning that CSOs and governments occupy different spheres of influence and decision making. The Komeito, a Japanese political party founded by him served as the bridge between the governments of Japan and China in regard to normalization of their relations. It made it clear that nuclear disarmament was its main diplomatic policy and served as the bridge between anti-nuclear CSOs and the MOFA. The SGI's legal organisation in Japan, the Soka Gakkai Japan, serves as the corporate body supporting the political party as constituent voters, their management however is completely separate. CSOs cannot make political decisions for the government. The SGI itself remains an NGO in UN Advisory Status and undertakes activities as a CSO and maintains distance from political matters. It has been undertaking activities that emphasize strengthening collaboration with the UN and other anti-nuclear CSOs.

Ikeda, a Buddhist Pacifist and a Japanese national who had also experienced atomic bombing, has an extremely strong commitment to promoting nuclear abolition. During the Cold War period, he conducted private diplomacy based on cultural, educational and art exchanges with China and the USSR and other communist countries at a time when diplomatic channels were closed as well as with the US and many other countries. According to him, breakdown of relations between countries that could lead to developing nuclear weapons all stem from mutual distrust, from conflicts of political interests, and obsession with national and religious differences nurtured over time. He believed that overcoming those issues and nurturing mutual understanding would finally lead to abolition of nuclear arms. The example of the dialogue Ikeda conducted with leading figures in the world shows that 'low' politics consisting of cultural exchanges can at times be more efficient than 'high' politics in resolving nuclear issues, inter-state political tensions as well as the cold war context. Ikeda's private diplomacy is a deductive process that sets the conclusion first and works backwards towards achieving it, unlike the 'inductive' diplomatic negotiations that can often result in unintended outcomes depending on the progress of negotiation, changes in situation and conditions. For example, with regard to the normalization of relations between Japan and China, rather than starting deliberations at a low administrative level, he suggested that a summit level discussion be held first to reach an agreement for restoring diplomatic relations, and then to address individual issues. It was on Ikeda's 1968 recommendation that the Japanese government was able to restore normalization with China even before the US, although the start of negotiation was delayed due to Richard Nixon's sudden visit to China, and Ikeda was able to prevent diplomatic isolation in Northeast Asia.

Since CSOs hardly have any publically recorded reports of their activities, this study depended on first-hand materials produced and published by the organisations and those gained from personal interviews. Materials used were chosen carefully and limited to those with clear dates and events that actually took place. Diplomatic materials published by government offices were also referred to. An examination of these third-party materials confirmed that they were accurate and that the CSOs had not overstated their influence. In our highly information-oriented global society of today, it has become increasingly difficult to dispatch one-sided messages or make excessive appeals to the public or self-aggrandisements based on ambiguous information.

The immense confidence governments of China and the Soviet Union placed in Ikeda is proved by the sheer number of honours the two governments and their educational organisations awarded him among his countrymen. Michael Gorbachev saw it fit to confide in Ikeda what he shared with the Japanese government - a draft nuclear disarmament programme negotiated with the USA. Perhaps Gorbachev sensed that he could better maintain relationships with Japan through civilian contacts, such as with Ikeda and the SGI, rather than relying on diplomatic channels that can easily be interrupted by a flow of unrelated issues.

The Japanese government had always insisted that diplomacy was its exclusive responsibility, did not allow CSOs and private citizens to undertake private diplomacy and remains highly critical of it. In fact, hardly any mention is made of CSO activities on nuclear issues or relaxing inter-state tensions in government documents or records. That is to say, Ikeda's private diplomacy has been conducted entirely on his own without any collaboration from the Japanese government. It can be assumed that Ikeda had no national interest in mind in his involvement in relaxing tensions between China and the Soviet Union, for which the Japanese government had no direct involvement. Even today, the Japanese government claims that diplomacy remains its exclusive mandate and is negative about sharing it with civilians and the civil sector. However, in 1990 the government relied totally on Ikeda's private diplomacy to realize Michael Gorbachev's visit to Japan. This was an example of a successful case of private diplomacy helping its public counterpart get out from its impasse. This dissertation does not intend to point to the limitations of government diplomacy, rather to its narrowness, and suggests that in solving problems it will be more effective from a long-term perspective to seek comprehensive diplomacy in collaboration with the CSOs and civilians. Both governmental and private diplomacies are crucial to resolving highly political issues as well as those involving inter-state confrontations. At the 2013 Oslo Conference, an Egyptian delegate maintained that nuclear disarmament should be a vehicle that all involved parties could take on board. This study identifies the front and back wheels of the vehicle as government and private diplomacies respectively. While private diplomacy has different structures from that of the government, it is extremely efficient at improving inter-state relations and building foundations for relaxing tensions. This study suggests it is possible to build mutual understanding through CSO cultural exchanges in promoting political and economic exchanges.

Ikeda's private diplomacy was founded on the extension of his dialogues and is true to his commitment to "sustainability". He has received important statements in his person-to-person dialogues with leaders. For example, he received word from Alexei Kosygin that the USSR would not invade China. Henry Kissinger told Ikeda that more respect should have been paid to the Japanese government, referring to Richard Nixon's lightening visit to China. This was an example of how private diplomacy can draw out true intentions not necessarily made public in formal inter-state relations or between politicians. Ikeda also heard opinions that are opposite to his own beliefs. Richard Nikolaus von Coudenhove-Kalergi, for example, told him it was a waste of time for the Japanese government to expect advances in international nuclear disarmament, and André Malraux was definite in saying that there was no point in promoting nuclear disarmament. In spite of these negative reactions, Ikeda, who had based himself on the spirit of Buddhism, continued to believe in the importance of finding similarities rather than differences with his dialogue partners.

The SGI's anti-nuclear activities, based on Ikeda's commitment to dialogue, are successfully earning the trust of the Japanese government, often drawing attention to positive aspects of anti-nuclear logic that had escaped the attention of officials. The SGI believes that a CSOs' role is to make sure that government representatives are always present at international nuclear disarmament conferences, and to continue to encourage the government so that its commitment to nuclear disarmament does not retreat. There is no guarantee that an agreement can be reached through a dialogue. There can be breakups and failures in the short term. Ikeda, however, found value in sustaining the dialogue and in recognizing differences of views rather than necessarily arriving at conformity of opinions. This is the opposite of inter-state diplomacies where disagreement would result in a sudden cooling of relations. Needless to say, government diplomacy has priority in finding an outcome that will benefit national interests and would hesitate to place importance on friendly relations with the other country even at the loss of national interests. The government's priority is different from that of the CSOs.

The CSOs including the SGI cannot make political decisions for governments and parliaments, but they can produce outcomes that are at times above and beyond public diplomacies. Both the CSOs and governments are encouraged to utilize their respective uniqueness fully. It will be nothing but negative for governments to limit or deny CSOs their anti-nuclear activities either by words or by action. Nuclear disarmament would not go forward without their complementary involvements. To give an example in a very different case, it may even be effective for governments to depend on CSO's private diplomacy in paving the way for taxing inter-state communications. On the other hand, the anti-nuclear CSOs need to do more than shout slogans and conduct street demonstrations. By building their capacity and deepening their knowledge they should be able to discuss concrete disarmament policies with the government as equal partners. What is required today is to collaborate also with the government and to have sustained discussion and negotiation.

In that sense, establishment of the JNNNWA in 2010 symbolizes CSOs recognition of a need for continuous dialogue with the MOFA. However, the NGO network has constant concerns over the government's repeated negative attitude at the Conference on Humanitarian Impact of Nuclear Weapons (known as the Oslo Conference), as well as its repeated refusal to sign the Joint Declaration Concerning the Inhumanity of the Nuclear Weapons at the First Committee of the UN General Assembly. Moreover, absence of a MOFA representative at the NGO Network Meeting to which he was invited did not help MOFA and CSOs to reach agreement for collaboration at informal exchange meetings. The gulf remains large between the two. Under the circumstances, the SGI developed a new approach, which is-to address nuclear disarmament as a logical issue. Since the government's final objective is nuclear abolition, the SGI studied positive aspects of the government's positions and presented a logic-based argument to which the government would be able to agree.

This study has a number of limitations. Since most of the anti-nuclear movements gained momentum in the post-Cold War era, it is difficult to undertake effective historical evaluation due to the shortness of their history. Both the JPPNW and the MP were established towards the end of the cold war period. The SGI, in contrast, started its anti-nuclear activities immediately following the Second World War, thus providing an important model in producing efficient outcomes through a great deal of trial and error. The United States and the USSR (Russia later) have reduced the number of their nuclear weapons dramatically. In the 2000s, the nuclear disarmament momentum has been on the rise since President Obama's Prague Speech. In reality, however, the number of nuclear weapon states has been increased. CSOs, for example, are invited today to the Preparatory Sessions of NPT Review Conference, but the effect of their presence at such international conferences is little known, hence no evaluation can be made. The next stage of this study, after a given period, will be to follow up and examine the roles of CSOs particularly those of the Japanese anti-nuclear CSOs at the NPT Review Conference as well as at the Conference: Humanitarian Impact of Nuclear Weapons. Other studies to-date report that, due to the opposition from the US and the rest of the P5, the NPT Review Conference has not yielded any core outcome.

As soon as detailed research and enquiry were called for, the focus tended to shift to negative criticisms against nuclear weapons states. What is needed are more sensitive and detailed studies such as this one has attempted to be. It has focused on the attitudes and initiatives of CSOs not just during conferences, but also to check actions CSOs took beforehand, as well as off-conference sites in order to ensure their success. Given that nuclear disarmament is a complex diplomatic issue, the positive roles CSOs can play in dissolving inter-state conflicts have been demonstrated by Ikeda's private diplomacy. And further, once a concrete process for nuclear abolition is in sight, what roles would CSOs play? There will be a need to focus on the activities of anti-nuclear CSOs in Japan, including the SGI. This too, it is suggested, will be a topic for the next generation to pursue. With regard to the situation in Northeast Asia, Japan's relationships with China and Russia are worsening due to the post-Cold War exploitation of resources as well as territorial issues. Since the causes of the conflicts have moved on to economic competition and away from the ideological confrontation during the cold-war years, anti-nuclear CSOs will need to adjust their activities in the light of these changing circumstances and an analysis of the structure of nuclear disarmament will become necessary with that change in mind. Against this evolving background and emerging non-state actors, there is a need to see how the SGI will successfully produce effective nuclear disarmament in our global world of the post-Cold War period.

It is hoped that this study will assist in gaining wider recognition for the importance of collecting and making public records of the important roles private diplomacy has played in resolving global issues. The study of private diplomacy is an essential field of research, especially in today's increasingly borderless global era.

Bibliographies

Primary Sources

MOFA, Arms Control and Disarmament Division, Disarmament, Non-Proliferation and Science Department, *Japan's Disarmament and Non-Proliferation Policy (white paper, 2nd Edition, 2004)*, p23-p27 Chapter 1, Section 4: Japan's Basic Standpoint and Approach for Disarmament and Non-Proliferation

MOFA, Arms Control and Disarmament Division, Disarmament, Non-Proliferation and Science Department, Japan's Disarmament and Non-Proliferation Policy: Chapter 1 "Outline" of 1st (2002), 2nd (2004), 3rd (2006), 4th (2008), 5th (2010), and 6th edition (2013)

MOFA, Arms Control and Disarmament Division, Disarmament, Non-Proliferation and Science Department, Japan's Disarmament and Non-Proliferation Policy (white paper, 2nd Edition, 2004), Chapter 8: Role of Civil Society, Section 8: Symposium and Workshops, p237-p238

MOFA, Arms Control and Disarmament Division, Disarmament, Non-Proliferation and Science Department, Japan's Disarmament and Non-Proliferation Policy (white paper, 5nd Edition, 2011), Chapter 7: Dialogue and Cooperation with Civil Society, Section 4: Japan's Basic Standpoint and Approach for Disarmament and Non-Proliferation, Section 2: Symposium and Workshops, and Dialogue and Cooperation with Civil Society, "Side Event of the 3rd Preparatory Session for 2010 NPT Review Conference in 2009, sponsored by MOFA, UN Office of Disarmament Affairs, UN Institute for Disarmament Research, and Center for Nonproliferation Studies of Monterey Institute of International Studies" p129

Ibid, Chapter 3: Disarmament, Non-Proliferation, and Education, No 1: Submission of Working Papers about Disarmament and Non-Proliferation Education, p132

MOFA, Arms Control and Disarmament Division, Disarmament, Non-Proliferation and Science Department, Japan's Disarmament and Non-Proliferation Policy (white paper, 4nd Edition, 2008), Chapter 8: Role of Civil Society, Section 2: Symposium and Workshops, No 5: Collaboration to hold exhibitions regarding Atomic Bombs in Overseas, p148 "History of Japan's Exhibition regarding Atomic Bombs in the world"

Akira Kawasaki (Secretary-General of Japan NGO Network for Nuclear Weapons Abolition)'s Remark, Public Seminar "Towards Abolition of Nuclear Weapons: the World Situation and Japan – Report on 1st Preparatory Session for the 2015 NPT Review Conference and the Future", at Meiji Gakuin University, Tokyo, 12th May 2013

MOFA, Diplomatic Blue Book 1991, Chapter 1: Changing of International Situation and Japanese Diplomacy, Section 2: Issues to Japanese Diplomacy, No 3: Issues to Japanese Diplomacy

Accessed: 9 August 2011

MOFA and MOFA Diplomatic Archives, Nippon Gaiko Shuyo Bunsho Nenpyo (1) (Japanese Diplomatic Main Papers and Chronological Table (1)), p119-p112

MOFA, Joyakushu, 30-6. (Japan's Foreign Relations-Basic Documents Vol.1), p444-p448

Pema Gyalpo (Professor in Political Science, Toin University of Yokhama, Japan, Advisor to the Prime Minister of Bhutan, and former Representative of 14th Dalai Lama to Japan), *Lecture at Gakudo-kai Seminer "Japanese Original Power, Danger of China, and Possibilities of India"*, at Hibiya Library & Museum, Tokyo,

13th May 2013

Kazuhiro Tobisawa's Memo to Record Statements of Each Attendee, Oslo Conference Follow-up Meeting, which was held by Japan NGO Network for Nuclear Weapons Abolition at Meiji Gakuin University, Tokyo, 19th March 2013

Kazuhiro Tobisawa's Memo to Record Statements of Each Attendee, *Statement by Terumi Tanaka (Secretary-General, Japan Confederation of A and H bomb Suffers Organisations)*, Oslo Conference Follow-up Meeting, which was held by Japan NGO Network for Nuclear Weapons Abolition at Meiji Gakuin University, Tokyo, 19th March 2013

Kenichi Okubo's Answer to Kazuhiro Tobisawa, the Follow-up of Oslo Conference, JNNNWA at Meiji Gakuin University in Tokyo, 19th March 2013

MOFA, Diplomatic Blue Book No. 15, 1971, p412-p416

MOFA, Diplomatic Blue Book No. 31, 1987, p403-p404

List of SGI's Anti-Nuclear Exhibitions, which the SGI Peace Committee made and provided for this thesis

Soka Gakkai Office of International Affairs provided their remarks with copies of materials to this thesis

Soka Gakkai (SGI), *NGO Activity Report 2009*, SGI Office of Public Information 2009 p3, p30

MOFA, Gaiko Seisho 1972 (Diplomatic Blue Book 1972), 8th March 1972, p507-p508

MOFA Archives, Dai 2 Kai Takeiri Yoshikatsu Shu Onrai Kaidan Kiroku (Record of 2nd Meeting between Yoshikatsu Takeiri and Zhou Enrai) on 28th July 1972

MOFA Archives, Tanaka Sori Shu Onrai Sori Kaidan Kiroku (Record of Meeting between Prime Minister Tanaka and Prime Minister Zhou

Enrai) between 25th and 28th September 1972

MOFA Archives, Dai 1 Kai Takeiri Yoshikatsu Shu Onrai Kaidan Kiroku (Record of Meetings between Yoshikatsu Takeiri of Komeito and Zhou Enrai No1), 27th July 1972

MOFA Archives, Dai 2 Kai Takeiri Yoshikatsu Shu Onrai Kaidan Kiroku (Record of Meetings between Yoshikatsu Takeiri of Komeito and Zhou Enrai No2), 28th July 1972

MOFA Archives, Dai 3 Kai Takeiri Yoshikatsu Shu Onrai Kaidan Kiroku (Record of Meetings between Yoshikatsu Takeiri of Komeito and Zhou Enrai No3), 29th July 1972

MOFA Archives, Tanaka Sori Shu Onrai Sori Kaidan Kiroku (Record of Meetings between Prime Minister Tanaka and Prime Minister Zhou), 25th – 28th September 1972

MOFA Archives, the Soviet-Japanese Neutrality Pact, 13th April 1941

Akira Kawasaki's Presentation, Report Session of Oslo Conference, which was held in support of the Japan NGO Network for Nuclear Weapons Abolition, 19th March 2013

Delivered by Ambassador Peter Woolcott, Australian Permanent Representative to the United Nations, Geneva and Ambassador for Disarmament, *Joint Statement on the humanitarian consequences of nuclear weapons*, 21st October 2013, p1

Secondary Sources

Books

Takuya Sasaki, Kokusai Shakai Ni Okeru NGO No Tenkai: 1, Amerika Gaiko To NGO (NGO Activities in the International Society: 1, American Diplomacy and NGO), Minsai Gaiko No Kenkyu (Studies of People-To-People Diplomacy), Sanrei Shobo 1997, p75-p99

Claudia Kissiling, Civil Society and Nuclear Non-Proliferation: How do States Respons?, Ashgate 2008, p175

Sanseido Co., Ltd., Shin Roppo: Nihonkoku Kenpo (New Compendium of Laws Japan: Constitution), p11, 2001

Terumasa Nakanishi, Kimindo Kuasaka, Yoshiko Sakurai, Tsutomu Nishioka, Kan Ito, Nisohachi Hyodo, Nihon Kakubuso No Ronte – Kokka Sonritsu No Kiki O Ikinukutameni (Viewpoints of Japanese Nuclear Armament – To Survive in Crisis of the Nation's Existence), PHP Institute Office2006

Shintaro Ishihara (Governor of Tokyo Metropolitan City), *Nihon-yo (Japan), Sankei Newspaper*, 8th June 2010

Kajima Institute of International Peace, Nippon Gaiko Shuyo Bunsho Nenpyo 1 (Diplomatic Archives and Chronological Table of Japan' volume 1), Hara Shobo 1983, p784-p786

Editing Committee of the "Ikeda Daisaku No Kiseki", *Ikeda Daisaku No Kiseki (Track of Daisaku Ikeda volume 2)*, Ushio Shuppansha 2007, p138-p139

Takayuki Nakazawa, Gorubathofu To Ikeda Daisaku (Gorbachev and Daisaku Ikeda), Kadokawa Shoten 2004, p61-p62

Zhou Enrai School of Government, Nankai University (China), Edited by Kazuteru Saionji, *Shu Onrai To Ikeda Daisaku (Zhou Enrai and Daisaku Ikeda)*, Asahi Sonorama 2002 (published in Japanese), p73, p118, p285

Daisaku Ikeda, Seishin No Shiruku Rodo Wo Motomete (In Search of a Spiritual Silk Road), Ushio Shuppansha 2010

Daisaku Ikeda and Henry Kissinger, *Heiwa To Zinsei To Tetsugaku O Kataru (Philosophy of Human Peace)*, Seikyo Newspaper 2008, p163-p164 It was originally published in 1987

Takayuki Nakazawa, *Gorubathofu To Ikeda Daisaku (Gorbachev and Daisaku Ikeda)*, Kadokawa Shoten 2004, p61-p62, p67-p68, p79-p80, p190-p191, p205-p207, p218, p247

Daisaku Ikeda, Daido O Ayumu: Watashi No Zinsei Kiroku 3 (Taking Moral Principles: My Records of Life' Vol.3), Mainichi Newspaper Co. Ltd., 2002, p36, p40-p41, p48-p49

Masaru Sato, Kokka No Zibaku (Self-Locking of State), Fusosha 2010, p118-p119

Daisaku Ikeda and Viktor Sadovnichiy,

Japanese edition 1: *"Atarashiki Jinrui-wo, Atarashiki Sekai-wo"*, Ushio Shuppansha Co., Ltd., Tokyo, 2002

Japanese edition 2: *"Gaku-wa Hikari"*, Ushio Shuppansha Co., Ltd., Tokyo, 2004

Russian edition, Moscow State University Press, 2005

Chinese edition (orthodox), Cheng Yin Culture enterprise Co., Ltd., Taipei, 2006

Soka Gakkai, Toward an Era of Human Empowerment: Books on Buddhism and Humanity, 2007, p18

Daisaku Ikeda and Ved Prakash Nanda, *The Spirit of India – Buddhism and Hinduism*, The Institute of Oriental Philosophy 2005 (published only in Japanese)

Ikeda Daisaku No Kiseki Hensan Iinkai (The Editing Committee of the

Daisaku Ikeda's Track), Ikeda Daisaku No Kiseki III: Heiwa To Bunka No Daijo (tt 'The Daisaku Ikeda's Track III: The Great Castle for Promoting Peace and Culture'), Ushio Co., Ltd. 2008 p244-p245

Soka Gakkai Youth Peace Committee, *Mae! HIROSHIMA No Chocho: Hibakuchi Kara No Message*, Daisan Bunmeisha 2003

Daisaku Ikeda, Ikeda Daisaku Zenshu Dai 1 Kan (1st Volume of the Complete Works of Daisaku Ikeda), Seikyo Newspaper 1988, p473-p474

Daisaku Ikeda, New Waves of Peace Toward the Twenty-first Century: A Proposal Commemorating the Tenth Soka Gakkai International Day (Annual Peace Proposal 1985), January 26, 1985, p221-p222 (this copy was provided by the SGI Peace Committee)

Daisaku Ikeda, Shin Ningen Kakumei Vol. 7 (New Human Revolution' volume 7), Seikyo Newspaper 2004, p272-p273

Nichiren, Gift of Rice (Hakumai Ippyo Gosho), the Writings of Nichiren Daishonin Volume I, Soka Gakkai 1999, p1125 (English)

Nichiren, On Establishing the Correct Teaching for the Peace of the Land [Rissho Ankokuron], the Writings of Nichiren Daishonin Volume I, Soka Gakkai 1999, p 24 (English)

Nichiren, Offerings in the Snow [Ueno dono gohenji], the Writings of Nichiren Daishonin Volume II, Soka Gakkai 1999, p809 (English) Supervised by Koichi Miyata and Edited by Daisaibunmei-Sha, Inc, Makiguchi Tsunsaburo Gokuchu No Tatakai – Zinmon Chosho To Gokuchu Shokan O Yomu (Fighting of Tsunesaburo Makiguchi in Prison – The Records of Interrogations and His Letters in Prison), Daisanbunmei-Sha 2000, p132

Susumu Nishibe, Kakubuso Ron (Theory of Nuclear Armament), Kodansha 2007, p82-p88

Daisaku Ikeda, Ikeda Daisaku Zenshu 102 (The Complete Works of Daisaku Ikeda volume 102'), Bunmei Nishi To Higashi (Civilisations: West and East' dialogue with Richard Coudenhove-Kalergi), Seikyo Newspaper 2003, p70-p71, p74, p83-p84, p87, p94-p96, p168-p169 * the original book of its dialogue was published by Sankei Newspaper in 1972 (only available in Japanese)

Daisaku Ikeda and Norman Cousins, Sekai Shimin No Taiwa (Dialogue Between Citizens of the World), Seikyo Newspaper 2000, p76-p79, p121-p154, p125, p131-p133, p239-p240 It was originally published in 1991

Daisaku Ikeda and André Malraux, *Ningen Kaumei To Ningen No Joken (tt 'Changes within: Human Revolution and Human Condition')*, Seikyo Newspaper 1981, p77-p78, p89, p106 * it was originally published in 1976 (only in Japanese)

Daisaku Ikeda and Henry Kissinger, *Heiwa To Zinsei To Tetsugaku O Kataru (Philosophy of Human Peace)*, Seikyo Newspaper 2008, p137-p138, p140-p143, p165-p166, p168-p169 It was originally published in 1987

Richard Felix Star, *Foreign Policies of the Soviet Union*, Hoover Press 1991, p87

Ruud van Dijk, *Encyclopedia of the Cold War*, Taylor & Francis 2008, p645

Terumasa Nakanishi, Nippon Kaubuso No Ronten (Arguing Point of Japanese Nuclear Armament), PHP Kenkyujo 2006, p25, p39

Kan Ito, Chugoku No Kakusenryoku Ni Nihon Ha Kuppuku Suru (Japan will be Grovel before Chinese Nuclear Arms), Shogakkan Shinsho 2011, p204-p205

Kajima Institute of International Peace, Nippon Gaiko Shuyo Bunsho

Nenpyo 2 (Diplomatic Archives and Chronological Table of Japan: volume 2), Hara Shobo 1984, p525-p527

Kajima Institute of International Peace, Nippon Gaiko Shuyo Bunsho Nenpyo 1 (Diplomatic Archives and Chronological Table of Japan: volume 1), Hara Shobo 1983, p569-p570

Edited by the China Affairs Bureau of MOFA, Nicchu Kankei Kihon Shiryoshu 1949-1969 (Basic Document Collection in Relation between Japan and China 1949-1969), the Kazankai Foundation 1970, p50-p52, p215-p216, p231 Edited by the China Affairs Bureau of MOFA, Matsumura Kenzo Ziminto Komon To Shuonrai Chugoku Sori To No Kaidan Ni Kansuru Memo 1962 Nen 9 Gatsu 19 Nichi (Memorandum about Meeting between Kenzo Matsumura, Advisor to the Liberal Democratic Party Japan, and Zhou Enrai, the Chinese Prime Minister 19th September 1962'), Nicchu Kankei Kihon Shiryoshu 1949-1969 (Basic Document Collection in Relation between Japan and China 1949-1969), the Kazankai Foundation 1970, p214

Daisaku Ikeda, Shin Ningen Kakumei 20 (New Human Revolution volume Vol. 20), Seikyo Newspaper 2011, p71-p72

Paul Byrne, *Social Movements in Britain*, Routledge London 1997, p91 Translated by Fujiko Hara, with a foreword by Marius B. Jansen, *The Autobiography of Ozaki Yukio: The Struggle for Constitutional Government in Japan*, Princeton University Press 2001, p271

Kiichi Miyazawa, Tokyo-Washing No Mitsudan (The Secret Conversation between Tokyo and Washington), Chuokoronsha. Ltd 1999, p46-p47

Stuart Rees and Daisaku Ikeda, Heiwa To Tetsugaku To Shigokoro O Kataru (Dialogue on Peace, Philosophy and Poetic Inspiration), Daisan Bunmeisha, Co., Ltd 2014 p268-p269

Bibliographies

Newspapers

Asahi Newspaper, (21 countries admitted [illegality of use of nuclear weapons] and 35 countries made statements to the International Court of Justice"), 6th December 1994.

Asahi Newspaper, 1st August 2009 (evening edition), p2

Chugoku Shimbun (Chugoku Newspaper), Hiroshima Peace Media Center, Interview with Terumi Tanaka, head of the Japan Confederation of A-and H-Bombs Suffers Organizations, on nuclear disarmament conference in Oslo, 18th March 2013

Tokyo Shimbun (Tokyo Newspaper), 25th September 1974

Seikyo Newspaper, 27th May 1987, p1

Bernard Lown, Seikyo Newspaper, 27th May 1987

Seikyo Newspaper, 28th May 1987, p1

Seikyo Newspaper, Message from Gorbachev for 40th Anniversary of Ikeda's Visit the USSR, 8th September 2014, p1

(Gorbachev wrote) President Ikeda is a philosopher having a keen intellect, a humanist, and a man of letters"

Hirotsugu Terasaki, Chairman of Soka Gakkai Peace Committee, Shimin No Koe Koso Rekishi Kaiten No Gendoryoku (Voice of Ordinary People is Motive Force to Transform History), Seikyo Newspaper 16th November 2010 p2

UN, SGI, Hiroshima City, and Nagasaki City, *Review of Exhibition: Nuclear Arms: Threat to Our World*, Part 1 p2, p 5, Part 5 p1-p5

Seikyo Newspaper 13th April 1997

Seikyo Shimbun Newspaper 18th March 2013

Seikyo Newspaper, Beikoku De Kakuhaizetsu Heno Shukyokan Kaigi (SGI held an interfaith symposium in the United States to abolish nuclear weapons), 1st May 2014

Seikyo Newspaper, SGI Amerika Homondan Kakuheiki Haizetsu O Motomeru Kyodoseimei O NPT Saikento Kaigi No Junbi Iinkai Gicho Ni Teisyutsu (The SGI Visiting Group to the United States submitted the Joint Statement calling for nuclear abolition to the Chairman of the Preparatory Committee of the NPT Review Conference), 5th May 2014

Seikyo Newspaper, Beikoku De Kakuhaizetsu Eno Shukyokan Kaigi (SGI held an interfaith symposium in the United States to abolish nuclear weapons), 1st May 2014

Seikyo Newspaper, Oabama Daitoryo Ga Shunin: SGI Kaicho Ga Keishuku No Message (Mr. Obama became the new US President, and the SGI President sent his message for cerebration to Mr. Obama), 22nd January 2009

Seikyo Newspaper, Soka Gakkai No Hi Kinen Tokushu (Special Edition of Soka Gakkai Memorial Day), 4th May 2014, p2

Seikyo Newspaper, SGI Kaicho No Taiwaroku: Dai 23 Kai – Edward Kennedy, Amerika Join Giin (the 23rd Record of the SGI President's Dialogue with Leaders and People: Edward Kennedy, US Senator), 23rd December 2013 p3

Asahi Newspaper, 8th April 2014

Komei Newspaper, Kakuhaizetsuheno Choryu Tsuyoku (Strengthening Movement toward Abolition of Nuclear Weapons), 3rd April 2014

Komei Newspaper, NPDI Gaishokaigo Nihon De Kaisai (NPDI was held in Japan), 20th April

Interview with Katuko Kataoka, Secretary-General of JPPNW, 2012

Christopher S. Queen, Bunmei Wo "Shototsu" Kara "Kyosei" He To Hiraku Eichi (Wisdom to transfer civilization from "clash" to "co-exist), Seikyo Newspaper 16th September 2012, p3

Joseph Nye, Intabyu Shincho "Daitoryo No Lida-Sip To Amerika No

Zidai No Souzo" O Megutte (Interview regarding his new book "Presidential Leadership and the Creation of the American Era), Seikyo Newspaper, 1st January 2014, p6

Seikyo Newspaper, SGI Kaicho No Taiwaroku No. 27 André Malraux (SGI President's Record of Dialogue No. 27: André Malraux), 26th February 2014, p3

Japanese Communist Party, *Shimbun Akahata (Newspaper the Red)*, 20th September 2010

Komei Newspaper, To Hochudan Shu Kinpei Soshoki To Kaidan (The Komeito's Group to Visit China Met Xi Jinping), 26th January 2013, p1

Seikyo Newspaper, 11th September 2012, p3

Sankei Newspaper, Soka Gakkai No Minkan Gaiko O Kenen: Gaimusho Bei Ni Hyomei 68 (Ministry of Foreign Affairs Japan Expressed Serious Concern about the Soka Gakkai's Private Diplomacy in Meeting with the US Government, 1968), 16th February 1995

Seikyo Newspaper, 3rd October 2007, p3 (provided by the SGI)

Seikyo Newspaper, 28th June 2010, p3 (provided by the SGI)

Seikyo Newspaper, 7th June 1984, p1 (provided by the SGI)

Chiyako Sato, *Interview with Cheng Yonghua*, Mainichi Newspaper 17th September 2012 (in Japanese)

Komei Newspaper, *Kakuhaizetsu Sekai No Choryu Ni-Kakuchi De Shusenkinen Gaito Enzetsukai* (Let's make nuclear abolition as a worldwide common sense, New Komeito Party gave speeches in cities and towns in Japan for the memorial day of finishing of the Second World War,), 16th August 2011, p1

Komei Newspaper, Kokusai Giron O Shudo Seyo, Kakuheiki Hizindosei Meguri Kinkyu Teigen, To Kaku Haizetsu Suishin Iinkai

(Komeito Party Committee on Promoting of Nuclear Abolition called Japanese government should lead discussion about humanitarian consequences of nuclear weapons in the international society), 20th October 2012

Nihon Keizai Shimbun (Japanese Economic Newspaper Co., Ltd), *Shuin Sen*

Koyaku Shuu (Manifestos of All Political Parties on the Diet for General

Election 2012), 15th December 2012

The Nikkei, Kaku Gunshuku Kokuren Ketsugi Mezasu (Nuclear Disarmament: Aiming to Reach an UN Resolution) 26th July 2015, p2

Yomiuri Shimbun 8th November 2006, Shasetsu: "Kaku Rongi" Giron Sura Fuziru No Ha Okasii (Leading Article: "Discussion for Nuclear Armament: it is strange to even prohibit discussing about nuclear armament")

Mainichi Shimbun 27th November 2006, Kaku Hoyu No Giron Ha Yonin – Saita No 6Wari Shimeru (No to Nuclear Armament But Accept to Discuss about That – This Opinion Poll Reached 60%)

Articles

Hiroshima Ishikai Sokuho (Dai 2053 Go) (tentative translation: 'Report of Hiroshima Prefectural Medical Association (No. 2053)', 2009, p3

Hiroshima Ishikai Sokuho (Dai 2022 Go) (Report of Hiroshima Prefectural Medical Association (No. 2022), Hiroshima Nanao Kamata (Member of JPPNW Board of Directors, and Professor emeritus Hiroshima University), '*Dai 18 Kai IPPNW Sekai Taikai Waku Shopu* (18th IPPNW World Conference Work Shop)', 5th September 2008, p1-p3

Hiroshima Ishikai Sokuho (Dai 2048 Go) (Report of Hiroshima Prefectural Medical Association (No. 2048)', p2

Japan Medical Association, '*Nihon Ishikai Soritsu Kinenshi: Sengo Gojunen No Ayumi* (Magazine of 50th Anniversary of Japan Medical Association), 1997, p220

Hiroshima Prefectural Medical Association, *Hiroshimaken Ishikai Sokuho No. 2083* (Report of Hiroshima Prefectural Medical Association No. 2083), 2010, p2

Hiroshima Prefectural Medical Association, *Hiroshimaken Ishikai Sokuho No. 2019* (Report of Hiroshima Prefectural Medical Association No. 2019), 2008, p1

Hiroshima Prefectural Medical Association, *Hiroshimaken Ishikai Sokuho No. 2018* (Report of Hiroshima Prefectural Medical Association No. 2018), 2008, p2

Hiroshima Prefectural Medical Association, *Hiroshimaken Ishikai Sokuho No. 2112* (Report of Hiroshima Prefectural Medical Association No. 2112), 2011, p1

Hiroshima Prefectural Medical Association, *Hiroshimaken Ishikai Sokuho No. 2103* (Report of Hiroshima Prefectural Medical

Association No. 2103), 2010, p3

Hiroshima Prefectural Medical Association, Hiroshimaken Ishikai Sokuho No. 2109 (Report of Hiroshima Prefectural Medical Association No. 2109), p2

Hiroshima Prefectural Medical Association, Hiroshimaken Ishikai Sokuho No. 2156 (Report of Hiroshima Prefectural Medical Association No. 2156), 2012, p4

Hiroshima Prefectural Medical Association, Hiroshimaken Ishikai Sokuho No. 2090 (Report of Hiroshima Prefectural Medical Association No. 2090), Attended Inter Action Council, 25th July 2010 p1-p2

Mayors for Peace, Dai 3 Kai Heiwa Shicho Kaigi Sokai Hokokusho (Report of Mayors for Peace General Conference), 1993 Accessed: 20 November 2013

JALANA, Hankaku Horitsuka (bulletin of JALANA) No 76, Kokusai Hankaku Horitsuka Kyokai (IALANA) Rizikai Giziroku, Raina Buraun (Record of IALANA Board of Directors by Reiner Braun), p39 2013

JALANA, Hankaku Horitsuka (bulletin of JALANA) No74, p16-p19, Spring 2013

JALANA, *Hankaku Horitsuka No 76*, p10-p11, Summer 2013

JALANA, *Hankaku Horitsuka No 77*, p12-p13, pp16-pp18, Autumn 2013

Kenichi Okubo, *Oslo Kaigi (Oslo conference)*, Hankaku Horitsuka (bulletin of JALANA) No 76, p24-p25, Summer 2013

JALANA, Hankaku Horitsuka (bulletin of JALANA), Datsu Genpatsu O Kimeta Doitsu No Keiken Ni Manabu (Learning German experience which has determined to abolish nuclear reactors), 2012, p33-p37 Accessed: 1 December 2013

Ivan Kovalenko, *Daibyaku Renge volume 11* (appeared in Japanese), November 1994

Daisaku Ikeda, Sunday Mainichi (a magazine of Mainichi Newspaper), 11 February 1979

Ushio Shuppansha, *Ushio (Monthly Magazine)*, November 2007, p110

Masaru Sato, Ikeda SGI Kaicho No Minkan Gaiko Ga Hatasu Igi (The Meaning of Private Diplomacy by SGI President Ikeda), Magazine Ushio, Ushio Shuppansha, November 2007, p205-p206

Jiji Press, Gaiko (Diplomacy", a journal) Vol. 18, Kantaro Oguri: Ongaku To Gaiko (Music and Diplomacy), p118, March 2013

Seikyo Newspaper, SGI Kaicho No Taiwaroku: Dai 23 Kai – Edward Kennedy, Amerika Join Giin (the 23rd Record of the SGI President's Dialogue with Leaders and People: Edward Kennedy, US Senator), 23rd December 2013, p3

Hiroshima Soka Gakkai News Vol. 13, Dai16kai Gakusei Heiwa Ishiki Chosa (16th Survey of Students on Awareness of Peace), 2012 p23-p24

Daisaku Ikeda, *Annual Peace Proposal 1987*, p22-p23 (this copy was provided by the SGI)

Hiroyasu Kobayashi (President of Min-On Concert Association, Japan), Chugoku To No Bunka Koryu: the Min-On Concert Association, Ikeda Daisaku To Nichu Yuko No Ayumi (Cultural Exchange with China: Min On Concert Association, Daisaku Ikeda's Track for Japan-Chinese Friendship), People's Daily Overseas Edition Japan Monthly 2012, p60

People's Daily Overseas Edition Japan Monthly, Ikeda Daisaku To Nicchu Yuko No Ayumi: Nicchu Kokou Seijouka 40 Shunen Kinen (Daisaku Ikeda and History of Japan-China Friendship: The 40th Anniversary of Diplomatic Normalization between Japan and

China), 2012, p5, p18, p34-p35, p50-p51, p52, p53, p64, p68-p69, p73-p76

Hirotomo Teranishi (Professor of Soka University), Ikeda Daisaku No Ningen Shugi Gaiko (Daisaku Ikeda's Diplomacy for Humanism: Example of His First Visit to China and the USSR in 1974), Soka Kyoiku Dai 3 Go (Soka Education No 3), p3, p9

Komei Graphic Winter 2014, Comment by Nobumasa Akiyama, Professor of Hitostusbashi University and former senior research fellow of the Centre for the Promotion of Disarmament and Non-Proliferation Japan, January 2014, p10-p11

The House of Commons, Research Paper 98/91, The Strategic Defence Review White Paper, 15th October 1998

Internet Sources

The National Conference of Catholic Bishops, *The Challenge of Peace: God's Promise and Our Response – A Pastoral Letter on War and Peace*, 3rd May 1983, p3 http://www.usccb.org/upload/challenge-peace-gods-promise-our-response-1983.pdf

Accessed: 17 December 2012

Hiroshima City, List of *hibakusha* (official information) http://www.city.hiroshima.lg.jp/www/contents/0000000000000/1283234802275/index.html

Accessed: 15 December 2011

Nagasaki City, List of *hibakusha* (official information) http://www1.city.nagasaki.nagasaki.jp/gentai/irei_tuitou/houan.html

Accessed: 15 December 2011

Ministry of Foreign Affairs Japan (MOFA), Gunshuku To Waga Kuni No Torikumi: Gaikan (Japan's Approach for Disarmament and Non-Proliferation)

http://www.mofa.go.jp/mofaj/gaiko/fukaku/torikumi.html

Accessed: 6 May 2010

MOFA, Arms Control and Disarmament Division, Disarmament, Non-Proliferation and Science Department, *Japan's Disarmament and Non-Proliferation Policy (white paper, 1st Edition, 2002)*, p13 http://www.mofa.go.jp/mofaj/gaiko/gun_hakusho/2002/hon1_1.pdf

Accessed: 8th October 2011

MOFA, Resolution at the Japanese Diet regarding the Three Non-Nuclear Principles

Resolution approved by House of Representative Committee on Foreign Affairs, 27th April 1976, following the Nuclear Non-Proliferation Treaty

(NPT)
http://www.mofa.go.jp/mofaj/gaiko/kaku/gensoku/ketsugi.html
Accessed: 26 March 2012

Formal Questioning Session at the House of Representative Japan by Komeito (political party), *Minutes of Plenary Session of the House of Representatives Japan [094/099]57-Shu-Honkaigi-4Go, 8th December 1967,*
http://kokkai.ndl.go.jp/cgi-bin/KENSAKU/swk_dispdoc.cgi?SESSION=24165&SAVED_RID=2&PAGE=0&POS=0&TOTAL=0&SRV_ID=3&DOC_ID=23407&DPAGE=5&DTOTAL=99&DPOS=94&SORT_DIR=1&SORT_TYPE=0&MODE=1&DMY=28412
Accessed: 14 September 2011

MOFA, *Diplomatic Blue Book 2002, Section 3: Approaches to Global Issues, No 6: Human Security*
http://www.mofa.go.jp/mofaj/gaiko/bluebook/2003/gaikou/html/honpen/index.html
Accessed: 7 May 2010

MOFA, *Diplomatic Blue Book 2002, Chapter 1: Outline "International Situation and Japanese Diplomacy 2002*
http://www.mofa.go.jp/mofaj/gaiko/bluebook/2003/gaikou/html/honpen/index.html

Ibid, *Chapter 3: Diplomacy in Each Field, No 7: Arms Control, Disarmament, and Non-Proliferation*
http://www.mofa.go.jp/mofaj/gaiko/bluebook/2003/gaikou/html/honpen/index.html
Accessed: 7 May 2010

MOFA, Japan-China Relations: Japan-China Summit Meeting, 10th November 2014
http://www.mofa.go.jp/a_o/c_m1/cn/page4e_000151.html

Accessed: 14 November 2014

MOFA, Arms Control and Disarmament Division, Disarmament, Non-Proliferation and Science Department, Japan's Disarmament and Non-Proliferation Policy (white paper, 1nd Edition, 2002), Chapter 8: Role of Civil Society, Section 2: Symposium and Workshops, p157-p159 http://www.mofa.go.jp/mofaj/gaiko/gun_hakusho/2002/hon8.pdf

Accessed: 7 May 2010

MOFA Archives 1994

http://www.mofa.go.jp/mofaj/gaiko/un_cd/gun_un/ketsu_94.html

Accessed: 8 January 2013

MOFA Archives 1999 http://www.mofa.go.jp/mofaj/gaiko/un_cd/gun_un/ketsu_99.html

Accessed: 8 January 2013

MOFA Archives 2000-2001 http://www.mofa.go.jp/mofaj/gaiko/un_cd/gun_un/ketsu_2001.html

Accessed: 8 January 2013

MOFA Archives 2002-2012 http://www.mofa.go.jp/mofaj/gaiko/un_cd/gun_un/archive.html#ketsugian_others

Accessed: 8 January 2013

MOFA Archives 2001: Disarmament and Non-Proliferation – Japan's Proposal at the UN Assembly 2001 titled "Approach to Abolition of Nuclear Weapons"

http://www.mofa.go.jp/mofaj/gaiko/un_cd/gun_un/ketsu_2001.html

Accessed: 8 January 2013

Japan NGO Network for Nuclear Weapons Abolition, Kokuren Sokai Daiichi Iinkai Oyobi Raishun No Osuro Kaigi Ni Kansuru Shitumon (Questions on No 1 Committee of the UN Assembly and the Oslo

Conference in Spring Next Year), p2 http://nuclearabolitionjpn.files.wordpress.com/2012/11/20121119_ngoquestions.pdf

Accessed: 19 April 2013

House of Councillors Japan, Sangiin Shitumon Dai 82 Go “”Kakuheiki No Ikaku Mataha Shiyo No Gohosei Ni Kansuru Kokusai Shiho Saibansho Kankokuteki Iken No Follow UP” Ni Kansuru Shitumon Shui” – Migi No Shitumon Shuisho O Kokkai Ho Dai 74 Jo Ni Yotte Teishutsu suru. Heisei 22 Nen 11 Gatsu 4 Ka, Hamada Masayoshi. Nishioka Takeo Sangiinn Gicho Ate.

(No 82 of Question at the House of Councillors Japan “Memorandum on Questions regarding UN Resolution “Follow up of ICJ Advisory Opinion on Legality of Threat or Use of Nuclear Weapons”. Interpellator: Masayoshi Hamada, a member of the House and Komeito, to Speaker Takeo Nishioka, 4th November 2010) http://www.sangiin.go.jp/japanese/joho1/kousei/syuisyo/176/syup/s176082.pdf

Accessed: 7 January 2012

House of Councillors Japan, Sangiin Tobeinsho Dai 82 Go “Naikaku Sanshitsu 176 Dai 82 Go Heisei 22 Nenen 11 Gatsu 12 Nichi, Naikaku Sori Dajin Rinji Dairi Kokumu Daijin Sengoku Yoshito. Nishioka Takeo Sangiin Gicho Ate.

(No 83 of Written Answer [176-No82, 12 November 2011] from Acting Prime Minister / Minister of State Yoshito Sengoku to Speaker of the House of Councillors Takeo Nishioka)

http://www.sangiin.go.jp/japanese/joho1/kousei/syuisyo/176/toup/t176082.pdf

Accessed: 7 January 2012

Ministry of Defense Japan, “Kenpo To Zieitai” 2, Kenpo 9 Jo No Shushi Ni

Tsuite No Seifu Kenkai, (2) Zieiken Hatsudo No Yoken (Constitution and Self-Defense Force" 2, Japanese Government's Opinion on Meaning of Article 9 of the Constitution, (2) Conditions for Invoking Right of Self-Defense)
http://www.mod.go.jp/j/approach/agenda/seisaku/kihon02.html
Accessed: 23 February 2012

MOFA, Diplomatic Blue Book 1991, Chapter 2: Gulf War and Japanese Diplomacy, Section 2: Response to Gulf War, No 3: Support to Restore Peace in the Area of Gulf, No 5: Evaluation by the International Society
http://www.mofa.go.jp/mofaj/gaiko/bluebook/1991/h03-2-2.htm
Accessed: 9 August 2011

Prime Minister of Japan and His Cabinet (Prime Minister's Office Japan), Tero Taisaku Tokuso Ho Ni motozuku Taio Sochi No Zissi Oyobi Taio Sochi Ni Kansuru Kihon Keikaku Ni Tsuite, Anzenhosho Kaigi Kettei, Kakugi Kettei (Cabinet Decision and Decision of Security Council of Japan on Basic Plan of Measures for Action and Measures based on Special Anti-Terrorism Law)
http://www.kantei.go.jp/jp/kakugikettei/2001/1116keikaku.html
Accessed: 9 August 2011

Ministry of Defense Japan, Shokan Horei To – Shitsumon Shuisho Tobensho – 2008 Nen 4 Gatsu 27 Nichi No Nagoya Koto Saibansho Kakutei Hanketsu Ni Kansuru Shitsumon Ni Taisuru Tobensho (Fukuda Yasuo Naikaku Sori Daijin) (Related Laws – Memorandum on Questions and Written Response – Written Response to Questions on Final Judgement of Nagoya High Court on 27th April 2008 (by Prime Minister Yasuo Fukuda)
http://www.mod.go.jp/j/presiding/touben/169kai/syu/tou352.html
Accessed: 9 August 2011

MOFA, *Nichibei Kankei – 1, Nichibei Kankei Soron (Japan-US Relation -1 ,*

Outline of Japan-US Relation)
http://www.mofa.go.jp/mofaj/area/usa/kankei.html
Accessed: 24 January 2013

Kajima Institute of International Peace, Gaiko Shuyo Nenpyo 1 (Chronological Table of Japanese Diplomacy Vol. 1 [1941-1960]), Hara Shobo Co., Ltd., 1983, p718-p719

Sankei Newspaper, Kita Chosen No Taichu Boeki Izon, Hazimete 7 Wari Ni (Ratio of North Korean Dependency on Trade with China reached 70%), * this article appeared analysis of South Korean National Statistical Office, 27th December 2012
http://sankei.jp.msn.com/world/news/121227/kor12122723290005-n1.htm
Accessed: 5 March 2013

World News 15th April 2013, *Kerry: China must to do more to resolve North Korean missile crisis*
http://worldnews.nbcnews.com/_news/2013/04/15/17757742-kerry-china-must-do-more-to-resolve-north-korean-missile-crisis?lite
Accessed: 19 April 2013

Chugoku Newspaper, Nihon, Kaku Higohoka No Shomei Kyohi: Kokureni No 16Kakoku Seimeian (Japan refused to sign a document that describes nuclear weapons as inhumane, which was submitted by 16 countries to the UN committee), Masakatsu Oota (Kyodo Press Co., Ltd.), 19th October 2012
http://www.chugoku-np.co.jp/News/Sp201210190065.html
Accessed: 21 October 2012

Shultz, Perry, Kissinger, Nunn, *A World Free of Nuclear Weapons*, Wall Street Journal 2007,
http://online.wsj.com/news/articles/SB116787515251566636
http://www.pugwash.org/reports/nw/nuclear-weapons-free-statements

/NWFW_statements_USA.htm

Accessed: 11 October 2010

Katsuya Kodama (Vice-President Professor, Mie University, Japan), Hiroshima Nagasaki Purosesu: Kaku Haizetsumade No Genzitsuteki Gutaitekina Rodo Map (Hiroshima Nagasaki Process: A Realistic Road Map for Nuclear Abolition), 2013 http://bylines.news.yahoo.co.jp/kodamakatsuya/20130807-00027073/

Accessed: 3 June 2013

Obama's Prague Speech on Nuclear Weapons: FULL TEXT http://www.huffingtonpost.com/2009/04/05/obama-prague-speech-on-nu_n_183219.html

Accessed: 3 February 2010

US Department of State, South Pacific Nuclear Free Zone Treaty http://www.state.gov/www/global/arms/treaties/spnfz.html

Accessed: 5 January 2013

Association of Southeast Asian Nations, SANWFZT http://www.aseansec.org/asean-anthem/

Accessed: 5 January 2013

US Department of State, *African Nuclear Weapons Free Zone Treaty,* http://www.state.gov/www/global/arms/treaties/afrinwfz.html#1

Accessed: 5 January 2013

United Nations Office for Disarmament Affairs, *Treaty on a Nuclear-Weapons-Free-Zone (CANWFZ)* http://disarmament.un.org/treaties/t/canwfz/text

Accessed: 5th January 2013

INESAP, *Nuclear Weapons Conventions* http://www.inesap.org/publications/nuclear-weapons-convention

Accessed: 5 January 2013

Katsuya Kodama, Hiroshima Nagasaki Purosess: Kakuheikihaizetsu

Madeno Genzitsuteki Gutaiteki Na Rodomapu 1 (Hiroshima Nagasaki Process: Drawing A Roadmap to the Total Abolition of Nuclear Weapons 1), 2013
http://bylines.news.yahoo.co.jp/kodamakatsuya/20130807-00027073/
Accessed: 13 June 2013

ICBL, *Ban History*
http://www.icbl.org/index.php/icbl/Treaty/MBT/Ban-History
Accessed: 13 June 2013

Katsuya Kodama, 1, 2013
http://bylines.news.yahoo.co.jp/kodamakatsuya/20130807-00027073/
Accessed: 13 June 2013

Mayors for Peace, *Mayors for Peace 2020 Vision Campaign*
http://www.2020visioncampaign.org/en/about-us.html
Accessed: 13 June 2013

Katsuya Kodama, *Hiroshima Nagasaki Process: Kakuheikihaizetsu Madeno Genzitsuteki Gutaiteki Na Rodomapu* 2 (In English 'Hiroshima Nagasaki Process: Drawing A Roadmap to the Total Abolition of Nuclear Weapons 2'), 2013
http://bylines.news.yahoo.co.jp/kodamakatsuya/20130807-00027074/
Accessed: 13 June 2013

Kokkai Kaigiroku Kensaku Sisutemu, *Hamayotsu Toshiko Ni Yoru Komeito Daihyo Shitsumon*, Kokuritsu Kokkai Toshokan 3rd October 2008
(Search System of Record of the Proceedings of the Diet (Japan), Query by Representative of Komeito (Toshiko Hamayotsu, Acting Representative of Komeito) at Plenary Session of the House of Councillors, Japan, National Diet Library, 3rd October 2008')
http://kokkai.ndl.go.jp/cgi-bin/KENSAKU/swk_dispdoc.cgi?SESSION=13227&SAVED_RID=2&PAGE=0&POS=0&TOTAL=0&SRV_ID=9&DOC_ID=5123&DPAGE=1&DTOTAL=1&DPOS=1&SORT_DIR=1

&SORT_TYPE=0&MODE=1&DMY=15438

Accessed: 10 July 2010

Kokkai Kaigiroku Kensaku Sisutemu, *Aso Taro Naikaku Soridaijin No Toben*, Kokuritsu Kokkai Toshokan 3rd October 2008

(Search System of Record of the Proceedings of the Diet (Japan), Answer by Prime Minister Taro Aso to Toshiko Hamayotsu (Komeito), National Diet Library, 3rd October 2008) http://kokkai.ndl.go.jp/cgi-bin/KENSAKU/swk_dispdoc.cgi?SESSION=13227&SAVED_RID=2&PAGE=0&POS=0&TOTAL=0&SRV_ID=9&DOC_ID=5123&DPAGE=1&DTOTAL=1&DPOS=1&SORT_DIR=1&SORT_TYPE=0&MODE=1&DMY=15438

Accessed: 10 July 2010

Kokkai Kaigiroku Kensaku Sisutemu, Hamada Masayoshi (Komeito) No Shitsugi, Sangin Gaiko Boei Iinkai, 2009nen 7gatsu 2ka

(Search System of Record of the Proceedings of the Diet (Japan), Questions by Masayoshi Hamada (Komeito) , Committee on Foreign Affairs and Defence, House of Councillors, National Diet Library, 2nd July 2009) http://kokkai.ndl.go.jp/cgi-bin/KENSAKU/swk_dispdoc.cgi?SESSION=1333&SAVED_RID=2&PAGE=0&POS=0&TOTAL=0&SRV_ID=9&DOC_ID=5846&DPAGE=1&DTOTAL=3&DPOS=2&SORT_DIR=1&SORT_TYPE=0&MODE=1&DMY=2222

Accessed: 10 July 2010

Kokkai Kaigiroku Kensaku Sisutemu, Nakasone Hirofumi Gaimudaijin No Hamada Gin Heno Toben *, 2009nen 7gatsu 2ka*

(Search System of Record of the Proceedings of the Diet (Japan), Answer by Minister of Foreign Affairs Hirofumi Nakasone to Hamada, Committee on Foreign Affairs and Defence, House of Councillors, National Diet Library, 2nd July 2009) http://kokkai.ndl.go.jp/cgi-bin/KENSAKU/swk_dispdoc.cgi?SESSION

=1333&SAVED_RID=2&PAGE=0&POS=0&TOTAL=0&SRV_ID=9&DOC_ID=5846&DPAGE=1&DTOTAL=3&DPOS=2&SORT_DIR=1&SORT_TYPE=0&MODE=1&DMY=2222

Accessed: 10 July 2010

Komeito News, *To Suishi-ni Nichigokyodosengen De Iken Kokan: NGO Mo Sanka* (KCPANW held a session on the Joint Statement of Japanese and Australian Governments, and NGO joined the session), 20th February 2010 https://www.komei.or.jp/news/detail/20100220_496

Accessed: 18 August 2010

MOFA, The Report of the Tokyo forum for Nuclear-Non Proliferation and Disarmament

http://www.mofa.go.jp/mofaj/gaiko/t_forum99/tokyo_f.html

Accessed: 8 August 2010

Arms Control and Disarmament Division, Disarmament, Non-Proliferation and Science Department, MOFA, Japanese Disarmament and Non-Proliferation Diplomacy 2002 (White Paper), Chapter 8: Role of Civil Society,

http://www.mofa.go.jp/mofaj/gaiko/gun_hakusho/2002/hon8.pdf

Accessed: 25 October 2010

MOFA, *Report of Tokyo Forum: Part 1, The New Nuclear Dangers*, MOFA Archives, http://www.mofa.go.jp/policy/un/disarmament/forum/tokyo9907/report-1.html

Accessed: 25 October 2010

MOFA, *Financial Contribution to the United Nations 2003,* http://www.mofa.go.jp/mofaj/kids/ranking/un.html

Accessed: 25 October 2010

MOFA Archives, *Report of Tokyo Forum: Part 2, Mending Strategic Relations to Reduce Nuclear Dangers* http://www.mofa.go.jp/policy/un/disarmament/forum/tokyo9907/report-2.html

Accessed: 25 October 2010

Arms Control and Disarmament Division, Disarmament, Non-Proliferation and Science Department, MOFA, Japanese Disarmament and Non-Proliferation Diplomacy 2013 (White Paper), Chapter 8: Dialogue and Collaboration with Civil Society, p1
http://www.mofa.go.jp/mofaj/gaiko/gun_hakusho/2013/pdfs/hon1_8.pdf

Accessed: 9 November 2013

Arms Control and Disarmament Division, Disarmament, Non-Proliferation and Science Department, MOFA, *Japanese Disarmament and Non-Proliferation Diplomacy 2011 (White Paper), Chapter 7: Role of Civil Society,* p7
http://www.mofa.go.jp/mofaj/gaiko/gun_hakusho/2011/pdfs/hon1_7.pdf

Accessed: 9 November 2013

Arms Control and Disarmament Division, Disarmament, Non-Proliferation and Science Department, MOFA, Japanese Disarmament and Non-Proliferation Diplomacy 2013 (White Paper), Chapter 8: Dialogue and Collaboration with Civil Society, p157-p158
http://www.mofa.go.jp/mofaj/gaiko/gun_hakusho/2013/pdfs/hon1_8.pdf

Accessed: 9 November 2013

ICNND

http://icnnd.org/Pages/default.aspx

Accessed: 9 November 2013

MOFA, *List of Attendees at Meeting between ICNND and NGOs,*
http://www.mofa.go.jp/mofaj/gaiko/icnnd/

Accessed: 9 November 2013

Declaration calling for the abolition of nuclear arms by Soka Gakkai Second President

http://www.joseitoda.org/vision/declaration/
Accessed: 1 December 2012
PSR official website
http://www.psr.org/about/
Accessed: 1 December 2012
IPPNW official website, *IPPNW Affiliate Directory*
http://www.ippnw.org/affiliates-directory.html
Accessed: 1 December 2012
Nobel Peace Prize 1985
http://www.nobelprize.org/nobel_prizes/peace/laureates/1985/press.html
Accessed: 1 December 2012
Tadatoshi Akiba, Specially Appointed Professor, University of Hiroshima, Former Mayor of Hiroshima, *the 29th Seminar on International Cooperation, "Elimination of Nuclear Weapons by 2020! Peace and the Role of Citizens"*, at the University of Tokyo, 21st October 2011
http://inter.k.u-tokyo.ac.jp/seminar_event/is_seminar/pdf/event_29.pdf
Accessed: 1 December 2012
IPPNW Japan Chapter, *About us,*
http://www.hiroshima.med.or.jp/ippnw/nihonshibu/index.html
Accessed: 14 October 2012
Research Institute for Radiation Biology and Medicine, Hiroshima University
http://www.rbm.hiroshima-u.ac.jp/
Accessed: 14 October 2012
IPPNW Japan Chapter, *About us*,
http://www.hiroshima.med.or.jp/ippnw/nihonshibu/index.html
Accessed: 14 October 2012
Japan Medical Association

http://www.med.or.jp/english/about_JMA/index.html

Accessed: 1 December 2012

Kakuheiki Haizetsuni Kansuru Ketsugi (Resolution of Japan Medical Association for Elimination of Nuclear Weapons), 2009

http://www.antiatom.org/Gpress/?p=470

Accessed on 16 December 2012

PNND Japan

http://www.pnnd.jp/about.html

Accessed: 16 December 2012

Kita Azia Chiiki Kaigi (North Asia Regional Conference)
http://www.hiroshima.med.or.jp/ippnw/ippnwnitsuite/kitaasia.html

Accessed: 22 November 2012

JPPNW, *Dai Ikkai Kita Azia Chiiki Kaigi (1st North Asia Regional Conference)*
http://www.hiroshima.med.or.jp/ippnw/ippnwnitsuite/1ippnw19971123.html

Accessed: 22 November 2012

JPPNW, *Dai Nikai Kita Azia Chiiki Kaigi (2nd North Asia Regional Conference)*
http://www.hiroshima.med.or.jp/ippnw/ippnwnitsuite/2ippnw19991016.html

Accessed: 22 November 2012

JPPNW, *Kita Azia Chiiki Kaigi (North Asia Regional Conference)*
http://www.hiroshima.med.or.jp/ippnw/ippnwnitsuite/kitaasia.html

Accessed: 1 December 2012

JPPNW, *Dai Yonkai Kita Azia Chiiki Kaigi (4th North Asia Regional Conference)*
http://www.hiroshima.med.or.jp/ippnw/ippnwnitsuite/4ippnw2003105.html

Accessed: 1 December 2012

JPPNW, *Dai Gokai Kita Azia Chiiki Kaigi* (tt '5th North Asia Regional Conference') http://www.hiroshima.med.or.jp/ippnw/ippnwnitsuite/5ippnw2005821.html

Accessed: 1 December 2012

JPPNW, *Statement on Nuclear-Weapon-Free Zones*, IPPNW 6th North Asia Regional Meeting Ulaanbaatar, Mongolia, 22th June 2007 http://www.hiroshima.med.or.jp/ippnw/ippnwnitsuite/6ippnw2007622.html

Accessed: 1 December 2012

Japanese Government, Headquarters for the Abduction Issue, Government of Japan, *Seifu Nintei 17 Mei Ni Kakawaru Zian* (Abduction Issue of 17 People by the North Korea)

http://www.rachi.go.jp/jp/ratimondai/jian.html

Accessed: 21 May 2013

MOFA, Rachi Mondai No Kaiketsu: Sonota Kitachosen Tokyoku Niyoru Zinken Shingai Mondai He No Taisho Ni Kansuru Seifu No Torikumi Ni Tsuite No Hokoku (Report of Japanese Government Policy and Activities regarding Issues of Abduction and Abuse of Human Rights by the North Korea) http://www.mofa.go.jp/mofaj/press/pr/pub/pamph/pdfs/rachi_torikumi.pdf

Accessed: 28 February 2014

Japan Prime Minister's Office Archives, Koizumi Sori No Enzetsu Kishakaiken Tou, Nichou Pyongyang Sengen (Prime Minister Koizumi's speech and press conference, the Japan-North Korea Pyongyang Declaration), 2002 http://www.kantei.go.jp/jp/koizumispeech/2002/09/17sengen.html

Accessed: 28 February 2014

National Police Agency Japan, Tokutei Shissousha Mondai Chosaikai (Investigation Commission on Missing Japanese Probably Related to North Korea), *Keisatsu No Tokutei Shissousha Lisuto* (List of Missing People by the National Police Agency Japan'), 2012, http://www.chosa-kai.jp/121230.html

Accessed: 28 February 2014

United Nations Information Centre, Kitachosen No Zinken Ni Kansuru Kokuren Chosa Iinkai, Hokokusho O Happyo, Kohani Ni Wataru Zindo Ni Taisuru Tsumi O Shiteki (UN Commission on DPRK's Abuse of Human Rights made the final document and indicated its broad crime against human rights), 2014

http://www.unic.or.jp/news_press/info/6912/

Accessed: 21 May 2014

JPPNW, *The 8th IPPNW North and South Asia Joint Regional Conference, Kathmandu Declaration*, 6th March 2011 http://www.hiroshima.med.or.jp/ippnw/ippnwnitsuite/8ippnw201036.html

Accessed: 7 December 2012

ECRR

http://www.euradcom.org/

Accessed: 7 December 2012

John Loretz, *IPPNW has been a constant voice against nuclear energy*, IPPNW Peace and Health Blog, 17th March 2011 http://peaceandhealthblog.com/2011/03/17/reject-nuclear/ Accessed: 7 December 2012

IPPNW European Affiliate, Nuclear Energy and Security http://www.ippnw-europe.org/en/nuclear-energy-and-security.html

Accessed: 7 December 2012

InterAction Council (IAC), About Us
http://www.interactioncouncil.org/about-us
Accessed: 7 December 2012
IAC, 2010 List of Participants
http://interactioncouncil.org/2010-0
Accessed: 7 December 2012
IAC, *The Hiroshima Declaration: A plea for zero nuclear weapons*, publications, 19th April 2010
http://interactioncouncil.org/hiroshima-declaration-plea-zero-nuclear-weapons-0
Accessed: 7 December 2012
IAC, *Accomplishments: The Cold War Era*
http://interactioncouncil.org/accomplishments
Accessed: 7 December 2012
The Elders: Independent Global Leaders Working Together for Peace and Human Rights
http://theelders.org/
Accessed: 3 May 2012
International Conference Center Hiroshima
http://www.pcf.city.hiroshima.jp/icch/english.html
Accessed: 20 November 2013
Hiroshima Peace Culture Foundation (HPCF), *About HPCF*
http://www.pcf.city.hiroshima.jp/hpcf/english/about/index.html
Accessed: 20 November 2013
Mayors for Peace, *Heiwa Shuchokaigi Kiyaku (MP's Covenant)*
http://www.mayorsforpeace.org/jp/outlines/agreement.html
Accessed: 20 November 2013
Mayors for Peace, *Map Showing Member Cities*
http://www.mayorsforpeace.org/english/membercity/map.html

Accessed: 20 November 2013

United Nations, The Secretary-General, *Message to the General Conference of Mayors for Peace, Hiroshima 3rd August 2013* http://www.mayorsforpeace.org/jp/activites/meeting/8th/statements/UN_Secretary_General_en.pdf

Accessed: 20 November 2013

Mayors for Peace, Protocol complementary to the Treaty on the Non-Proliferation of Nuclear Weapons for achieving a nuclear-weapon-free world by the year 2020 http://www.mayorsforpeace.org/jp/activites/others/100625_hn_giteisho/h_n_protocol.pdf

Accessed: 20 November 2013

Mayors for Peace, *Hiroshima Nagasaki Protocol* http://www.2020visioncampaign.org/en/about-us/history/hiroshima-nagasaki-protocol.html

Accessed: 20 November 2013

Mayors for Peace, *2020 Vision Campaign* http://www.mayorsforpeace.org/jp/ecbn/index.html

Accessed: 20 November 2013

Mayors for Peace, Hiroshima Nagasaki Giteisho Sando Shomei ZichitaiIchiran (Kaigai) (List of Foreign Cities signed to support the Hiroshima Nagasaki Protocol) http://www.mayorsforpeace.org/jp/activites/others/100625_hn_giteisho/cities_appeal.pdf

Accessed: 20 November 2013

Mayors for Peace, *Hiroshima Nagasaki Giteisho (Hiroshima Nagasaki Protocol)* http://www.mayorsforpeace.org/jp/activites/others/100625_hn_giteisho/index.html

Accessed: 20 November 2013

Mayors for Peace, 2020 Vision Kakuheiki Haizetsu No Tameno Kinkyukodo (Urgently Taking Action for 2020 Vision Campaign)

http://www.mayorsforpeace.org/jp/ecbn/index.html

Accessed: 20 November 2013

Mayors for Peace, *Hiroshima Appeal,* 2013 http://www.mayorsforpeace.org/jp/activites/meeting/8th/20130805_hiroshima_appeal.pdf

Accessed: 20 November 2013

Mayors for Peace, *Responses from the UN and national governments to the Hiroshima Appeal adopted at the 8th General Conference* http://www.mayorsforpeace.org/english/activities/meeting/8th/res_to_appeal/index.html

Accessed: 20 November 2013

The United States Conference of Mayors, *About USCM* http://www.usmayors.org/about/overview.asp

Accessed: 20 November 2013

The United States Conference of Mayors, Legislation and Programs, International

http://usmayors.org/international/

Accessed: 20 November 2013

Mayors for Peace, *USCM Dai 77 Kai Nenzi Sokai Heno Shusseki 2009 Nen 6 Gatsu (Attended the 77th USCM Annual Conference, June 2009)* http://www.mayorsforpeace.org/jp/gallery/2009_uscm.html

Accessed: 20 November 2013

Mayors for Peace, Full text of a resolution in support of Mayors for Peace, Adopted at the 79th US Conference of Mayors annual meeting, Baltimore, MD, June 20 2011 http://www.mayorsforpeace.org/english/topic/2011/110712_us_conferen

ce_of_mayors/index.html

Accessed: 20 November 2013

Mayors for Peace, Full text of a resolution in support of Mayors for Peace, Adopted at the 80th US Conference of Mayors annual meeting, Orlando, Florida, June 16 2012

http://www.mayorsforpeace.org/english/topic/2012/201206_us_conference_of_mayors/index.html

Accessed: 21 November 2013

Mayors for Peace, Full text of a resolution in support of Mayors for Peace, Adopted at the 81st US Conference of Mayors annual meeting, Las Vegas, Nevada, June 24 2013

http://www.mayorsforpeace.org/english/topic/2013/20130624_us_conference_of_mayors/index.html

Accessed: 21 November 2013

Kamakura Kyujo No Kai (Association For Protecting Article 9 of Japanese Constitution in Kamakura City), Tadatoshi Akiba's Lecture "To Become World Without Nuclear Energy and Weapons After Great East Japan Earthquake [11th March 2011]", November 2011

http://kamakura9-jo.net/cn17/pg151.html

Accessed: 21 November 2013

Osaka City Official Website, *All Population Data is from November 2010 (in Japanese)*,

http://www.city.osaka.lg.jp/toshikeikaku/cmsfiles/contents/0000014/14987/H22-11-H23-9suikei.pdf

Accessed: 24 November 2013

Chugoku Newspaper, Heiwa Shicho Kaigi Kamei "Shiranai" Hashimoto Osaka Shicho (Hashimoto, Mayor of Osaka City said he does not know the City is a member of MP) 16th November 2011

Chugoku Newspaper, Hikakusangensoku "Minaoshimo" Hashimotoshi

"Mocikomasezu" De Genkyu (Mr. Hashimoto referred to amend the Three Antinuclear Principles)
http://www.hiroshimapeacemedia.jp/mediacenter/article.php?story=20121112103358265_ja
Accessed: 24 November 2013

Mayors for Peace, *Agenda item 3, Measures for strengthening Mayors for Peace's management system*, 2013
http://www.mayorsforpeace.org/english/activities/meeting/8th/Agenda3_Measures_for_strengthening_Mayors_for_Peaces_management_system.pdf
Accessed: 24 November 2013

ICAN, *Campaign overview*
http://www.icanw.org/campaign/campaign-overview/
Accessed: 26 November 2013

ICAN, *Partner Organisations*
http://www.icanw.org/campaign/partner-organizations/
Accessed: 26 November 2013

ICAN, hear the stories
http://www.icanw.org/category/hear-the-stories/
Accessed: 26 November 2013

ICAN, Don't Bank on the Bomb
http://www.dontbankonthebomb.com/
Accessed: 26 November 2013

ICAN, Parliamentary Appeal
http://www.icanw.org/projects/appeal/
Accessed: 26 November 2013

Kenichi Okubo (JALANA Secretary-General, Advocate of Japan), *Kakuheiki No Ihousei No Kakuritsu No Tameni ! (To Establish Illegality of Nuclear Weapons!)*, JALANA Official Website, 2007

http://www.hankaku-j.org/infomation/data/080923_02.html
Accessed: 27 November 2013

IALANA Official Website, *About us*
http://en.ialana.de/about-us/
Accessed: 27 November 2013

IALANA Official Website, About us, 'United States, Canada, Germany, the Netherlands, New Zealand, India '
http://en.ialana.de/about-us/
Accessed: 27 November 2013

Kenichi Okubo, *Genbaku Nintei Saiban Ni Tsuite (About Trials to Certify Radiation Sickness)*, JALANA Official Website
http://www.hankaku-j.org/data/jalana/002.html
Accessed: 27 November 2013

Ministry of Health, Labour and Welfare Japan, *Genbaku-sho Nintei (About Certifying Radiation Sickness*,
http://www.mhlw.go.jp/bunya/kenkou/genbaku09/08.html
Accessed: 27 November 2013

Ministry of Justice Japan, *Genbaku-sho Nintei Sosho (Trials to Certify Radiation Sickness)*,
http://www.moj.go.jp/shoumu/shoumukouhou/shoumu01_00027.html
Accessed: 27 November 2013

Kenichi Okubo, *Genbaku Nintei Saiban Ni Tsuite (About Trials to Certify Radiation Sickness)*, JALANA Official Website
http://www.hankaku-j.org/data/jalana/002.html
Accessed: 28 November 2013

Japan Federation of Bar Associations (JFBA), *Declaration of a Call to Action Toward Achieving a World Without Nuclear Weapons*, 2010
http://www.nichibenren.or.jp/en/document/statements/year/2010/20101008_4.html

Accessed: 28 November 2013

JFBA, *Declaration of a Call to Action Toward Achieving a World Without Nuclear Weapons*, 2010 http://www.nichibenren.or.jp/en/document/statements/year/2010/20101008_4.html

Accessed: 28 November 2013

Nihon Hidankyo (Japan Confederation of A-and H-Bomb Suffers Organisations), T*okyo Genbaku Saiban (Tokyo Trial on Dropping Atomic Bombs)* http://www.ne.jp/asahi/hidankyo/nihon/rn_page/menu_page/side_menu_page/saiban_sosyou/tokyosaiban.htm

Accessed: 28 November 2013

JALANA, *Shin Genbaku Saiban Koso (Plan of New Trial Accusing Dropping Atomic Bombs by the United States) by Kenichi Okubo*, 20th August 2006 http://www.hankaku-j.org/data/hoka/004.html

Accessed: 28 November 2013

Japan NGO Network for Nuclear Weapons Abolition [JNNNWA] http://nuclearabolitionjpn.wordpress.com/

Purpose http://nuclearabolitionjpn.wordpress.com/about/

Accessed: 19 August 2013

JNNNWA, *Gaimusho tono Iken Kokankai (Meetings with MOFA, Nuclear Regulatory Agency, and Nuclear Regulatory Committee)* http://nuclearabolitionjpn.wordpress.com/?s=%E6%84%8F%E8%A6%8B%E4%BA%A4%E6%8F%9B%E4%BC%9A

Accessed: 29 November 2013

JNNNWA, Kokurensokai Daiichi Iinkai Oyobi Raishun No Osuro Kaigi Ni *Kansuru Sitsumonsho (Written Inquiry to Foreign Minister on the UN 1st Committee Resolution and Oslo Conference)*, 19th November 2012 http://nuclearabolitionjpn.files.wordpress.com/2012/11/20121119_ngoq

uestions.pdf
Accessed: 29 November 2013

JNNNWA, *Kakuheiki No Higohoka O Meguri Gaimusho To Ikenkoukankai O Okonaimashita* (JNNNWC and MOFA held a meeting for discussion how to make use of nuclear weapons illegal'), 22nd November 2012
http://nuclearabolitionjpn.wordpress.com/2012/11/22/mofaroundtable_report20121121/
Accessed: 29 November 2013

Chatham House, Experts, Dr. Patricia Lewis, Research Director of International Security
http://www.chathamhouse.org/about-us/directory/182053
Accessed: 29 November 2013

ICAN, *ICAN Civil Society Forum*
http://www.icanw.org/campaign-news/norway/oslo-civil-society-forum/
Accessed: 29 November 2013

ICAN, *Report : ICAN Civil Society Forum 2013*
http://goodbyenukes.wordpress.com/
Accessed: 29 November 2013

HPCF Heiwa Bunka (Japanese Newsletters) No. 83, *Noruwe Osuro De Kaisai Sareta Shiminshaki Foramu Heno Shusseki (Attended to a Civil Society Forum in Oslo, Norway)*
http://www.pcf.city.hiroshima.jp/hpcf/heiwabunka/pcj183/Japanese/02J.html
Accessed: 29 November 2013

People's Decade for Nuclear Abolition (SGI's special website for nuclear weapons abolition), *Exhibition Tour, SGI Participates in Oslo Conference on Humanitarian Impact of Nuclear Weapons*, 2013
http://www.peoplesdecade.org/decade/exhibition/eyt/2013/130305.html
Accessed: 29 November 2013

Kenichi Okubo, *Kitachosen no Kakubuso Kyoka o Kaerutameni (To Stop Escalation of the North Korean Nuclear Armament)*, JALANA 2009 http://www.hankaku-j.org/data/hoka/007.html

Accessed: 1 December 2013

Kenichi Okubo, Kakuhaizetsu Joyaku Soki Zitsugen No Tame Ni – Kokusai Minshu Horitsukyokai Hanoi Taikai De No Zimukyokucho Speech (To Make the Nuclear Weapons Conventions to Force Immediately – Speech by JALANA's Secretary-General at the Conference of International Association of Democratic Lawyers [IADL] in Hanoi),

JALANA Official Website, 2009

http://www.hankaku-j.org/infomation/data/090619.html

Accessed: 1 December 2013

Kenichi Okubo, *Kitachosen no Kakubuso Kyoka o Kaerutameni (To Stop Escalation of the North Korean Nuclear Armament)*, JALANA 2009 http://www.hankaku-j.org/data/hoka/007.html

Accessed: 1 December 2013

Seikyo Online, Goaisatsu (Greeting)

http://www.seikyoonline.jp/seikyo/

Accessed: 1 December 2013

George Shultz, [Document Type: Commentary] Cold War: Reykjavik (Reagan-Gorbachev) Summit (Shultz memoirs), Margaret Thatcher Foundation, 12th October 1986

http://www.margaretthatcher.org/document/110620

Accessed: 1 December 2013

Nivedita Das Kundu, *Celebrating the 25th Anniversary of the Delhi Declaration, Russia & India Report*, 25 November 2011 http://in.rbth.com/articles/2011/11/25/celebrating_the_25th_anniversary_of_the_delhi_declaration_13302.html

Accessed: 7 June 2012

MOFA, *Diplomatic Blue Book 1991*,
http://www.mofa.go.jp/mofaj/gaiko/bluebook/1991/h03-4-4.htm
Accessed: 20 March 2010

Seikyo Online, Rosia Kokka Ga Jokun O Kettei Ikeda SGI Kaicho Ni Yuko Kunsho (Russian Government decided to confer its Order of Friendship to SGI President Ikeda), 1st February 2008
http://www.seikyoonline.jp/news/headline/2008/02/1185504_2144.html
Accessed: 19 March 2010

MOFA, Nichiro Kenzin Kaigi Dai 1 Kai Kaigo Kekka Gaiyo (Result Summary: The 1st Conference of Japanese-Russian High-Level Expert Group), 14th April 2004
http://www.mofa.go.jp/mofaj/area/russia/kenjin01_gai.html
Accessed: 4 February 2010

MOFA, Nichiro Kenzin Kaigi Dai 2 Kai Kaigo: Nichiro Shinzidai Ni Mukete (The 2nd Conference of Japanese-Russian High-Level Expert Group: Toward A New Era of Japanese-Russian Relationship), 2nd February 2005
http://www.mofa.go.jp/mofaj/area/russia/kenjin02_b3.html
Accessed: 4 February 2010

MOFA, Nichiro Kenzin Kaigi Dai 3 Kai Kaigo Kekka Gaiyo (Result Summary: The 3nd Conference of Japanese-Russian High-Level Expert Group), 27th March 2006
http://www.mofa.go.jp/mofaj/area/russia/kenjin03_gai.html
Accessed: 4 February 2010

BOBGELDOF.COM, *Live Aid*,
http://www.bobgeldof.com/content.asp?section=31
Accessed: 17 October 2013

CatholicHerald.co.uk, *Geldof attacked Howe*, originally printed in the 6th June 1989 http://archive.catholicherald.co.uk/article/6th-june-1986/3/geldof-attacks-howe

Accessed: 4 February 2010

BBC News, *Geldof nominated for Nobel Prize*, 6th July 2005 http://news.bbc.co.uk/2/hi/entertainment/4657627.stm

Accessed: 17 October 2013

SokaNet, Zindo Shien (Humanitarian Aid)

http://www.sokanet.jp/hbk/heiwa.html

Accessed: 17 October 2013

Soka net, SGI No Gaiyo (Overview of SGI)

http://www.sokanet.jp/sgi/gaiyo.html

Accessed: 17 October 2013

Association of Youthful Priests Dedicated to the Reformation of Nichiren Shoshu, *Dai Ku Kanki No Uta Ha Gedo Raisan (Singing the Beethoven's 9th Symphony is Praising Non-Buddhist Teachings)*, 16th December 1990 http://www.nichiren.com/jp/organ/organ02/org02_2.html

Accessed: 4 May 2012

Josei Toda, *Declaration Calling for the Abolition of Nuclear Weapons*, http://www.joseitoda.org/vision/declaration

Accessed: 9 January 2010

Daisaku Ikeda, Leonardo's Universal Vision and the Parliament of Humanity, 1994

http://www.daisakuikeda.org/sub/resources/works/lect/lect-05.html

Accessed: 9 January 2010

WMDC http://www.un.org/disarmament/education/wmdcommission/index.html

Accessed: 19 May 2011

WMDC Report, *Recommendation 26, etc, Weapons of Terror - Freeing the World of Nuclear, Biological and Chemical Arms,* 2006
http://www.isn.ethz.ch/Digital-Library/Publications/Detail/?ord588=grp2&ots591=0C54E3B3-1E9C-BE1E-2C24-A6A8C7060233&lng=en&id=26614
Accessed: 19 May 2011

DERASAT
http://www.derasat.org.bh/
Accessed: 19 May 2011

Ministry of Foreign Affairs Mexico, *Second Conference on the Humanitarian Impact of Nuclear Weapons 2014*,
http://www.sre.gob.mx/en/index.php/humanimpact-nayarit-2014
Accessed: 21 August 2014

United Nations Office for Disarmament Affairs, Third Session of the Preparatory Committee for the 2015 Review Conference of the Parties to the Treaty on the Non-Proliferation of Nuclear Weapons (NPT) 28April-9 May 2014,
http://www.un.org/disarmament/WMD/Nuclear/NPT2015/PrepCom2014/index.shtml
Accessed: 21 August 2014

SGI, Joint Statement of US Religious Committees on the Humanitarian Consequences of Nuclear Weapons – Making a Difference: Faith Communities and the Humanitarian Impact of Nuclear Weapons, 24th April 2014
http://www.sgi.org/assets/pdf/Joint-Faith-Statement-Antinukes.pdf
Accessed: 21 August 2014

SGI, *Press Release: US Faith Group Unite to Call for Nuclear Weapons Abolition, Stressing Devastating Humanitarian Impact*, 25th April 2014 http://www.sgi.org/news/press-releases/press-release-2014/us-faiths-call-for-nuclear-weapons-abolition.html

Accessed: 27 April 2014

Seikyo Online, Obama Daitoryo Enzetsu Ni SGI Kaicho O Shotai: Harada Kaicho Ga Dairi Shusseki (tt, The SGI President was invited to the President Obama's Speech, and President Harada of the Soka Gakkai Japan attended instead), 15th November 2009 http://www.seikyoonline.jp/news/headline/2009/11/1186692_2447.html

Accessed: 2 February 2011

Reuters, Kissinger, Shultz back Obama to push eliminate nuclear arms, 20th May 2009 http://blogs.reuters.com/talesfromthetrail/2009/05/19/kissinger-shultz-back-obama-push-to-eliminate-nuclear-arms/

Accessed: 16 January 2010

Hiroshima Heiwa Media Center of Chugoku Shimbun (Hiroshima Peace Media Center of the Chugoku Newspaper), *Hiroshima No Kiroku 1978 1Gatsu (The Records of Hiroshima in January 1978)* http://www.hiroshimapeacemedia.jp/mediacenter/article.php?story=20100628120059236_ja

Accessed: 18 November 2012

The United States Senate Committee on Foreign Relations, *Statement by Ms. Caroline Kennedy, Nominee for U.S. Ambassador to Japan, Senate Foreign Relations Committee*, September 19, 2013, pp3 http://www.foreign.senate.gov/imo/media/doc/Kennedy_Testimony.pdf

Accessed: 17 October 2013

Committee on Disarmament, Peace and Security of CoNGO

http://disarm.igc.org/

Accessed: 14 July 2011

NGOCDPS, *"Deleted Uranium Weapons – A Continuing Challenge in Working Toward a Ban"*

http://disarm.igc.org/index.php?view=article&id=351%3Adepleted-uranium-weapons-a-continuing-challenge-in-working-toward-a-ban&option=com_content&Itemid=77

Accessed: 3 November 2011

SGI, *The Oneness of Mentor and Disciple*,

http://www.sgi.org/buddhism/buddhist-concepts/the-oneness-of-mentor-and-disciple.html

Accessed: 3 November 2011

SGI, *Peace and Disarmament: "Transferring the Human Spirit" Shown at Roehampton University, UK*, Jan 24 2011

http://www.sgi.org/news/peace/peace2011/transforming-the-human-spirit-shown-at-roehampton-university-uk.html

Accessed: 3 November 2011

SGI, *Peace and Disarmament: Hiroshima Peace Day Event Held in UK*, Sep 3 2011

http://www.sgi.org/news/peace/peace2011/hiroshima-peace-day-event-held-in-uk.html

Accessed: 3 November 2011

SGI-UK, Youth Peace Committee,

http://www.sgi-uk.org/peace/youth-peace-committee

Accessed: 3 November 2011

Daisaku Ikeda, President of SGI, *Nuclear Abolition Proposal 2009: Building Global Solidarity Toward Nuclear Abolition*,

http://www.daisakuikeda.org/assets/files/disarm_p2009.pdf

Accessed: 3 November 2011

Hiroshima Soka Gakkai Official Website, *Peace Wave from Hiroshima ~1979* and 1990~

http://www.hiroshima-soka.jp/ayumi/ayumi_1.html

Accessed: 28 November 2012

Chugoku Newspaper, Kakuheiki Mitomenai 63% Soka Gakkai Gakusei Chosa (Research by Soka Gakkai Students Division: Only 63% said 'Using Atomic Bombs to Hiroshima and Nagasaki is not Acceptable), 24th August 2013 http://www.hiroshimapeacemedia.jp/mediacenter/article.php?story=20130828104735439_ja

Accessed: 30 September 2013

The People's Decade for Nuclear Abolition, *Survey: International Survey by SGI Youth Shows 91%Consider Nuclear Weapons Inhumane*, 2013 http://www.peoplesdecade.org/decade/survey/2013/130424.html

Accessed: 2 November 2013

People's Decade for Nuclear Abolition

http://www.peoplesdecade.org/

Accessed: 2 November 2013

Kokkai Toshokan (National Diet Library Japan), Kokkai Kaigiroku Kensaku Sisutem (Search System of Minutes of the Diet), *Takehisa Tsuji's Query to Prime Minister Eisaku Sato at the Plenary Session of the House of Councillors 26th November 1964*, (Komeito's first query at the Diet), only in Japanese

http://kokkai.ndl.go.jp/cgi-bin/KENSAKU/swk_dispdoc.cgi?SESSION=8922&SAVED_RID=1&PAGE=0&POS=0&TOTAL=0&SRV_ID=3&DOC_ID=12629&DPAGE=1&DTOTAL=17&DPOS=17&SORT_DIR=1&SORT_TYPE=0&MODE=1&DMY=11524

Accessed: 8 August 2010

Komeito Official Website, *Yamaguchi Vision 2010* https://www.komei.or.jp/policy/policy/vision.html

Accessed: 25 September 2011

Komeito Official Website, Kenpo 9 Jo Kenzi Subeki (We should keep

Article 9 of the Constitution), 15th March 2013

https://www.komei.or.jp/news/detail/20130315_10593

Accessed: 11 April 2013

Office of the Press Secretary, the White House, *Remarks by President Barack Obama at Suntory Hall, Tokyo, Japan*, 14th November 2009 http://www.whitehouse.gov/the-press-office/remarks-president-barack-obama-suntory-hall

Accessed: 27 May 2010

Komeito Official Website, *Kakuhaizetsu No Ridoyakuni (tt 'Komeito Leads to Promote Nuclear Abolition')*, 20th February 2010 https://www.komei.or.jp/news/detail/20100220_496

Accessed: 11 April 2013

MOFA, *Foreign Minister Kishita's Attendance at 8th NPDI Ministerial Meeting (Hiroshima, April 11-12, 2014)*, 2014 http://www.mofa.go.jp/dns/ac_d/page23e_000232.html

Accessed: 12 August 2014

Kokkai Toshokan (National Diet Library Japan), Kokkai Kaigiroku Kensaku Sisutem (Search System of Minutes of the Diet), *Masayoshi Hamada's Query to Foreign Minister Koichiro Genba at the Budget Committee of the House of Councillors 5th April 2012*, only in Japanese

http://kokkai.ndl.go.jp/cgi-bin/KENSAKU/swk_dispdoc.cgi?SESSION=8922&SAVED_RID=2&PAGE=0&POS=0&TOTAL=0&SRV_ID=9&DOC_ID=9157&DPAGE=1&DTOTAL=8&DPOS=6&SORT_DIR=1&SORT_TYPE=0&MODE=1&DMY=1963

Accessed: 3 February 2013

Soka Gakkai, Daihyo Teki Na Gosho: Rissho Ankokuron (the Most Major Writing of Nichiren "Rissho Ankokuron [On Establishing the Correct Teaching for the Peace of the Land]"), http://www.sokanet.jp/kaiin/kisokyogaku/gosho/01.html

Accessed: 16 July 2011

SOKAnet, *Soka Gakkai Ni Tsuite (About Soka Gakkai), Shodai Kaicho Makiguchi Tsunesaburo (First President Tsunesaburo Makiguchi)* http://www.sokanet.jp/info/president/makiguchi.html

Accessed: 16 July 2011

SOKAnet, Gairon (Outline)

http://www.sokanet.jp/info/gaiyo.html

Accessed: 6 January 2010

SOKAnet, Nichiren Daishonin No Goshogai: Rissho Ankoku Ron To Hounan (Life of Nichiren: "On Establishing the Correct Teaching for the Peace of the Land" and Religious Persecution), http://www.sokanet.jp/kaiin/kisokyogaku/nichiren/03.html

Accessed: 16 July 2011

Daisaku Ikeda, *Mahayana Buddhism and Twenty-First Century*, Ikeda Center for Peace, Learning, and Dialogue (based in Boston, USA) http://www.ikedacenter.org/20th-anniversary/founding-lecture

Accessed: 16 July 2011

Hidenori Tozawa (Professor of Graduate School of Law, Tohoku University), *Coudenhove-Kalergi To Soka Gakkai (Coudenhove-Kalergi and Soka Gakkai)*, RCK Forum http://www.law.tohoku.ac.jp/~tozawa/RCK%20HP/RCKjap3.htm

Accessed: 24 December 2012

Interviewed by Harry Kreisler, *The Quest for Peace: Conversation with Norman Cousins <Kennedy and Khrushchev>*, 12 September 1984 http://globetrotter.berkeley.edu/conversations/Cousins/cousins3.html

Ibid, *<The Dropping of the Atomic Bomb>* http://globetrotter.berkeley.edu/conversations/Cousins/cousins1.html

Ibid, *<Political Leaders and Public Opinion>* http://globetrotter.berkeley.edu/conversations/Cousins/cousins2.html

Ibid, <*The Peace Movement*>
http://globetrotter.berkeley.edu/conversations/Cousins/cousins4.html
Accessed: 11 August 2012

Delegate of Egypt, *Conference on Disarmament Discusses Nuclear Disarmament, News & Media UNOG*, 5 March 2013
http://www.unog.ch/80256EDD006B9C2E/%28httpNewsByYear_en%29/CA654DA3242244FAC1257B250067B11F?OpenDocument
Accessed: 3 April 2013

Kyoko Hamagawa, Chosa To Joho: Issue Brief No 547: Higashi Shina Kai Ni Okeru Nicchu Kyokai Kakutei Mondai (Research and Information: Issue Brief No 547: Issue of the Line of Demarcation between Japan and China in East China Sea), Section of Diplomacy and Defence, National Diet Library Japan, 16th June 2006, p1, p4
http://www.ndl.go.jp/jp/diet/publication/issue/0547.pdf
Accessed: 28 April 2013

MOFA, Higashi Shina Kai Ni Okeru Shigenkaihatsu Ni Kansuru Wagakuni No Hoteki Tachiba (Our Country's Legal Standpoint regarding the Issue of Developing Natural Resources in East China Sea), November 2008
http://www.mofa.go.jp/mofaj/area/china/higashi_shina/tachiba.html
Accessed: 8 December 2013

MOFA, *Japanese Territory: Senkaku Islands*,
http://www.mofa.go.jp/region/asia-paci/senkaku/index.html
Accessed: 8 December 2013

Jeremy Page and Norihiko Shirouzu, *Toyota Faces Fine in China at Sensitive Time for Ties*, The Wall Street Journal, 20th September 2010,
http://online.wsj.com/news/articles/SB10001424052748703399404575505601971499626?mg=reno64-wsj&url=http%3A%2F%2Fonline.wsj.com%2Farticle%2FSB10001424052748703399404575505601971499626.html

Accessed: 8 December 2013

The Epoch Time (English Edition), *Behind China's Anti-Japan Protests, the Hand of Officials*, 19th September 2012 http://www.theepochtimes.com/n2/china-news/behind-chinas-anti-japan-protests-the-hand-of-officials-292859.html

Accessed: 8 December 2013

The White House (Office of the Press Secretary), *Joint Press Conference with President Obama and Prime Minister Abe of Japan (at Akasaka Palace in Tokyo, Japan)*, 24th April 2014 http://www.whitehouse.gov/the-press-office/2014/04/24/joint-press-conference-president-obama-and-prime-minister-abe-japan

Accessed: 12 May 2014

Irib World Service, *Chugoku, Amerika Daitoryo No Senkaku Hatsugen Ni Hanpatsu (China Offended US President's Speech Regarding Senkaku Islands)*, 24th April 2014 http://japanese.irib.ir/news/latest-news/item/44769

Accessed: 12 May 2014

MOFA, Senkaku Shoto Ni Tsuite (About Senkaku Islands'), March 2013, p10

http://www.mofa.go.jp/mofaj/area/senkaku/pdfs/senkaku.pdf

Accessed: 5 June 2013

MOFA, Nicchu Shuno Kaidan (tt 'Japan-China Top-Level Meeting'), 13th May 2012

http://www.mofa.go.jp/mofaj/area/jck/summit2012/jc_gaiyo.html

Accessed: 12 May 2014

Stephen Harner, *After Yasukuni, China Closes The Door On Abe: Why Is He Smiling*, Forbes 1st February 2014 http://www.forbes.com/sites/stephenharner/2014/01/02/after-yasukuni-china-closes-the-door-on-abe-why-is-he-smiling/

Accessed: 12 May 2014

Sankei Newspaper, Nicchugiren Hochu O Chushi Chukinpei Shuseki Menkai Medo Tatazu (tt 'The Japan-China Friendship Parliamentarian's Union Gave Up To Visit China Because They Could Not Arrange Meeting With Xi Jinping'), 22nd April 2013 http://sankei.jp.msn.com/politics/news/130422/stt13042214000002-n1.htm

Accessed: 12 May 2014

Sankei Newspaper, Nicchugiren No Komura Shi Cho Shi To Senkaku Rekishi De Hageshii Oshu Nicchu Shuno Kaidan No Michisuji Miezu (Mr. Komura of the Japan-China Friendship Parliamentrian's Union and Mr. Zhang Traded Barbs Over History and Senkaku Island), 6th May 2014

http://sankei.jp.msn.com/politics/news/140506/plc14050608000003-n1.htm

Accessed: 12 May 2014

MOFA, *Meeting between Prime Minister Yoshiko Noda (Japan) and Prime Minister Wen Jiabao (China)*, 13th May 2012, Beijing http://www.mofa.go.jp/mofaj/area/jck/summit2012/jc_gaiyo.html

Accessed: 12 May 2014

Stephen Harner, *After Yasukuni, China Closes The Door On Abe: Why Is He Smiling*, Forbes 1st February 2014 http://www.forbes.com/sites/stephenharner/2014/01/02/after-yasukuni-china-closes-the-door-on-abe-why-is-he-smiling/

Accessed: 12 May 2014

MOFA, Dai 3 Sho: Waga Kuni To Kakkoku Tono Shomondai – Azia Nishi Azia O Nozoku (Issues between Our State and Other States – Asia except West Asia), Gaiko Seisho (Diplomatic Blue Book), 1963 http://www.mofa.go.jp/mofaj/gaiko/bluebook/1963/s38-3-5.htm#2

Accessed: 12 May 2014

People's Daily Online, Gaiko Bu: "Chugoku Ha Kaku Danto 250 Patsu Hoyu" To No Hokoku Ni Tsuite (Ministry of Foreign Affairs China: "About the Report that China is possessing 250 Nuclear Warheads"), 4 January 2013 http://j.people.com.cn/94474/8269873.html

17 December 2013

China-Japan Friendship Association http://211.144.130.250/index.php?m=content&c=index&a=show&catid=9&id=1433

Accessed: 19 January 2013

Tokyo Fuji Art Museum, *Tenran Kai Shosai: Maki-e Lacquer & Oriental Ceramics* http://www.fujibi.or.jp/exhibitions/profile-of-exhibitions.html?exhibit_id=2199709181

Accessed: 18 April 2014

The Nagasaki Shimbun (Nagasaki Newspaper), Chunichi Chugoku Taishi Ga Bakushinchi De Kenka "Rekishi Kyokun Ni Heiwa Kosei He" (Chinese Ambassador to Japan Offered Flowers at the Hypocentre: To Transmit the Historic Lesson to Posterity), 19th December 2010 http://www.nagasaki-np.co.jp/news/peace/2010/12/19124557.shtml

Accessed: 27 March 2011

The Elders: Independent Global Leaders Working Together for Peace and Human Rights http://www.theelders.org/

Ibid, *What do the Elders stand for?* http://www.theelders.org/about

Ibid, How Do They Work?

Ibid, How Can I Support The Elders' Work?

Ibid, On the delegation: Ela Bhatt, Gro Harlem Brundtland, Fernando Henrique Cardoso, Jimmy Carter, Mary Robinson and Desmond Tutu. http://theelders.org/israel-palestine/elders-work

Accessed: 13 October 2013

The Elders Report 2009, p9, p11-p12, p14 http://www.theelders.org/docs/middle-east/People-and-Peace-in-the-Middle-East.pdf

Accessed: 13 October 2013

Japan External Trade Organization, *Kisha Happyo (Press Release)*, 19th August 2014

http://www.jetro.go.jp/news/releases/20140819742-news

Accessed: 21 September 2014

The Elders, "A Just and Secure Peace for All: Report of The Elders' visit to Egypt, Gaza, Israel, Jordan, Syria, and the West Bank 15-22 October 2010" , p1-p2, p4 http://www.theelders.org/docs/middle-east/The_Elders_Middle_East_Trip_Report-October-2010.pdf

Accessed: 13 October 2013

The Elders, Press Release: We are heading towards a one-state outcome, 22 October 2012

http://theelders.org/article/we-are-heading-towards-one-state-outcome

Accessed: 13 October 2013

Shintaro Ishihara (Author & Japan Restoration Party), *Lecture at Japan Foreign Correspondence Club*, 20th November 2012

https://www.youtube.com/watch?v=ixXjZI-G5hA

Accessed: 5 May 2013

MOFA, Kishita Gaimu Daizin Kaiken Kiroku 2013 October 11th 12:35pm-Daijin Kaikenshitsu Mae (Record, Press Conference of Foreign Minister Kishita, 12:35pm in front of the Meeting Room of Foreign Minister Japan), October 2013

http://www.mofa.go.jp/mofaj/press/kaiken/kaiken4_000011.html

Accessed: 10 December 2013

Asahi Shimbun Digital (Asahi News Paper Digital), Kaku Fushiyou No Kyodo Seimei Ni Nihon Hatsusando (Japan signed the joint statement of non-use of nuclear weapons for the first time), 16th November 2013

http://www.asahi.com/articles/TKY201311160069.html

Accessed: 10 December 2013

Satomi Kyuko (National Diet Library Japan), Eikoku No Kaku Seisaku O Meguru Keii To Giron –Trident Koshin O Chushin Ni – (Process and Discussion about the British Nuclear Policy –Updating the Trident System -), National Diet Library Japan, November 2011, p94 http://ndl.go.jp/jp/diet/publication/refer/pdf/073005.pdf

Accessed: 21st July 2015)

CND, *171 arrests at Faslane nuclear base*, 1st October 2007, http://www.cnduk.org/cnd-media/item/465-171-arrests-at-faslane-nucle ar-base

Accessed: 21st July 2015

The Committee stood candidates in the British general election 1964 in Bromley and Twickenham, but they achieved only 1,534 votes.

Hawaii Book Library, *Radical Alliance* http://www.hawaiilibrary.com/articles/radical_alliance

Accessed: 21st July 2015

IWJ Independent Web Journal, *Interview with Kate Hudson (CND Secretary-General) in London 21st February 2013 (written in Japanese)* http://iwj.co.jp/wj/open/archives/60424

Accessed: 21st July 2015

British American Security Information Council, *US-UK Nuclear Cooperation, 1958 US-UK Mutual Defence Agreement* http://web.archive.org/web/20041221225546/http://basicint.org/nuclear/ 1958MDA.htm

Accessed: 21st July 2015

Atomic Weapons Establishment (AWE), *UK/US Agreement* http://web.archive.org/web/20080118030158/http://www.awe.co.uk/main_site/about_awe/history/timeline/1958/

Accessed: 21st July 2015

UK Government, *Announcement, Strategic Defence and Security Review Published, 19th October 2015* https://www.gov.uk/government/news/strategic-defence-and-security-review-published--2

Accessed: 21st July 2015

Political Stuff Site, *Archive of Labour Party Manifesto 1983* https://web.archive.org/web/20150330053201/http://www.labour-party.org.uk/manifestos/1983/1983-labour-manifesto.shtml

Accessed: 21st July 2015

UK Labour Party MP Gerald Kaufman

BBC News, *Foot's message of hope to left*, 14th July 2003 http://news.bbc.co.uk/2/hi/uk_news/politics/3059773.stm

Accessed: 21st July 2015

Labour CND, *Labour PPCs say Scrap Trident* http://www.labourcnd.org.uk/2015/02/labour-ppcs-say-scrap-trident/

Accessed: 22nd July 2015

Weekly Standard, *State Dept: U.S. Nukes Down 85%, From 31,255 to 4,804*, 19th December 2014 http://www.weeklystandard.com/blogs/state-dept-us-nukes-down-85-31255-4804_821888.html

Accessed: 1st August 2015

CNN, *U.S. reveals it has 5,113 nuclear warheads*, 3rd May 2010 http://edition.cnn.com/2010/POLITICS/05/03/us.nuclear.warhead.count / Accessed: 1st August 2015

G8 Information Centre, 1992 Munich Summit, *Political Declaration: Shaping the New Partnership*, Munich, 7 July 1992 http://www.g8.utoronto.ca/summit/1992munich/political.html

Accessed: 7th July 2015

Technical Secretariat on Cooperation for the Elimination of Nuclear Weapons Reduced in the Former Soviet Union, G8 Global Partnership: Nichiro Hikakuka Kyoryoku Russia Taeki Sensuikan Kaitai Kyoryoku Zigyo: Kibo No Hoshi (G8 Global Partnership: Russo-Japanese Cooperation on Denuclearization: Russo-Japanese Cooperation on Demolishing Retired Nuclear Submarines), September 2008 http://tecsec.org/pdf/kibounohoshi_j.pdf

Accessed: 7th July 2015

G8 Information Centre, 2002 Kananaskis Summit Documents: Statement by G8 Leaders: The G8 Global Partnership Against the Spread of Weapons and Materials of Mass Destruction, 27th June 2002 http://www.g8.utoronto.ca/summit/2002kananaskis/arms.html

Accessed: 19th July 2015

MOFA, Russia Taieki Gensen Kaitai Kyoryoku Zigyo "Kibo No Hoshi" (Cooperation on Demolishing Russian Retired Nuclear Submarines "Star of Hope"), 5th April 2010 http://www.mofa.go.jp/mofaj/gaiko/kaku/kyuso/star_of_hope.html#4

Accessed: 19th July 2015

Masanobu Inoue (Member of the JALANA Board of Directors), *Hiroshima Hanketsu No Gani (Meaning of the Judicial Decision in Hiroshima)*, JALANA official website http://www.hankaku-j.org/data/jalana/001.html Accessed: 19th July 2015

BBC News, *Enola Gay crew 'have no regrets'* 4th August 2005 http://news.bbc.co.uk/2/hi/americas/4743061.stm

Accessed: 20th July 2015

UN, C*harter of the United Nations* http://www.un.org/en/documents/charter/chapter3.shtml

Accessed: 20th July 2015

MOFA, Agreed Official Minutes Relating to the Agreement Regarding the Status of the United Nations Forces in Japan (signed at Tokyo, February 19, 1954. Published, June 1, 1954) http://www.mofa.go.jp/mofaj/gaiko/treaty/pdfs/B-S38-P1-3_4.pdf

Accessed: 20th July 2015

Kadena Air Base (US Stationary Forces in Japan), *Base hosts 1st RAAF training in Japan (by Tech. Sgt. Rey Ramon: 18th Wing Public Affairs)* 10th November 2007 http://www.kadena.af.mil/news/story.asp?id=123071589 Accessed: 9th August 2015

Thomas C. Schelling, *A world without nuclear weapons?*, On the Global Nuclear Future Vol. 1, American Academy of Arts & Sciences, Fall 2009 https://www.amacad.org/content/publications/pubContent.aspx?d=945 Accessed: 27th June 2015

Mari Izuyama & Shinichi Ogawa, Nuclear Policies of India and Pakistan, Bulletin Vol 5 of the National Institute for Defence Studies Japan (Ministry of Defence Japan), August 2002 p44 http://www.nids.go.jp/publication/kiyo/pdf/bulletin_j5-1_3.pdf

Accessed: 1st July 2015

BBC News, *Surviving Mumbai gunman convinced over attacks*, 3 May 2010 http://news.bbc.co.uk/2/hi/south_asia/8657642.stm

Accessed: 1st July 2015

BBC News, *Ukraine conflict: Putin 'was ready for nuclear alert'*, 15th March 2015 http://www.bbc.com/news/world-europe-31899680

Accessed: 1st July 2015

BBC News, *Putin: Russia to boost nuclear arsenal with 40 missiles*, 16th June 2015 http://www.bbc.com/news/world-33151125

Accessed: 1st July 2015

Steven Pifer, *Putin's nuclear saber-rattling: What is he compensating for?*, the Brookings 17th June 2015 http://www.brookings.edu/blogs/order-from-chaos/posts/2015/06/17-put in-nuclear-saber-rattling-pifer

Accessed: 1st July 2015

Josei Toda, *Declaration Calling for the Abolition of Nuclear Weapons*, Josei Toda Website Committee http://www.joseitoda.org/vision/declaration Accessed: 1st July 2015

The Nikkei (Newspaper) 15th May 2014, The Philippines, Chugoku No Minami Sina Kai Umetate Shashin Kokai (The Philippines exposed photos that China making reclaimed land in the South China Sea) http://www.nikkei.com/article/DGXNASGM1502R_V10C14A5FF1000 / Accessed: 3rd July 2015

MOFA, The 13th IISS Asian Security Summit – The Shangri-La Dialogue – Keynote Address by Shinzo ABE, Prime Minister, Japan "Peace and prosperity in Asia, forevermore, Japan for the rule of law, Asia for the rule of law, And the rule of law for all of us", 30th May 2014 http://www.mofa.go.jp/fp/nsp/page4e_000086.html

Accessed: 3rd July 2015

U.S Department of Defense, *Secretary of Defense Speech, IISS Shangri-La Dialogue,* 31st May 2015 http://www.defense.gov/speeches/speech.aspx?speechid=1857

Accessed: 3rd July 2015

MOFA, *The Three Principles on Transfer of Defence Equipment and Technology*, 1st April 2014

http://www.mofa.go.jp/press/release/press22e_000010.html
Accessed: 3rd July 2015

Reuters, Nihon Ga Tsuyomeru Minami Sina Kai He No Gunziteki Kanyo Chugoku Kensei No Nerai (Japan strengthens its military collaboration in the South China Sea, it aims to contain China), 16th March 2015, http://jp.reuters.com/article/marketsNews/idJPL4N0WE1YA20150316 Accessed: 4th July 2015

The Nikkei (newspaper) 1st August 2014, Seifu, Vietnam Ni Senpaku 6Seki Kyoyo Gaisho Kaidan De (Japanese government agreed to give 6 boats to Vietnam at the meeting between the Japanese and Vietnam government) http://www.nikkei.com/article/DGXLASDE01004_R00C14A8PP8000/ Accessed: 4th July 2015

Reuters, Nihon Ga Tsuyomeru Minami Sina Kai He No Gunziteki Kanyo Chugoku Kensei No Nerai (Japan strengthens its military collaboration in the South China Sea, it aims to contain China), 16th March 2015, http://jp.reuters.com/article/marketsNews/idJPL4N0WE1YA20150316 Accessed: 4th July 2015

Iskander Rehman, *Dragon in a Bathtub: Chinese Nuclear Submarines and the South China Sea*, Carnegie Endowment for International Peace, 9th March 2013 http://carnegieendowment.org/2013/03/09/dragon-in-bathtub-chinese-nuclear-submarines-and-south-china-sea
Accessed: 4th July 2015

Financial Times (FT), *US diplomat angers Seoul with comments on regional tension, 2nd March 2015* http://www.ft.com/cms/s/0/9e78bf88-c0b8-11e4-9949-00144feab7de.html#axzz3hDLvigMt
Accessed: 21st July 2015

United Nations, *2015 Review Conference of the Parties to the Treaty on the Non-Proliferation of Nuclear Weapons (NPT)*, 27th April to 22nd May 2015 http://www.un.org/en/conf/npt/2015/index.shtml

Accessed: 21st July 2015

Kyodo News, *Japan to keep urging world leaders to visit Hiroshima and Nagasaki*, 25th May 2015 https://english.kyodonews.jp/news/2015/05/354521.html

Accessed: 21st July 2015

Kazutaka Hisada, Public Diplomacy To Bunka Hasshin Kyoten: Nihon To Kankoku No Hikaku O Chushin Ni (Public Diplomacy and Basis of Culture Creation: Comparison between Japan and South Korea), No 180 Bulletin of Society of Humanities 2013, Kawagawa University (Japan) http://human.kanagawa-u.ac.jp/gakkai/publ/pdf/no180/18004.pdf

Accessed: 2nd August 2015

Record China, Nichukan Ha "Higashi Asia Kokyo Gaiko Kyodotai" No Kakuritu O: Seifu O Koeta Minkan No Chikara De Ittai To Naru (Japan, China and South Korea should create an "East Asian Public Diplomacy Community": Unify with Private Powers over Governments), 2nd August 2013 http://www.recordchina.co.jp/a75035.html

Accessed: 2nd August 2015

Kazutaka Hisada, Public Diplomacy To Bunka Hasshin Kyoten: Nihon To Kankoku No Hikaku O Chushin Ni (Public Diplomacy and Basis of Culture Creation: Comparison between Japan and South Korea), No 180 Bulletin of Society of Humanities 2013, Kawagawa University (Japan) http://human.kanagawa-u.ac.jp/gakkai/publ/pdf/no180/18004.pdf

Accessed: 2nd August 2015

UN Information Centre, Funso Yobo (Preventing Disputes)

http://www.unic.or.jp/activities/peace_security/conflict_prevention/
Accessed: 2nd August 2015

SHARE (a NGO that engages in international cooperation through health promotion), Interview with Professor Michio Ito of Rikkyo University Graduate School of Social Design Studies, Ima NGO Ga Hatasu Yakuwari Vol. 1 (Role of NGO Today Volume. 1), http://share.or.jp/opinion_advocacy/think/ito_michio_interview01.html Accessed: 1st May 2015

AAR Japan, History of AAR Japan the Ministry of Justice http://www.aarjapan.gr.jp/english/about/history.html
Accessed: 15th June 2015

Ministry of Justice Japan, *Press Release: Immigration Bureau of Japan 20th March 2014: Number of Refugee Status 2013 (in Japanese)* http://www.moj.go.jp/nyuukokukanri/kouhou/nyuukokukanri03_00099.html Accessed: 15th June 2015

Ministry of Justice Japan, *Press Release: Immigration Bureau of Japan 11th March 2015: Number of Refugee Status 2014 (in Japanese)* http://www.moj.go.jp/nyuukokukanri/kouhou/nyuukokukanri03_00103.html Accessed: 15th June 2015

The Network Aiming at the Coexistence with the Refugees in Japan http://www.rafiq.jp/event/101205nanmin_report.pdf
Accessed: 15th June 2015

NewsSphere 13th March 2015, Nihon No Nanmin Nintei 5000Nin Chu 11Nin To Senshinkoku Chu Saitei Shimaguni Ha Iiwakeni Naranai Kaigai Kara Hihan (Japanese Government gave only 11 people the refugee status out of 5,000. Their word "island country" cannot become a reason to refuse refugees)

http://newsphere.jp/politics/20150313-1/

Accessed: 15th June 2015

The Nikkei (newspaper) 13th February 2015, Kaigoshoku No Fukushoku Shien Nado Teian (30Man Nin Busoku De Koro Sho (It will be 300,000 employees short: the MHLW suggested supporting staffs, who were in nursing or care for aged, to reinstate)

http://www.nikkei.com/article/DGXLASFS13I14N_T10C15A2EE8000/

Accessed: 15th June 2015

CNN Politics, *Kerry: U.S. to accept more Syrian Refugees*, 20th September 2015

http://edition.cnn.com/2015/09/20/politics/syrian-refugees-john-kerry/index.html

Accessed: 21st September 2015

Asahi Shimbun Digital, Syria Nanmin Ukeire O Nihon Seifu Ni Yosei UNHCR Kyokucho (Director of UNHCR requested the Japanese government to receive Syrian refugees) 21st June 2015

http://www.asahi.com/articles/ASH6N443BH6NUHBI00D.html

Accessed: 5th July 2015

Gakudo-kai Official Website http://gakudo-kai.com/

Accessed: 20th June 2015)

The House of Representatives Japan, Questions from Jintaro Yokota (Member of the House) on 13th December 1950 and Answer from Prime Minister Yoshida on 11th January 1951,

http://www.shugiin.go.jp/internet/itdb_shitsumona.nsf/html/shitsumon/010025.htm

Accessed: 28th April 2015

Cabinet Office of Japanese Government, *Tokutei Hieiri Katsudo Towa*

(What is the Activities of Non-Profit Organisation?) https://www.npo-homepage.go.jp/about/npo-kisochishiki/nposeido-gaiyou Accessed: 1st May 2015

Professor Michio Ito of Rikkyo University Graduate School of Social Design Studies, *Ima NGO Ga Hatasu Yakuwari Vol. 1 (Role of NGO Today Volume. 1)*, SHARE (a NGO that engages in international cooperation through health promotion) http://share.or.jp/opinion_advocacy/think/ito_michio_interview01.html Accessed: 1st May 2015

Cabinet Office of Japanese Government, Hokokusho: Heisei 25Nendo Shimin No Shakai Koken Ni Kansuru Zittai Chosa (Report: Factual Survey of People's Contribution to Society 2015), p11 https://www.npo-homepage.go.jp/uploads/h25_shimin_chousa_all.pdf Accessed: 1st May 2015

Cabinet Office of Japanese Government, *Tokutei Hieiri Katsudo Hojin No Ninteisu No Suii (Transition of Number of Certified Non-Profit Organisations)*, https://www.npo-homepage.go.jp/about/toukei-info/ninshou-seni

Accessed: 1st May 2015

Professor Michio Ito of Rikkyo University Graduate School of Social Design Studies, *Ima NGO Ga Hatasu Yakuwari Vol. 1 (Role of NGO Today Volume. 1)*, SHARE (a NGO that engages in international cooperation through health promotion) http://share.or.jp/opinion_advocacy/think/ito_michio_interview01.html Accessed: 1st May 2015

MOFA, *ODA Budget (13th May 2015)* http://www.mofa.go.jp/mofaj/gaiko/oda/shiryo/yosan.html

Accessed: 10th May 2015)

MOFA, PALM http://www.mofa.go.jp/mofaj/area/ps_summit/

Accessed: 1st June 2015

MOFA, "A Beacon for Diplomacy toward PICs: Working to Establish a Society of Pacific Citizens" Keynote Speech by Prime Minister Shinzo Abe during the Opening Session of the Seventh Pacific Islands Leaders Meeting (PALM7) May 23, 2015 Iwaki, Fukushima http://www.mofa.go.jp/mofaj/files/000081724.pdf

Accessed: 1st June 2015

Hiroshi Nakanishi (Professor of Kyoto University), *Wangan Senso To Nihon Gaiko (The Gulf War and Japanese Diplomacy)* http://www.nippon.com/ja/features/c00202/

Accessed: 12th June 2015

Mainichi Shimbun 27th October 2014, Yureru Okoku: Thai "Kai Kaku" No Yukue /2 Sizi Eru Gunsei "Minshuka" (Shaking Kingdom: Thai "Road for Reformation" Part 2, Military Government is getting support) http://mainichi.jp/shimen/news/20141027ddm007030127000c.html

Accessed: 12th June 2015

Mainichi Shimbun 27th October 2014, Yureru Okoku: Thai "Kai Kaku" No Yukue /2 Sizi Eru Gunsei "Minshuka" (Shaking Kingdom: Thai "Road for Reformation" Part 2, Military Government is getting support) http://mainichi.jp/shimen/news/20141027ddm007030127000c.html

Accessed: 12th June 2015

MIAC, *2011 White Paper: Information and Communications in Japan* http://www.soumu.go.jp/johotsusintokei/whitepaper/ja/h23/html/nc213230.html

Accessed: 18th June 2015

MIAC, *2012 White Paper: Information and Communications in Japan* http://www.soumu.go.jp/johotsusintokei/whitepaper/ja/h24/html/nc1212c0.html

Accessed: 18th June 2015

Tomoyuki Yoshida of University of Tokyo, *Amerika Ni Okeru Ideorogi Teki Bunkyokuka To Sinku Tank (Ideological Polarization: American Think Tanks)*, US-Japan Research Institute (USJI) 21st July 2011 http://www.us-jpri.org/en/reports/seminar/miyata20110721_2.pdf

Accessed: 17th June 2015

Andrew Rich, War of Ideas: Why mainstream and liberal foundations and the think tanks they support are losing in the war of ideas in American politics, Stanford Social Innovation Review, Graduate School of Business, Stanford University Spring 2005 p24 http://www.ssireview.org/pdf/2005SP_feature_rich.pdf

Accessed: 17th June 2015

Tomoyuki Yoshida of University of Tokyo, *Amerika Ni Okeru Ideorogi Teki Bunkyokuka To Sinku Tank (Ideological Polarization: American Think Tanks)*, US-Japan Research Institute (USJI) 21st July 2011 http://www.us-jpri.org/en/reports/seminar/miyata20110721_2.pdf

Accessed: 17th June 2015

National Institute for Research Advancement (Japan) [NIRA], Outline of Survey Result of "Information of Think Tanks 2014", http://www.nira.or.jp/pdf/tt2014_gaiyo.pdf

Accessed: 17th June 2015

Ed Hale, White House Does Not Meet with Iran President Ahmadinejad during UN General Assembly Meeting But a Small Group of American Citizens Does, Peace with Iran 25th April 2007 http://www.peacewithiran.com/white-house-does-not-meet-with-iran-president-ahmadinejad-during-un-general-assembly-meeting-%E2%80%93-but-a-small-group-of-american-citizens-does/#more-86

Accessed: 16th June 2015

National Cherry Blossom Festival http://www.nationalcherryblossomfestival.org/

Accessed: 17th June 2015

The Japan-American Society of Washington DC, *55th Annual Sakura Matsuri Japanese Street Festival* http://www.sakuramatsuri.org/japanese/

Accessed: 17th June 2015

Sankei Shimbun 29th March 2015, "Nihon No Isan O Hokori Ni Sogo Rikai O" Zenbei Sakura Matsuri De Nikkeizin No Rekishi O Kataritsugu Shikiten (Be proud of Japanese legacy and promote mutual trust: holding event to share history of Japanese American at the National Cherry Blossom Festival) http://www.sankei.com/world/news/150329/wor1503290024-n1.html Accessed: 17th June 2015

Japan Audit Bureau of Circulations http://www.jabc.or.jp/

Accessed: 4th May 2015

Asahi Shimbun 27th January 2015, Soka Gakkai Ikeda Shi Ga Heiwa Teigen O Happyo (Mr. Ikeda of Soka Gakkai presented his peace proposal),

http://www.asahi.com/articles/DA3S11571431.html

Accessed: 3rd May 2015

Mainichi Shimbun 26th January 2015, Soka Gakkai: Ikeda Shi Ga Teigen (Soka Gakkai: Mr. Ikeda proposed),

http://mainichi.jp/shimen/news/20150126ddm041040100000c.html

Accessed: 3rd May 2015

Sankei Shimbun 26th January 2015, *Soka Gakkai No Ikeda Meiyo Kaicho Ga Heiwa Teigen (Honorary President of Soka Gakkai Ikeda presented his peace proposal),* http://www.sankei.com/life/news/150126/lif1501260028-n1.html Accessed: 3rd May 2015

The Yomiuri Shimbun 25th January 2014, Ikeda Meiyo Kaicho Datsu Genpatsu Izon He: Komeito Ni Eikyo Mo (Honorary President Ikeda will propose abandoning nuclear power generation: It will influence the Komeito),

http://www.yomiuri.co.jp/politics/news/20120125-OYT1T01096.htm

Accessed: 25th January 2014

The Yomiuri Shimbun 26th November 2014, *Summary of Manifesto: Liberal Democratic Party Japan*

http://www.yomiuri.co.jp/election/shugiin/2014/commitment/20141126-OYT8T50052.html

Accessed: 5th May 2015

Hiroshima Peace Media Centre (Chugoku Shimbun)

http://www.hiroshimapeacemedia.jp/?lang=ja

Accessed: 3rd May 2015

Hiroshima Peace Media Centre (Chugoku Shimbun), Kakuheiki Haizetsu He Renkei Yakusoku Peru Taishi Ga Hiroshima Shicho Hyokei (Agreed to cooperate for the nuclear abolition: Ambassador of Peru to Japan visited Mayor of Hiroshima City) 27th May 2013,

http://www.hiroshimapeacemedia.jp/?p=9821&query=%E5%89%B5%E4%BE%A1%E5%AD%A6%E4%BC%9A

Accessed: 3rd May 2015

Hiroshima City 23rd January 2015, *Request to US President Obama to visit Hibakuchi*,

http://www.city.hiroshima.lg.jp/www/sp/contents/1422240749304/index.html Accessed: 3rd May 2015

Shizuoka Shimbun 3rd March 2015, Fukushima Ziko Rinken Demo Kojosen Kensa O Ishidantai Ni Shisa (The Accident in Fukushima, A group of medical doctors (IPPNW) indicated that it needs to hold thyroid function test in neighbour prefectures),

http://www.at-s.com/news/detail/1174173295.html Accessed: 6th May 2015

Mainichi Shimbun, IPPNW Sekai Taikai: Seimei Ni 'Datsu Genpatsu' Morazu Heimaku Hiroshima (IPPNW World Congress: It did not add 'abandoning nuclear generation' in the final document. Hiroshima)
http://mainichi.jp/select/news/20120827k0000m040076000c.htm
Accessed: 30th August 2012

Kyotanabe City (in Kyoto Prefecture), *Heiwa Toshi: Heiwa Shucho Kaigi Ni Tsuite (Peace City: About the Mayors for Peace)*, http://www.kyotanabe.jp/0000004984.html
Accessed: 6th May 2015

Takarazuka City (in Hyogo Prefecture), *Hiewa Shyucho Kaigi Heno Kamei Ni Tsuite (About Joining the Mayors for Peace),* http://www.city.takarazuka.hyogo.jp/kyoiku/jinken/1000113/1000479.html Accessed: 6th May 2015

Sankei Shimbun 16th December 2010, *Opinion: Nippon No Kaku Buso (Opinion Poll on Japanese Nuclear Armament)* http://sankei.jp.msn.com/life/trend/101216/trd1012161852013-n1.htm Accessed: 3rd January 2010

Sankei Shimbun 14th February 2011, *Opinion: Nippon No Kakubuso (Opinion Poll on Nuclear Armament),* http://sankei.jp.msn.com/politics/news/110214/stt11021422510013-n1.htm Accessed: 19th August 2011

Ministry of Justice Japan, *Japanese Law Translation Database System, The Constitution of Japan* http://www.japaneselawtranslation.go.jp/law/detail_main?re=&vm=02&id=174
Accessed: 11th June 2015

Ryukyushinpo (a newspaper in Okinawa Prefecture) 8th May 2001, *Gaiko Ha Kuni No Senken Ziko: Hashimoto Okinawa Taishi (Diplomacy is State Monopoly by Hashimoto the Ambassador to Okinawa)*

http://ryukyushimpo.jp/news/storyid-112148-storytopic-86.html
Accessed: 5th June 2015

Asahi Shimbun 8th June 2014, Shugakuryokosei 5Nin Nagasaki No Hibakusha Ni Bougen Yokohama No Chugakko Shazai (5 students of school trip used offensive languages against a hibakusha in Nagasaki, their junior high school in Yokohama City apologized), http://www.asahi.com/articles/ASG673RG9G67TOLB001.html
Accessed: 7th May 2015

Hiroshima Peace Media Centre (Chugoku Shimbun), Genbaku No Hi Maeni Zenkoku Yoron Chosa (National Opinion Poll before Day of Atomic Bomb)
http://www.hiroshimapeacemedia.jp/abom/01abom/yoron/yoron.html
Accessed: 13th June 2015

NHK (Japan Broadcasting Corporation) Broadcasting Culture Research Institute, Shakai Ya Seiji Ni Kansuru Yoron Chosa: Genbaku Toka Kara 65Nen Kienu Kaku No Kyoi (Opinion Polls on Politics and Society: 65th Anniversary of Dropping Atomic Bombs – Fear of Nuclear Weapons has not been disappeared) October 2010
https://www.nhk.or.jp/bunken/summary/research/report/2010_10/101005.pdf Accessed: 12 June 2015

JPPNW, *IPPNW 18th World Congress, Delhi, India: DELHI DECLARATION March 9, 2008*,
http://www.hiroshima.med.or.jp/ippnw/sekaitaikai/18ippnw200839.html
Accessed: 7th May 2015

Asahi Shimbun Digital, Syria Nanmin No Wakamono Seifu Ga Gentei Ukeire O Kento (The Japanese government will accept young Syrian asylum seekers as international students not refugees) 25th September 2015
http://www.asahi.com/articles/ASH9S761TH9SUTFK025.html

Accessed: 1st October 2015

Asahi Shimbun Digital, Syria Nanmin Ukeire O Nihon Seifu Ni Yosei UNHCR Kyokucho (Director of UNHCR requested the Japanese government to receive Syrian refugees) 21st June 2015 http://www.asahi.com/articles/ASH6N443BH6NUHBI00D.html

Accessed: 5th July 2015

JNNNWA, *NGO Renraku Kai Ni Tsuite (About the Organisation)* https://nuclearabolitionjpn.wordpress.com/about/

Accessed: 7th May 2015

Appendix: Interviews and Statements

(1) SGI Peace Committee (9th and 29th March 2010)

Interview Place: Soka Gakkai Office of International Public Relations, Soka Gakkai Toda International Memorial Centre, 15-1 Samon-cho, Shinjuku-ku, Tokyo, Japan

Hirotsugu Terasaki: Soka Gakkai Vice-President, and Chair of SGI Peace Committee, which is the section in charge of SGI's NGO activity against nuclear weapons
Kimiaki Kawai: Secretary-General of SGI Peace Committee

9th March 2010
Tobisawa: Thank you very much for making the time to meet with me today. Our time is rather limited, so I hope you do not mind if I proceed with the interview right away. The questions I would like to ask today relate to SGI's antinuclear movement, its relationship with the Japanese government, and its relationship and cooperation with other CSOs. First of all, in regard to SGI's antinuclear movement, I believe you are actively engaged in holding antinuclear exhibitions and activities in many countries around the world. However, there are many governments in various regions that possess or promote nuclear armament. Moreover, I believe that political decision-making on security is considered an exclusive right of each government. What are your thoughts on how CSOs in their role can contribute to nuclear disarmament and the abolition of nuclear weapons? Please tell us your thoughts in terms of specific initiatives carried out by SGI.

Kawai: With a network encompassing 192 countries worldwide, we are an organisation based on the principles of peace and humanity according to Nichiren Buddhism. As you may know, we are involved in a wide range of educational activities, including organizing and holding anti-nuclear exhibitions, publishing books on anti-war themes, documenting the experiences of atomic bomb victims in Hiroshima and Nagasaki, promoting awareness of the enormity of the devastation caused by nuclear weapons as well as their cruelty, and trying to prevent these memories from fading from the minds of new generations by passing them on to the next generation. We are also recognised as an NGO with consultative status by the United Nations Economic and Social Council (UNESCO), and have promoted antinuclear activities to date centred on the UN including an exhibition entitled "Nuclear Arms: Threat to Our World (ENATOW)," which was held at the UN Headquarters worldwide. In activities such as the Ottawa Process for eradicating landmines and banning cluster bombs, the role of NGOs is growing quite significantly, I believe. Earlier you mentioned the role of CSOs in nuclear disarmament. I believe promoting dialogue with people of different walks of life at the grass roots level is one of the most significant characteristics of SGI. We hold regular regional discussion meetings almost once a month in groups of 10 to 20 members in towns and areas with SGI organisations in various countries. These are open meetings for all people including non-SGI members. Whilst we learn about Buddhism in these meetings, we also learn together about current social problems and peace issues including nuclear weapons, and actively engage in discussions. Of course, it stands to reason that there will be differences in opinions but our members are promoting mutual understanding by listening to the opinions of others as well as expressing their own opinions. By having people of different cultural backgrounds, living environments, and professions discuss peace on an equal footing through a discussion on the issue of nuclear weapons, for example, I believe that we can form a meaningful public opinion.

Tobisawa: My next question is in regard to your relationship with the Japanese government. Is there any relationship of cooperation between SGI and the Japanese government in regard to nuclear disarmament?

Terasaki: We do not have any specific relationship with the Japanese government. On the other hand, we do have a strong relationship of cooperation with the United Nations in the ENATOW and various other activities. We have established SGI-UN liaison offices in cities where the UN has a prominent presence such as New York, Geneva, and Vienna, and we are constantly stepping up efforts in exchanges of opinions and our cooperation with the UN. In recent years, however, the Japanese government has begun to listen to the opinions of the civil community. In the past, when we visited other countries to hold exhibitions or other events, local Japanese embassy staff made perfunctory visits more or less as a customary courtesy to a Japanese organisation holding a local event. Although there was no overt objection to our activities, we could detect an attitude that they would prefer us not to get involved in such activities because they were already engaging in diplomatic relationships and friendly relations with the countries concerned, and preferred that non-government organisations like ours not meddle in their affairs. In recent years, when CSOs hold antinuclear symposiums or conferences and send invitations to the Ministry of Foreign Affairs, the relevant officials have begun to attend such events. However, they still seem to merely express views from the standpoint of the Japanese government. Nevertheless, I believe the stance of the Japanese government towards civil society will eventually change.

Tobisawa: What exactly makes you think that the stance of the Japanese government will change? The Japanese government holds a firm nuclear policy, which it has done for a long time, in matters such as nuclear deterrence under a U.S. nuclear umbrella. I wonder if there is a possibility such government will listen to the opinions of civil society or reflect their opinions in policy?

Terasaki: Take, for example, the Convention on the Prohibition of Anti-Personnel Landmines. This is also called the Ottawa Treaty, and the process leading up to its establishment is commonly known as the Ottawa Process. This is a treaty that was spearheaded by NGOs from countries that actually suffered damages from landmines. After the NGOs provided results of their own research and other information that reflected the views of the local people, the treaty was established with the cooperation of the respective governments. This is an example that demonstrates CSOs and governments can cooperate with one another. In terms of the banning of weapons of mass destruction, we can also cite an example of the banning of cluster bombs. Currently, the joint goal for anti-nuclear CSOs is to establish the Nuclear Weapons Convention[1] submitted to the UN by the governments of Costa Rica and Malaysia. The time has come for banning weapons like anti-personnel landmines and cluster bombs that cause devastating bloodshed under international law. Therefore, I believe the Nuclear Weapons Convention should also be established.

---

[1] Nuclear Weapons Convention
http://lcnp.org/mnwc/ （in English）
http://inesap.org/sites/default/files/inesap_old/mNWC_2007_Unversion_English_N0821377.pdf (in English)

Tobisawa: Although I am asking about cooperation and relationships with other CSOs, since SGI has a well-established membership and network, I imagine SGI engages in activities independently.

Kawai: We interact with major antinuclear organisations, engage in exchanges of opinions and, on occasion, co-host exhibitions of antinuclear weapons. Of course, these respective organisations have their own particular approach and strong convictions, and at present we hardly see any agreement in opinions. Amongst the various organisations, we have a strong partnership with the International Campaign to Abolish Nuclear Weapons (ICAN). We sometimes hold joint exhibitions for the abolition of nuclear weapons. It is important to edify international public opinion.

Tobisawa: Today we live in an era of globalization and, as you are well aware, our society is saturated with information to a high degree. To highlight the cause of antinuclear public opinions, have you considered utilizing vehicles such as media and the Internet? Of course, I am aware that SGI's network covers 192 countries and that SGI engages in large-scale exhibitions and publishing activities. At the same time, however, we live in an era where the overwhelming majority of the younger generation receives information via the Internet.

Kawai: I think it is a very important suggestion. In addition to our official websites for SGI and the Soka Gakkai Japan, we have established the People's Decade for Nuclear Abolition, a website dedicated to nuclear disarmament. At that site, we actively publish results of public opinion questionnaire surveys on antinuclear matters as well as news about exhibitions. We also publish first hand accounts of the experiences of atomic bomb victims.

Tobisawa: Well, thank you very much for your time today.

29th March 2010

Tobisawa: Thank you very much for again making the time for today's interview.

Kawai: You are welcome. Please feel free to ask any questions. I would like to introduce one of our staff – Ms. Emiko Kubo, who is in charge of matters concerning your research. From now on, may I ask that you contact Ms. Kubo if you require any materials or information for your work.

Tobisawa: Thank you very much and appreciate your consideration. Well, I would like to commence the interview right away, if you do not mind. If I may, I will start with basic matters. SGI and Soka Gakkai Japan are both religious organisations, and are involved in activities for nuclear disarmament under a special section, such as the SGI Peace Committee. What is the reason, or shall I say fundamental reasons, for establishing a nuclear disarmament movement?

Kawai: First of all, the Soka Gakkai is a Japanese organisation, and SGI has a network of 192 countries throughout the world. In this context, the Soka Gakkai in Japan basically serves as the Japan branch of SGI. The reason why we engage in total abolition of nuclear weapons is based on the history of the Soka Gakkai and its objective to respect the dignity of human life. Although the Soka Gakkai was established in 1930 before

World War II, it was basically annihilated as a result of the crackdown of the military government during the war. This oppression manifested itself in suppression of religious freedom and pacifism under Japan's extreme nationalism and the evil of power. After the war, following through with the intentions of Tsunesaburo Makiguchi, Soka Gakkai (Japan's) first president, Josei Toda, Soka Gakkai (Japan's) second president rebuilt the Soka Gakkai. The third president, Daisaku Ikeda, continued these efforts by developing the Soka Gakkai into the global organisation of today.

Tobisawa: Compared with the movements of other antinuclear CSOs, SGI's antinuclear movement has a very long history. What is your opinion of the activities of antinuclear CSOs in Japan?

Kawai: The total abolition of nuclear weapons is a borderless issue. Therefore, I believe the time has come for CSOs to engage not only in domestic but also in borderless activities. The activities of other antinuclear CSOs in Japan have been mainly domestic in nature and have made little progress in expanding their activities to the international community. In recent years, however, we are beginning to see gradual changes in antinuclear CSO activities in Japan through the networking of concerted antinuclear CSO activities. In this context, we can say that the antinuclear CSO movement in Japan is at the developmental stage.

Tobisawa: I understand that the Declaration Calling for the Abolition of Nuclear Weapons (DCANW) by second President Toda and President Ikeda's antinuclear ideology and popular diplomacy form the basis of SGI's antinuclear movement. However, about how long has Soka

Gakkai Japan engaged in antinuclear activities as an NGO?

Kawai: Whilst DCANW represents President Toda's ideology regarding antinuclear weapons, President Ikeda has continued its spirituality and has developed it into SGI's antinuclear activities of today. In 2009, SGI President Ikeda announced the Nuclear Abolition Proposal. Please refer to it, as the details of this announcement dedicated to the antinuclear weapons movement are separate from the Peace Proposal announced on 26th January every year. DCANW also clearly stated that the acceptance of nuclear weapons was the destruction of the dignity of human life. In this declaration, President Ikeda insisted on the need for a change in the way of thinking of the international community, stating that nuclear weapons would never be a means of deterrence but instead would only heighten the tension between countries in bilateral or multilateral relationships. This need for a change in people's ways of thinking is the underlying theme of SGI's antinuclear movement.

Since the dropping of the atomic bombs in 1945, the Japanese government has continued to submit resolutions for the abolition of nuclear weapons in the Diet and in the United Nations, but efforts of the Japanese government stop at merely making pronouncements.

It can be said that SGI's activities as an antinuclear NGO began in earnest from 1980 onwards. It was around this time that SGI concluded a formal agreement of cooperation with the United Nations. The 1980s can be described as the dawn of the rise of CSOs, including other organisations that tackled peace issues. Since 1982, in a tie-up with the UN Department of Public Information (UNDPI), SGI has held ENTOW at the UN Headquarters. UN Secretary-General Javier Perez de Cuellar and Yasushi Akashi, former UN Undersecretary-General in charge of Public Information, Disarmament, and Humanitarian Issues have also shown strong interest and offered their cooperation in these activities. Based on a proposal by President Ikeda in 1971, the Soka Gakkai Youth Division (Japan) in 1973 started the “10 Million Signature Campaign for the Abolition of Nuclear Weapons” and in 1975, President Ikeda presented the signatures of 10 million people directly to UN Secretary-General Kurt Josef Waldheim at UN headquarters. This was the beginning of SGI’s ongoing relationship with the United Nations. In light of President Ikeda’s proposal to “preserve and promote truth,” Soka Gakkai began conducting interviews and recording the personal experiences of World War II of people all over Japan with a view to passing these on to the next generation. Accordingly, the testimonies of people were collected in a total of 80 volumes over a period of 12 years and include the testimonies of atomic bomb victims. These activities, which were held all over Japan, evolved into the anti-war, antinuclear exhibitions sponsored by the Soka Gakkai and further developed into the ENTOW held on a global scale. The Toda Peace Memorial Hall (Former British No. 7 Building) located in Yokohama, Kanagawa Prefecture has a permanent display of antinuclear weapons, and combined with the antinuclear weapons exhibitions held on a world scale, these exhibitions are held with considerable frequency.

Tobisawa: Other CSOs promote the antinuclear movement based on a particular affiliation of their groups such as legal, medical, or local government administration, etc. In that respect, what do you see as the antinuclear movement of SGI on its own?

Kawai: As an organisation, SGI is not solely dedicated to antinuclear activities. Therefore, I do not believe it can be categorised as a so-called antinuclear organisation in the conventional sense. SGI is an organisation based on Buddhism's principles of peace, and engages in the antinuclear movement entirely as a cultural corporation and cultural movement. SGI is not a group of antinuclear specialists but a gathering of ordinary people who have different occupations and home environments. The members of SGI, however, do share a sense of mission to pray for and achieve happiness for themselves and others. Moreover, they study together and discuss with each other on a daily basis peace, culture, education, and events in society, and they share an awareness of issues. SGI can also be described as a gathering of all kinds of people and a platform for sharing awareness. All of SGI's antinuclear movements have an educational aspect, and even national issues and technical aspects of national security have to be at a level that ordinary people can understand and discuss in order to contribute to human security. These local grass roots peace movements centred on ordinary people have resulted in the formation a network of antinuclear public opinion spread across 192 countries. I believe this is the unique contribution that SGI is capable of making.

Tobisawa: How would you describe the reaction of the Japanese government and the governments of other countries in regard to SGI's antinuclear exhibitions? Earlier you stated that SGI is a group of ordinary people, but how do you unify or share their opinions?

Terasaki: The response of the Japanese government has been very cool. When we hold antinuclear exhibitions in the UN or other countries, the local Japanese embassy staff often pay courtesy visits. In countries where we hold exhibitions we often receive congratulatory telegrams from presidents or top-level officials of local governments, and government ministers or officials at vice-minister level, renowned scholars and highly educated people also visit the exhibitions as special guests. Due to the significance of the exhibitions' impact and scale, and at the same time as events organised and held by a Japanese organisation, I believe both the Ministry of Foreign Affairs in Japan and the local Japanese embassy cannot ignore them. Whilst they greet us on the surface, they always wear an expression as if to advise us not to be meddling in their affairs. In short, I guess they believe that diplomacy and international exchanges are the sole domain of government, and private citizens should not be sticking their noses into business that does not concern them. Furthermore, the Japanese government has its policies in areas such as diplomacy and defence, and I guess it puts them in an awkward position if groups like ours adopt a stance in their activities that differs from their policies. Whilst they visit our exhibitions to pay their respects, we never receive any kind of cooperation from either the Japanese government or the Japanese embassy. We do not hold antinuclear exhibitions or engage in any antinuclear activities in cooperation with the Japanese government.

Kawai: SGI's antinuclear movement is based on transnationalism. As I stated before, SGI is a group of ordinary people. That said, it is an enormous network with a membership of people hailing from widely diverse backgrounds and, therefore, there may be occasions when the opinions of SGI members may not agree on fine points in regard to antinuclear issues. Naturally, our members are free to have various opinions of their own. Whilst maintaining tolerance both inside and outside the organisation, SGI promotes its antinuclear movement based on the activities, declarations, and proposals made by the first, second and third presidents.

Tobisawa: Whilst you may not have any relationship with the Japanese government, do you cooperate at all with Japanese political circles or so-called law-makers, as well as with antinuclear CSOs within Japan?

Kawai: If the opportunity arises, we never refuse from our side. Of course, our association with another organisation would depend on the basic principles and stance of that organisation. The Komeito, of which the Soka Gakkai is the main supporting block, has a Committee in Promoting Nuclear Abolition. In other political parties – although I do not know about individual members of the parliament – I do not believe there are any political parties to have established either a section or committee for the abolition of nuclear weapons.

(2) Komeito Committee for Promoting Nuclear Abolition (21st July 2010)

Interview Place: Members' Office Building of the House of Councillors of Japan, 2-1-1 Nagata-cho, Chiyoda-ku, Tokyo 100-0014, Japan
Masayoshi Hamada: Member of the House of Councillors, Chairman of Komeito Committee for Promoting Nuclear Abolition, Former Vice-Minister of Foreign Affairs, former Director of Bio-Industry Division, Ministry of Economy, Trade and Industry

Tobisawa: Councilor Hamada, what is your understanding of the role of CSOs in nuclear disarmament and the abolition of nuclear weapons? We have been reminded that this issue is an arbitrary matter for the government's diplomacy.

Hamada: It is not appropriate to exclude CSOs from the issue of nuclear weapons. CSOs, for example, can lobby the governments of their respective countries for nuclear disarmament. In a country like Japan, for example, the government may find it difficult to make statements regarding certain matters to the U.S. government or other nuclear powers due to its alliances. In such cases, there is a way for Japanese CSOs cooperating with their counterparts in the United States to convey various messages to the U.S. government via CSOs in the United States. When it comes to matters that could create hard feelings between governments, I believe CSOs, taking advantage of their borderless relationships, have a significant role to play. The reality in the political world in Japan is that there is a dearth of Japanese politicians who have personal relationships with politicians in nuclear powers including the United States, which are close enough to allow for the frank exchange of opinions concerning vital matters, particularly the issue of nuclear weapons. In this context, relationships and cooperation with antinuclear CSOs in various countries are crucial.

Tobisawa: So do you consider specific approaches such as policy planning that adopts the views of CSOs?

Hamada: Whilst I believe there is a role for CSOs, I also believe that it is difficult for the Japanese government to suddenly respond to the appeals of CSOs to have governments of countries sign the Nuclear Weapons Convention. It is not possible to suddenly and instantly abolish all nuclear weapons. CSOs need to understand this too.

An important point here is determining what kind of process needs to be put in place for realistic diplomatic negotiations and discussions to proceed. The focus has been solely on whether or not to ratify the convention, but it is important to start examining how to pave the way for establishing the convention. One good example is the Nagasaki Hiroshima Process, about which Mrs. Toshiko Hamayotsu, Acting Representative of Komeito, raised questions in the House of Councilors.

Tobisawa: Councilor Hamada, what kind of initiatives do you think the Japanese government could take as preparatory steps for the Nuclear Weapons Convention?

Hamada: As a start, I believe the Ottawa Treaty (Convention on the Prohibition of the Use, Stockpiling, Production and Transfer of Anti-Personnel Mines and on Their Destruction) and the Oslo Treaty (the Convention on Cluster Munitions), which the Japanese government positively ratified, are some good examples for paving the way towards establishing international law prohibiting weapons of mass destruction. The next question, however, is what we should to prohibit nuclear weapons. Idealistic arguments serve no purpose. We need to think in concrete terms about what we can do now. As a road map, I believe the Nagasaki Hiroshima Process proposed by Professor Katsuya Kodama of Mie University is a good example. This was raised in a parliamentary question of the Committee on Foreign Affairs and Defense in the House of Councilors. You can find this in the minutes of the proceedings.

Tobisawa: I believe the Japanese government originally positioned nuclear deterrence under the U.S. nuclear umbrella, as its central policy of the national security. Do you think it is possible for Japan to promote the Nuclear Weapons Convention under such a policy?

Hamada: I believe we need to change our basic way of thinking in regard to this matter. Originally it was believed that promotion of nuclear disarmament would be contradictory to Japan's security policies. Therefore, it was believed that promotion of nuclear disarmament would make maintaining Japan's security untenable. Although this is the view held by many, it is not correct. Rather, if we intend to strengthen Japan's security, we need to first reduce the nuclear threat of China and North Korea. This is not contradictory to enhancing the security of our country. It is a viewpoint that insists reduction in the value and number of nuclear weapons as national security will result in improving Japan's security.

Tobisawa: Does the Komeito actually cooperate with CSOs?

Hamada: The Komeito Committee for Promoting Nuclear Abolition holds meetings for exchanging opinions with many of Japan's CSOs promoting the abolition of nuclear weapons. Very lively discussions take place at these meetings. Recently the United States agreed to supply nuclear fuel to the Indian government. India has been undertaking nuclear development outside of the NPT framework, and the United States has a history of vehemently criticizing India for this. This is clearly a double standard on the part of the United States, and we intend to take up this issue as an agenda item in the next meeting for exchanging views.

Tobisawa: Could you please give specific examples of Komeito's initiatives for nuclear disarmament including when they started and their background?

Hamada: For specific details, I suggest that you do your own online research by searching the minutes of the Diet, which are available to the public. But to give you a quick overview, the Komeito, since its establishment in 1964, has consistently promoted peace and welfare as its bottom line. In recent years, the party has also taken a clear stand on promoting the abolition of nuclear weapons in its foreign policy as framed in the "Yamaguchi Vision," one of its national election manifestos.

(3)SGI-UN liaison office in New York (10th September 2010)

Interview Place: SGI-UN Liaison Office in New York, 211 East 43rd Street, Suite 1104, New York, NY 10017, USA

Hiro Sakurai: Representative of SGIUNLO in New York
Professor Richard Langhorne joined this interview

Tobisawa: Thank you so much for taking time today. I hope to introduce my supervisor Professor Richard Langhorne.

Sakurai: Thank you so much for your coming.

Langhorne: Mr. Tobisawa is a DPhil student of the University of Buckingham and is researching about civil society organisation's influence on nuclear disarmament. My question is that whether SGI has been collaborating with politics such as governments. If so, how have you been working with them? And hope to know some examples.

Sakurai: Our anti-nuclear weapon activities are the core of our peace activities. But we do not have any collaboration with governments, and we are not a political organisation. I have been serving as the President of the Committee on Disarmament, Peace and Security, of CoNGO [CDPSCONGO]. But the title 'President' is not suitable, I am thinking it is a coordinator to harmonise discussions of its member NGOs. The CDPSCONGO is a counterpart of the First Committee of the United Nations, and has been working for the series of NPT Review conference.

Langhorne: I think you (Tobisawa) now ask your questions. In Japanese is fine and more convenient for you. I do not mind, it is for your thesis.

Tobisawa: Thank you, professor. I will now continue in Japanese. First of all, I would like to ask about the function and role of SGI liaison offices. When were they established and what kind of role do they play in the antinuclear CSO movement of SGI? In addition, as I understand that you are also the president of the CDPSCONGO, could you please comment on the role and significance of such an NGO alliance?

Sakurai: Yes, both SGIUNLO in New York and SGIUNLO in Geneva were established in 1997. SGI has developed peace activities on a wide range of disarmament issues. In addition to disarmament, we are also tackling environmental issues such as sustainable development. In peace activities of SGI, nuclear disarmament is its symbol. In NGO alliances, I am not only the president of the CDPSCONGO but I also serve as the president of the Committee of Religious NGOs at the United Nations (CRNUN).[2] The religious aspect is also very important in disarmament activities.

Tobisawa: When NGOs of different religions come together to discuss the abolition of nuclear weapons, do they reach any form of consensus? Also, in what specific way is the religious aspect important?

Sakurai: CRNUN and the CDPSCONGO are the same, and the majority of the participating groups have their own strong beliefs and arguments. There are some groups that are not cooperative and refuse to

---

[2] CRNUN http://rngos.wordpress.com/

compromise in any way. To create a groundswell for resolving issues in nuclear development and wars in the real world, we need as many NGOs and government organisations as possible to build cooperative relationships. The aim of SGI's activities is to create such a groundswell of solidarity for peace. In specific terms, as I mentioned to Professor Langhorne before, it is important for the presidents of NGO alliances to act as coordinators and determine how to facilitate discussion and communication so that they proceed in a smooth, constructive and progressive manner without people leaving or quitting.

Tobisawa: Are you saying that whilst the CSOs to date have merely persisted with their own principles and policies, in the future this will not be the case?

Sakurai: Of course, beliefs or principles and policies are important. SGI also has its own strong principles regarding peace and the abolition of nuclear weapons. However, harmony is crucial.

Tobisawa: So, it seems the challenge is to get as many organisations and people as possible to agree to peace and abolition of nuclear weapons.

Sakurai: Therefore, whilst I am in the position of president as well as chairman of an NGO alliance, there are times when I refrain from expressing my own opinion as a coordinator. I make every effort to have our meetings become venues for mutual understanding and harmony, where all persons are respected.

Tobisawa: That seems to be different from the traditional stance of antinuclear CSOs. My impression is that the majority of groups see putting forward their own arguments as their top priority. I wonder if yours is a Buddhist attitude, and that is why you say that the religious aspect is important.

Sakurai: I guess you could say that, but I feel the thrust of SGI's efforts lies in changing the way people think, including rulers and leaders of countries, so that we can make a transition from an era characterised by war and violence to an era of peace. To do that, we have to change people's spirituality. For example, the Preamble of Rome Statute of the International Criminal Court is rich in spirituality due to the campaigning of religious NGOs, which assert that international crime is not a crime but an intrinsic problem of human beings. We believe the essential questioning of why international crime needs to be condemned, and why nuclear weapons must be abolished is important.

Tobisawa: There has been some movement toward reducing nuclear weapons such as the U.S.-Russia Strategic Arms Reduction Treaty (START). This is said to be largely due to the pressure placed on national finances stemming from the enormous costs involved in maintaining nuclear weapons developed during the Cold War. In other words, it is a policy aimed at reducing nuclear weapons due to economic and financial problems, not for the sake of humanity or human rights. If this is the case, there is a possibility nuclear development will recommence once financial conditions improve, and I do not believe this will lead to the fundamental abolition of nuclear weapons. Having said that, you may find this manner of speaking unpleasant, but I believe it would be difficult to influence political decision-making based on the abstract idealism and humanism that

CSOs proclaim. When I speak with people from various antinuclear CSOs, they are passionate in telling me their antinuclear principles and claims, but I believe they have very little concrete practice in achieving their principles. I believe nuclear disarmament is not a security issue but a diplomatic issue. Various countries are caught up in the background of various historical confrontations over nuclear weapons issues. Unless these issues are resolved, I do not believe we can achieve nuclear disarmament. I do not think we can abolish nuclear weapons simply by discussing the right and wrong of nuclear weapons. Although forums for resolving nuclear issues have been established bilaterally and multilaterally, including the Six-Party Talks on North Korea Nuclear Program, all government-to-government talks are in a deadlock situation at present. I understand very well that SGI has established a network of antinuclear CSOs and arms reduction CSOs, and I believe this is the most beneficial example of a bottom-up approach aimed at abolition of nuclear weapons by shoring up antinuclear public opinion internationally. On the other hand, I would appreciate knowing whether there are top-down initiatives to abolish nuclear weapons, in other words, are there any initiatives for approaching or cooperating with governments?

Sakurai: All SGI's efforts at abolishing nuclear weapons are based on the principles of human security. President Ikeda repeatedly campaigned for human security in past peace proposals and other approaches. In terms of specific SGI antinuclear activities where SGIUNLO in New York was involved, we held an exhibition in 2007 entitled "From a Culture of Violence to a Culture of Peace: Transforming the Human Spirit."[3] This was organised and executed by

[3] SGI, Antinuclear exhibition: "From a Culture of Violence to a Culture of

SGI to commemorate the 50th anniversary of DCANW initiated by Second President Toda in 1957. In addition, to shore up international public opinion for the abolition of nuclear weapons, we held a civil society forum and a workshop where we had atomic bomb victims from Hiroshima and Nagasaki talk about their experiences. This exhibition was organised specifically to pass on the principles and activities for abolishing nuclear weapons to the younger generation. It was held in 200 venues in 24 countries including the UN Office in Geneva and the Parliament House of New Zealand. In 2009, during the preparatory conference (4th-15th May) for the 3rd NPT Review Conference held at the UN Headquarters, SGI with support from ICAN held the Symposium "Nuclear Abolition and Human Security". We also held a simultaneous workshop for listening to the experiences of seven victims of the atomic bomb, who were invited from Hiroshima and Nagasaki. As a result, over 400 citizens of New York City engaged in exchanges with the atomic bomb victims. Building networks of mutual understanding amongst the United Nations, government organisations and NGOs, as I mentioned earlier, is the main activity and goal of the SGI liaison offices.

Tobisawa: Indeed. Thank you very much for your time today.

Peace: Transforming the Human Spirits"
http://www.sgi.org/resource-center/ngo-resources/peace-disarmament/transforming-the-human-spirit.html

(4) Permanent Mission of Japan to the International Organisations in Vienna, Ministry of Foreign Affairs Japan (6th October 2010)

Interview Place: The office of the Permanent Mission in Vienna, Austria
Yasuyuki Ebata: First Secretary in charge of nuclear policy

Tobisawa: I am grateful that you have agreed to give me time you're your busy schedule.

Ebata: Not at all, you're welcome.

Tobisawa: I would like to ask you about the Japanese government's nuclear policy and relationships with CSOs. I believe issues of nuclear weapons belong to state diplomacy and for the government to develop policies and to negotiate with other states. However, today things are different as was the case in Otawa process concerning the s such it is the state that conducts negotiations, developed policies and made decisions on the issue. Today, however, as was the case with the Otawa Process dealing with the Convention to Ban Anti-personnel Land Mines, the role of CSOs have increased from humanitarian perspective over the unnecessary sufferings and indiscriminate killings of the weapons. Is it the thinking of the government that it should collaborate with CSOs on issues of nuclear weapons? And if there is already collaboration I would like to hear about it.

Ebata: I invite you to look at our pamphlets, "Japan's Disarmament and Nonproliferation Diplomacy" prepared and updated every 4 to 5 years by the Ministry of Foreign Affairs, Disarmament and Non-proliferation, Science Department, Arms Control and Disarmament. I will have them sent to you from the Arms Control and Disarmament Section. Coping with nuclear weapons is an issue that demands prompt address from the security perspective and also in consideration of the safety of our allies during deliberations at the United Nations, for example. The basic stance of the government of Japan is that nuclear disarmament and security are the two wheels of our nuclear weapons policy. Needless to say, the matter of security will have to be decided by the government alone, but on nuclear disarmament we believe collaboration with CSOs important. Pushing for nuclear disarmament alone, however, is not enough. In terms of our activities here at Japan's Permanent Mission in Vienna, it must be said first of all that Vienna is home to IAEA, International Atomic energy Agency that oversees global nuclear energy, including control of imports and exports of nuclear power, deliberations on the peaceful use of nuclear energy as in nuclear power plants. Nuclear non-proliferation is, however, concerned, not a matter for collaboration with CSOs. Naturally, there are contacts with researchers from civilian research institutes as well as nuclear physicists. We believe in this area collaboration with CSOs is difficult. I might say that there have been no CSOs that came forward to state their anti-nuclear position or engage us in dialogue. Their foremost interest is, I believe, nuclear disarmament. On that matter, the Ministry of Foreign Affairs sends officers in charge to be at the annual Peace Ceremonies that take place in Hiroshima and Nagasaki as well as events organized by local governments and CSOs to exchange views.

Tobisawa: Don't you feel there are strong views that Japan, as the only country with the experiences of atomic bombings should take the initiative towards nuclear weapons elimination in a more visible manner?

Ebata: Ambassador Ohno from our Ministry of Foreign Affairs is the new IAES Secretary General. The government of Japan provides cancer therapy to about 120 developing countries (not allied with Japan). We are prompting them to live up to their obligations for nuclear non-proliferation through supporting them rather than controlling them. The three pillars of the NPT regime are disarmament, non-proliferation and peaceful use. Vienna is the home base if you will for non-proliferation and peaceful use but I have yet to meet any CSO that will come to talk to us about their views. The stance of the Japanese government is not to increase nuclear weapons from the present level. NPT's three pillars must be balanced. One must not specialize on a single pillar or carry it forward. Further, there are issues of security and nuclear terrorism. Policies and decisions must be made in balance with those considerations. I believe the international community appreciates Japan's ability to coordinate. It is important for us to coordinate while keeping the balance.

Tobisawa: I thank you for giving me your precious time.

(5) Arms Control and Disarmament Division, Disarmament, Non-Proliferation and Science Department, Ministry of Foreign Affairs Japan (2nd November 2010)

Interview Place: The Ministry of Foreign Affairs, Japan

Haruna Abe (Ms): Officer of Arms Control and Disarmament Division

Tobisawa: Thank you for giving me your time today and for the materials on "Japan's Disarmament and Non-Proliferation Policies".

Abe: We should thank you for choosing as your research subject diplomacy on disarmament and non-proliferation. We appreciate it.

Tobisawa: I am looking into the roles of CSOs in nuclear disarmament. Mr. Ebata, the First Secretary at the Embassy in Vienna told me that the Foreign Ministry sends its staff to take part annually in Peace Memorial Services in Hiroshima and Nagasaki and to engage in exchanges of views. Do you have contacts and relations with CSOs at other times?

Abe: True, the role of civic societies is gaining importance. The Ministry of Foreign Affairs also sends *hibakusha* as special envoys throughout the world to have them share their experiences.

Tobisawa: The US nuclear umbrella under the Japan-US alliance protects Japan. I received your material "Japan's disarmament and Non-proliferation Diplomacy", but is it the government's policy to deny the US nuclear umbrella?

Abe: As you know, Japan-US alliance is the cornerstone of the government's defense diplomacy. Our section of arms control and disarmament makes policies dedicated to disarmament and non-proliferation. The Ministry of Defense and other ministries and agencies have their opinion, so we have within our Ministry posts specialized in Japan-US Alliance. The policies of the government are not limited to disarmament and non-proliferation. I believe the government will eventually determine the nuclear weapons policy by adjusting views of other agencies.

Tobisawa: You are saying that there are posts that acknowledge the nuclear umbrella?

Abe: Yes.

Tobisawa: CSOs are aiming at total abolition of nuclear weapons and establishment of Convention Banning Nuclear Weapons by 2020. How is the government of Japan copying with these approaches?

Abe: In any case we will need a realistic approach. As it is stated in NPT's Article 6 it is clear that we must go forward towards nuclear disarmament. However, I believe that we should make our decisions considering carefully all matters including the situation surrounding Japan.

Tobisawa: I will certainly refer to the materials I have received. Thank you for your time.

Appendices

(6)SGI-UN Liaison Office in Geneva (10th June 2011)

Interview Place: SGI-UN liaison office in Geneva, World Council of Churches Building, Route de Ferney 150, 1218 Le Grand-Saconnex, Suisse

Kazunari Fujii: Representative of SGIUNLO in Geneva

Tobisawa: Thank you very much for arranging time to talk with me despite your busy schedule.

Fujii: Thank you for making the long trip here today. Please feel free to ask any questions you like.

Tobisawa: Thank you. If you don't mind, I'll start right away. First of all, could you please tell me when and how the SGIUNLO in Geneva was established, and what kind of activities they engage in? Could you also say if there are other activities relating to nuclear disarmament that SGI is promoting as mainstays of its peace movement.

Fujii: Sure. To answer your first question, Geneva is the hub of the UN's human rights activities. SGI, which engages in activities centred on the importance of human rights and human rights education, appointed a representative in 1996. Needless to say, in addition to human rights activities, we are involved in the Geneva Conference on Disarmament. At present, the UN Headquarters in New York is considered the heartland of the United Nations, but the UN Office in Geneva was the headquarters of the former League of Nations and is still used as a meeting place for discussions of many UN matters. I think we can consider New York as the place for making resolutions and Geneva as the place for specific working groups and for technical and specialist discussions, planning, and action plans. Furthermore, since Switzerland is a permanent neutral country, representatives from countries that do not always have a good relationship with the United States can enter the country to attend conferences of the UN Office in Geneva. Attending conferences at the United Nations Headquarters in New York means entering the United States, and there are many cases where people of various countries are unable to attend due to difficulties in having entry visas to the United States issued. In this regard, conferences held in Geneva afford more countries the opportunity to express their opinions. Therefore, our activities in Geneva are significant. Mr. Tobisawa, I understand that you are studying nuclear disarmament. As far as activities in Geneva are concerned, human rights-related activities are more pronounced than activities relating to disarmament. In 1997, the SGI UN liaison office in Geneva was established. Until about 1998 or1999, we had a small office in a multi-tenant building in front of a train station. Thereafter, until around July 2005, the office was located in one of the rooms at Centro Culturale SGI Suisse, the SGI Centre in Switzerland. We then moved to the current building in the World Council of Churches (WCC).

Tobisawa: As SGI is an organisation based on Buddhism, it was somewhat of a surprise to find it located in a building belonging to the Christian Federation.

Fujii: That's right. Some of our guests who come to visit our office are also surprised to find a Buddhist-affiliated NGO organisation in a building like this, after seeing a large cross at front of the building.

However, as many UN-related NGOs have offices in this building, I am very happy that we moved into this building. The fundamental principle of the SGI liaison office is to reflect the opinions of as many NGOs as possible in global policy decision-making. That is our real mission. In the Centro Culturale SGI Suisse, the central base of SGI-Switzerland[4] where our previous office was located, we rarely had opportunities to cooperate with or have exchanges of opinions with other NGOs. As an aside, I would just like to mention that having an office in this WCC building is also a status of sorts for UN-related NGOs, and gives credibility. Of course, our NGO activities make no distinctions of religion or race. Transcending such differences, we look for ways of collaboration to cooperate in human rights and disarmament issues. Through exchanges of opinions with other NGOs in this building, we achieve synergistic effects.

Tobisawa: Since you already had the Centro Culturale SGI Suisse, what was the reason for establishing SGIUNLO in Geneva?

Fujii: In Geneva, thousands of UN and NGO meetings are held every year, especially in relation to human rights activities. We set up our liaison office to accommodate these meetings. Long before establishing the SGI liaison office, SGI was involved in grass-roots civil social activities. SGI President Ikeda has been writing peace proposals to present to the United Nations every year for some time. In 1983, the UN Economic and Social Council's advisory status was bestowed on SGI. Due to these various circumstances, however, we needed to set up an office dedicated to UN-related matters. The Swiss government's policy and laws also make it possible for UN-related NGOs to engage in

---

[4] SGI-Switzerland http://www.sgi-ch.org/

activities in Switzerland even if they are organisations headquartered outside the country.

Tobisawa: Excuse me for getting caught up in minor details, but I have another question about SGI as an organisation. Since SGI is headquartered in Tokyo, am I correct in assuming it is a Japanese NGO?

Fujii: For SGI's UN-related activities and activities as a NGO, the headquarters is Tokyo. SGI Headquarters in Tokyo takes initiative in promoting UN-related activities and shares information with the respective SGI-UN liaison offices. SGI's organisations, which spread across 192 countries, promote peace, cultural, and educational activities based on Buddhism. With the SGI Charter's[5] basic policy that incorporates its motto calling on all members to "contribute to society as good citizens" in their local communities, SGI encourages members to engage in activities freely in accordance with laws, society, and customs of their respective countries. The role of SGI Headquarters in Tokyo is to support these activities. In terms of NGO activities, SGI is a network oriented international NGO. There are three types of NGOs: (1) domestic local NGOs that conduct activities limited to within the country, (2) international regional NGOs that conduct activities within their respective regions such as Asia, Middle East, or Europe, and (3) international NGOs that conduct their activities in locations all over the world. Amnesty Japan is the Japan branch of Amnesty International and conducts its own seminars and training and engages in activities in cooperation with the headquarters of Amnesty International. In the same way, the ICRC has also established branches in every country. SGI

[5] SGI, *SGI Charter 1995*
http://www.sgi.org/resource-center/introductory-materials/sgi-charter.html

adopts a similar system.

Tobisawa: What about nuclear arms reduction activities? What kind of activities does the SGIUNLO in Geneva engage in?

Fujii: To answer your question, I need to first explain the historical background of cooperative UN and NGO activities in Geneva. All of the activities our office currently engages in are activities concerning human rights, the overwhelming majority of which are related to human rights education. Currently Geneva is the UN hub for conducting activities relating to human rights. In 2006 the United Nations Human Rights Council became the UN Human Rights Commission (UNHRC) located at the UN Office in Geneva. This is also an area where human rights departments are concentrated, such as the Office of the UN High Commissioner for Human Rights and the Office of the UN High Commissioner for Refugees. In the past Geneva was the hub for disarmament, and the Geneva Conference on Disarmament actively engaged in activities. Disarmament talks by Regan and Gorbachev were also held in Geneva. Many nuclear disarmament NGOs established their offices and formed a community in Geneva, but this nuclear disarmament NGO community has retreated and moved their activities to the United States. Until recently, SGI and the International Peace Bureau[6] were the only NGOs still engaged in activities including nuclear disarmament in Geneva. Since around 2009 or 2010, however, there has been a resurgence in NGO activities for disarmament there. This is due to a growing global call for nuclear disarmament, including U.S. President Obama's speech in Prague, and the Geneva Conference on Disarmament has started attracting attention again. Many NGOs for

[6] IPB http://www.ipb.org/web/

nuclear disarmament have also begun to establish offices in Geneva including, for example, ICAN and the Nuclear Age Peace Foundation. Our office has become an NGO of long standing and, as such, is often asked by other NGOs that are establishing new offices in Geneva for advice about various matters such as ways of conducting activities in the UN Office in Geneva and methods of exchanging information with other NGOs. In areas where UN offices are located, there are always NGO networks and alliances in respective fields, and SGI serves in the capacity of a committee member or chairperson in most of these networks and alliances. Our SGI UN liaison offices also engage in exchanges of opinions and cooperation with international organisations and government representatives of various countries.

Tobisawa: So, SGI plays a role in supporting NGOs aiming to establish a presence in Geneva. And what is the situation with NGO alliances, or what kind of activities is SGI involved in? Could you also please describe the role SGI plays exactly? During the Geneva Conference on Disarmament or when official conferences are held at the First Committee of the UN General Assembly in New York, do NGOs play a role similar to that of lobbyists outside the venue when it comes to nuclear disarmament? I heard that NGOs and private organisations are not allowed either to engage in discussions or to enter the venues at the disarmament conferences at the United Nations.

Fujii: This is a topic that touches on essential facts, so I would like to answer clearly in an orderly sequence. An NGO alliance is a collective of NGOs. The largest NGO collective amongst UN-related NGOs is the so-called collective CoNGO, which promotes activities like a counterpart of the United Nations, and it has about 3,000 NGOs including SGI as members. In the CoNGO, working groups and committees are divided into specialist areas and established. The committees of the CoNGO are established in each UN city (New York, Geneva, and Vienna) and engage in different activities in line with the activities of the UN Headquarters and other UN offices in New York. In relation to disarmament, in New York there is the NGO Committee on Disarmament, Peace and Security, the CoNGO, which Representative Hiro Sakurai of the SGI UN liaison office heads as president. The CoNGO in Geneva has the NGO Committee on Disarmament, and in the CoNGO in Vienna, the NGO Committee in Peace. No particular rules apply to the activities of these organisations, which take on the characteristics of their respective cities. SGI and the International Peace Bureau have participated in the NGO Committee on Disarmament of the CoNGO in Geneva as committee members since the beginning of its establishment, and recently ICAN and the Women's International League for Peace and Freedom have also participated. However, in many cases it is difficult to integrate opinions in discussions and information exchanges of these NGO collectives not only in relation to disarmament. Because the assertions and contents of activities of the respective NGOs are different, it is not easy to summerise these in a coherent manner. There are some groups that will never modify their assertions and threaten to pull out from the committee if their assertions are not accepted.

Tobisawa: Representative Mr. Hiro Sakurai of the SGI UN liaison office in New York made the same comment. Mr. Sakurai is also the president of the NGO Committee on Disarmament, Peace and Security and said that his position is more that of a coordinator. Consequently, he seems to avoid expressing his own opinions as much as possible and throw himself into the role of listening to and summing up the opinions of others. I guess this may be attributable to his Japanese nature in placing importance on cooperativeness, as well as the peace principles of the Buddhist organisation. I feel I have come to understand the circumstances of SGI's NGO activities. At any rate, am I correct in saying that your aim is to promote the formation of an NGO collective for nuclear disarmament and formation of global opinion? At SGI, President Ikeda promotes dialogue and interviews with knowledgeable people from countries all over the world, and establishes the fundamental principles with themes such as dialogue amongst civilisations and understanding different cultures. If I am correct, this seems to be the basis of SGI's NGO activities.

Fujii: That is correct. However, in Geneva, in contrast to the CoNGO, there is the Geneva Forum. This is an organisation specialising in disarmament issues, and engages in all kinds of disarmament activities. Its operating organisation is the UN Institute for Disarmament Research. This is a venue specialising in affairs at the political level and in academic areas and technology. SGI has participated in this forum and engaged in exchanges of opinions since its inception. This is a highly diplomatic meeting ground where the Graduate Institute of International Studies (an organisation with which SGI cooperates), the University of Geneva, ambassadors of various countries, research directors of academic institutions, and Ms. Rebecca Johnson, the Co-Chair of ICAN all participate. Rather than participating, SGI attends the Geneva Forum solely for the purpose of updating its knowledge of the latest information in the world. The disarmament movement is also showing a recent upsurge in Geneva. NGOs and civil organisations are engaging in lobbyist activities at the Geneva Conference on Disarmament, and SGI is engaging in dialogue. It appears that a system allowing for such activities is being put in place.

Tobisawa: What kinds of lobbying activities do the disarmament NGOs engage in?

Fujii: I will explain so that there will be no misunderstanding, but I would like to start by saying that SGI is not an organisation dedicated to disarmament or any other political activity. An organisation for humanity and human rights is perhaps a more appropriate description of SGI. In our lobbying activities, we draw the line at interest groups like those that lobby the U.S. Congress or UN Headquarters. From beginning to end, our lobbying is through dialogue and the exchange of opinions with other groups and other government organisations, and such initiatives are not for political gain. SGI's stance, as defined by President Ikeda, is to broadly reflect world opinions at the international political level. SGI's exhibitions for the abolition of nuclear weapons held at the UN Headquarters in New York and at the UN Office in Geneva have been well received by visitors including the NGO Committee in Disarmament and the CoNGO, with visitors commenting that SGI's exhibition and affirmations reflect and represent the voices of civil society. Furthermore, SGI is neither a specialist nor a technical organisation. We create networks for promoting nuclear disarmament and human rights education whilst working together and cooperating with various individuals and groups. At times we do form networks with specialist groups, and we co-host these with other groups when we hold seminars or exhibitions for the abolition of nuclear weapons. I believe promoting networking like this is SGI's most significant contribution.

Tobisawa: I received an invitation to the opening of the antinuclear weapon exhibition "From a Culture of Violence to a Culture of Peace", which was held at the UN Office in Vienna from 4th to 15th October in 2010 last year, and I had the honour of attending. That exhibition was also co-hosted by SGI, the NGO Committee on Peace, and the CoNGO. I recall that many leaders showed interest including Ms. Ana Maria Cetto, Deputy Director of the IAEA, who made a speech, and the mayor of Vienna who sent a message. Nuclear disarmament, however, requires political decision-making. As an NGO, what kind of relationship does SGI have with the governments of various countries including the Japanese government? Is SGI in cooperative relationships with any government?

Fujii: I am well aware that you are studying nuclear disarmament, but I would like to address your question concerning SGI's relationships with governments of countries in the context of the SGIUNLO's activities in Geneva. Therefore, please allow me to concentrate on activities in human rights education, the main activities of the SGIUNLO in Geneva. The United Nations designated the ten years from 1995 to 2004 as the UN Decade for Human Rights Education (UNDHRE),[7] and undertook activities for planning and capacity building in human rights education in international society, local areas, schools, and communities. SGI also cooperated in these activities. However, in the Peace Proposal President Ikeda presents every year on 26th January, he suggested that these activities should not come to an end in 2004 but should continue in a second UN Decade for Human Rights Education. As a result, SGI took on this initiative and prepared the World Program for Human Rights

[7] United Nations Human Rights, *United Nations Decade for Human Rights Education*
http://www.ohchr.org/EN/Issues/Education/Training/Pages/Decade.aspx

Education (WPHRE)[8] in cooperation with the US Human Rights Education Network in the United States. The Costa Rican government accepted this program and proposed it to the UN General Assembly, and it was adopted in 2004. The UN Commission on Human Rights (UNCHR) has been coordinating this program since 2005. During the First Phase from 2005 to 2010, the aim of the program was to promote human rights education in primary schools and secondary schools. During the Second Phase from 2010 to 2014, the aim was to promote human rights education in institutes of higher education and amongst teachers, public servants, legal professionals, and military personnel. During the Third Phase from 2015 to 2019, it will aim to promote human rights education on a national level in individual countries and will focus on specific groups and national sections. Making an appeal to numerous NGOs throughout the world, SGI has been actively promoting this program. At the drafting stage of WPHRE, many cooperating groups put forward proposals. For example, Plan A was to simply extend the UNDHRE for 10 more years. SGI proposed Plan B with more specific operations for WPHRE, and this was adopted. However, as a matter of course, the proposer of WPHRE to the United Nations is established as the Costa Rica government. The SGIUNLO in Geneva has a close cooperative relationship with the Costa Rican government and its UN representative. Through the history of such initiatives, the Working Group on Human Rights Education was established in 2006 in the Commission on Human Rights, the CoNGO in Geneva, and I was appointed chairman. This group at present is more highly regarded than CHR, and the President of the CoNGO recognises it as being an active group. People from Amnesty International often

[8] United Nations Human Rights, *World Program for Human Rights Education* (2005-ongoing)
http://www.ohchr.org/EN/Issues/Education/Training/Pages/Programme.aspx

pay visits to SGIUNLO in Geneva to consult on matters of human rights education. Through these NGO alliances, we engage in strategic discussions with other groups. In terms of discussions with various governments, SGI is cooperating with the Costa Rican government and the Italian government in public relations for human rights. In 2007, SGI commenced discussions on human rights education with the Swiss government and the Moroccan government. In the spring of 2008, the seven countries of Costa Rica, Italy, Switzerland, Morocco, the Philippines, Senegal, and Slovenia established the Platform for Human Rights Education and Training (PHRET) as an intergovernmental organisation. The Commission on Human Rights, the CoNGO in Geneva, acts as a channel for liaising between PHRET and NGOs. Whilst it is officially stated to be the Commission on Human Rights, the CoNGO in Geneva, in reality the SGIUNLO in Geneva is in charge of its operations.

Meetings and panel discussions co-hosted by the Commission on Human Rights, CoNGO in Geneva, and PHRET are held in March and September every year, and SGIUNLO in Geneva is always in attendance either as chair or as a panelist. The SGIUNLO in Geneva actually drafts the final documents, etc. organised at these meetings. However, SGI's name is always withheld, and any pronouncements that are forthcoming from these meetings take the form of a joint statement issued by all members in attendance. I believe our stance of throwing ourselves into the role of support personnel behind the scenes is the reason many government organisations and NGOs place their confidence in SGI. Simply asserting oneself will never solve problems or advance any cause.[9] The Commission on Human Rights, the

[9] On 19 December 2011, UN General Assembly adopted the Declaration on Human Rights Education and Training. The draft was made in collaboration of PHRET and CHRCNGOG. SGI played a crucial role to make the Declaration.

CoNGO in Geneva, effectively prepares the reports of these conferences, and the ministries of education and the relevant departments in charge of education in the governments of over 100 countries read these reports. Whilst the Council of Europe actively promotes human rights education, SGI has conducted exhibitions and workshops on human rights education eight times to date at the Council of Europe.

Tobisawa: Like government organisations, NGOs thoroughly promote their own principles and policies. In many NGO movements, I get the impression there is a prevailing belief that making a strong appeal will accelerate the momentum of a movement, and more or less confronting government organisations will solve problems. What is your relationship with the Japanese government as you conduct your activities? I recall that human rights education itself has never been incorporated in school education in Japan. As you know, I am currently studying nuclear disarmament. However, Mr. Fujii, how do you assess the stance taken by the Japanese government at the UN in Geneva and its cooperation with NGOs?

Fujii: First of all, the Japanese government representatives never make any statements even when they attend UN conferences on human rights education, and they leave the venue right away after a conference. Therefore, there are no opportunities for dialogue with NGOs. Perhaps they are not interested in human rights education itself. Consequently, there are no points of contact for cooperation. This is not a criticism of

---

SGI, Human Rights: The General Assembly adopts the UN Declaration on Human Rights Education and Training
http://www.sgi.org/news/human-rights/hr2011/the-un-declaration-on-human-rights-education-and-training.html
UN Resoltion 66/137.
http://daccess-dds-ny.un.org/doc/UNDOC/GEN/N11/467/04/PDF/N1146704.pdf?OpenElement

these representatives as such, and there is no way I am able to comment on the Japanese government. As you pointed out, human rights education has not been incorporated into the curriculum of schools in Japan. This is only my personal impression, but the Japanese government perhaps believes it is sufficient to act in concert with the United States and allies at the United Nations. On the other hand, the Costa Rican government is the only UN member country that does not have a military and is putting significant effort into education. It can be called an advanced country in human rights. Costa Rica engages in advanced initiatives in nuclear disarmament and, as you may know, it is also amongst the countries proposing a Nuclear Weapons Convention. Italy is also involved in activities such as playing an active role at the UNCHR, and the Italian government regards SGI-Italy as an outstanding human rights organisation. Certainly, a significant gap exists in the opinions of the various NGOs. Our stance, however, is to place emphasis on dialogue and harmony based on Buddhism. At times, other groups express their respect for our stance as "Great Buddhism." My belief is that there is no respect without making a contribution. Therefore, I believe words like "constant, substantial contribution, and recognition" describe our attitude in activities based on the principles of President Ikeda. Through his Peace Proposal and other guidance, President Ikeda always affirms that the 21st century is a global era and that our only pathway is to raise international opinion to establish political decision-making on a global scale in both the United Nations and governments. We position SGI's NGO activities as our activities for achieving this.

If you have more questions about human rights education, I am available to answer them for any number of hours after this. However, I believe that what I have just explained is an overview of the role SGI plays in relationships between government organisations and NGOs.

Tobisawa: Thank you very much for spending such a long time with me.

(7) Mayors for Peace (31st October 2012)

Interview Place: Chairman's Office, Hiroshima Peace Culture Foundation, Hiroshima Peace Memorial Museum, 1-2 Nakajima-cho, Naka-ku, Hiroshima City, Hiroshima Prefecture 730-0811, Japan

Steven Leeper: Chairman of Board of Directors, Hiroshima Peace Culture Foundation (Secretary-General of Mayors for Peace)

Tobisawa: Thank you very much for making the time to meet with us today.

Leeper: Not at all. The pleasure is mine. I understand that you are studying about antinuclear CSOs.

Tobisawa: Yes, I am currently writing my doctoral thesis, and today I would like to ask you some questions about MP.

Leeper: You can view most information on MP on the official MP website. I suggest that you visit the site.

Tobisawa: Yes, I heard about it from Mr. Murakami. Today, however, I would still like to ask you a few questions about the significance of the MP and its relationship with the Japanese government, as well as its relationship and cooperation with other antinuclear CSOs.

Leeper: The significance of MP is that its members are comprised of local governments from all over the world. The mayors, who represent their respective cities, are officially elected public figures, and the MP may be considered the only antinuclear CSO to have true political legitimacy. That's what makes it so different in nature from other organisations, and at the same time, it has an advantage that other organisations do not have. Since all members as individuals have political legitimacy, the statements they make can be said to carry more weight.

Tobisawa: I see. What about the organisation's relationship with the Japanese government? As an organisation with political legitimacy, does it cooperate closely with the Japanese government?

Leeper: The Japanese government's policy on nuclear weapons and the MP's arguments are different. The Japanese government's policy and stance regarding nuclear weapons also differ from those of the city of Hiroshima. It can also be assumed that the Japanese national government's view concerning nuclear disarmament differs from the views of municipal governments.

Tobisawa: What about cooperation and relationships with other nuclear CSOs?

Leeper: In the past, antinuclear NGOs promoted their own activities independently. Recently, however, these organisations are seeking global cooperation and making efforts at establishing networks. It was Abolition 2000 that started this. Whilst MP participates in this network, there is in fact little agreement amongst NGOs regarding the essence of Abolition 2000. The respective organisations differ in both their approaches and activities, and there are rather fierce collisions of opinions within Abolition 2000, so I believe we cannot hope for further advances in the movement.

Tobisawa: Despite their unequivocal common goal to abolish nuclear weapons, I am surprised to hear that even NGOs fall victim to rigidity and breakdowns over opinions to the point that their differences become irreconcilable.

Leeper: That is quite right. At present, ICAN is playing a major role. It can be said that IPPNW, which initiated the establishment of ICAN, is a hero of antinuclear CSOs.

Tobisawa: Japan is currently facing unstable conditions in Northeast Asia, with North Korea's nuclear development and difficult diplomatic relations with China amongst others. Under the circumstances it seems that the Japanese government is of the opinion that it cannot promote abolition of nuclear weapons so lightly.

Leeper: The Japanese Government should take a stand and declare that it is a peace-loving nation. In short, I believe the Japanese government should, at its own initiative, abandon its territorial rights to the Senkaku Islands. It should tell the Chinese side that they can have the Senkaku Islands and that Japan has no intention of contesting its claims. The Japanese government should also take action by sending out a strong message to surrounding countries and the world that it has no intentions of being party to a conflict with any country and completely rejects circumstances that cause conflict.

Tobisawa: This is still an ongoing issue, and it seems there are many different opinions. Regrettably, we have run out of time. Thank you very much for your cooperation.

Leeper: Thank you too. Good luck with your doctoral thesis.

(8) Japan Physicians for the Prevention of Nuclear War (JPPNW) (31st October 2012)

Interview Place: Hiroshima Prefectural Medical Association

Katsuko Kataoka (Ms.): Secretary General of JPPNW, Professor Emeritus University of Hiroshima, Doctor of Medicine, Member of Pugwash Conference on Science and World Affairs
Jitsuro Yanagida: Board Member of JPPNW, Organizing Committee Chairman, 20th IPPNW World Congress in Hiroshima, 2012, IPPNW Headquarters International deputy trustee

Tobisawa: Thank you for giving me your precious time. My question to you has to do with basic activities of your organization, its relationships with the IPPNW Headquarters (located in the USA) and the government of Japan.

Yanagida: Thank you. I was looking forward to welcoming you today. I brought you some materials and books that are basic to us for you to be able to refer to them.

Tobisawa: That's very kind of you, thank you.

Kataoka: Our activities are not political; they are geared at genuinely supporting *hibakushaa* (A-bomb victims) in Hiroshima and Nagasaki. As physicians we focus on their dreadful state of health that resulted from atom bombs. Indeed, our activities are focused on eliminating the worst kinds of materials that damage human health. Health is not a political issue. We believe it has no relation with political confrontations.

Having said that, we believe we should collaborate and work together with a broad range of persons including those in politics. We participate as Japan Chapter at every World Convention that IPPNW organize by IPPNW headquarters since 1981 with notable personalities such as Tadatoshi Akiba, former Mayor of Hiroshima and the Chair of Mayors for Peace and Ms Nanami Shiono, a popular author.

Tobisawa: I saw in your official website that your membership consists of 3,000 physicians. What kinds of activities at what frequencies do you organize throughout the country? Do you have any collaborative relationship with the Government of Japan?

Kataoka: Majority of the members of IPPNW Japan Chapter are physicians from Hiroshima Prefectural Doctors' Association and that Association is the largest support organization of our Chapter. The Japan Doctors Association has become a strong supporter as well in recent years. The IPPNW World Congress took place in Hiroshima this year after 23 years with enormous support from the national association of doctors[10]. We also enjoy good relations with Parliamentarians for Nuclear Non-Proliferation and Disarmament, Japan (PNND Japan), its Chair Taro Kono, M.P. and Co-Chair Hideo Hiraoka, M.P. We also with the InterAction Council established by the Honorable Takeo Fukuda, former Prime Minister as well as with the Ministry of Foreign Affairs. I believe that the United Nations is the most important forum to deliberate on nuclear abolition. Recently, a good number of NGOS are working to establish Nuclear Weapons Convention (NWC). We are

[10] The 20th IPPNW World Congress (in Hiroshima) was managed by the IPPNW Japan Chapter Organizing Committee. The 20th IPPNW World Congress - From Hiroshima to Future Generations http://ippnw2012.org/default.htm (in English)

indeed in favour of it and wish it were realized but we do not confront political and other groups head-on. We believe we should amicably reach our goals through exchanging our opinions.

Tobisawa: You have all sorts of activities including organizing IPPNW World Congress, but what may I ask is the signature activity of IPPNW Japan Chapter?

Kataoka: We do not just wave flags opposing nuclear arms and nuclear bombs but we undertake initiatives based on scientific grounds whether they are activities regarding A-bomb damages, health damages from radiation, and educational activities. One such major initiative is the issue of residual radiation. Through scientific evidence we are working to win legal recognition of victims who are today not covered by existing law.

For example, Shizuteru Usui, Chairman of Japan Chapter has been to Chernobyl for research and stocktaking. In collaboration with University of Hiroshima, Research Institute for Radiation Biology and Medicine, and IPPNW Headquarters to study consequences of nuclear power plant explosions in Fukushima and the neighbouring Miyagi prefecture. Our Chapter, based on our fundamental principles dedicated to protecting health of the humankind, we conduct education and provide medical support in many developing countries. Our activities in the developed countries are mainly focused on nuclear power plants. The IPPNW Headquarters take strong views against nuclear power plants aiming at decommissioning of all nuclear power plants.

Tobisawa: IPPNW has its headquarters located in the USA. Isn't it a challenge for IPPNW to have its Headquarters located in a country that is a leading nuclear power, and to clearly take a stance against nuclear power plants? Does this not create difficulty in terms of its relation with the US Administration?

Kataoka: IPPNW has its Chapters in many countries around the world. Yes, its headquarters is in the USA, but it is Japan Chapter that is most active. Japan Chapter continues to provide financial assistance to IPPNW Headquarters at its request. Dr. Yanagida who is here with us today serves as a deputy on the board of trustees at the Headquarters, and I am elected as a member of Pugwash Conference on Science and World Affairs. Pugwash Conference is composed of scientists and enjoys high international esteem as an anti-nuclear organization. As you know there is strict examination to its member. These I believe are evidences of the high international esteem Japan Chapter enjoys. It is my experience that there are people even in the United States of America who understand and support non-nuclear activities. When I was a student in the USA conversation tended to be about atom bombs since I came from Hiroshima and was a student of Hiroshima University. Most Americans I met at that time were sympathetic of the damages done to Hiroshima and Nagasaki. That is different from the experience of the former Mayor Tadatoshi Akiba (Chair of Mayors for Peace) as a student in the USA. In his student days many Americans apparently told him that A-bomb was necessary to end the war. As a result, he apparently felt that most Americans approved of dropping the atom bombs. On this point I differ from Mr. Akiba. While IPPNW Headquarters has its own policy, the activities are more or less left to the discretion of each national chapter. In regard to the Fukushima Nuclear Power issue, most of the anti-nuclear power lobby demand decommissioning of plants due to physical and mental distress. As you may know, there are anti-nuclear demonstrations surrounding the parliament building every week. Nothing comes out of just shouting in vain. Given the power supply chain at present, if all nuclear power plants were to be decommissioned all at once, where would the needed power come from when there is no adequate alternative energy supply in place. We differ on this point with the views of the IPPNW Headquarters; Japan Chapter does not stand for decommissioning of all plants. We believe we ought to have realistic solutions. We must therefore not just confront the government but do our best to work to have politicians to come on our side. For instance, I believe it was a big step forward for the ICNND (International Commission on Nuclear Non-proliferation and Disarmament)[11], co-chaired by Ms Yoriko Kawaguchi (the Minister of Foreign Affairs at the time), to have established a forum where ongoing dialogue can take place between civil society and the government. Going back to the 20th IPPNW World Congress, there were many NGOs and government officials as well as physicians present. Each had different opinion but in the end a final statement was adopted through ironing out the differences and deliberating on what could be agreed[12]. Also, we have a zealous

---

[11] On INNCD: http://www.mofa.go.jp/mofaj/gaiko/iennd/ A website (in Japanese) of the Ministry of Foreign Affairs posts an explanation. * This was a time-limited joint project set up for the 2010 NPT Review Conference by Japan ad Australia in an attempt to have exchange of views with NGOs (please refer to Chapter 2 for details).

[12] The Final Statement did not include denuclearization.
Hiroshima Peace Appeal (Final Statement adopted) 5th September 2012, Hiroshima Doctors' Association Quick Report No. 2166: "The 20th International Doctors World Conference on Prevention of Nuclear War (IPPNW) Ends – Hiroshima Peace Appeal Adopted" 5th September 2012.
http://www.hiroshima.med.or.jp/ippnw/sokuho/docs/2166_001.pdf
(In Japanese)
The Mainichi Shimbun, 16th August 2012; Hiroshima, "IPPNW World Congress closes without referring to"de-nuclearization" in its final statement". "The 20th IPPNW closed on 26th with Hiroshima Peace Appeal as its final

member in Sokagakkai which is grappling with nuclear issues and engaged in an all out anti-nuclear campaigns. As everyone knows Sokagakkai is the supporting body of the Komei-to party. Reflecting the enthusiasm of Sokagakkai, the Komei-to members are deeply involved in nuclear issues at the local level as well as members of the national parliament. Sokagakkai is the supporting body of Komei-to party. As such, Komei-to members are involved both at the local assemblies and national parliament. Tetsuo Saito, a former minister of environment elected from a proportional representation constituency of the Chugoku region, which includes Hiroshima prefecture, is sympathetic to what we have to say and often drops in at the Japan Chapter to talk with us. When all is said and done, Sokagakkai was the first organization in Japan that came out against nuclear weapons. Its founding chairman was an educator and the organization heads anti-nuclear movement with its numerous publications on testimonies of *higaisha* and anti-war. I was invited to write and article on anti-nuclear weapons movement for publication in Pumpkin, a magazine published by Ushio Publishers closely associated with the Soka Gakkai. They have time for someone

---

statement. The statement pointed out that "nuclear chain from uranium mining and processing, nuclear power generation based on atomic fission, pollution caused by nuclear wastes and nuclear weapons is filled with danger". It also declared it will take further actions towards elimination of nuclear weapons and to provide full support to forthcoming international conference in Oslo, Norway in March of the following year at which inhumanity of nuclear weapons will be discussed.

On this day, a plenary session was held debating the nuclear power plant accident of Tokyo Electric Power Company's Fukushima Dai-ichi power plant and the pros and cons of nuclear energy. There were also mixed evaluation regarding health risks of nuclear power plants and radiation. The Congress in its final declaration stated, "tragedy must not be forgotten" referring to the accidents in Fukushima, but stopped short of declaring "denuclearization--stop nuclear power plants". The 3-day congress was participated by an aggregate number of 1,600 physicians from 45 countries."

like me from other organizations and care enough to introduce activities. Mr. Ikeda, the Chairman Emeritus, encourages us by issuing peace message every year and organizing large scale anti-nuclear weapons movements.

Tobisawa: Thank you indeed for giving me your precious time today.

(9) Soka Gakkai Hiroshima Peace Committee (1st November 2012)

Interview Place: Soka Gakkai Hiroshima Ikeda Peace Centre, Hiroshima City, Japan

Daisaku Shiode: Chairman of Soka Gakkai Hiroshima Peace Committee
Tohru Hidaka: Senior Manager of Soka Gakkai Hiroshima Peace Committee

Tobisawa: Thank you very much for sparing your precious time for me today. I was recently able to interview Mr. Terasaki, the Chairman, and Mr. Kawai, the Secretary-General of the SGI Peace Committee. When I heard of the existence of the Soka Gakkai Hiroshima Peace Committee within Soka Gakkai (Japan), I requested an interview today. I understand that in Hiroshima at present there are some centres for antinuclear CSOs that represent Japan. I also understand that Hiroshima and Nagasaki, the two cities that were victims of atomic bombs, are symbolic presences in the antinuclear movement. Therefore, I would appreciate it if you could tell me the relationship of the SGI Peace Committee and the Soka Gakkai Hiroshima Peace Committee. Is there any division of roles between the two organisations?

Shiode: First of all, thank you for coming such a long way to visit us. We have prepared some booklets and other reference materials that we have published. I am sorry to weigh you down with these on your way home, but please take them with you.
First, the basic stance of SGI's peace movement may be described as

following two lines: a realistic line and a dialogue line. The Soka Gakkai Hiroshima Peace Committee is basically in a position to give support to the SGI Peace Committee. President Ikeda always strongly emphasises the significance of Hiroshima as the place where the first atomic bomb was dropped, and a decision was made to establish a Peace Committee in Hiroshima as well. SGI considers Hiroshima as a very important place for communicating antinuclear ideology and philosophy. When time permits, President Ikeda speaks about the dropping of the atomic bomb on Hiroshima to leaders and persons of culture from countries around the world, who visit Japan to meet with him. As a result, many of these dignitaries visit Hiroshima after attending various events in Tokyo. During their visits, we show them the narratives of personal experiences of victims of the atomic bomb and other reference materials displayed in our hall. As for our own specific activities, we hold seminars under the title "Lectures on Hiroshima Study for Peace" and we invite knowledgeable people from both Japan and overseas as lecturers. We also actively hold meetings to exchange opinions with the Hiroshima Peace Culture Museum, the Mayors for Peace, the JPPNW, and atomic bomb victims. We also hold the "Three Prefectures Peace Summit" with the Soka Gakkai Youth Division. This includes the three prefectures of Hiroshima, Nagasaki as the second location that was victim to an atomic bomb, and Okinawa, the only prefecture to experience a land battle on Japanese soil during World War II. At this summit, we engage in activities for publishing antiwar materials, interview atomic war victims and people who experienced war, hold peace exhibitions and lecture meetings, and conduct attitude surveys of Japanese people today in regard to nuclear weapons. We hope to create a groundswell for the dignity of life, which is a motto of SGI.

Tobisawa: Could you please tell me in detail your reasons for conducting interviews of atomic war victims and people who experienced war?

Shiode: Already 60 years have passed since the dropping of the atomic bombs on Hiroshima and Nagasaki. Fortunately, during this time no atomic bombs or other nuclear weapons were used again. However, the generation that actually experienced the horrors of atomic weapons is decreasing due to old age, and the history of the dropping of the atomic bombs is gradually fading from memory. Therefore, we decided to preserve the living voices of the victims of the atomic bomb. The results of our interviews have been compiled in a book called "Fly! Butterflies of Hiroshima – Message from the Land that was Victim to Atomic Bombs" (Daisanbunmei-sha, 2003) and published. People's experiences include not only suffering caused by radiation sickness but also suffering caused by discrimination. Simply because they were victims of atomic bombs, some people were unable to get employment. These people lived their lives without talking about their experiences of the atomic bomb. During our interviews, some victims spoke for the very first time about their experiences, which they had kept shut within them with heavy feelings. We do not want people to view what happened in history simply as "the use of cruel weapons". These atomic bomb victims lived truly harsh lives, and we believe it is our obligation to pass on their experiences to the next generation.

Tobisawa: Being in a special place like Hiroshima, what is your relationship like with other antinuclear CSOs? Do you sometimes cooperate with them?

Shiode: We often exchange opinions with the JPPNW, the Mayors for Peace, the Hiroshima Peace Memorial Museum, the Hiroshima Peace Culture Foundation, and the successive mayors of Hiroshima City.

Tobisawa: You mean to say you also cooperate with political leaders?

Shiode: Our cooperation is not limited to mayors only. We actively engage in exchanges of opinions regarding antinuclear views with the media such as the Chugoku Shimbun, for example, and all kinds of people. The mayors themselves have different approaches to antinuclear issues. Former mayor Akiba actively traveled from Hiroshima to appeal to international society about nuclear issues. The current Mayor Matsui took the opposite approach and instead going out of Hiroshima, he invited many people from around the world to visit Hiroshima. He wants people of other countries to visit the Hiroshima Peace Memorial Museum and experience first hand the history of the dropping of the atomic bomb and the presence of Hiroshima. I believe SGI's antinuclear movement will gain more momentum from now on.

Tobisawa: What exactly do you mean by gain more momentum from now on?

Shiode: SGI's antinuclear movement is something that President Ikeda built up based on the Declaration 1957 by the President Toda, the second president of SGI. I believe we will pass this achievement on to the next generation and further promote our global antinuclear movement through various approaches.

Tobisawa: Thank you very much for sparing some of your precious time today.

(10) SGI Peace Committee (19th March 2013)

Interview Place: Meiji Gakuin University, Tokyo (following the Reporting Meeting on Oslo Conference on its campus)

Kimiaki Kawai: Secretary-General of SGI Peace Committee

Tobisawa: At the same time as the Reporting Meeting of the Oslo Conference I noted NGOs were also reporting on their own activities through their own exhibitions and panel discussions near where the Oslo meeting was taking place. It was interesting to note the changes in CSO attitudes from singularly criticizing governments through mass demonstrations. Instead, I was impressed in seeing a different kind of demonstration with Kim Maria of Peace Depot holding up with young people, a banner that read "Thank you for coming to the Oslo Conference!" calling out to government representatives of participating countries as they found their way to the conference venue. My question to you is, when you shared (addressed the audience under the heading,) 'the views of the government of Japan' why you took all your speaking time, in effect defending your government and said, although the government refused to sign the UN Resolution on Inhumanity of nuclear weapons it is in support of the principle?

Kawai: We believe that nuclear arms are by their very nature inhuman weapons. However, their elimination must follow a rational process. Bureaucrats everywhere, not just at the Japanese ministry of foreign affairs, are professionals in their narrow area of responsibilities. We tend to lack flexible skills in our use of language. When a decision is made that Japan will not put its signature to the resolution condemning nuclear weapons as inhuman, anyone speaking to it tends to emphasize that part of the issue alone. This consequently invites criticism focused merely on the refusal as if the Japanese government has no intention of abolishing nuclear weapons. I thought that someone should read into the statement and find small areas that are open to negotiation and offer, if you will, an exit. Nothing will come out of criticizing the government. We should ensure that the Japanese government would not leave any discussion, domestic or international, on abolition of nuclear weapons. Most of the CSOs see nuclear arms as absolute evil and see them as unethical. The recommendation on nuclear abolition made to the Wall Street Journal by the four wise men including Henry Kissinger and James Shultz was made from a security perspective.

Tobisawa: President Obama's Plague speech can be said to have the security undertone. Neither President Obama nor the US administration is saying that nuclear weapons are inhuman weapons.

Kawai: That is one way of looking at it. If possession and the use of nuclear weapons are defined as unethical, the P5 countries in possession of nuclear weapons can be said to be responsible over the years for their unethical deeds. They would not easily accept that said about them. Nuclear weapons abolition sought from a security point of view will all together leave out the question of them being absolutely evil or inhuman.

Tobisawa: Well, if a security perspective is adopted, it would mean that if and when the environment is in place, though that is easier said than done in our globalized world of logistics and distribution, but again if and when the fear of terrorists getting hold of nuclear weapons is erased, it would start an argument that countries may undertake nuclear arms development.

Kawai: Neither of the two standpoints is unacceptable for both the civil society and the governments. Rather than jumping to the conclusion that nuclear weapons are unethical or that they do not involve ethical issues, what is important is to carefully examine the logic and find common grounds acceptable to each organization and government. With regard to the present case, we should appreciate that the Japanese government is in support of the principle that the weapons are inhuman. We should commend it for its presence at the Oslo Conference after it had refused to put its signature on the UN resolution on "inhumanity". The CSOs should have the mind to understand that the government might be feeling a bit shy and welcome its presence at the international conference calling for support for the inhumanity of the weapons. On the other hand, if it only expected to be criticized by CSOs and fellow governments it may stiffen its attitude. That will bring us no solution. We want the Japanese government to send its representative to the next Mexican conference. I believe one of the roles of CSOs is to assist the government of Japan, which is slow to come to a decision due to current situation, being under the US nuclear umbrella and the recent developments in East Asia. What we want is the elimination of nuclear weapons, isn't that our ultimate objective? We should not let the process stagnate just because we do not agree on every opinion.

Logically, all we need is an international agreement to abolish nuclear weapons. Who would gain by accusing Japanese government and the P5s? One of the roles of CSOs is to assist governments by seeking out common issues and explain and find the logical way of going forward.

Tobisawa: SGI has produced and organized an Exhibition "Challenge towards Abolition of Nuclear Weapons" in Bahrain from 12th to 23rd March this year[13] in collaboration with International Campaign on Annihilation of Nuclear Weapons (ICAN), Bahrain Strategic International Energy Research Center (DERSAT), United Nations Public Relations Center Gulf States Office and Inter Press Services (IPS). Bahrain's Foreign Minister H.E. Hariffer, H.E. Dr. Abdul Ghaffar, Adviser to HM for Diplomatic Affairs, Foreign Affairs Advisor to His Majesty Abdul Gaphal, Ambassador Plenipotentiary from Japan HE Shigeki Sumi as well as diplomatic corps from 18 countries and UN representatives were present at the Opening Ceremony that took place at Bahrain National Museum in Manama City. How were you able to put together this anti-nuclear exhibition involving governments and UN organizations at a time when Iranian nuclear development issue continues to be a concern, and where Arab Spring has made the area less stable? Do you have diplomatic and other routes to constantly achieve these great turnouts?

Kawai: We directly contact embassies and related organizations of countries in which we hope to organize events and explain what we wish to do rather than going through third parties and connections. We believe this to be the best way. This time as well, we made an appointment with the Bahrain Embassy in Tokyo and explained what we hope to do and explained each step of the way. We explained to our Foreign Ministry the nature of the exhibition we intended to organize in Bahrain. We also shared what we stated at the Oslo Reporting Meeting today concerning the analysis we made of the governments thinking with the people at the Foreign Ministry's Disarmament Nonproliferation,

---

[13] Seikyo Online 18th March 2013
http://www.seikyoonline.jp/news/headline/2013/03/1206630_4427.html

Science Department Arms Control Nonproliferation Section including its director. We have been doing this for some time so that MOFA people tell us these days, "your analysis and interpretation of the issues are extremely interesting and we learn much from them." Since we have developed relations that enables us to frankly exchange opinions, we did the same this time, explained what we wished to do, and discussed them and finally had Japanese Ambassador to Bahrain, H.E. Shigeki Sumi to be present. We did the same with other embassies, we simply visited them, explained what we wished to do and invited them to "please come and see for yourself". What is important is our attitude to invite everyone to become our collaborators.

Tobisawa: I appreciate your willingness to explain things frankly, but can you be sure you will succeed every time? Particularly in Middle East where it is politically quite sensitive? To organize an anti nuclear arms exhibition there must have been a challenge. What do you think made it a success? I suppose other CSOs to have opportunities to discuss with governments and Japanese foreign office, but they are likely to assert their own positions and rarely get their acts together to succeed.

Kawai: I suppose it has much to do with our commitment to explain, to engage the other in a dialogue and the way we go about doing that. Over the years, SGI's Chairman, Dr. Daisuke Ikeda has been promoting dialogue between religions and civilizations. He has shown us through his dialogue with leading national opinion leaders, social and political leaders that it is important to listen to what the other party has to say and for him to respect and understand their positions, religion and culture before stating his own

Tobisawa: I believe Dr. Ikeda has published a book, "Choices towards the 21st Century" from Ushio Publishers Co. Ltd. in 2000, a collection of his dialogue on commonalities between Buddhism and Islam with Professor Majit Teheranian of Iran from Harvard University. They discussed the commonalities between Buddhism and Islam. Professor Teheranian was invited to serve as the first director of Toda Memorial International Peace Institute that Dr. Ikeda established. Professor Richard Langhorn, the tutor for my doctorial thesis I am writing at Buckingham University is a good friend of Professor Teheranian as he serves as an international advisor to Toda Institute. Dr. Ikeda has also published his dialogue with Professor Do Waymin (Entwin Institute at Harvard University) entitled "Civilizations of Dialogue – On Hopeful Philosophy of Peace" from Daisan Bunmei-sha publisher in 2007.

Kawai: I believe our respect for different cultures and religions has helped us build mutual trust in every country and region. Dr. Ikeda has ingrained in us young people that we should look for common values as humans in every difference.

Tobisawa: What impressed me at the Oslo Reporting Meeting today was to see heads of CSOs deeply and amicably engaged with each other. I would expect each organization to have different approach to nuclear disarmament. How did you build the cooperative system?

Kawai: Actually we all got together, including us organizers, to decide in detail what each of us would say. Actually all of us were committed today to cooperate more than ever before. Above all we have become personal friends. It is a result I think of us taking the trouble to get together after each symposium to have informal discussion over evening meals. We may not completely agree with each other but that we were always able to share our honest feelings had gone a long way to establishing Japan NGO Network for Nuclear Weapons Abolition (JNNNWA)[14]. We constantly exchange opinions with Professors Kataoka and Yanagida of IPPNW and Mr. Okubo of JALANA.

Tobisawa: Is that so, but each CSO does have different background and methodology and area of expertise. I meet with various persons from anti-nuclear NGOs and get the feeling that they have strong and convincing arguments. At times they have harsh things to say against views and methods of other organizations, if not emotional. How do you build such amicable relations with each other? With JNNNWA, you even have an anti-nuclear NGO Alliance in Japan. Today's Oslo Reporting Meeting clearly showed how CSOs are increasing their collaboration and partnerships. What issues do you think NGO alliance (JNNNWA) should be taking on going forward?

Kawai: Well, I think today's Reporting Meeting of the Oslo Conference was an exceptional success. I feel that CSO partnerships are growing stronger. And that has to do also with the passage of time. We started to exchange opinions about 10 years ago. Naturally, there were some groups that were not going to concede their arguments. And of course there were cold stares and critical opinion against religious organizations like ours. But as I said, our attitude for dialogue with respect for the other, to cease every opportunity to be at their meetings, and to continue our discussion over receptions following meetings, have created the basis for mutual understanding. Now with regard to

[14] http://nuclearabolitionjpn.wordpress.com/

JNNNWA's activities, I believe what I presented at the Reporting Meeting of the Oslo Conference will be the pillar of the nuclear abolition movement in the future, that is to say, what the Egyptian delegate had said at the Oslo Conference on Disarmament; " …The Treaty Prohibiting Nuclear Weapons must be a vehicle that all can participate…[15]". With the risk of repeating myself, the idea is to create an international framework to prohibit nuclear weapons just with an international law, neither from an ethical framework that condemns them as unethical and absolute evil nor from a security framework. If you start with the thought that nuclear weapons involve issues of humanity, therefore they are absolute evil and are unethical, try and add to them a security point of view, it will simply end up without any point of contact or commonality, and result in becoming a three dimensional confrontation. Through such an endless theological exercise we will never achieve abolition of nuclear weapons. We should start with simple wordings such as 'nuclear weapons must be prohibited'. JNNNWA should be a place where parties could discuss what should be done to see that the Japanese government would continue to participate at the Mexico Conference.

Tobisawa: I believe you have given me a new perspective on civil society's nuclear disarmament and nuclear abolition movements. I thank you most cordially.

---

[15] Delegate of Egypt, Conference on Disarmament Discusses Nuclear Disarmament, News & Media UNOG 5 March 2013
http://www.unog.ch/80256EDD006B9C2E/%28httpNewsByYear_en%29/CA654DA3242244FAC1257B250067B11F?OpenDocument
"...The Treaty on the Non-Proliferation of nuclear weapons could be **a vehicle** to achieve nuclear disarmament as long as nuclear weapon States fulfilled their obligations under Article VI of the Treaty and started negotiating in good faith on nuclear disarmament, and the universality of the Treaty was achieved... "

Appendices

(11) Japan Association of Lawyers Against Nuclear Arms (JALANA) (27th March 2013)

Interview Place: Headquarters, Japan Federation of Bar Associations

Kenichi Okubo: Secretary General of JALANA, Vice-Chairman, Constitutional Investigation Committee of the Japan Federation of Bar Associations and Head of the Working Group on Abolition of Nuclear Weapons Committee Project Team.

Tobisawa: Thank you for giving me your precious time. Let me broach the subject without delay. I was at the Reporting Meeting of the Oslo Conference the other day and was impressed at seeing how freely and cordially CSO representatives were engaging each other in discussions in a most straightforward manner and in good humour. I expect them to have approaches of their own but I believe they have now established Japan NGO Network for Nuclear Weapons Abolition (JNNNWA).

Okubo: Yes, we are now collaborating with all kinds of organizations, including Soka-gakkai. JNNNWA was established for the purpose of exchanging opinions with the Japanese Ministry of Foreign Affairs. Japan does not have nuclear weapons but it is protected under the US nuclear umbrella. The long and short of it is that our country is reliant on nuclear weapons. While approaches differ from organization to organization I believe we share a strong common will to abolish nuclear weapons and a common wish that our government will take lead in eliminating nuclear weapons as the government of the only country victimized by atom bombs

Tobisawa: What sort of issues do you discuss at your coordination meetings with the Ministry of Foreign Affairs? I believe Professor Okubo, you chaired a symposium in 2010 sponsored by Japan Federation of Bar Associations' Constitution Committee Nuclear Proliferation Project Team aiming at "The world without nuclear arms – Outcome of the Non Nuclear Proliferation Treaty (NPT) Review Conference and Our Challenges"14 June, 2010.[16] I believe Mr Hideo Suzuki, Director of Science Department, Arms Control/Arms Reduction, Disarmament and Non-proliferation from the Foreign Ministry participated in the panel from "a position of the Japanese Government".

Okubo: Unfortunately, we have not gone beyond stating our conventional positions. It is the position of the Japanese government that while it believes nuclear weapons should be abolished but at the same time it feels that the US nuclear umbrella and Japan-US alliance are also important. The government had recently started a joint project with the Australian government in the light of the NPT Review Conference 2010, to have exchange of view meetings with NGOs but there has been no change with regard to its conventional claims. When I ask a government representative whether as the only A-bombed country's government the present attitude is correct. The answer has always been, "Tell me, Mr. Okubo, if there is a way to protect peace and security of our country without relying on the US nuclear umbrella." The reality is we continue to remain far apart.

Tobisawa: Let me ask you the question I raised at the Reporting

[16] Japan Federation of Bar Associations, Constitution Investigation Committee, Nuclear Abolition Project Team
http://www.nichibenren.or.jp/activity/human/constitution_issue.html

Meeting of the Oslo Conference[17]. Suppose that the inhumanity to mankind of the nuclear weapons is recognized, and the Treaty prohibiting nuclear weapons is signed, what good would that do if there is no penalty provided in international law? Do you still think there would be anything to be gained by passing laws against inhumanity?

Okubo: I think the absence of P5 at the Oslo Conference is because they knew only too well what is at stake in case the international law was enacted. If they were on the scene when the international law that recognized nuclear arms as the weapons of inhumanity, they would have to face criticism of the international community if they did not abandon nuclear arms having established the law. They will lose their standing in the international community, and set an example for making all other international laws the US and others have put in place little more than mere names. To be criticized and driven into such circumstances amount to a punishment for violating international law, and this I believe is in effect the binding power.

Tobisawa: The present nuclear challenge in Northeast Asia is North Korea but there are no prospects in sight for reopening the Six-Party Talks. What do you think should be done from a lawyer's point of view?

Okubo: First of all, we must not under any circumstance allow North Korea to use nuclear weapons. The only relevant legal instrument in Japan regarding nuclear weapons is one of Bomb Disease Certification Litigation. As Japanese lawyers we can start a litigation process on behalf of the Koreans who were in Japan in 1945 and have returned to

---

[17] Reporting Meeting of Oslo Conference organized by PRIME Support Study Group, took place at the Meiji Gakuin University on 19 March 2013. http://www.meijigakuin.ac.jp/event.20130408/archive/2013-03-15-1.html

the North after the war having being exposed to radiation disease. North Korea is criticized for pulling out of NPT but it points to the inequality of the NPT itself that recognizes the P5 alone the right to possess nuclear weapons. P5 for their part should not rest on the legality of their situation. They are clearly neglecting their duty to implement NPT article 6[18].

Tobisawa: At the November 2012 JALANA general meeting there was a discussion regarding a model Non-Nuclear law. In other words, enacting domestic laws in line with the declared Three Non-Nuclear Principles. It was announced then that the Constitution Committee of the Japan Federation of Bar Associations would likely be deliberating on the issue this year. The Constitution Committee has a Project Team on abolition of nuclear weapons. I would like to know why and when the abolition of nuclear weapons PT was established in the Constitution Committee. And also after the deliberation last year on the non-nuclear model law you told me, "Even when it is submitted to the Constitution Committee I am afraid it will be past through quickly." What did you mean by that?

Okubo: Actually (Tobisawa sensei,) we plan to hold a meeting right here (at the headquarters of Japan Federation of Bar Associations immediately after your interview to discuss what we should be doing about passing the non-nuclear law. Actually right after this interview we plan to hold a meeting here (at the headquarters of Japan Federation of

---

[18] NPT Article 6 http://www.ne.jp/asahi/nozaki/peace/data/kaku_npt_all.html
"Each member state promises to undertake negotiation with integrity, based on effective measures concerning the early suspension of nuclear arms race and the reduction of nuclear arms, as well as on conventions concerning total and complete arms reduction under strict and effective international control."

Lawyers), to decide what the Constitution Committee should be doing about having the non-nuclear law enacted. To start with, the establishment of non-nuclear PT was determined by a resolution passed at the Human Rights Convention in Morioka City, Iwate Prefecture that was sponsored by Japan Federation of Bar Associations in 2010. What we like you to know is the basic principles of JALANA's objectives; enactment of non-nuclear act in Japan, establishment of nuclear free zone in Northeast Asia and the institution of a treaty to ban nuclear weapons. You may ask why we have non-nuclear PT in our Constitution Committee. The answer is that pacifism and respect for basic human rights, two of the three principles of the Constitution we believe are closely related with abolition of nuclear arms. The mission of us lawyers is the respect of basic human rights and realizations of permanent peace and social justice. As lawyers our mission is to respect basic human rights, realize permanent peace and social justice. At the next human rights convention we hope to discuss the proposed revision of the Constitution by the ruling party, in particular to state the self-defense forces as national security forces. Anti-war, peace and abolition of nuclear arms must be considered as a set. Originally, we had planned to discuss the enactment of non-nuclear law but establishment of national security forces and constitutional revision are likely to take precedence.

Tobisawa: Did we not dispatch self-defense forces to Afghanistan and Iraq on the strength of the preamble of our Constitution to maintain peace of the international community--"We desire to occupy an honored place in an international society striving for the preservation of peace, and the banishment of tyranny and slavery, oppression, and intolerance for all time from the earth"

Okubo: The Nagoya District court ruled that the SDF dispatch to Iraq was unconstitutional.[19] Given the anti-war Article 9 of the Constitution I believe it is unreasonable to dispatch forces solely on the grounds of the Preamble. War is the greatest infringement of human rights. Russell-Einstein Declaration regarding hydrogen bomb is bent on treating it as human rights issue. This is the reason for regarding war and nuclear abolition as a set. Having said this, it is difficult for Nichibenren (Japan Federation of Bar Associations) to have a single opinion on matters concerning whether or not self-defense forces are lawful and whether the use of nuclear weapons will lead to violation of human rights.

Tobisawa: Why is that?

Okubo: It is because Nichibenren membership is compulsory. That is to say, all lawyers in Japan are legally obliged to join it. Lawyers have different opinions and our legal interpretation may also be different. It is impossible, therefore, to integrate diverse views into a single opinion. It follows that Nichibenren, as an organization is not able to issue an opinion stating that the use of nuclear weapons will result in violation of human rights. Also, if one were to promote human rights education to understand what are basic human rights and what constitutes violation of human rights in Japan it is more than likely to be associated with the "dowa (burakumin) issue"(social discrimination of certain groups of people). This will again result in losing sight of the original purpose of discussion.

---

[19] Nagoya High Court ruling as unconstitutional (Ruling: 17 April 2008, confirmed on 2 May 2008.
http://www.kyodo-center.jp/ugoki/kiji/080417.htm

Tobisawa: Two years ago (2011) I went to Geneva to visit among others the United Nations Headquarters to meet the Head of Working Team of Human Rights Education of the Conference of NGOs (CoNGO). The person was a Japanese and I recall him (her) telling me that there is hardly any education given in Japan on human rights. Last week I was at a study group, Gakudo-kai, organized by Ms Fujiko Hara, who is an international-minded person. This group invites leading lecturers to address a broad range of topics from nuclear abolition, international issues and constitution among them. The lecturer was Nassrine Azimi, Special Advisor (formerly its director) to United Nations Training and Research Institute whose topic on "Remembering Beate Sirota Gordon (who had died a few months earlier) - Women and Constitution". After the lecture a time was allocated for group discussion and I had a chance to exchange views with a university student sitting in front of me. She had absolutely no knowledge of the Constitution, neither its contents nor its spirit. As you have said Okubo sensei, I felt that Constitution is no longer close to the hearts of the Japanese people to the extent that few are able to engage in any discussion regarding it. Schools do not teach constitution and there are no places to study it.

Okubo: That is an interesting lecture meeting. Constitution is not part of the curriculum in teacher training courses in Japan. It is not that the Constitution is not taught at schools, teachers know very little about the Constitution nor has any knowledge about it.

Tobisawa: I believe the Japanese government claims the importance of Japan-US Alliance basically due to the feeling of uncertainty it has regarding the situation of Northeast Asia. Two nuclear powers in the region, China and Russia both have territorial issues with Japan. Of course, the Japanese government takes the position that territorial issues do not exist with regard to the Senkaku islands. Media, however, report from time to time on frequent visits made to the area by Chinese fishing and naval ships situations and in February 2013, the Chinese Navy focused its fire control system on the Japanese escort ship from the Maritime Self Defense Forces. What are your thoughts on our relationships with China or with Russia?

Okubo: Although the government denies it, I believe the Senkaku islands are territorial issues. The government will do well by acknowledging it in the first place. And it should institute a case for action at the International Court of Justice (ICJ) to determine to which country the islands belong. Conventionally, it required agreements of the contesting parties to take legal action but today it is possible for Japan alone to present the case to the ICJ. What is important is not to allow wars and conflicts to occur. That should be the fundamental premise. This is not an issue that can be resolved by exchange of blows.

Tobisawa: As there is little time left I would like to ask you the last question, and that is on your relationship with IALANA. Can I take it that JALANA is a branch of IALANA? Is it correct to assume that the information and objectives are constantly shared between the two?

Okubo: No, that's not quite right. JALANA was not created by ILANA as its branch. IALANA had been established in Germany, a leader in non-nuclear issues. Japanese lawyers also felt a strong need to do something as the only country with atom bomb experience as well as support the victims of atomic radiation. It was the lawyers in the Kanto region who spontaneously got together to establish JALANA and IALANA. That is how it started.

Tobisawa: Since JALANA's activities are based on supporting atomic bomb victims I thought that it was originated in Hiroshima or Nagasaki.

Okubo: Actually it was lawyers from the Kanto Region who were keen to organize the group. The differences between IALANA and ours is, while IALANA pursues anti-nuclear activities worldwide, JALANA uniquely provides support to *hibakusha*, the A-bomb victims. Another commitment of JALANA is its initiative to have an anti-nuclear act put in place. IALANA we believe follows with interest our regular report on this particular development. Also, Kenji Urata, professor emeritus of University of Waseda is a director both of JALANA and IALANA and I believe he participated in the IALANA Congress in Poland in 2011. IALANA does have a great impact on establishing an international non-nuclear act. For instance, the IALANA Committee on nuclear policy has made recommendations (or has provided views that amount to a recommendation) regarding the use of nuclear weapons to the 1996 International Court of Justice and it has also drafted a model treaty on non-use of nuclear weapons.

Tobisawa: IALANA's website does not post the number of its membership. What is its size and membership?

Okubo: IALANA must be envious of our JALANA which has a membership today of 400. IALANA and its national anti-nuclear lawyers' associations probably have membership of less than one hundred. JALANA is actively involved in diverse initiatives including support of *hibakusha* and establishing a non-nuclear act. IALANA may not be all that much interested in the number of its membership or its size.

Tobisawa: Thank you Mr. Okubo for your time. I look forward to learning more from you.

Statements

A.P. Okonishnikov (USSR)

"The government of the Soviet Union must pay attention to the unfriendly actions against our Union regarding the so-called the Northern Territories. The facts that the movement is encouraged and led by persons in public positions speak of its nature. At the end of last year, a special government office for Okinawa and Northern Territories was established. In both Houses of Parliament there are committees on the Northern Territories. As of October 1969 "Committee regarding the Northern Territories Issue has started its activities and its mission is to develop concrete policies regarding the Soviet territories. Maps, textbooks and other materials have been published with the approvals of the Ministries of Education and Ministry of Construction indicating Soviet territories of Habomai, Shikotan, Kunashiri and Etorofu as Japanese territories. Similarly, the Soviet Union cannot overlook the government of Japan's attempt to involve other states regarding the so-called "territorial issue". That is through Japan's diplomatic representatives in foreign countries, what is distorting already known historic facts and calling the Soviet territories Japan is through Japan various materials containing groundless demands (among which is (are) found those published by Japan's Ministry of Foreign Affairs are distributed. In April 1970, the Permanent Mission of Japan to the United Nations official distributed the pamphlet on this issue to Permanent Missions of UN member states. This year two special representatives were sent to the US and attempted to win support for Japan's position from the US Department of State and Permanent Missions of some countries. That Japan's Prime Minister Sato has thought possible to use the rostrum of the UN General Assembly to demand its territorial issues from the Soviet Union would not in any sense conform to the purposes of developing Japan-Soviet relations or relaxing international tensions. At present, with assistance from public organizations "a month long campaign for the return of Northern Territories" is conducted. During this month assemblies, conferences, collection of signatures and fund-raising campaigns as well as TV and radio programmes are carried out. With the intention of drawing attention to Japan's demand for the southern islands of the Chishima chain of islands located north of Hokkaido, that belong to the Soviet Union, members of parliament and representatives of public organizations participate in trips conducted to "inspect" the islands from the sea. It must be pointed out from the Soviet-Japan relations, to artificially create the so-called "territorial issue" as well as constantly sensationalize it is against developing good neighborly relations between the Soviet Union and Japan, and contribute only to the interests of Japan and other foreign forces that are against strengthening peace in Asia and East Asia. That movement in Japan supporting territorial demands against the Soviet Union is gaining strength will only make difficult resolution of real issues that concern both our countries, of which Japan must clearly have an interest in."

(The USSR government's opening declaration concerning the Northern Territories, 11 November 1970)[20]

(Translated by Fujiko Hara)

Haruki Mori (Japan)

"The Government of Japan regrets that even after passage of 25 years since the end of the war we have no peace treaty between our countries,

[20] MOFA, Diplomatic Blue Book No. 15, 1971, p412-p414

and wish that peace treaty would be concluded as soon as possible in order that the bilateral relations may develop on truly stable foundation. After all, the Japan-Soviet Joint Declaration of 1956 stipulates that after diplomatic relations are restored between our two states, negotiations regarding the peace treaty will be continued. Recovery of the Japan-USSR diplomatic relations did not develop into a negotiation for the peace treaty is due to the lack of agreement between the two states concerning the territorial issue except for Habomai group of islands and Shikotan island, thus postponing the issue to later day negotiations. Since then, the Government of Japan has taken every opportunity to emphasize to the Government of the Soviet Union the need to conduct negotiations to promptly resolve the Northern Territories issue and thereby to conclude peace treaty. However, in spite of the positive attitude of the Japanese government the Soviet government not only continues to refuse negotiation agreed to by the Japan-USSR Joint Declaration Rather it sees the ardent aspiration of all the people of Japan for the return of the Northern Territories as a mere design perpetuated by certain groups of people, and to have further criticized series of internal measures by the government and the parliament is nothing but an attempt at intervening in domestic affairs of another state. Not only that, for the government of the Soviet Union to state in its declaration that the unfolding of the public movement to expedite the return of the Northern Territories is an unfriendly act against the Soviet Union and hampers resolution of practical issues concerning Japan-Soviet relations- these are putting the cart before the horse. (grossly wrong priorities) It is this kind of negative attitude that stalls development of stable Japan-Soviet relations".

(Japanese government's declaration of intent against the Soviet government declaration, 17 November 1970)[21]

(Translated by Fujiko Hara)

[21] Ibid, p414-p416

Abbreviations

AAR Japan: Association for Aid and Relief Japan

ABM: Anti-Ballistic Missile Treaty

ACDD: Arms Control and Disarmament Division

AEI: American Enterprise Institute

APEC: Asia-Pacific Economic Cooperation

ASEAN: Association of Southeast Asian Nations

CD: Conference of Disarmament (Geneva)

CDPSCONGO: Committee on Disarmament, Peace and Security, of CoNGO

CoNGO: Conference of NGOs

CND: Campaign for Nuclear Disarmament

CTBT: Comprehensive Nuclear Test Ban Treaty

CPAPM: Convention on the Prohibition of Anti-Personnel Mines

CRNUN: Committee of Religious NGOs at the United Nations

CSO: Civil Society Organisation

CEMR: Council of European Municipalities and Regions

CPDNP: Centre for the Promotion of Disarmament and Non-Proliferation

CFE: Treaty on Conventional Armed Forces in Europe

DCANW: Declaration Calling for the Abolition of Nuclear Weapons

DERSAT: Bahrain Strategic International Energy Research Center

DNPSD: Disarmament, Non-Proliferation and Science Department (MOFA Japan)

ECRR: European Committee on Radiation Risk

EEZ: Exclusive Economic Zone

EEC: European Economic Community

EP: European Parliament

ENATOW: Exhibition: Nuclear Arms: Threat to Our World

ENATH: Exhibition: Nuclear Arms: Threat to Humanity

EFCVCPTHS: Exhibition: From a Culture of Violence to Culture of Peace: Transforming the Human Spirit

FMCOT: Fissile Material Cut-Off Treaty

G7: Group of 7 (a governmental political forum of leading advanced economies in the world) [the United States, Japan, Germany, Italy, France, Canada and the United Kingdom]

G8: Group of 8 (a governmental political forum of leading advanced economies in the world) [the United States, Japan, Germany, Italy, France, Russia, Canada and the United Kingdom]

GALANA: German Association of Lawyers Against Nuclear Arms

GHQ: General Headquarters

HNP: Hiroshima Nagasaki Process

HPCF: Hiroshima Peace Culture Foundation

IAEA: International Atomic Energy Agency

IALANA: International Association of Lawyers Against Nuclear Arms

ICAN: International Campaign to Abolish Nuclear Weapons

ICBL: International Campaign to Ban Landmines

ICJ: International Court of Justice

ICC: International Criminal Court

ICT: Information and Communication Technology

INESAP: International Network of Engineers and Scientists Against

Proliferation

ICBBT: International Cluster Bomb Ban Treaty

ICNND: International Commission on Nuclear Non-Proliferation and Disarmament

IKF: Inter-denominational Peace Council

IPPNW: International Physicians for the Prevention of Nuclear War

IPS: Inter Press Service

ISIL: Islamic State in Iraq and the Levant

JACM: Japan Association of City Mayors

JALANA: Japan Association of Lawyers Against Nuclear Arms

JCG: Japan Coast Guard

JFK: John F. Kennedy

JPPNW: Japan Physicians for the Prevention of Nuclear War

JICA: Japan International Cooperation Agency

JFBA: Japan Federation of Bar Associations

JNNNWA: Japan NGO Network for Nuclear Weapons Abolition

KANPP: Korean Anti-Nuke Peace Physicians (North Korea)

KCPANW: Komeito Committee of Promoting the Abolition of Nuclear Weapons

LDP: Liberal Democratic Party (Japan)

MHLW: Ministry of Health, Labour and Welfare (Japan)

MOFA: Ministry of Foreign Affairs (Japan)

MP: Mayors for Peace

MPPNW: Mongol Physicians for the Prevention of Nuclear War

MIAC: Ministry of Internal Affairs and Communications (Japan)

NPDI: Non-Proliferation and Disarmament Initiatives
NATO: North Atlantic Treaty Organisation
NANWFTZ: Northeast Asia Nuclear-Weapon-Free Zone Treaty
NCJNFLA: National Council of Japan Nuclear Free Local Authorities
NGO: Non-Governmental Organisation
NPT: Nuclear Non-Proliferation Treaty
NPR: Nuclear Posture Review
NPO: Non-Profit Organisation
NWC: Nuclear Weapons Convention

ODA: Official Development Assistance

P5: [A Group of Five World Powers: Five Nuclear Weapon States: the United States, Russia, France, the United Kingdom, and China]
PALM: Pacific Islands Leaders Meeting
PHRET: Platform for Human Rights Education and Training
PRC: People's Republic of China
PSR: Physicians for Social Responsibility
PNND: Parliamentarians for Nuclear Non-Proliferation and Disarmament

SCIA: Standing Committee of International Affairs
SDF: Self-Defence Force
SGI: Soka Gakkai International
SGIUNLO: SGI UN Liaison Office
SNS: Social Networking Service
SSD: Special Session on Disarmament (of the United Nations General Assembly)

START: Strategic Arms Reduction Treaty

SALT: Strategic Arms Limitation Talk

UN: United Nations

UNGA: United Nations General Assembly

UNHCR: Office of the United Nations High Commissioner for Refugees

UNCLOS: United Nations Law of the Sea

UNDHRE: United Nations Decade for Human Rights Education

UNDPI: United Nations Department of Public Information

UNTAC: United Nations Transitional Authority in Cambodia

US: United States

USA: United States of America

USCM: United States Conference of Mayors

USSR: Union of Soviet Socialist Republics

USNCBM: US National Conference of Black Mayors

UK: United Kingdom

UCLG: United Cities and Local Governments

WCC: World Council of Churches

WMDs: Weapons of Mass-Destruction

WPHRE: World Program for Human Rights Education